This is a fantastic, fun, friendly way for students to understand what it truly means to have a relationship with Jesus Christ. But that's not all! Through real-life examples and easy-to-understand illustrations, they'll also learn how to grow spiritually and how to live in victory. Every ten- to fourteen-year-old student *needs* this book, and they'll *love* reading it!

SUSIE SHELLENBERGER
Full-time speaker and writer, SusieShellenberger.com

Regardless of age, there is nothing more impactful than daily time spent with, and learning about, our Lord and Savior, Jesus Christ. Through *The One Year Devotions with Jesus,* Joshua Cooley provides that opportunity to kids of all ages, mixing in practical ways to apply biblical truths to their lives and including interesting, Bible-based facts that they'll be excited to share with their friends—teaching others about their heavenly Father in the process. Cooley is a gifted writer whose heart is set on bringing anyone who reads his book closer to the one who inspires him, Christ the Lord.

CLAY MEYER
Editor, *FCA Magazine*, Fellowship of Christian Athletes

The introduction of this book says it all: "This book is all about Jesus." Joshua Cooley has provided a great opportunity for our kids to spend 365 days studying and learning to love Jesus. This devotional grows children in an understanding of who Jesus is so they can begin to have a relationship with him. This book weaves together the character of Jesus with theological doctrine. Well-thought-out sections break down what each doctrine means, provide next steps, and include fun things readers might not know. I'm looking forward to taking my kids through this book—there's no doubt good conversations will come from it.

JEFF HUTCHINGS
Pastor of family ministries, The Journey at Tower Grove

The One Year Devotions with Jesus will challenge your kids to think and will hold their attention with a ton of fun facts and activities. By the time your kids finish this devotional, they will know the gospel, understand what it means to become a Christian, and know what true faith looks like. That is exactly what I want for my children. Put a copy under the Christmas tree for each of your teens and preteens—they'll open it just in time to get started January 1.

MARTY MACHOWSKI

Family pastor and author of *Long Story Short: Ten-Minute Devotions to Draw Your Family to God, The Gospel Story Bible*, and *The Gospel Story* Sunday school curriculum

Joshua Cooley is a student of the Bible and a student of kids. He's a gifted writer and communicator who can connect the deep truths about Jesus and his redemptive story to the real world where kids live. *The One Year Devotions with Jesus* is biblical Christology unpacked in a way preteens can connect with. What a gift to the church!

JARED KENNEDY

Pastor of families at Sojourn Community Church in Louisville, KY

THE ONE YEAR® DEVOTIONS WITH JESUS

JOSHUA COOLEY

Tyndale House Publishers, Inc.
Carol Stream, Illinois

Visit www.cool2read.com.

TYNDALE and Tyndale's quill logo are registered trademarks of Tyndale House Publishers, Inc.

The One Year Devotions with Jesus: 365 Devotions to Help You Know and Love the Savior

Copyright © 2015 by Joshua Cooley. All rights reserved.

Cover illustration copyright © Aaron Garcia/Lightstock. All rights reserved.

Designed by Mark Anthony Lane II

Edited by Elizabeth R. Kletzing

Unless otherwise indicated, all Scripture quotations are taken from the *Holy Bible*, New Living Translation, copyright © 1996, 2004, 2007, 2013 by Tyndale House Foundation. Used by permission of Tyndale House Publishers, Inc., Carol Stream, Illinois 60188. All rights reserved.

Scripture quotations marked NIV are taken from the Holy Bible, *New International Version,*® *NIV.*® Copyright © 1973, 1978, 1984, 2011 by Biblica, Inc.® Used by permission. All rights reserved worldwide.

Scripture quotations marked ESV are taken from *The Holy Bible*, English Standard Version® (ESV®), copyright © 2001 by Crossway, a publishing ministry of Good News Publishers. Used by permission. All rights reserved.

For manufacturing information regarding this product, please call 1-800-323-9400.

ISBN 978-1-4964-0124-3

Printed in Canada

21 20 19 18 17 16 15
7   6   5   4   3   2   1

*To every adolescent reader who picks up this book,
wherever you are in your faith journey: may Jesus Christ
make himself gloriously known to you in these pages!*

Topics Addressed

Introduction

What do you think of when you hear the name *Jesus Christ*?

A good man? A moral teacher? Some ancient philosopher with long, brown hair, sandals, and a dusty robe? Perhaps you lump him in with other famous religious leaders such as Buddha or Muhammad. Is he nothing more than an imaginary hero to you—an ancient Batman or Superman? Maybe you just picture him as a cute baby in a manger. Or a bloodied martyr on a Roman cross.

Many people have different opinions about Jesus. Ask ten people who he is and you might get ten different answers.

The same was true when Jesus lived on earth. Chapter 16 in the Gospel of Matthew gives us a fascinating look at what first-century Jews thought about the man they called "Jesus of Nazareth."

At that time, Jesus' fame was exploding. Thousands of people were flocking to him from all over ancient Israel. They had never heard anyone speak or perform miracles like he did. News of Jesus' growing fame had even reached Herod Antipas, the Roman-appointed ruler of Israel's Galilean district. Everyone wanted to know who this extraordinary man was.

So one day, during a rare quiet moment, Jesus asked his disciples, "Who do people say that I am?" Jesus' disciples answered, "Some say John the Baptist, some say Elijah, and others say Jeremiah or one of the other prophets." Interesting guesses, but all wrong.

Then Jesus looked directly at his disciples and asked, "But who do *you* say I am?" Peter, the boldest of the group, proclaimed in one of the most glorious confessions in Scripture, "You are the Messiah, the Son of the living God."

Peter got it right. But sadly, most of his countrymen didn't. Today, roughly two thousand years later, the world is still largely confused about Jesus' true identity. Jesus is the most famous person in history, but he is also the most misunderstood.

Some people think he was just a good man who taught us how to be nicer. Many think he was an important prophet of God, but nothing more. Others believe he possessed superhuman powers, but certainly not a fully divine status. Still others treat him like a heavenly buddy—a really nice guy to have around when you find yourself in a pinch. And then there are countless people who don't know, or care, if Jesus exists at all.

But your understanding of Jesus and what you do with that knowledge matters . . . *a lot*. In fact, the Bible says your eternal fate depends on it. In 1 Corinthians 15:3, the apostle Paul calls the gospel—the good news of Jesus' life, death, and resurrection and the salvation he offers—a message of "first importance" (NIV). Faith in Jesus brings forgiveness of sins and eternal life with God. Rejection of Jesus, or even indifference toward him, brings everlasting punishment. It's *that* important.

Do you *really* know who Jesus Christ is? Whatever your answer, this devotional is dedicated to helping you draw closer to him. Each day's devotion—all 365 of them—bears his name. This book is all about Jesus.

By reading on, you'll learn about his true identity, his incredible life and teachings, the amazing blessings he brings, and what you need to do about it.

So go ahead . . . turn the page and get started. The truth about Jesus Christ will change your life forever!

JANUARY 1

Christ is the visible image of the invisible God. He existed before anything was created and is supreme over all creation.
COLOSSIANS 1:15

Happy New Year!

To begin a new year and a devotional book about Jesus Christ, it's only natural to start at the beginning.

No, not at Jesus' birth. That's not even close. To find Jesus' beginning, you'd have to go back *way* further than that.

In fact, if you were in a time machine going backward through history, you'd have to zoom past the Bethlehem manger. You'd have to leave Daniel, David, Moses, and Abraham in your stardust. And when you finally reached the creation of the universe in Genesis 1, guess what? You'd have to fill up the fuel tank (time travel requires premium unleaded) and keep on truckin' backward into eternity past.

Ultimately, though, your mission would fail. That's because Jesus *had* no beginning. He has always existed. In other words, Jesus was alive *before* Mary gave birth to him in Bethlehem two thousand years ago.

Whoa. Talk about a brainteaser.

WHAT'S IT MEAN?

How can someone be alive *before* he or she is born as a baby?

For humans, it's impossible. Our lives begin in our mothers' wombs, we live seventy to eighty years on average, and then we die.

But not Jesus. Because he is fully God, Jesus is eternal and all-powerful. He has always existed, and his power is limitless. Today's verse says Jesus existed "before anything was created." (We'll discuss Jesus' human birth in the January 15 devotion.)

Jesus is not a created being. He never had a beginning. He has existed for all time with God the Father and God's Spirit, the other two persons of the Holy Trinity. If you were drawing a timeline for Jesus' existence, it would not have starting or ending points. The line would go forever in both directions!

This is difficult to understand. Our human brains can process only so much, and eternity is a tough concept. But Jesus *is* eternal because of who he is.

This is important to believe, because if Jesus was created, he would be limited in his power, like us. But he's not. He is fully God and all-powerful. And he's worthy of all our worship!

NOW WHAT?

Ask the oldest person in your family (probably a grandparent or great-grandparent) to share stories about what life was like when he or she was your age. Then remember that Jesus is infinitely older than your relative!

DID YOU KNOW?

The period before Jesus came to earth as a baby is called his "pre-incarnate state." *Incarnate* means to be flesh and blood like humans. So *pre-incarnate* means the time *before* Jesus became flesh and blood.

JANUARY 2

*God promised everything to the Son as an inheritance, and
through the Son he created the universe. The Son radiates
God's own glory and expresses the very character of God, and
he sustains everything by the mighty power of his command.*

HEBREWS 1:2-3

So if Jesus has existed forever (yesterday's devotion), what was he doing all
that time before being born in Bethlehem? Since he's all-powerful and all-
knowing, did he spend his days . . .

- beating every video game ever invented?
- playing golf on Pluto?
- helping the angels with their math homework?

Doubtful.

Here's what we know: at some point in eternity past, Jesus was actively
involved with God the Father in creating the universe. When Genesis 1:1
says, "In the beginning, God created the heavens and the earth," Jesus was
right there too!

Colossians 1:16 affirms this when it says, "Everything was created through
him [Jesus] and for him." And Hebrews 1:2 says, "Through the Son he [God]
created the universe."

Since Creation, Jesus also has kept the universe running smoothly.
Hebrews 1:3 says, "He sustains everything by the mighty power of his command." And "he holds all creation together" (Colossians 1:17).

It's by Jesus' infinite power that the earth revolves around the sun, planets
remain safely in their orbits, and stars twinkle in the nighttime sky. Amazing!

We also know that before coming to earth, Jesus enjoyed wonderful
fellowship with God the Father (John 17:24) and shared God's glory
(John 17:5). Otherwise, the Bible is mostly silent on Jesus' existence before
he came to earth.

WHAT'S IT MEAN?

Why doesn't the Bible tell us more about pre-Bethlehem Jesus? That's a mystery. But we know enough. The Bible provides everything God wants us to know about his Son. As 2 Timothy 3:15 says, "The holy Scriptures . . . have given you the wisdom to receive the salvation that comes by trusting in Christ Jesus."

Through God's Word, we know that Jesus is our eternal Creator, our loving Savior, and our almighty King. He made us, and he holds the entire universe together by simply speaking. That's incredible, praiseworthy power!

NOW WHAT?

Spend time making something special: build an Erector set, do a craft, or bake some cookies with your mom. Whatever you make, you need supplies or ingredients to create it, right? Now consider how Jesus created the entire universe out of nothing at all. Wow!

DID YOU KNOW?

The sun is one of Earth's closest celestial neighbors, yet NASA estimates that it is ninety-three million miles away. This should start to give you an idea of how big Jesus' universe is and how powerful he is!

In the beginning the Word already existed. The Word was with God, and the Word was God. JOHN 1:1

1 + 1 = 2

The earth is round.

What goes up must come down.

These are all simple facts that we take for granted. But at one point or another in history, they were either unknown, unexplained, or not accepted as truth. These facts help us understand life, and they remain true whether we believe them or not.

There is, however, another statement that far surpasses these others. It remains true regardless of our belief, and it will drastically change our lives—but only if we accept it. It's the simplest yet most profound statement ever: Jesus is God.

WHAT'S IT MEAN?

So what's the big deal with that? Why is it so important that Jesus is God?

First, if Jesus wasn't God,

- he was a liar and a fraud, since he claimed to be God.
- Scripture itself would be greatly diminished as error prone and misleading since it consistently presents Jesus as God.
- Jesus couldn't have taken away our sins, because only a sinless Savior could do that, and only God is sinless.

But Jesus *is* God! He claimed it many times, including in John 10:30 when he said, "The Father and I are one." He proved it with his miracles and resurrection. And Scripture affirms it in many other passages such as today's verse, Titus 2:13, and 2 Peter 1:1. Another key passage, Colossians 2:9, says, "For in Christ lives all the fullness of God in a human body."

This is where many people get confused. They wonder how a human can also be God. But don't let that throw you off. As we learned in the previous two devotions, Jesus has always existed and was with God the Father in eternity past. He can do all things. When Jesus came to earth, he took on human form while remaining God—fully God and fully man.

As God himself, Jesus was perfectly and uniquely qualified to become the sacrifice for the sins of humanity, including yours!

NOW WHAT?

Read some of the passages mentioned above about Jesus' deity (divine nature), and pray for God to give you understanding and faith in this most important area.

DID YOU KNOW?

There are dozens of instances in the New Testament (which was originally written in Greek) where the Greek words *theos* (God) and *kyrios* (Lord) are used to describe Jesus—more proof that Jesus is fully God and fully man.

JANUARY 4

May the grace of the Lord Jesus Christ, the love of God, and the fellowship of the Holy Spirit be with you all.

2 CORINTHIANS 13:14

Good things come in threes.

The Three Stooges set the standard for American comedy in the early twentieth century. In literature, you've got the three musketeers, three blind mice, and three little pigs—all classics. Isaac Newton gave us the three laws of motion, while Christopher Columbus and his crew sailed to the New World in the *Nina*, *Pinta*, and *Santa Maria*. If you're in the mood for some groovy music, look no further than Earth, Wind & Fire (ask your parents). And of course, let's not forget our favorite fearless trio from Hogwarts: Harry, Ron, and Hermione.

You get the point. It's cool to be three.

Of course, the greatest trio of all time is the Holy Trinity: God the Father, God the Son, and God the Holy Spirit. Even though Scripture never actually uses the word *Trinity*, it clearly teaches God's triune—or "three-in-one"—nature.

There is only one God (Deuteronomy 6:4). But God has three distinct persons—the Father, Son, and Spirit (see today's verse)—who are equal in divinity, yet separate in their roles.

WHAT'S IT MEAN?

If your head is swimming right now, don't worry. It's normal. This is the deep end of the theological pool.

No human can fully understand how one God is three equal persons with different functions. But the Bible clearly teaches the Trinity, so we need to believe it. Besides, if God is as awesome and mysterious as Scripture says, it only makes sense that we cannot totally comprehend his greatness or nature.

So what is Jesus' role in the Trinity? While God the Father reigns over all creation, and the Holy Spirit regenerates sinful hearts and sanctifies believers (both have other functions too), Jesus' main role was to come to earth and offer himself as a perfect sacrifice for our sins in order to make peace between us and God. As we've learned the last few days, Jesus was involved in creating the universe, and he still sustains it by his power, but the Son's chief role is reconciling lost sinners to a holy God.

Praise God for the Trinity! And praise God for the Trinity's second person, Jesus!

NOW WHAT?

The next time you do anything involving threes—such as watching a 3-D movie; eating a BLT sandwich; or playing rock, paper, scissors—remember the glorious truth of the Holy Trinity!

DID YOU KNOW?

While the Old Testament never specifically mentions the Trinity, it hints at it as early as Genesis 1:26, when God says on the sixth day of creation, "Let us make human beings in our image, to be like us." God didn't say, "Let *me* make . . ." He said, "Let *us* make . . ."!

JANUARY 5

Then the disciples worshiped him. "You really are the Son of God!"
they exclaimed. MATTHEW 14:33

One of the most popular titles for Jesus in Scripture is "Son of God." Jesus claimed it, the disciples believed it, the apostle Paul proclaimed it, a pagan Roman centurion at the Crucifixion admitted it, demons acknowledged it, and God the Father affirmed it.

There's no denying that Jesus is the Son of God. But this presents us with another doozy of a brainteaser: If Jesus is God, how can he also be the Son of God? Which is it? Is he God or God's Son?

Well, actually he's both.

WHAT'S IT MEAN?

As mentioned before, it's a doozy. But it's a question worth answering.

When Scripture refers to Jesus as the Son of God, it's a title that is always meant to highlight Jesus' deity, not imply that he is God's child. As discussed earlier in this book, Jesus is God. He is not a created being. He is equal to God the Father in divinity and has always existed.

Jesus is called the Son of God not because he is God's offspring but because he is perfectly like the Father in all his attributes: holiness, power, wisdom, eternal nature, etc. The title "Son of God" also means that Jesus became obedient to the Father, willingly taking the role of a servant in coming to earth. There are lots of verses in the Gospel of John that discuss this, such as John 5:19; 8:28; 10:18; 12:49; 14:24; and 15:10.

Like a human son obeys and submits to his father, Jesus gladly submitted to God's ultimate plan for humanity. When we as humans sinfully rebelled against God, instead of punishing us (as he had every right to do), God sent his Son—the second person of the Trinity—to accomplish his great rescue plan. Jesus willingly left heaven's glory to become a man and pay the price for our wickedness. It would cost Jesus his life. But it would provide new life for us.

The Son of God is truly worthy of all our praise!

NOW WHAT?

To learn more about Jesus' divine sonship, read Hebrews 1–2.

DID YOU KNOW?

Even some of Jesus' fiercest opponents, the Jewish religious leaders, acknowledged that his claim to be God's Son was really a declaration that he was God. That's why they wanted to kill him for blasphemy, or bringing disrespect (in their minds) to God (John 5:18; 10:33; and 19:7).

JANUARY 6

*There may be so-called gods both in heaven and on earth, and some
people actually worship many gods and many lords. But for us, there is
one God, the Father, by whom all things were created, and for whom
we live. And there is one Lord, Jesus Christ, through whom all things
were created and through whom we live.* 1 CORINTHIANS 8:5-6

The ancient world was teeming with idols. Most cultures in the Old and
New Testament eras were polytheistic. In other words, they believed in many
gods. The ancient Mesopotamians did. So did the Egyptians, Canaanites,
Assyrians, Babylonians, Greeks, Persians, and Romans. These pagan nations
worshiped gods such as Zeus, Poseidon, Jupiter, Apollo, Ra, Osiris, Baal,
Molech, Ashur, Anu, Marduk . . . the list goes on and on.

But these so-called "gods" are no more real than Batman, Bugs Bunny, or
Bigfoot. Scripture is very clear: there is only one true God.

Before the Israelites entered the Promised Land of Canaan, which was filled
with idol-worshiping nations, God reminded his people many times that he
alone was God. Deuteronomy 4:39 says, "Remember this and keep it firmly in
mind: The LORD is God both in heaven and on earth, and there is no other."

WHAT'S IT MEAN?

As we dive deeper into our study of Jesus, it's crucial to understand this truth:
there is only one true God, the God of the Bible, who exists in three equal
yet distinct persons—the Father, the Son, and the Holy Spirit. All other gods
are man-made ideas. They are false. Fake. Fictional. Phony.

The triune God of the Bible has no competitors. He is sovereign Creator
and Ruler of the universe. He sent his Son, Jesus, as the once-for-all sacrifice
for sins. And by his Spirit, he draws lost sinners to salvation.

NOW WHAT?

Ask God to increase your faith in him and his unique position as the only
true divine being that we are to worship.

DID YOU KNOW?

While most major religions in the world today aren't polytheistic, the belief in false gods still exists. Hinduism claims many deities. Islam, Sikhism, and Zoroastrianism are examples of other false religions that preach a god who isn't the true God of the Bible.

JANUARY 7

All have sinned and fall short of the glory of God.
ROMANS 3:23, NIV

A cool evening breeze rustled the leaves of Paradise. The trees in the Garden of Eden swayed back and forth. Everything on this day seemed perfect.

But it wasn't.

Adam and Eve, the first man and woman God created, were nowhere in sight. Unlike previous days, when they used to walk with God through his perfect creation, Adam and Eve now hid from their Creator in fear and shame. Earlier that day, they had been tempted by Satan—a.k.a. the devil, a fallen angel who is the chief enemy of God and all humanity—to disobey God. Adam and Eve gave in to temptation, choosing to eat fruit from the tree of the knowledge of good and evil, which God had forbidden.

Sin (breaking God's laws) had entered the world, and with it came sadness, pain, sickness, and death. We call this "the Fall." What's more, Adam and Eve were forced to leave the Garden forever.

WHAT'S IT MEAN?

Sin didn't stop with Adam and Eve, though. Like a deadly plague, it infected the whole world. Romans 5:12 says, "When Adam sinned, sin entered the world. Adam's sin brought death, so death spread to everyone, for everyone sinned."

Every human inherits a sinful nature. We are all sinful from birth (Psalm 51:5), rebelling against our Creator in our thoughts, words, and deeds.

As sinners, we fall short of God's standard of holiness (see today's verse). Sin separates us from our Creator and warrants eternal punishment (Romans 6:23).

Sin is serious. Really serious. It's a direct attack on our Creator. It's shaking our fist at God and saying, "No, I'm *not* going to do what you want me to do. I know best!" That's a pretty bold statement from created beings who can't even lift a finger apart from God's grace (his unmerited favor). We desperately needed a savior.

That's where Jesus comes in. As God's perfect Son, he was uniquely qualified to be the sacrifice for our sins. His death and resurrection satisfied God's wrath—his righteous anger—against sin.

The Fall is why we needed a savior. We all fall short of God's glory, but Jesus didn't. Our sin was great. But Jesus, our Savior, is greater!

NOW WHAT?

To learn more about the Fall, read Genesis 3. Then read Romans 5:18-21 to see how Jesus saved the day!

DID YOU KNOW?

Even as God punished Adam and Eve and sent them out of the garden, he still loved his children. Genesis 3:21 says God personally "made clothing from animal skins for Adam and his wife."

JANUARY 8

I will cause hostility between you and the woman, and between your offspring and her offspring. He will strike your head, and you will strike his heel. GENESIS 3:15

Paradise was lost.

Because of Adam and Eve's rebellion, life would never be the same for humanity. The Garden of Eden was no longer theirs. Humans were now separated from their Creator. Sin had marred everything in God's perfect creation.

In his righteous anger, God pronounced curses on man, woman, and the earth itself. Yet in the midst of the gloom, God made a glorious promise. And he did it in the form of a curse on Satan (see today's verse).

This unique curse-promise would change everything.

WHAT'S IT MEAN?

Sin's arrival didn't take God by surprise. God doesn't get caught off guard. In his sovereign wisdom, he knew what would happen and already had a marvelous plan of salvation ready because of his great love for us.

Genesis 3:15 foreshadows God's plan. It starts with a promise of "hostility," or conflict, between Satan and Eve's descendants. Someone was going to fight Satan.

This hero would "strike [Satan's] head," and Satan would "strike [the hero's] heel." Striking someone in the heel is never a fatal blow. But striking someone hard enough in the head is. In other words, while Satan would inflict a nasty injury, God's hero would ultimately destroy the devil.

Have you figured out who God's hero is yet? It's Jesus! Genesis 3:15 is the Bible's first prophecy (a prediction about the future) of a coming Savior! The eternal Son of God became one of Eve's "offspring" through his human birth in Bethlehem.

When Jesus came to earth, Satan knew what the stakes were. It would be an epic, winner-takes-all battle for the fate of humankind. If Satan won, we'd all be doomed to suffer God's wrath toward sin eternally.

Satan tried everything in his power to defeat Jesus. The "heel" injury he inflicted on Jesus was the Crucifixion. For a few days while Jesus was in the tomb, it looked like Satan was the winner. But when Jesus was resurrected in glory and power, he scored the knockout blow to Satan's "head" (Hebrews 2:14). He also defeated sin and death themselves (1 Corinthians 15:55-56).

Praise God for our victorious hero, Jesus Christ!

NOW WHAT?

Take a moment to reflect on the fact that before God even created the world, he had a plan in place to reverse sin's curse through Jesus. Wow!

DID YOU KNOW?

Satan still fights against God and his people today. But we don't need to fear him, because he is a defeated enemy whose "time is short" (Revelation 12:12, NIV).

The King will turn to those on the left and say, "Away with you, you cursed ones, into the eternal fire prepared for the devil and his demons." MATTHEW 25:41

When Adam and Eve rebelled against God in the Garden of Eden, the world changed drastically for the worse. Genesis 3 shows how sin brought shame, fear, pain, discord, struggles, and death into the human existence.

But those aren't the worst consequences of sin. The worst is hell.

WHAT'S IT MEAN?

Hell is a very misunderstood place.

Different religions have different ideas about hell. Cartoons, movies, and comic strips sometimes joke about hell. Some people think it's only make-believe.

But hell is very real. And it's no joking matter. Jesus mentioned hell many times, and he always spoke of it as an actual and terrifying place.

Hell is where God's enemies (people who don't trust in Jesus for the forgiveness of their sins) will be punished eternally after they die. It's the final destination of Satan and his demons, too.

The Bible describes hell as follows:

- "outer darkness" (Matthew 8:12)
- a "fiery furnace, where there will be weeping and gnashing of teeth" (Matthew 13:42)
- a place of "unquenchable fires" (Mark 9:43)
- "gloomy pits of darkness" (2 Peter 2:4)
- a place where "the smoke of their torment will rise forever and ever, and they will have no relief day or night" (Revelation 14:11)
- a "lake of fire" and "the second death" (Revelation 20:14)

This isn't meant to scare you. But it's very important to understand sin's grave effects. Unforgiven sin brings death, everlasting punishment, and separation from God.

But here's the good news: Jesus came to save us from hell! If you trust in him, he will clothe you in his righteousness and bring you to heaven to live with him forever.

Praise God that he loved us enough to send Jesus to save us from such a horrible place!

NOW WHAT?
Read Luke 16:19-31 for a parable Jesus told about heaven and hell.

DID YOU KNOW?
In the original Greek language of the New Testament, the word *hell* appears as *gehenna*. This refers to the Hinnom Valley outside Jerusalem where the Canaanites sacrificed their children in the fire to pagan idols in Old Testament times. By Jesus' day, the valley was used as a trash dump where rubbish was burned into ashes. The New Testament writers had the Hinnom Valley's constant flames in mind when they used *gehenna* to describe the place of eternal judgment.

Yes, Adam's one sin brings condemnation for everyone, but Christ's one act of righteousness brings a right relationship with God and new life for everyone. ROMANS 5:18

Let's talk about opposites.

High versus low. Fast versus slow. Rich versus poor. Less versus more. Wet versus dry. Earth versus sky. Happy versus sad. Good versus bad.

You get the point. There are lots of opposites in the world. Opposites are things that are completely different from each other. Kind of like Adam and Jesus.

Maybe you've never thought about Adam and Jesus as being opposites. But there's a striking passage of Scripture, Romans 5:12-21, that explains the extreme differences between the two.

Adam really blew it. He had a perfect setup—he lived in Paradise, for goodness' sake!—and he threw it all away by foolishly choosing to disobey God's command. After that, sin kicked down humanity's door and ruined everything. Humans have been struggling through a sin-stained existence ever since.

That's where Jesus comes in.

WHAT'S IT MEAN?

Jesus brings the opposite of what sin causes. Sin results in pain, anger, hatred, strife, death, and eternal separation from God in hell. Jesus, on the other hand, provides healing, joy, love, peace, life, and eternal fellowship with God in heaven. The difference between the two, if you'll forgive the expression, is night and day.

As horrible as the consequences of Adam's sin are, the blessings of Jesus' sacrifice are even more wonderful (see today's verse). If Adam's sin ranks as a 10 on the 1-to-10 scale of terribleness, Jesus' act of love ranks as a 100 on the 1-to-10 scale of blessing!

As Romans 5:15 says, "There is a great difference between Adam's sin and

God's gracious gift. For the sin of this one man, Adam, brought death to many. But even greater is God's wonderful grace and his gift of forgiveness to many through this other man, Jesus Christ."

One man's sin brought pain, punishment, and death. Another man's sacrifice brought love, forgiveness, and life. It doesn't get more beautifully opposite than that.

NOW WHAT?

Read Romans 5:12-21 to learn more about how Adam and Jesus stand as opposites.

DID YOU KNOW?

Could Old Testament believers such as Noah, Abraham, Moses, David, and Daniel—all who lived between Adam's sin and Jesus' sacrifice—be saved? Yes! Even though Jesus' coming was a long way off during the Old Testament period, salvation was still available to Old Testament individuals through faith in God's promise of a coming Savior. Check out Hebrews 11, especially verse 13, to learn more.

I have sworn an oath to David, and in my holiness I cannot lie:
His dynasty will go on forever; his kingdom will endure as the sun.
PSALM 89:35-36

One day, around 1000 BC, King David got a grand idea.

Relaxing in his beautiful new palace in Jerusalem, Israel's greatest monarch lamented the fact that he lived in luxury while God's "house," the Tabernacle, was nothing more than a large, transportable tent. So he decided to build God a temple.

It was a noble desire, but God said no. But God then made an astounding promise to David: "Your house and your kingdom will continue before me for all time, and your throne will be secure forever" (2 Samuel 7:16).

This "Davidic covenant" was like no other guarantee in history. David's family line would always have a ruler in Israel.

For roughly four hundred years, Davidic kings reigned in Jerusalem. But then a wee little snafu occurred. In 586 BC, Babylon's King Nebuchadnezzar conquered Israel's southern kingdom of Judah and deported many of the people. To this day, about 2,600 years later, no human descendant of David has ever ruled again. Did God's promise fail?

Not in the least. God's promise was fulfilled in Jesus, the true Son of David!

WHAT'S IT MEAN?

Today and for the next three days, we're going to see how Jesus completely fulfilled all Old Testament prophecy. We start with God's promise to David.

How was Jesus, the eternal Son of God, also the Son of David? The term "Son of David" is a symbolic title (Matthew 1:1) given to Jesus to show his Jewish heritage and royal heredity (from a human perspective).

Joseph, Jesus' earthly father, "was a descendant of King David" (Luke 2:4). When the angel Gabriel foretold Jesus' birth to Mary, he told her, "The Lord God will give to him the throne of his father David, and he will reign over the house of Jacob forever, and of his kingdom there will be no end" (Luke 1:32-33, ESV).

God's promises about Jesus never fail (2 Corinthians 1:20). Jesus completely fulfilled the Davidic covenant because he is the eternal Son of God who reigns forever. As Isaiah 9:7 says, "His government and its peace will never end. He will rule with fairness and justice from the throne of his ancestor David for all eternity."

Jesus is the Son of David, the Son of God, and the "King of all kings and Lord of all lords" (Revelation 19:16)!

NOW WHAT?

Check out Jesus' human ancestry in Matthew 1:1-17 and Luke 3:23-38.

DID YOU KNOW?

Starting with David's son, Solomon, twenty kings from David's lineage reigned for a total of about four hundred years until Jerusalem fell.

He was pierced for our transgressions, he was crushed for our iniquities; the punishment that brought us peace was on him, and by his wounds we are healed. We all, like sheep, have gone astray, each of us has turned to our own way; and the LORD has laid on him the iniquity of us all. ISAIAH 53:5-6, NIV

After the Fall, life moved on for the human race.

Humans increased on the earth and grew so wicked that God sent a worldwide flood to destroy humanity and start over again with Noah. Hundreds of years later, God called a pagan named Abram from the Mesopotamian land of Ur, told him to resettle west in the land of Canaan, and promised one day to make his descendants into a great nation (Israel).

Even when the Israelites rebelled against God throughout their history, he mercifully provided prophets who called the nation to repent. These prophets also spoke of a coming Savior who would save the people from their sins and turn their hearts back to God.

One of these prophecies, though, stands out above all the rest: the "Suffering Servant" prophecy of Isaiah 52:13–53:12.

WHAT'S IT MEAN?

No Old Testament prophecy is as extensive or vivid in its descriptions of Christ as Isaiah's "Suffering Servant" prophecy. In fifteen verses, Isaiah discusses the following about Jesus and his sacrifice:

- his sinless nature
- how people rejected him
- his grief and sorrow
- his humility
- the unjust condemnation he endured
- the torture he suffered
- the toll his torture took on his physical appearance

- how he died in our place
- how he took God's wrath for our sins upon himself
- how he freely gives his righteousness to us
- how his death was part of God's plan
- his resurrection
- how he intercedes between sinful humans and a holy God

What a prophecy! What a passage! What a Savior!

NOW WHAT?

Read the entire Suffering Servant prophecy in Isaiah 52:13–53:12 and memorize today's verse.

DID YOU KNOW?

Isaiah lived about seven hundred years before Jesus came to earth. And yet by God's power, everything he prophesied about Jesus came true. Amazing!

JANUARY 13

As my vision continued that night, I saw someone like a son of man coming with the clouds of heaven.   DANIEL 7:13

Shivers ran down Daniel's back. His face turned white. The vision of the future he had just seen terrified him.

First, a lion with eagles' wings emerged from the raging sea. Then came a ferocious bear. Next came a four-headed leopard with four wings on its back. Finally, a mysterious beast with iron teeth and ten horns appeared, stronger and more vicious than the others.

What did it all mean?

About 550 years before Jesus came to earth, Daniel, one of the Jews forced into exile by Babylon's King Nebuchadnezzar, received a frightening glimpse of things to come. Daniel saw chaos on earth as four beasts rose to power and eventually fell. Meanwhile, the "Ancient of Days" (Daniel 7:9, NIV) sat on a glorious throne, exalted above all the turmoil below.

Then Daniel saw someone approach the throne. This mysterious figure came "with the clouds of heaven" (today's verse). Daniel didn't know how to describe this breathtaking individual. He appeared human, but only a divine being could approach the holy Ancient of Days. So Daniel described him as "someone like a son of man."

WHAT'S IT MEAN?

What an incredible vision! The beasts in Daniel's vision are generally thought to represent the last four great Old Testament empires—Babylon (lion), Medo-Persia (bear), Greece (leopard), and Rome ("terrifying" beast)—as these bloodthirsty kingdoms battled for power. The "Ancient of Days," meanwhile, is God, who rules over everything.

Are you wondering who the "son of man" was? It was Jesus!

Jesus is the Son of God, Savior, Messiah, and many other titles. But "Son of Man" was Jesus' favorite name for himself. It's a title that shows both

Jesus' divinity (as shown in Daniel's vision) and his humanity as the humble Servant who sacrificed his life to save us.

At the end of Daniel's vision, he saw God give Jesus "authority, honor, and sovereignty over all the nations of the world, so that people of every race and nation and language would obey him." And Daniel saw that unlike the kingdoms of earth that rise and fall, Jesus' rule "will never end" (Daniel 7:14).

Jesus possesses all of God's power, wisdom, and holiness. Everything that God rules Jesus also rules—forever! Jesus, the divine, eternal Son of Man, is worthy to be praised!

NOW WHAT?

Read Daniel chapter 7. Then use a Bible concordance to locate and read some stories where Jesus calls himself the "Son of Man."

DID YOU KNOW?

Jesus calls himself the "Son of Man" more than eighty times in the Gospels!

You, O Bethlehem Ephrathah, are only a small village among all the people of Judah. Yet a ruler of Israel, whose origins are in the distant past, will come to you on my behalf. MICAH 5:2

In a couple of months, March Madness will begin once again. It's the time of year when sports talk turns to "mid-majors," "5-vs.-12 games" and "bracketology."

The NCAA men's basketball tournament is one of the most exciting annual sporting events in America, largely because of its unpredictability. Whether it's Northern Iowa's second-round win over top-seeded Kansas in 2010, eleventh-seeded George Mason's Final Four run in 2006, or North Carolina State's still-amazing championship win over Houston's "Phi Slamma Jamma" superteam in 1983, the tournament is always filled with unexpected twists.

It's virtually impossible to fill out a perfect NCAA tournament bracket. That's why billionaire Warren Buffett and Quicken Loans offered $1 billion to anyone who nailed every pick during the 2014 tournament! Alas, no one who took the challenge even made it out of the first round without a loss.

Predicting the future is a tough business. Unless, of course, it's the Bible.

WHAT'S IT MEAN?

God's Word contains thousands of predictions—also known as prophecies—and not a single one has been incorrect. Hundreds of these prophecies are about Jesus. Micah 5:2 contains a particularly unique one. It predicts that "a ruler of Israel" will be born in Bethlehem. Matthew 2:1 and Luke 2:4-7 confirm this prophecy's accuracy.

Micah nailed it, which is remarkable since he spoke those words perhaps 750 years before Jesus' birth. That would be like an English Crusader in the thirteenth century AD predicting that Barack Obama, the forty-fourth president of the United States, would be born in Hawaii.

Micah's Bethlehem prophecy is just one more proof of the Bible's complete inerrancy (Psalm 119:89). Scripture's perfect trustworthiness and unity is extraordinary, considering it's a sixty-six-book collection written by about forty different authors over thousands of years.

How is that possible? Because God inspired all Scripture (2 Timothy 3:16). God is perfect, and so is his Word. We can believe everything it says, including every word about Jesus, the only Savior from our sins.

When it comes to accuracy, you could say the Bible is a slam dunk!

NOW WHAT?

Start a plan to read through the Bible in one year and begin a Scripture memory plan. Perhaps you can choose some of your favorite verses in this devotional to memorize, and you can find a one-year Bible reading plan here: http://www.oneyearbibleonline.com/readingplan/oneyearbiblereadingplan.pdf.

DID YOU KNOW?

Of all the biblical authors, the apostle Paul wrote the most books (thirteen).

Look! The virgin will conceive a child! She will give birth to a son,
and they will call him Immanuel, which means "God is with us."
MATTHEW 1:23

Considering his menacing scowl, black mask, and intimidating body-armor suit, Batman might not be a guy you'd bring home to Sunday dinner with the family. But compared to most of his crime-fighting buddies, the Dark Knight almost seems normal.

In the comic book universe, Bruce Wayne is one of the few superheroes who is fully human, devoid of any special powers. Most of the other costumed, muscle-bound do-gooders of the world are more than human.

Superman, for instance, is a human-looking alien from the planet Krypton who possesses otherworldly strength, X-ray vision, and the ability to fly. Spider-Man can spin sinewy webs, thanks to a radioactive spider's bite. Wonder Woman is a warrior princess of Greek mythology's all-female race of Amazons. And then, of course, there's the big, green fella himself, the Hulk, whose exposure to gamma rays didn't really help him in the anger management department but seriously improved his bench press.

These, of course, are all fictional characters of comics, TV shows, and movies. There is, however, a real person who possesses superhuman abilities. Know who?

His name is Jesus.

WHAT'S IT MEAN?

Jesus is the world's only true superhero. But he is not make-believe. He and his limitless powers are 100 percent real because he is the Son of God.

Jesus is fully God and fully man. When he came to earth, it was literally God walking around in human form. This is history's most amazing miracle!

Today's verse from Matthew 1:23 reflects this. It's the apostle Matthew quoting a long-ago prophecy in Isaiah 7:14 about the promised child named "Immanuel." Jesus is Immanuel, a name that means "God is with us."

Theologians (smart guys who study the Bible for a living) call Jesus' coming to earth as a man "the incarnation." It's hard to understand how Jesus was both fully God and fully human. But it's critical to believe this. If Jesus weren't fully God, he couldn't have remained sinless. And if Jesus weren't fully man, he couldn't have died a human death in our place.

But the Son of God really *did* live a perfect human life. That's why Jesus—and only Jesus—could pay for our sins on the cross.

Now *that's* superpower!

NOW WHAT?

Next time you watch a superhero movie, remember how much greater Jesus is than that guy or girl in a mask and a cape!

DID YOU KNOW?

Isaiah's "Immanuel" prophecy was part of a speech against the wicked Israelite king Ahaz, more than seven hundred years before Jesus' birth.

JANUARY 16

There is no sin in him.   1 JOHN 3:5

On June 12, 1880, J. Lee Richmond made history. The slender, five-foot-ten left-hander from Sheffield, Ohio, pitched Major League Baseball's first perfect game, leading the Worcester (MA) Ruby Legs to a 1–0 win over the Cleveland Blues.

To earn a perfect game, a pitcher must record a victory in a game of at least nine innings in which he does not allow a single hitter from the opposing team to reach base.

The "perfecto," as it's called, is one of baseball's rarest feats. From 1869, the start of professional baseball, through 2014, there have only been twenty-three perfect games recorded—an average of one every 6.3 years.

Only once has a perfect game occurred in the playoffs—New York Yankees legend Don Larsen's famous 2–0 win over the Brooklyn Dodgers in Game 5 of the 1956 World Series.

Being perfect as a pitcher is tough. But being perfect as a human is impossible. It simply can't be done. Every human is born into sin. We have inherited Adam's sinful nature (Romans 5:12).

Jesus, though, is different. Jesus' miraculous birth kept him from human corruption.

WHAT'S IT MEAN?

The Bible says Jesus experienced a virgin birth (Matthew 1:18-25). In other words, Mary didn't become pregnant with Jesus the normal human way. Having previously existed as the eternal Son of God, Jesus entered Mary's womb through a miracle of the Holy Spirit (Matthew 1:20; Luke 1:35).

This is one of the greatest, most mysterious wonders of the Bible. But it's critical that we believe it. Because of Jesus' virgin birth, he didn't inherit a sinful nature like regular humans. As today's verse and many others like it proclaim, Jesus never sinned. His holiness uniquely qualified him—and only him—to pay the penalty for sins that we deserved (Hebrews 9:14).

Jesus threw a perfect game on earth, and we get the eternal win!

NOW WHAT?

Reread Matthew 1:18-25 and Luke 1:26-38 with new eyes, thinking about the miracle of the virgin birth and Jesus' sinless nature.

DID YOU KNOW?

In 2012, San Francisco's Matt Cain, Chicago White Sox's Philip Humber, and Seattle's Felix Hernandez all threw perfect games, marking the first time in baseball history that three occurred in one season.

JANUARY 17

She will have a son, and you are to name him Jesus, for he will save his people from their sins.   MATTHEW 1:21

Do you know what your name means? Have you ever wondered why your parents gave you your name? You probably have, especially if your first name is Humperdinck or Hortense.

Names were really important in biblical times. People often named their children to commemorate big events in their lives or praise God for something.

When Isaac's wife, Rebekah, gave birth to twins, she named the younger twin Jacob (meaning "he takes by the heel") after he came out of the womb clutching his older brother Esau's foot (Genesis 25:26). When Pharaoh's daughter lifted a Hebrew baby out of a basket floating on the Nile River, she named him Moses, which means "draw out" (Exodus 2:10). And when God gave Hannah a son after she had endured many childless years, she named him Samuel, which means "name of God," to honor the Lord (1 Samuel 1:20).

So when the angel Gabriel visited Mary and told her to call her future child Jesus, Mary knew something amazing was about to happen. *Jesus*, the Greek form of the Hebrew *Joshua* or *Yeshua*, means "the Lord saves."

WHAT'S IT MEAN?

Jesus has dozens and dozens of names in the Bible. He is called Son of Man, Son of David, Son of God, Lamb of God, Lord, Messiah, Savior, Prince of Peace, the Good Shepherd, the Word, the Alpha and the Omega, the King of kings and the Lord of lords, and many more.

Each name tells us something about Jesus. Together, his names show us that there is no one like Jesus in all creation. That's why the apostle Paul writes in Philippians 2:9-11, "Therefore, God elevated him to the place of highest honor and gave him the name above all other names, that at the name of Jesus every knee should bow, in heaven and on earth and under the earth, and every tongue declare that Jesus Christ is Lord, to the glory of God the Father."

The name of Jesus is worthy of all our praise!

NOW WHAT?

Ask your parents what your name means and why they gave it to you.

DID YOU KNOW?

Jesus is often referred to as Jesus Christ. The word *Christ* is not Jesus' last name. It's a title describing who Jesus is. *Christ* is a Greek word meaning "anointed" and is equivalent to the Hebrew title *Messiah*. When you read the name *Jesus Christ* in the New Testament, it's acknowledging that Jesus is the one whom God anointed to be the Savior of the world.

JANUARY 18

This foolish plan of God is wiser than the wisest of human plans.
I CORINTHIANS 1:25

What if everything in your life was opposite?

Imagine if you went to sleep at ten in the morning and got up for the day at seven at night. Or if you clipped your teeth and flossed your toenails. Or if you craved lima beans and spat out ice cream. Or if you hated video games and loved homework.

Weird. Very weird.

What if you paid your parents an allowance? Or if you wanted to be the most unpopular kid in school? Or if your dog walked you?

You get the point. Life would be pretty strange if you did things opposite.

But did you know that God often loves to do what is the opposite of human wisdom? It's true. Jesus' coming proves it.

WHAT'S IT MEAN?

God called a bunch of helpless slaves out of Egypt to be his treasured people. He transformed a shepherd boy (David) into Israel's greatest king. And he turned a wicked persecutor of Christians (Paul) into history's greatest missionary.

But all these examples pale in comparison to how God flipped the script with Jesus. When humankind needed a sacrificial Savior, God offered his own Son. Who in the world would do that? God would!

When Jesus—the eternal, exalted Son of God—came to earth as a human child, his first baby crib was a feeding trough for smelly livestock. The King of kings had "nothing beautiful or majestic about his appearance, nothing to attract us to him" (Isaiah 53:2). The Lord of lords was "a man of sorrows" (Isaiah 53:3).

Many years later, when Jesus rode into Jerusalem during the Triumphal Entry, he entered not as a conquering emperor standing atop a golden chariot but as a humble servant sitting on a young donkey. He hadn't come to be crowned king but to die on a cruel Roman cross. The Lion of Judah became the Lamb who was slain (Revelation 5:5-6).

None of this makes sense from a human perspective. But human wisdom is foolishness to God (1 Corinthians 3:19).

God's wonderfully opposite way of thinking means hope and salvation for us. Praise the Lord!

NOW WHAT?

Read 1 Corinthians 1:18-31 to see how Jesus' great sacrifice for us is the opposite of human wisdom.

DID YOU KNOW?

When Paul talks about the "foolish plan of God" in 1 Corinthians 1:25, he isn't speaking literally. God is perfectly wise. He knows all things and doesn't make mistakes. This reference to God's "foolish plan" is describing how the sinful world views God's thoughts. Ironically, that so-called foolishness actually represents greater wisdom than any human is capable of.

You know the generous grace of our Lord Jesus Christ. Though he was rich, yet for your sakes he became poor, so that by his poverty he could make you rich. 2 CORINTHIANS 8:9

Imagine for a moment that you are the most powerful emperor in the world. You rule over a perfect kingdom where nothing bad ever happens. You are rich beyond description. You eat the most delicious foods at every meal. You have servants who exist to do your bidding. And you can do whatever pleases you.

Sounds like a pretty amazing life, right?

Now imagine thinking to yourself one day, *I'm going to leave my kingdom and go to a poor, dark, wicked country. I'm going to surrender many of my royal privileges and live like a peasant in this foreign land. I'll invite others to return with me to my own kingdom, where they, too, can enjoy eternal blessings. A few will say yes, but I know most will hate me. They'll insult me, reject me, torture me, and eventually kill me. But I'm still going to go.*

That sounds crazy! Who in the world would do that?

Jesus would. In fact, that's what he did when he came to earth.

WHAT'S IT MEAN?

We are really good at taking care of ourselves. Think about it: When was the last time you grabbed a hammer and started smashing your fingers? Or jumped into a water tank with great white sharks? Or ate a rock sandwich?

That's ridiculous. We'd never do that. Most people don't do things that they know will cause them harm.

But Jesus did.

As the omniscient (all-knowing) Son of God, Jesus knew exactly what awaited him before coming to earth. Jesus traded heaven's glory for a smelly manger. He left his exalted position as Creator and Ruler of the universe for life as a poor carpenter. He gave up perfect fellowship with God the Father to stand before a bloodthirsty mob who shouted, "Crucify him!"

Jesus knew he'd experience all this beforehand. And yet he came anyway, all because he loved us. All because we desperately needed forgiveness for our sins. As today's verse says, "For your sakes he became poor, so that by his poverty he could make you rich" in salvation.

What a Savior!

NOW WHAT?

Is there anyone you know whom you can "become poor" for? Consider befriending an unpopular classmate at school or giving some money to an organization that helps underprivileged kids.

DID YOU KNOW?

Often in his earthly life, Jesus didn't even have a place to sleep (Luke 9:58)! He gave up so much glory and privilege to be your Savior.

The Lord declares, "I have placed my chosen king on the throne in Jerusalem, on my holy mountain." PSALM 2:6

"Kill all the infants and toddlers—*ALL OF THEM!*"

It was a horrific command, but it wasn't all that surprising. Herod the Great was an evil, ruthless king. This, though, was the most monstrous decree of his long reign.

For thirty-three years until his death in 4 BC, Herod ruled as "King of the Jews," the Roman-appointed monarch of the entire region of Judea. He was notoriously protective of his throne and suspicious of others, even murdering his wife, several sons, and other relatives to retain his position. He was a brutal, power-hungry dictator.

So when the wise men came to him and said, "Where is the newborn king of the Jews? We saw his star as it rose, and we have come to worship him" (Matthew 2:2), Herod was greatly troubled. He wasn't about to relinquish his power.

By this time, Jesus was a toddler living in Bethlehem. Herod tried to trick the wise men into telling him Jesus' exact location so Herod could destroy him. But when the wise men didn't follow Herod's plan, he furiously ordered his soldiers to slaughter all the boys age two and under in and around Bethlehem.

Tragically, dozens of baby boys were killed, but Herod's wicked scheme failed. Joseph and Mary escaped with Jesus to Egypt, thanks to an angel's warning.

WHAT'S IT MEAN?

Herod eventually died a painful, disease-ridden death, while Jesus survived and grew up to become the King of kings and the Lord of lords (Revelation 17:14). Jesus' coming had been determined before creation itself. Nothing was going to stop God's plan of salvation, not even violent, powerful tyrants.

Psalm 2 says, "The rulers plot together against the LORD and against his anointed one" (verse 2). But God, the almighty Creator and Ruler of the universe, "rebukes them, terrifying them with his fierce fury" (verse 5).

God's plan, as today's verse notes, was to place his "chosen king," Jesus, on his rightful, royal throne—all for our sake. And when God plans something, it's as good as done.

NOW WHAT?

Read Matthew 2:18. It's a quotation of Jeremiah 31:15. Now read all of Jeremiah 31 to see the original prophecy. Jeremiah 31 is a wonderful promise of the hope God promised to Israel (and us!) through Jesus.

DID YOU KNOW?

Herod was not a first name but a title used by different kings of the ancient Herodian Dynasty. For instance, Herod the Great (also known as Herod I) was different than the Herod who beheaded John the Baptist (Herod Antipas).

JANUARY 21

*We turned our backs on him and looked the other way. He was
despised, and we did not care.* ISAIAH 53:3

Herod the Great was dead.

The wicked ruler of Judea who had tried to kill young Jesus had died a
miserable death from an apparent kidney disease. But the threat to Jesus'
life wasn't over. Herod's son Archelaus had succeeded his father, and he was
a violent chip off the old Herodian block. So as Joseph and Mary traveled
back from their safe haven in Egypt, an angel warned them not to return to
Bethlehem, which was located in Archelaus's jurisdiction.

Here's where things get interesting. Matthew 2:23 picks up the story with
a prophecy that, uh, wasn't really a prophecy. The verse says, "So the family
went and lived in a town called Nazareth. This fulfilled what the prophets
had said: 'He will be called a Nazarene.'"

But here's the catch: there's no prophecy in the Old Testament that links
Jesus to Nazareth. In fact, the Old Testament doesn't mention Nazareth at all.

So what gives?

WHAT'S IT MEAN?

In Jesus' day, the town of Nazareth was a small village of no distinction or
importance. To call someone a Nazarene was an insult. It was like saying,
"You're a nobody."

So when the apostle Matthew wrote in his Gospel, "This fulfilled what
the prophets had said: 'He will be called a Nazarene,'" he wasn't referring to a
specific prophecy about Jesus. He was thinking about all the Old Testament
prophecies about people scorning Jesus (Psalm 22:6; Isaiah 49:7; and today's
verse, among others) and summing them all up by using a term—*Nazarene*—
that would've been familiar to his first-century readers as a put-down. Even
one of Jesus' own disciples, Nathanael, mocked the Lord's upbringing in
Nazareth before meeting him (John 1:43-46).

Here's the point: by worldly standards, Jesus was a nobody. He didn't live in the Beverly Hills district of ancient Judea or travel in a kingly chariot. He had no bling, swag, or fame. Many people mocked him, and few believed in him. The Savior was despised—*a Nazarene, of all things!*—by the people he came to save.

Jesus didn't come to earth to win a popularity contest, though. Celebrity status didn't matter to him. What matters to Jesus is you! He gave up heaven's glory and endured humans' shame to offer you salvation.

Praise God for Jesus of Nazareth!

NOW WHAT?

Do you know someone from a poor or rough neighborhood—a modern-day Nazareth? Show Jesus' love to that person.

DID YOU KNOW?

Not even the people of Jesus' hometown believed in him. Check out the stories in Matthew 13:53-58 and Luke 4:14-30.

When you obey my commandments, you remain in my love,
just as I obey my Father's commandments and remain in his love.
JOHN 15:10

Joseph and Mary were terrified. Their young boy was lost in a huge city.

Or so they thought. Actually, Jesus was exactly where he was supposed to be.

Luke 2 tells a unique story about Jesus when he was twelve years old. Joseph and Mary, his earthly parents, had taken him to Jerusalem for the annual Passover celebration but unknowingly left the city without Jesus. They had come with so many friends and relatives that they didn't even realize Jesus wasn't with them.

After traveling a while, they noticed Jesus' absence. They slammed on the brakes—if donkeys or horse-drawn carts have brakes—and rushed back to Jerusalem. Finally, after three days, they found Jesus in the Temple, speaking to the religious leaders and amazing everyone with his knowledge.

Both exasperated and relieved, Mary scolded Jesus for not staying by their sides. Jesus' answer was quite interesting: "But why did you need to search? . . . Didn't you know that I must be in my Father's house?" (verse 49).

WHAT'S IT MEAN?

Jesus wasn't talking about Joseph's house in Nazareth. He was talking about the house (Temple) of his heavenly Father. Young Jesus—not even a teenager yet—was providing his earthly parents with a reminder of who he really was. He is the eternal Son of God, who always does the will of the Father.

As we've discussed earlier, Jesus is God. Within the Holy Trinity, the Son is equal to the Father in all respects. But the Son willingly took a submissive role to the Father by coming to earth to act as a sacrifice for sinful humanity.

As today's verse says, Jesus always obeyed God's commands. He did everything God asked him to do on earth, culminating with his death on the cross.

This is great news for us. If Jesus had veered off course at all, his mission of salvation would've failed. But he obeyed God the Father perfectly, even as a twelve-year-old!

NOW WHAT?

Read the whole story of twelve-year-old Jesus in Luke 2:41-52.

DID YOU KNOW?

The Temple mentioned in the Gospels was actually a massive complex of many buildings. At the center was the Temple building itself, which was rebuilt and finished in 515 BC after the Babylonian exiles returned to Jerusalem. Herod the Great significantly expanded the Temple and its surrounding buildings, starting around 20 BC.

Children, obey your parents in everything, for this pleases the Lord.
COLOSSIANS 3:20, NIV

After the great "Missing Child at Passover Mystery" in Luke 2 had been solved, Joseph, Mary, and young Jesus left Jerusalem and returned to Nazareth. During Jesus' childhood in Nazareth, Jesus, the firstborn of Mary, grew up with at least six younger siblings and probably learned the carpentry trade of Joseph (Matthew 13:55-56).

Other than this, we know virtually nothing of Jesus' upbringing. But Luke 2:51 does offer one small, vitally important detail about Jesus' childhood after his twelve-year-old Passover trip. It says, "Then he returned to Nazareth with them and was obedient to them."

This short verse—coupled with the rest of what Scripture says—tells us a great deal about Jesus. As the eternal, all-powerful, all-knowing Son of God, he could have easily lorded it over Mary and Joseph with an attitude of, "Hey, Mom and Dad, *you* should be obeying *me*!" But he didn't.

Jesus never disobeyed his parents. Not once. We know that because of his sinless nature (see the January 16 devotion). He never lied to them. He never talked back. He never even refused to give the family donkey a bath.

Wow!

WHAT'S IT MEAN?

Jesus' perfect obedience toward his parents is a tough act to follow. Because we were born into sin, disobeying our parents comes naturally to us. Take toddlers, for example. They like to say no and throw tantrums, but their parents certainly didn't teach them to do that. They started life with a natural desire to rebel.

Obeying your parents isn't always easy. But as today's verse says, it pleases God. He notices how you treat Mom and Dad. Obeying your parents is so important that God included it as one of the Ten Commandments (Exodus 20:12).

Ultimately, obeying your parents requires Jesus' help. You need the Savior to transform your sinful heart into one that wants to say yes, not no. This is the first step in learning to obey God. After all, how can you obey God (whom you can't see) if you can't obey your parents (whom you *can* see)? The Bible makes such a big deal of obeying your parents, because this action teaches you how to obey your Creator.

So ask Jesus to forgive your disobedience and help you to obey!

NOW WHAT?

Say "Yes, Mom" or "Yes, Dad" right away when one of your parents asks you to do something. It's a great habit to get into!

DID YOU KNOW?

"Obey your parents" was the first command God gave ancient Israel that included a promise for us when we follow it. See Exodus 20:12 and Ephesians 6:1-3 to find out what it is!

Jesus grew in wisdom and in stature and in favor with God and all the people. LUKE 2:52

Sixteen words. That's it. Today's verse, Luke 2:52, is all that the Bible provides to summarize eighteen years of Jesus' life.

After the story of twelve-year-old Jesus being left behind by his parents in Jerusalem, the next mention of Jesus, in Luke 3:21, is when he was baptized and began his public ministry of teaching and performing miracles at age thirty. None of the other Gospels—Matthew, Mark, or John—record anything of Jesus' adolescence or early adulthood either.

There are so many fascinating unknowns about Jesus. What did he look like? Was he short or tall? What color was his hair? Did he have a beard like all the modern-day illustrations show?

What kind of childhood friends did Jesus have? What did he enjoy most in school? What was his favorite food? Did he have any hobbies? Was he good at sports? Did he play a musical instrument?

How exactly did his status as fully God and fully human work? Jesus clearly knew he was the Son of God at age twelve (Luke 2:49). But what about at age seven? Or five? Or two?

We know that Jesus' first recorded miracle was turning water to wine at a wedding in Cana (John 2:11). But could he have done a miracle as a kid?

For all these questions, we simply don't know.

WHAT'S IT MEAN?

Jesus lived about thirty-three years on earth. Scripture, though, gives us significant details about only the last three.

The Bible never explains why it remains silent on most of Jesus' life. But honestly, we don't need to know more.

God's Word is perfectly sufficient for all our needs. As we read in 2 Timothy 3:15, "The Holy Scriptures . . . are able to make you wise for salvation through faith in Christ Jesus" (NIV). Even though the Bible doesn't tell us everything about Jesus, it tells us everything we *need* to know.

Don't worry about what the Bible *doesn't* tell you about Jesus. Just be amazed and live your life according to what it *does* tell you. It's more than enough!

NOW WHAT?

There's lots of misinformation out there about Jesus. Commit to believing only what God's inspired, perfect Word tells us about him.

DID YOU KNOW?

The four Gospels aren't a full account of Jesus' last three years on earth. The Gospel of John ends by saying, "Jesus also did many other things. If they were all written down, I suppose the whole world could not contain the books that would be written" (John 21:25).

He wore a robe dipped in blood, and his title was the Word of God.
REVELATION 19:13

Of the Bible's many different titles for Jesus, one of the most interesting, profound, and, honestly, a bit confusing at first, is found in John 1.

The apostle John starts his Gospel with these well-known words: "In the beginning was the Word, and the Word was with God, and the Word was God. He was with God in the beginning. Through him all things were made; without him nothing was made that has been made" (John 1:1-3, NIV). Eleven verses later, John continues the theme: "The Word became flesh and made his dwelling among us. We have seen his glory, the glory of the one and only Son, who came from the Father, full of grace and truth" (John 1:14, NIV).

"The Word" is Jesus. But why did John use this unique name to describe him?

WHAT'S IT MEAN?

The entire Bible starts with this famous sentence in Genesis 1:1: "In the beginning God created the heavens and the earth." Now compare it to John 1:1: "In the beginning was the Word" (NIV). See the similarity? By using the familiar phrase "In the beginning" to talk about "the Word," John is pointing to Jesus' eternal nature, deity, and his active role in Creation (see the January 1 and 2 devotions).

As for calling Jesus "the Word," here's why: God communicates and relates to his creation through words. He created the universe through words. He spoke ("Let there be light" and "Let the land produce living creatures") and things immediately came into being (Genesis 1:3, 24, NIV).

The rest of Scripture affirms God's interpersonal, loving, and communicative nature. He spoke to the patriarchs—Abraham, Isaac, and Jacob—through physical appearances and visions. He spoke to Moses on Mount Sinai, giving the Israelites written commands to follow. And he spoke to the Israelites through the words and writings of prophets.

So when John calls Jesus "the Word," he's showing that Jesus is God's greatest revelation of himself. That's because Jesus *is* God! All the visions, commands, and prophecies—*every single word!*—that God used to speak to Old Testament Israel are fulfilled in the true Word, Jesus.

To know Jesus, the true Word of God, is to know God himself!

NOW WHAT?
Read Genesis 1; John 1:1-18; and 1 John 1:1-4 and look for the similarities.

DID YOU KNOW?
John loved referring to Jesus as "the Word" in his other writings too. He called Jesus "the Word of life" in 1 John 1:1 and "the Word of God" in Revelation 19:13 (today's verse).

JANUARY 26

Everyone was expecting the Messiah to come soon, and they were eager to know whether John might be the Messiah. LUKE 3:15

The people flocked in droves to the hot, arid region of eastern Israel. All around them, the earth was dry and parched as the scorching, Middle Eastern sun blazed overhead. As sweat beaded on their foreheads, anticipation bubbled inside of them.

They couldn't wait to see the Wilderness Man.

The Israelites had been waiting, thousands of years, literally, for God's promised Messiah. But for the last four centuries or so, God had remained silent. No prophecies. No books of the Bible written. Nothing. Only wars, political upheaval, and oppression from stronger empires. So the people waited . . . and waited . . . and waited.

Then John the Baptist appeared. John was like no one they had ever seen before. Unlike the arrogant religious leaders of the day who walked around with rich, flowing robes and upturned noses, John lived in the wilderness, wore camel-hair clothing, and ate honey-dipped locusts for lunch.

But John wasn't just a weirdo. There was a piercing forcefulness to his words. As he baptized people in the Jordan River, he shouted, "Repent of your sins and turn to God, for the Kingdom of Heaven is near" (Matthew 3:2). His powerful voice echoed across the barren landscape.

All of Israel was abuzz. Could this strange, dynamic desert dweller actually be the Messiah?

No, John told them, but they would see the Savior soon enough.

WHAT'S IT MEAN?

The ancient Jews were desperate for a savior. They had been subject to foreign rule for most of the previous six hundred years.

Sadly, when Jesus revealed himself as the Messiah, the majority of Israel didn't believe in him. He didn't fit their preconceived ideas.

This yearning for spiritual truth—for something, or someone, to believe in—is still prevalent today. That's why there are so many religions out there. People all over the world want to know why they're here and what to believe in. Many people might not want to admit it, but all of us need to be made right with our Creator.

Jesus is the answer. God's Son revealed himself in person to the people of Israel, and he reveals himself to us today through God's Word.

The people of Jesus' day largely rejected him. What will you do?

NOW WHAT?

Read all the Gospel accounts of John the Baptist's ministry—Matthew 3:1-17; Mark 1:1-8; Luke 3:1-20; and John 1:15-42—and compare them.

DID YOU KNOW?

Many other religions besides Christianity acknowledge Jesus' existence, but only Christianity teaches that salvation from sins comes exclusively through faith in Jesus' sacrificial work on the cross.

JANUARY 27

He will baptize you with the Holy Spirit and with fire.

MATTHEW 3:11

With his camel-hair outfits, flying-insect diet, and propensity for calling Israel's hypocritical religious leaders a "brood of snakes" to their faces (Matthew 3:7), John the Baptist could have certainly hosted his own reality TV show.

John was a brutally honest man. He didn't mince words, especially when it came to eternal matters. He boldly called people to repent and prepare their hearts for the coming Savior. His whole mission, in fact, was to announce the Messiah's coming (Matthew 3:3).

But John's description of Jesus might surprise you. As huge crowds gathered around John at the Jordan River, here's what he said: "Someone is coming soon who is greater than I am—so much greater that I'm not worthy even to be his slave and carry his sandals. He will baptize you with the Holy Spirit and with fire. He is ready to separate the chaff from the wheat with his winnowing fork. Then he will clean up the threshing area, gathering the wheat into his barn but burning the chaff with never-ending fire" (Matthew 3:11-12).

Not exactly warm and fuzzy words, huh?

WHAT'S IT MEAN?

Yes, it's true that Jesus is loving, patient, and kind. He had a heart for children. He healed the sick and hurting. He wept over people's pain. And he died in our place.

But there's also a distinct seriousness to Jesus. Just like farmers in ancient times used to toss their harvest into the air to separate the wheat (good) from the chaff (bad), the holy Son of God separates people into two categories: the righteous and the wicked, those who are his true followers and those who aren't. There's no middle ground.

As today's verse tells us, following Jesus brings forgiveness of sins, the blessing of God's Spirit, and eternal life; however, rejection of Jesus brings eternal separation from God in the "never-ending fire" of hell that John the Baptist mentioned. It might sound shocking, but that's what our sin deserves.

As you read this devotional, you'll hear a great deal about Jesus' love and kindness. But it's also important to remember that denying Jesus brings terrible consequences.

So you have a choice to make: Will you follow Jesus?

NOW WHAT?

Following Jesus requires repentance (turning from your sins) and faith (believing that Jesus is the only one who can save you from your sins). If you haven't already, commit your life to following Jesus today!

DID YOU KNOW?

Herod Antipas eventually beheaded John the Baptist for condemning the wicked king's immoral marriage (Matthew 14:1-12).

Christ, our Passover Lamb, has been sacrificed for us.
I CORINTHIANS 5:7

John the Baptist couldn't contain his excitement. His entire life had been building toward this moment. His mission was simple: point people to the Messiah. And now, the Messiah was here. Jesus was walking his way.

John immediately stopped what he was doing, pointed at Jesus, and shouted, "Look! The Lamb of God who takes away the sin of the world!" (John 1:29).

Now *there's* an interesting description of Jesus! Let's think about lambs for a moment. Like other livestock, they smell. They are weak, defenseless, and quite honestly, not very bright.

Lambs—and sheep in general—don't take charge; they follow. If someone calls you a sheep, it's not a compliment. It probably means you are a follower, not a leader.

People raise lambs for their meat, skin, wool, and milk. In other words, lambs are bred to be slaughtered. It's a bummer to be a lamb.

So why did John refer to Jesus as one?

WHAT'S IT MEAN?

By calling Jesus "the Lamb of God," John was connecting thousands of years of Israel's history to Jesus. In Exodus 12, God commanded the Israelites to kill a young, pure lamb and smear its blood on the doorposts of their homes before he delivered them from Egyptian slavery—the first Passover. Shortly thereafter, God gave his people the Old Testament law, which required them to offer spotless animals as sacrifices for their sins. Lambs were an acceptable option.

Why did God tell the Israelites to kill so many innocent animals? Because as Hebrews 9:22 says, "Without the shedding of blood there is no forgiveness of sins" (ESV). To save a life from sin, a life must be taken. Through animal sacrifices, God was mercifully sparing his sinful people from his righteous judgment.

But the death of smelly livestock cannot truly forgive sins. This was God's temporary solution until the true sacrifice arrived. That sacrifice is Jesus!

Eventually, Jesus went to the cross "like a lamb to the slaughter," fulfilling Isaiah 53:7. As the "sinless, spotless" Savior (1 Peter 1:19), he was able to make a once-for-all sacrifice for sins.

Today, there's no more need for Passover celebrations or animal sacrifices. Thanks to the death and resurrection of Jesus, the true Lamb of God, our sins can be completely forgiven!

NOW WHAT?

Learn how Jesus perfectly fulfilled the requirements of the Passover lamb in Exodus 12 by looking at John 19:33-36 and Hebrews 4:15.

DID YOU KNOW?

The book of Revelation alone refers to Jesus as "the Lamb" nearly thirty times.

A voice from heaven said, "This is my dearly loved Son, who brings me great joy." MATTHEW 3:17

In Romans 3, the apostle Paul writes some sobering words about the human race. Using some Old Testament passages from Psalms, Proverbs, and Isaiah, Paul tells us that "no one is righteous—not even one. No one is truly wise; no one is seeking God. All have turned away; all have become useless. No one does good, not a single one" (verses 10-12).

Yikes.

That's bad news for us humans. But Paul is right. In fact, in the history of the world—including the gazillions of people who have lived on earth— no one has fully pleased God with 100-percent-perfect obedience.

Except Jesus.

We see evidence of this in Jesus' baptism. As Jesus came up out of the water, Matthew 3:16-17 says that the Holy Spirit descended on him like a dove and God spoke these words from heaven: "This is my dearly loved Son, who brings me great joy."

WHAT'S IT MEAN?

So what, exactly, did Jesus do to bring God great joy? Did he overthrow the Roman Empire, which was oppressing God's people? Did he end world hunger? Did he help little old ladies cross the street every day?

No, none of those things was his ultimate mission.

Jesus pleased God by perfectly obeying his heavenly Father and fulfilling his calling to become humanity's sin-sacrifice. Jesus mentioned this in a prayer to the Father in John 17:4: "I brought glory to you here on earth by completing the work you gave me to do."

Sometime in eternity past, well before the creation of the world, God decided on a perfect rescue plan for corrupt humanity. We need help to please God, because we can't do it on our own. So the sinless Son of God willingly submitted himself to God's plan and pleased the Father on our behalf. He came to earth in human form and paid the price for our sins.

This gave God great joy, and it should do the same for you! Rejoice that Jesus fully accomplished his mission and pleased God for your sake! And rejoice that there's a God in heaven who loved you enough to sacrifice his own Son to save you!

NOW WHAT?

Through Jesus, you can now please God—not by good works, but by faith and obedience. Trust in Jesus and live to glorify God.

DID YOU KNOW?

The prayer Jesus prayed in John 17 is often called the "High Priestly Prayer." Check out Hebrews chapters 4–10 for an amazing description of why Jesus is our great High Priest. Also make sure to read the February 3 and June 16 devotions.

Andrew went to find his brother, Simon, and told him, "We have found the Messiah" (which means "Christ").   JOHN 1:41

What do you anticipate most each year? Christmas? Your birthday? The last day of school? A sweet summer vacation?

Early in the first century AD, the Jewish people were eagerly anticipating the Messiah. By the start of Jesus' public ministry somewhere around AD 26, the Jews had been subject to foreign powers like Babylon, Persia, Greece, and Rome for the better part of six hundred years. God's people were hungry for freedom, desperate for the Messiah. Luke 3:15, set in the story of Jesus' baptism, says, "Everyone was expecting the Messiah to come soon, and they were eager to know whether John [the Baptist] might be the Messiah."

So in John 1:41, you can almost hear the excitement in the voice of Andrew (the apostle Peter's brother) when he told Peter (also called Simon) about his first encounter with Jesus. "We have found the Messiah!" Andrew exclaimed.

WHAT'S IT MEAN?

If you've been around church awhile, you've probably heard Jesus described as "the Messiah." But do you know what that word means?

Messiah doesn't mean "savior" or "lord." The term comes from the Hebrew term *mashiach*, used during the Old Testament era. Literally translated, it means "anointed."

To be anointed meant to be chosen by God for a special purpose. Old Testament kings such as Saul, David, and Solomon were anointed. So were Old Testament priests.

As the Israelites found out, no human king could totally fulfill God's laws and perfectly shepherd God's people. Even the greatest kings like David had serious flaws. A divine "anointed one" was needed instead. Eventually, Isaiah, Jeremiah, and other divinely inspired prophets started predicting a perfect *mashiach* who would save God's people and restore God's Kingdom.

If your head is spinning a bit, don't sweat it. We just compressed thousands of years' worth of Jewish history into a few hundred words. Here's what you need to know: Jesus is God's promised Messiah. Through his death and resurrection, he completely fulfilled every messianic prophecy in the Bible. He is God's true anointed one, the perfect divine king!

NOW WHAT?

There are scores of messianic prophecies in the Old Testament. To check out a few, read Isaiah 7:10-17; 9:1-6; 61:1-2; Jeremiah 23:5-6; Daniel 9:24-27; and Zechariah 3:8.

DID YOU KNOW?

The Old Testament prophets who spoke of a coming Messiah were given only partial knowledge about what they were predicting. They "wanted to know more about" Jesus and "wondered what time or situation" he would arrive in (1 Peter 1:10-11). God told them that "their messages were not for themselves, but for you" (1 Peter 1:12).

JANUARY 31

Then Jesus was led by the Spirit into the wilderness to be tempted there by the devil. MATTHEW 4:1

We love to celebrate big events with parties. We throw birthday parties, graduation parties, Halloween parties, Christmas parties, New Year's Eve parties, and Super Bowl parties. We even have parties to celebrate parties (like prom after-parties).

Jesus' baptism was a really big event. Through it, God announced that Jesus was God's Son and the long-awaited Messiah.

Do you know how Jesus celebrated this momentous occasion? Immediately after his baptism, Jesus traveled alone into the desert, where he fasted for forty days and confronted his greatest enemy.

That's right—Jesus went into the wilderness for an epic showdown with the devil.

WHAT'S IT MEAN?

So who, exactly, is the devil?

First, let's clear up some confusion: he isn't red with a sinister goatee, horns, or a pointy tail. And he definitely does not carry a pitchfork.

But the devil is real. The Bible is very clear about that. He is often called Satan, which means "adversary." Scripture also refers to him as "the evil one" (John 17:15), "the god of this world" (2 Corinthians 4:4), the "prince of demons" (Matthew 12:24), and "the dragon" (Revelation 12).

Satan is not eternal or all-powerful like God (Job 1:12). He is a created being and a fallen angel. Some Bible scholars believe that Isaiah 14:12-15 describes how God kicked him out of heaven after he rebelled.

Satan's chief goal is to destroy God's people and creation through sinful temptations, deceit, accusations, slander, and strife. In 1 Peter 5:8, he is called our "great enemy" who "prowls around like a roaring lion, looking for someone to devour." He is a "murderer" and "the father of lies" (John 8:44)—evil through and through.

That's why he disguised himself as a serpent and tempted Adam and Eve in the Garden of Eden. And it's why he tempted Jesus in the wilderness. Satan knew that Jesus was our only hope for salvation, so he tried as hard as he could to ruin Jesus' mission.

It didn't work. Jesus won the battle when he rose from the grave. Death couldn't beat Jesus, and neither could Satan! Now the devil "is filled with fury, because he knows that his time is short" (Revelation 12:12, NIV). He is a defeated foe, doomed to hell (Revelation 20:10). All because of Jesus!

NOW WHAT?

Thank Jesus for his victory over Satan, which is a victory for you!

DID YOU KNOW?

The Bible's first reference to "Satan" came either in Job 1 or 1 Chronicles 21, depending on which was written first. The phrase "the devil" first appears in the story of Jesus' temptation in Matthew 4.

FEBRUARY 1

When he lies, it is consistent with his character; for he is a liar and the father of lies. JOHN 8:44

Here's a shocking fact: Satan knows the Bible.

Hard to believe, huh? But it's true. When Satan tempted Jesus three times in the wilderness, he actually quoted Scripture on his second attempt (Matthew 4:5-6).

After taking Jesus to the highest point of the Temple in Jerusalem and challenging him to jump off to display his power, Satan recited Psalm 91:11-12, which says, "He will order his angels to protect you wherever you go. They will hold you up with their hands so you won't even hurt your foot on a stone."

But those verses weren't written to encourage anyone to pull a really dangerous stunt. Satan was trying to trick Jesus into misusing his power. Jesus saw right through the deception and answered by quoting Deuteronomy 6:16: "You must not test the LORD your God."

WHAT'S IT MEAN?

The devil loves to twist God's words. He's been doing it since the Garden of Eden. Remember how God gave Adam and Eve specific instructions not to eat from the tree of the knowledge of good and evil? Then along came Satan, who asked Eve, "Did God really say you must not eat the fruit from any of the trees in the garden?" (Genesis 3:1).

It's important to understand how the devil works. Just like a soldier benefits from knowing how the enemy army operates, Christians can fight the devil's temptations better when they know his methods.

Satan loves to lie. It's in his nature. Sometimes he will blatantly lie to you. Other times, he will insidiously twist God's words so his falsehoods sound pretty close to the truth. Either way, he wants to deceive you and lead you into sin since "he has always hated the truth, because there is no truth in him" (John 8:44).

To defeat Satan, you must know and believe the truth. Like Jesus did in the wilderness, you must combat Satan's lies and temptations by following the truth of Scripture. In 2 Samuel 7:28, we read, "You are God, O Sovereign LORD. Your words are truth."

Follow God's Word and you'll defeat the liar!

NOW WHAT?

Memorize Scripture! In light of today's devotion, a good passage to memorize is 1 Peter 5:8-9. In our battle against Satan, Ephesians 6:17 calls the Bible "the sword of the Spirit." God's Word is an offensive weapon that we can use to defeat the enemy.

DID YOU KNOW?

While Satan is the father of lies, Jesus is the essence of truth. In John 14:6, Jesus says, "I am the way, the truth, and the life. No one can come to the Father except through me."

FEBRUARY 2

This High Priest of ours understands our weaknesses, for he faced all of the same testings we do, yet he did not sin.   HEBREWS 4:15

Here's a challenge: Try to go through today without sinning.

Sound easy? It's not. Today, you will be bombarded with chances and temptations to sin. Even on a great day, your sinful nature eventually will kick in and start pulling you toward evil.

Anger, pride, lying, greed, impatience, envy, unkindness, selfishness, bitterness, hurtful speech, disobedience to your parents . . . at some point today, you will probably fall prey to one of these things. As God told Cain in Genesis 4:7, "Sin is crouching at your door; it desires to have you, but you must rule over it" (NIV). That's true for all of us.

Now try wrapping your mind around this: Jesus never sinned.

Not only did Jesus overcome all of Satan's temptations in the desert, but he never sinned before or afterward, either. Not once. Nada. Never.

Jesus never said no to his parents. He never hit his younger siblings. He never lied or cheated or stole. He never said a bad word or entertained an impure thought.

He was perfect.

WHAT'S IT MEAN?

Jesus' sinless nature is simply amazing. Even though he was fully God (and God is sinless), the Bible says he was also fully human. He wasn't immune to temptation. Today's verse makes that clear.

Jesus was tempted to sin in the same ways we are. He was tempted to yell, lie, and hit someone. He got tempted to cheat, argue, and disobey his parents. But he never gave in.

This is a profound truth with huge implications for us today. If Jesus sinned even once, he would've been disqualified as our Savior. That's why Satan tempted him. But Jesus remained perfect, meeting God's holy standard for a sin-sacrifice. No one else could've died for our sins.

The benefits of Jesus' sinless nature don't stop there, though. Read today's verse again. Because Jesus experienced temptations like we do, he's able to empathize with us. When sinful cravings attack us, he can help. Hebrews 2:18 says, "Since he himself has gone through suffering and testing, he is able to help us when we are being tested." We have a Savior who understands temptation!

NOW WHAT?

When temptations to sin come, pray for help to the Savior who defeated sin!

DID YOU KNOW?

Jesus even got angry without sinning. For an example, read the story of Jesus cleansing the Temple in John 2:13-17.

FEBRUARY 3

Let us come boldly to the throne of our gracious God. There we will receive his mercy, and we will find grace to help us when we need it most. HEBREWS 4:16

Access in this world is often restricted.

You've probably seen Do Not Enter signs at school, banks, restaurants, and stores. Football fans aren't allowed to just mosey into NFL locker rooms and get autographs from their favorite players. And if you jump the fence at the White House and start running across the grass, you'll be arrested faster than you can say, "Secret Service."

In the Old Testament, access to God was limited at times too. Before God descended on Mount Sinai in a terrifying cloud of smoke and fire to provide the Ten Commandments, he told Moses, "Be careful! Do not go up on the mountain or even touch its boundaries. Anyone who touches the mountain will certainly be put to death" (Exodus 19:12).

Later, when the Jews worshiped at the Tabernacle and the Temple, only the high priest could enter the Most Holy Place—the place representing God's presence—once a year. God was teaching the people that sinners cannot approach his holiness on their own.

That's why Jesus came.

WHAT'S IT MEAN?

When Jesus died on the cross, the Temple curtain restricting access to the Most Holy Place tore in two (Matthew 27:51). Suddenly, free access to God was possible through the Savior who was sinless (see yesterday's devotion).

Approaching God should no longer cause fear or trembling. Yes, God is still just as awesome and holy as he was in the Old Testament. And yes, we are to revere and honor him. But because he is a loving heavenly Father who sacrificed his own Son for us, we can have confidence that he wants to be near to us.

Faith in Jesus gives us a personal relationship with the almighty Creator of the universe! Our sins have been forgiven forever. We have no reason to fear. That's why Hebrews 4:16 encourages us to "come boldly to the throne of our gracious God."

How do we approach God? That's simple: through prayer, reading his Word, and worship. We can worship him freely, speak honestly with him, and ask for his help. You have access to God through Jesus!

(But please stay off the White House lawn.)

NOW WHAT?

When you pray, you can make bold requests of God—not selfishly bold requests, but requests for God to increase your faith, help you, and bless others.

DID YOU KNOW?

The Israelites had to ceremonially purify themselves before approaching Mount Sinai. We are purified through Jesus!

FEBRUARY 4

Do not love this world nor the things it offers you, for when you love the world, you do not have the love of the Father in you.

1 JOHN 2:15

Today's devotional is a scouting report.

In professional sports, teams send out scouts to watch future opponents and write reports about their style of play. It's the same in war. Military forces learn about the enemy by secretly sending soldiers or spying equipment ahead to gather information about a foe prior to a battle.

When it comes to our spiritual lives, we need a scouting report on the enemy too. We need to know what we're up against. According to the Bible, Christians actually have not one . . . not two . . . but three main enemies: Satan, the world, and the flesh.

WHAT'S IT MEAN?

We've already discussed Satan several times. He is our biggest enemy, and he wants to ruin God's plans and lead people astray. But he will ultimately be destroyed.

Let's discuss the other two. When the Bible refers to "the world," it's not saying the earth is our enemy. "The world," as defined by Scripture, is the system of sinful humanity that opposes God and promotes ungodly values, such as movies that include inappropriate material, or schools that promote evolution as the origin of life, or countries that outlaw Christianity. This is "the world" (see today's verse).

Likewise, when the Bible talks about "the flesh," it's not saying skin is our enemy. "The flesh" refers to our sinful nature—the natural desires of our hearts as fallen human beings. It's caring more about what your body will enjoy than about what God says. Romans 8:8 says, "Those who are in the realm of the flesh cannot please God" (NIV).

All three of these enemies tempt us in different ways. Satan tempts us to doubt and disobey God. The world tempts us to live for ourselves. And the flesh tempts us to satisfy our sinful desires.

All Christians must battle Satan, the world, and the flesh daily. Sometimes we win, and sometimes we don't. But take heart! According to Scripture, Christians are already victorious over all of them.

Thanks to his death and resurrection, Jesus defeated Satan (1 John 3:8), overcame the world (John 16:33), and broke the power of the flesh (Galatians 5:24). Through Christ, we win!

NOW WHAT?

Pray to God for help against the temptations of Satan, the world, and the flesh. He will be faithful to help you.

DID YOU KNOW?

The book of Revelation describes the destruction of Satan and the world. As for the flesh, its defeat is seen in the fact that Jesus will one day give believers new, perfect bodies (1 Corinthians 15).

*The temptations in your life are no different from what others
experience. And God is faithful. He will not allow the temptation
to be more than you can stand. When you are tempted, he will show
you a way out so that you can endure.* 1 CORINTHIANS 10:13

In the classic 1985 movie *Rocky IV*, boxer Rocky Balboa agrees to fight Soviet super-fighter Ivan Drago after Drago literally beat Rocky's friend Apollo Creed to death in an earlier bout. Creed didn't have to die. But as Creed was taking a deadly pounding, he stubbornly refused to allow the referee to stop the fight.

Of course, *Rocky IV* is only Hollywood fiction, but that part of the movie rings true: no fighter ever wants to give up.

Yielding to an opponent is the worst feeling in the world for a fighter. In boxing, it's called "throwing in the towel." In various forms of martial arts, it's called "tapping out." It's when a competitor admits defeat because he's in an inescapable submission hold or he's unable to physically continue the match.

When it comes to temptations, sometimes the urge to disregard God's rules and give in to sin can feel overwhelming, like fifteen grueling rounds with an elite fighter. It can feel impossible to win, as if throwing in the towel is the only option.

But it's just not true.

WHAT'S IT MEAN?

When temptations come, tapping out and giving in to sin is never our only choice. That's another lie from Satan. Today's verse makes that clear.

While God never tempts us (James 1:13), he does allow temptations to come. In his divine wisdom, he does this to teach us to depend on him. And he never allows us to experience any inescapable temptations. He always provides an escape route. He always gives us the strength and ability to say, "No, I choose to obey God."

This is possible through Jesus. Because God's Son perfectly obeyed the

Father, we can too. The same power that Jesus possessed to avoid sinful temptation and obey God is also available to all who trust in him as their Savior.

Don't tap out to sin . . . tap *in* to Jesus' power to obey!

NOW WHAT?

Memorizing Scripture (and recalling it in times of trouble) is a great way to overcome temptations. Start with Psalm 119:11. Hiding God's Word in your heart helps to defend against sin.

DID YOU KNOW?

The *Rocky* movie franchise includes six films spanning thirty years (1976–2006), with actor Sylvester Stallone playing the title character in all of them. Stallone was nearly sixty years old when number six, *Rocky Balboa*, was released. That's a senior citizen boxer!

"The time promised by God has come at last!" he announced.
"The Kingdom of God is near! Repent of your sins and believe the
Good News!" MARK 1:15

The time had come.

Jesus had been baptized. He had overcome Satan's temptations. Now he was ready to start his public ministry. So he started traveling throughout Israel, telling people, "The Kingdom of God is near! Repent of your sins and believe the Good News!"

Maybe you've read that verse many times and it doesn't mean much to you. But to a Jew living in first-century Israel, those words were fascinating—and probably somewhat mysterious.

The religious leaders of the day—the Pharisees, Sadducees, priests, and scribes—weren't teaching the people about repentance and "Good News." Instead, they were telling the people that God would show favor to you if you (a) were a descendant of Abraham (a Jew) and (b) tried your best to keep the Old Testament laws. They preached a false religion of heritage and works.

Then along came a man named Jesus who spoke a completely different message. The people marveled at his unique teaching and authority. Sadly, though, few people really understood who he was and what he was talking about.

WHAT'S IT MEAN?

Jesus' message was simple. He was telling the people to turn away from their sins ("repent") and trust in him, because the Kingdom of God had arrived.

Many of Jesus' listeners probably looked around and said, "I don't see the Kingdom of God. Where is it? We're still living under the oppressive rule of the Romans."

But the "Kingdom of God" that Jesus mentioned wasn't a physical realm with a human king fighting for Israel's freedom. When Jesus spoke about the Kingdom of God, he was referring to himself! Jesus was the fulfillment of all the Old Testament promises of a coming Savior. Jesus could tell people "the Kingdom of God is near" because the Son of God was literally walking among the people!

Sadly, most people who initially were captivated by Jesus' words didn't actually put their faith in him. They never truly understood that the Kingdom of God isn't about earthly empires; it's about Jesus changing people's hearts through faith in his death and resurrection.

Even today, Jesus still calls out through Scripture, "The Kingdom of God is near! Repent of your sins and believe the Good News!" Will you believe?

NOW WHAT?

If you haven't repented of your sins and trusted in the good news of salvation through Jesus, do it today!

DID YOU KNOW?

At first, even Jesus' disciples had a hard time understanding what the true Kingdom of God was all about (Acts 1:4-9).

FEBRUARY 7

At daybreak he called together all of his disciples and chose twelve of them to be apostles. LUKE 6:13

As Jesus began his public ministry, he called twelve men to be his closest friends—his apostles (they were sometimes called his disciples). An "apostle" is someone who is sent by someone else to represent the sender and fulfill a specific mission.

You'd think that the sinless, eternal Son of God would choose the nicest, most amazing, superholy guys when choosing his inner circle, right?

Wrong.

Jesus' apostles were Andrew, Peter, James, John, James (another one!), Philip, Bartholomew, Thomas, Matthew, Thaddaeus, Simon, and Judas Iscariot (Matthew 10:2-4). These guys were no Boy Scouts.

Matthew was a tax collector for the Romans, a profession filled with thievery and dishonesty. Peter viciously cut off a man's ear in the garden of Gethsemane and later denied that he knew Jesus. Simon probably once belonged to a violent, politically motivated group called the Zealots. James and John once asked Jesus if they could call down fire from heaven to destroy some inhospitable Samaritans. Thomas infamously doubted Jesus' resurrection at first. And then, of course, there was Judas Iscariot, who betrayed God's Son for a measly thirty pieces of silver.

The apostles were a ragtag bunch. They often argued, lacked faith, and struggled to understand Jesus' teachings. They were angry, hardheaded, and deceitful. They lied, cheated, stole, and maybe even murdered. And in Jesus' greatest moment of need in Gethsemane, they all deserted him (Matthew 26:56).

Yet Jesus still loved them.

WHAT'S IT MEAN?

Jesus' choice of friends is a powerful reminder that he can use *anyone* for his glory, even weak sinners like the apostles . . . and us.

Look how he changed the apostles:

- Matthew wrote the first Gospel.
- John became a loving pastor and wrote five books of the Bible.
- James was martyred for his courageous faith.
- Peter wrote two books of the Bible and became an important church leader.

It's not who you are that matters to God. It's who you trust. So if you're feeling weak or worthless, cheer up! You're just like the apostles, who ended up doing great things for God. Through faith in Jesus, you can too!

NOW WHAT?

Make a list of why Jesus *shouldn't* use you. . . . Done? Good. Now cross out everything and remember: Jesus still loves you and wants to use you for his glory!

DID YOU KNOW?

Other than Peter, John, and James, the Bible remains largely silent on the lives of Jesus' apostles after his return to heaven. Sadly, Judas Iscariot hanged himself (Acts 1:16-20).

Jesus called out to them, "Come, follow me, and I will show you how to fish for people!" MATTHEW 4:19

These days, the sport of fishing is a competitive, multibillion-dollar industry. Professional bass fishermen travel all over the country with state-of-the-art equipment to compete in elite tournaments for a chance to win huge prize money.

It's a far cry from the fishing of Jesus' day. Back then, no one fished for recreation. There were no powerboats, lucrative sponsorships, high-tech rods and reels, or ESPN coverage. Fishermen in ancient times threw crude nets into the water and hoped to haul in a big catch. Otherwise, their family wouldn't eat. Fishing was their livelihood.

When Jesus chose his disciples, he first called two sets of fishermen brothers—Andrew and Peter, and James and John. One day, Jesus saw these men fishing in the Sea of Galilee. So he called out to them, "Come, follow me, and I will show you how to fish for people!" (today's verse). Without hesitation, they all left their boats and followed Jesus.

WHAT'S IT MEAN?

Fortunately, when Jesus mentioned "fishing for people," he wasn't speaking literally. After all, who wants to have a sharp hook sticking through his or her cheek? Or to flop around with a bunch of other people while stuck in a slimy net? No thanks.

Jesus was speaking figuratively. He was telling his new disciples, "Just as you once pulled in fishnets for a living, now I want to teach you how to draw in people with a message of God's love and forgiveness."

Jesus wanted these men—and the rest of his disciples—to trust in him and learn from him so that, after he returned to heaven, they could continue spreading the gospel message that God forgives sins through Jesus. As the book of Acts tells us, the disciples (minus Judas Iscariot) faithfully carried out Jesus' plan once he ascended.

But two thousand years later, the job isn't finished. Jesus still wants his followers today to fish for people. If you've put your faith in Jesus, you have a job to do: tell others the good news that Jesus died for their sins and rose from the dead.

Being a fisher for people also means that you live what you preach. If you say you're a Christian but don't show it by the way you act and speak, no one will listen.

Speak and live out the gospel toward others, and you will be a modern-day people-fisher!

NOW WHAT?

Do you know someone who's not a Christian? Give that person a Bible or strike up a conversation with him or her. Talk about what your friend believes, and point him or her to Jesus.

DID YOU KNOW?

Early Christians used a fish symbol, called an *ichthys*, to identify themselves as followers of Jesus. You may have seen this symbol on a car bumper sticker before.

Obviously, I'm not trying to win the approval of people, but of God.
If pleasing people were my goal, I would not be Christ's servant.
GALATIANS 1:10

On a scale of 1 to 10 (with 10 being the greatest), how popular are you?

If you said 10, you probably need a little dose of humility. If you said 1, you probably need a hug. If you said somewhere in between, you are probably pretty close to being accurate.

When Jesus was on earth, he buried the 1-to-10 popularity needle somewhere beyond 100. As Jesus started traveling throughout Israel, Luke 5:15 says "vast crowds came to hear him preach and to be healed of their diseases." Matthew 4:23-25 says Jesus' fame spread across Israel's borders into neighboring regions. He got so popular, in fact, that the crowds wanted "to force him to be their king" (John 6:15).

But Jesus' interest in being popular registered at a big, fat zero. He didn't feed off fame or crave attention, even though he literally had thousands of people flocking to him and hanging on his every word. John 2:24 says, "Jesus would not entrust himself to them, for he knew all people" (NIV).

WHAT'S IT MEAN?

Jesus understood that popularity is empty and fame is fleeting. He knew that getting caught up in fame would detract from his true mission: sacrificing himself on the cross for our sins.

We need to be wary of popularity too. There's nothing necessarily wrong with being popular, but it's not something we should strive for. Popularity is a human reaction that is usually impulsive, fickle, and short lived. And it certainly doesn't bring any eternal reward.

The apostle Paul addressed this issue in today's verse. According to Galatians 1:10, trying to win a popularity contest makes it tough to follow Jesus. That's because when you want to be popular with people, your attention shifts to yourself instead of the Savior. That's not good.

Instead, Paul says we should seek God's approval. His approval, after all, will determine our eternal fate.

You don't earn God's approval by works. It starts with a heart that acknowledges your need for a Savior. Jesus won God's approval for you by dying on the cross for your sins, a debt you could never pay on your own.

So forget about personal fame, and trust in the Savior who cared little about popularity but cares greatly about you!

NOW WHAT?

Seek to make Jesus famous in your life by living for him and spreading the good news about him to others.

DID YOU KNOW?

Jesus often reacted to the huge crowds gathering around him by withdrawing to quiet places to pray (Luke 5:16).

The Father gave me these works to accomplish, and they prove that he sent me.   JOHN 5:36

Lots of people can do card tricks or pull a rabbit out of a hat. But anyone who can make the Statue of Liberty disappear qualifies as a pretty amazing magician.

In 1983, world-famous conjurer David Copperfield performed this stunt on Liberty Island in New York before a live crowd and a TV audience of millions. It's just one of the many grand illusions that Copperfield has pulled off in a remarkable four-decade career that has produced twenty-one Emmy Awards and his own star on the Hollywood Walk of Fame.

Some of his other more memorable illusions include walking through the Great Wall of China, levitating over the Grand Canyon, and escaping from Alcatraz prison. It's pretty cool stuff. But then again, it's all fake.

There was, of course, another man who accomplished never-before-seen acts of wonder that shocked his audiences and staggered the imagination. His name is Jesus Christ. But Jesus was no magician. The miracles he performed were not by sleight of hand nor were they optical illusions. They were real, and they came from a source of power that no one else can claim.

WHAT'S IT MEAN?

Jesus' first miracle was turning large amounts of water into wine at a wedding feast in the town of Cana (John 2:1-11). He changed water into a completely different liquid without touching a single jug. Take a moment to wrap your mind around *that*.

As time went on, Jesus' miracles inspired even more awe: he calmed a storm, walked on water, fed thousands with one small meal, cast out demons, gave sight to the blind, and even raised the dead. The list could go on and on. We'll talk more in depth about some of these in future devotions.

But Jesus didn't perform miracles to wow audiences or show off. He did amazing signs and wonders to reveal his true identity.

Jesus is the Son of God, and his miracles prove it. He gave people small glimpses of his limitless power to show who he is. Only the eternal, all-powerful Messiah can do what he did.

Best of all, Jesus has the power to miraculously transform rebellious, sinful hearts into those acceptable to a holy God through faith. He is worthy of all worship and praise!

And that's no hocus-pocus.

NOW WHAT?

Ask your parents to show you a David Copperfield performance on the Internet. As you watch, remember that, while Copperfield's feats are illusions, Jesus' miracles were real.

DID YOU KNOW?

Jesus sometimes refused to perform miracles when people lacked faith in him (Matthew 12:38-40; 13:53-58).

One day as he saw the crowds gathering, Jesus went up on the
mountainside and sat down. His disciples gathered around him,
and he began to teach them. MATTHEW 5:1-2

As Jesus' popularity grew throughout Judea, huge crowds started following him. So one day, he climbed up a mountain to teach the masses from an elevated spot. We call this the Sermon on the Mount; it's found in Matthew chapters 5–7.

For the next three-plus weeks, we're going to dig into the Sermon on the Mount to unearth its treasures. The wealth of spiritual knowledge found there is rich and deep.

Jesus started his discourse with a series of statements that Bible scholars call the "Beatitudes." That's not a term we really use these days. If you're scratching your head asking, "What on earth is a Beatitude?" don't worry—you've come to the right place!

WHAT'S IT MEAN?
The word *beatitude* means "blessed" or "happy." Each Beatitude in Matthew 5:3-11 starts off with the phrase "Blessed are . . ." (NIV).

When the Bible uses the word *blessed*, it doesn't mean, "Life will be all peaches and cream if you do such-and-such." Being "blessed" in Scripture is a state of peace and well-being with God because your sins are forgiven and you're living for him. It's like saying, "God's blessings will be upon you if you do such-and-such out of a heart of faith."

Jesus was trying to change the thinking of his first-century listeners. For nearly 1,500 years, ever since God gave the Ten Commandments to Israel in Exodus 20, the Jews had been trying to earn God's favor by obeying the law. But the law was never meant to forgive sins. It was only meant to show the people how sinful they were and how much they needed a Savior (Romans 3:20).

The arrival of Jesus, the Messiah, marked a new era—the "Kingdom of God" that Jesus mentioned in Mark 1:15. No longer was it necessary to perform religious rituals and sacrifice animals. Jesus kept the law perfectly, and he died on the cross as a perfect sacrifice. Forgiveness and righteousness come only through him.

So in essence, Jesus was telling the people on the mountain that day, "You want God's true blessings? It's a matter of the heart, not the law. Follow me and my example, and you will be blessed."

NOW WHAT?

Read all the Beatitudes in Matthew 5:3-11 to prepare for the next week's devotions.

DID YOU KNOW?

There's a similar, but slightly different, discourse that Jesus gave to a large crowd of people in Luke 6:17-49, which some Bible scholars refer to as the "Sermon on the Plain."

Blessed are the poor in spirit, for theirs is the kingdom of heaven.
MATTHEW 5:3, NIV

Jesus was sitting on a mountain. Thousands of captivated followers surrounded him below. Many had already seen his miracles and listened to his unique teachings. Others had come out of sheer curiosity, wanting to see who this man from Nazareth was.

The large crowd eagerly awaited what Jesus would say or do next. The Sermon on the Mount was about to begin. And then, Jesus opened his mouth and said, "Blessed are the poor in spirit, for theirs is the kingdom of heaven."

Huh?

WHAT'S IT MEAN?

At first glance, Jesus' first beatitude might be a bit confusing. "Poor in spirit" is not a phrase commonly used today.

What does it mean to be "poor in spirit"? Is that when you flip your wallet upside-down, shake it out, and don't get a single drop of spirit to fall out?

Well, not exactly.

Being poor in spirit has nothing to do with money. It has everything to do with humility—not thinking too highly of yourself. It means having a heart that acknowledges your need for God.

The opposite of being poor in spirit is having a haughty, or prideful, spirit—being arrogant and thinking you've got everything figured out. But Proverbs 16:18 says, "Pride goes before destruction, and a haughty spirit before a fall" (NIV).

To please God and be blessed by him, you need to admit your helpless state apart from him. Without God, we can't even draw a single breath (Isaiah 42:5). But being poor in spirit goes further than that. It means confessing that you are a sinner condemned to eternal punishment apart from God's saving mercy and grace, which he showed to us through his Son's death and resurrection.

Be poor in spirit, and you will be rich in God's blessings!

NOW WHAT?

One way to cultivate a "poor in spirit" heart is by kneeling down and praying the following prayer: "Dear God, I admit that I'm a sinner who needs a Savior. Thank you for sending Jesus to take my sins away on the cross. Help me to love you and to remain humble before you."

DID YOU KNOW?

As the eternal, all-powerful Son of God, Jesus had every right to think highly of himself. But even Jesus was poor in spirit. To understand this wonderful truth more, see 2 Corinthians 8:9 and Philippians 2:5-8.

Blessed are those who mourn, for they will be comforted.
MATTHEW 5:4, NIV

If you thought the first of Jesus' beatitudes ("Blessed are the poor in spirit") during the Sermon on the Mount needed an explanation, then wait till you hear the second!

As he sat on the mountain, Jesus told the crowd, "Blessed are those who mourn, for they will be comforted."

Hmmm. Let's think about that for a minute. Was Jesus telling people that being sad will make you happy? That sounds like an oxymoron.

Does this verse mean that churches should cut prayer, worship music, the pastor's sermon, and the offering out of Sunday services so the congregation can cry on one another's shoulders all morning? Should all Christians quit school or their jobs to devote their time to mourning effectively? . . . *Okay, people, time to weep, wail, and cover yourself with sackcloth and ashes and wander through the streets moaning about your terrible plight in life!*

Uh, no. That's not what Jesus meant.

WHAT'S IT MEAN?

Jesus isn't telling us to walk around all mopey every day. Jesus, as usual, is talking about the posture of our hearts—in this case, as it relates to sin.

Here's a news flash: you are a big sinner. You've broken God's laws more than you can count. So has everyone else.

Some people feel sorry when they sin. Many don't. And often, even those who do are only sorry that they got caught or for the pain their bad choice caused, but not for the deed itself.

Sin, though, is serious business. It's a direct attack against our Creator. Sin is like shaking our fists at God and saying, "I don't want to obey you. I know better!" That's not good.

Sin deserves death (Romans 6:23), and it should produce godly sorrow.

This is what Jesus is talking about in the second beatitude. God blesses those who feel genuinely sorry for their sin and repent of it.

A great verse on godly sorrow is 2 Corinthians 7:10. It says, "The kind of sorrow God wants us to experience leads us away from sin and results in salvation. There's no regret for that kind of sorrow. But worldly sorrow, which lacks repentance, results in spiritual death."

NOW WHAT?

When you sin, remember to ask for God's forgiveness and for his help to change.

DID YOU KNOW?

The Bible provides some good, specific examples of worldly sorrow (Matthew 27:3-5) and godly sorrow (Luke 18:13). Check them out!

FEBRUARY 14

There is no greater love than to lay down one's life for one's friends.
JOHN 15:13

Ahhh, Valentine's Day.

Here we are once again at the annual holiday celebrating love. It's a big day, so we've taken a one-day break from our study of the Beatitudes to talk about the "L word."

Emotions today are as plentiful as greeting cards and rose bouquets. There's probably not another day on the calendar when "I love you" is said more often.

Love, though, has become a pretty loosely defined word over the years. Have you ever said any of the following?

- I love going to the beach!
- I love video games!
- I love playing basketball!
- I love it when I get money for my birthday!
- I love pizza!

Of course you've said some of those. We all have. But they don't really help us define love.

The *Merriam-Webster Dictionary* offers nearly a dozen different definitions for love. It's the subject of countless standup comedy routines, sermons, books, movies, and TV shows. Yet a quick scan of the often-sobering daily newspaper headlines reveals how little true love there is in the world.

How can we know what true love is?

WHAT'S IT MEAN?

God's Word is the ultimate authority on love. Why? Because "God is love" (1 John 4:8), and he inspired every word of Scripture (2 Timothy 3:16). To fully understand love, we must study the Bible and understand our Creator.

Other than the Old Testament's Song of Solomon, which describes romantic love between a man and woman, Scripture almost always refers to love as an action, not an emotion. The Bible defines love as something you do rather than something you feel (1 Corinthians 13).

Love involves devotion and concern for others. Most of all, love involves sacrifice. Read today's verse again. It comes from a long discussion Jesus had with his disciples the night before he was crucified. As Jesus said, the greatest sacrifice you can make for someone else is giving your life for his or her life. That's what Jesus did for you on the cross.

To love Jesus, you must sacrifice your own sinful desires and submit to his lordship in your life. To love others, you must sacrifice what you want for their good.

Today and every day after, love Jesus and others with biblical, sacrificial love!

NOW WHAT?

Want to give someone a true valentine? Forget the heart-shaped box of chocolates and put that person's needs above yours in a specific way.

DID YOU KNOW?

Historians debate how Valentine's Day got started. One popular theory says that it was Catholic Pope Gelasius I's attempt to "Christianize" a pagan Roman festival called Lupercalia in the fifth century AD.

FEBRUARY 15

Blessed are the meek, for they will inherit the earth.
MATTHEW 5:5, NIV

Gentleness is not really in vogue these days. We like our athletes brash, our movie stars muscle bound, and our cars dripping with horsepower. We like our music loud, our video games violent, and our comedians sarcastic.

When was the last time you watched a football game involving defensive linemen who apologize every time they drill the quarterback into the turf? Or a superhero movie starring little old ladies? Or a NASCAR race featuring little girls in pigtails rolling around the track on bikes with training wheels?

No, gentleness isn't really our thing. But it was Jesus' thing. In fact, he encouraged it.

Jesus' third beatitude during the Sermon on the Mount is reflected in today's verse: "Blessed are the meek, for they will inherit the earth."

WHAT'S IT MEAN?

The word *meek* means "humble," "quiet," and "gentle." Meekness is a character trait greatly valued in Scripture. Psalm 37:11 says, "The meek will inherit the land and enjoy peace and prosperity" (NIV). And the Bible contains many passages that promote humility and condemn pride (for example, Matthew 23:12).

People who are meek show love, put others first, and don't try to advance their own causes. They are better listeners than talkers. They don't think highly of themselves or selfishly seek their own good. They realize their own weaknesses and their desperate need for God.

The ultimate example of meekness, of course, is Jesus. In Matthew 11:29, he describes himself as "humble and gentle at heart." You can't get any more humble than temporarily giving up your rights as the Son of God to pay for the sins of humanity.

Meekness brings great spiritual rewards. Jesus says those who are meek "will inherit the earth." This could be a way of saying that humble Jesus followers, in general, will enjoy a peaceful life on earth, as Psalm 37:11 says.

Perhaps this promise also alludes to the future blessings that believers will receive at Jesus' second coming (Revelation 20–21).

So choose to be meek like Christ. Just don't expect to watch a movie about grandmas fighting supervillains anytime soon.

NOW WHAT?

Memorize Matthew 11:28-30, a great passage about Jesus' meekness.

DID YOU KNOW?

The modern-day word *meek* is of Scandinavian origin, dating back to at least the thirteenth century AD. It comes from Middle English words meaning "gentle" and "soft."

Blessed are those who hunger and thirst for righteousness, for they will be filled. MATTHEW 5:6, NIV

Life in Israel during Jesus' day was difficult. The daily necessities of food and water weren't always a given.

Israel, a rural, farming society, was under Roman rule at the time, and Rome heavily taxed its subjects. Many people were poor, and food was often scarce.

So it's not surprising that after Jesus fed five thousand people and then miraculously walked across the Sea of Galilee that night, the crowd eagerly looked for him the next day. When Jesus saw them, he exposed their true motives: "I tell you the truth, you want to be with me because I fed you, not because you understood the miraculous signs" (John 6:26).

There are other examples too. Hunger was a major theme in Jesus' story of the Prodigal Son (Luke 15:11-31). He mentioned bread in many parables (Matthew 7:9; Luke 11:5-8; and Luke 13:20-21), and in John 6:35, he called himself "the bread of life." In John 4:10, he promised a woman "living water" if she trusted in him.

Jesus knew his audience. That's probably one of the reasons why, when giving his fourth beatitude, he said, "Blessed are those who hunger and thirst for righteousness, for they will be filled."

WHAT'S IT MEAN?

Jesus knew his listeners would understand the feeling of going without enough food and water. But he wants his true followers to desire something even more than bodily nourishment. He wants us to actively pursue righteousness as if our lives depend on it—because, well, they do.

The word *righteous* means "morally good." Because he is holy, God is the ultimate standard of righteousness—what is good and fair. Deuteronomy 32:4 says, "He is the Rock; his deeds are perfect. Everything he does is just and fair. He is a faithful God who does no wrong; how just and upright he is!"

To be like Jesus, we are to pursue what is right, good, and fair. We must live according to God's righteous standards in our private lives and toward others.

This, of course, is impossible for sinners on their own. But through the cross, Jesus imputes (or credits) his righteousness to us (Romans 5:19), making it possible for imperfect people to be righteous before God and live righteously among others.

That's amazing food for thought!

NOW WHAT?

Ask God for help in your pursuit of righteousness. Truly righteous people realize that moral goodness is possible only through the God who is good.

DID YOU KNOW?

In the Bible's original languages of Hebrew (Old Testament) and Greek (New Testament), the word *righteousness* is synonymous with "justice."

Blessed are the merciful, for they will be shown mercy.
MATTHEW 5:7, NIV

In the classic 1984 movie *The Karate Kid*, a newcomer to a Southern California high school (Daniel) turns to a wise martial-arts expert (Mr. Miyagi) to learn to defend himself against some violent bullies.

One day, Daniel and Mr. Miyagi get a glimpse of why Daniel's tormentors are so aggressive, when they enter the bullies' karate dojo, which is run by a ruthless sensei named John Kreese. As Daniel and Mr. Miyagi look on, Kreese barks at his pupils, "We do not train to be merciful here. Mercy is for the weak!"

Apparently, John Kreese never read Matthew 5:7!

WHAT'S IT MEAN?

Mercy sometimes seems like a foreign concept in the world today, whether in movies or real life. Have you ever heard any of these popular phrases?

- "He got what he deserved."
- "Do the crime; do the time."
- "Eye for an eye."

Not much mercy there. Mercy, as defined by the *Merriam-Webster Dictionary*, is "compassion or forbearance shown, especially to an offender." In other words, it means not getting a penalty that you deserve. The fifth beatitude shows us that Jesus loves mercy.

We are to show mercy to others because we have received far greater mercy ourselves. No matter how someone else has wronged us, it's nothing compared to the wrongs we've piled up against God.

Humans don't deserve mercy. Our sins against God deserve death and eternal punishment (Romans 6:23). But Ephesians 2:4-5 brings good news: "God is so rich in mercy, and he loved us so much, that even though we were dead because of our sins, he gave us life when he raised Christ from the dead."

God showed the supreme example of mercy by sacrificing his own Son for lost, undeserving sinners. With that example as our guide, we should be merciful to others when they wrong us.

The alternative is scary. James 2:13 speaks about the fate of those who withhold mercy: "There will be no mercy for those who have not shown mercy to others. But if you have been merciful, God will be merciful when he judges you." Facing God's judgment without mercy is terrifying indeed.

Pay no attention to what movie villains from '80s karate movies say. Mercy is not for the weak. Mercy is for the godly!

NOW WHAT?

Has someone wronged you? Show that person mercy by letting him or her know you're offering forgiveness.

DID YOU KNOW?

Karate Kid became one of the most popular movies of the 1980s, spawning three sequels and an entire reboot of the franchise in 2010, starring Jaden Smith as the main character.

Blessed are the pure in heart, for they will see God.
MATTHEW 5:8, NIV

In stating the Beatitudes during his Sermon on the Mount, Jesus set the bar high—really high. In fact, he set the bar so high, not even a world-class pole-vaulter could reach it.

Take today's verse, for instance. Jesus says that God will bless the "pure in heart." The *Merriam-Webster Dictionary* describes *pure* as "not mixed with anything else" and "clean and not harmful in any way." Jesus is talking about a clean heart that is untainted by sin.

And that's a problem for us.

WHAT'S IT MEAN?

Humans aren't pure. Not one single person. Sin has contaminated all of us (Romans 3:10).

But we can *become* pure. Psalm 119:9 says, "How can a young person stay pure? By obeying your word." God's Word says that we can become pure in God's sight when we trust in Jesus for the forgiveness of our sins (1 John 1:9) and pursue righteous living. That's what it means to be "pure in heart."

But Jesus' sixth beatitude didn't stop there. He added a promise to the end: those who are pure in heart "will see God." This is nothing short of astounding!

Since the creation of the world, no one has ever fully seen God (John 1:18). Oh sure, certain people in the Bible caught glimpses of him, such as Moses in Exodus 33:21-23 or Isaiah in Isaiah 6:1. But no one has ever beheld God's full glory. It's too overwhelming for fallen mortals like us (Exodus 33:20).

The Bible, though, promises that the pure in heart will see God face-to-face one day! Listen to the amazing promise of Revelation 22:3-4: "The throne of God and of the Lamb will be there, and his servants will worship him. And they will see his face, and his name will be written on their foreheads."

This is possible only because of Jesus' work on the cross, turning lost sinners into purified, forgiven children of God. Thank you, Jesus!

NOW WHAT?

Those who are "pure in heart" not only trust in Jesus but also seek to live for him. Live for Jesus by reading and obeying his Word.

DID YOU KNOW?

Like Revelation 22:3-4, 1 John 3:2-3 talks about how the pure in heart will one day see the Lord: "Dear friends, we are already God's children, but he has not yet shown us what we will be like when Christ appears. But we do know that we will be like him, for we will see him as he really is. And all who have this eager expectation will keep themselves pure, just as he is pure."

Blessed are the peacemakers, for they will be called children of God.
MATTHEW 5:9, NIV

Peace is a wonderful thing.

It's a state of harmony, tranquility, and quiet. It's the absence of disturbance, conflict, or war. And whether in current or ancient times, peace worldwide is as rare as a fish in the desert.

Other than the Garden of Eden, there has never been complete peace on earth. The human race was barely two generations old before history's first murder—Cain against his brother Abel in Genesis 4—shattered any illusions of lingering peace from God's original perfect creation.

The first war in recorded history happened in approximately 2700 BC between the ancient Middle Eastern kingdoms of Sumer and Elam. The Bible's first recorded military conflict—a battle between various regional Canaanite kings, found in Genesis 14—dates back to about 2000 BC. But it's likely that the pre-Flood "human wickedness on the earth" mentioned in Genesis 6:5 included wars between people groups.

Fighting has always been a part of human history. But in his seventh beatitude, Jesus calls us to peace.

WHAT'S IT MEAN?

Peace isn't easy. It takes hard work, both for nations and individuals. Due to indwelling sin in human hearts, our natural tendency is toward conflict (James 4:1-2).

But true Christians are marked by a love of peace. That's because Jesus, our greatest example, is the Prince of Peace (Isaiah 9:6). During his time on earth, he taught people to live peacefully together. He achieved peace between a holy God and rebellious humanity on the cross. And at his second coming, he will destroy all evil, set up his eternal Kingdom, and bring everlasting peace (Revelation 19–21).

To love Jesus is to love peace. Peacemaking often starts with humility—

taking that first step toward reconciliation and harmony, whether you're at fault or not. As Romans 12:18 says, "Do all that you can to live in peace with everyone."

When you do, today's verse says, you will be called a child of God. In other words, God will acknowledge that you are his because you are reflecting his peace-loving character.

Well, today's devotion is nearly finished. Peace out!

NOW WHAT?

Have you been fighting with someone—a parent, a sibling, or a schoolmate? Pursue peace by asking for that person's forgiveness and showing kindness to him or her.

DID YOU KNOW?

The well-known peace sign—where the index and middle fingers of someone's hand are raised in a *V* shape—originated as the sign for victory among Allied Forces in World War II. By the time of the Vietnam War in the 1960s, hippies and antiwar activists had transformed the gesture into a protest symbol for peace.

FEBRUARY 20

Blessed are those who are persecuted because of righteousness,
for theirs is the kingdom of heaven. MATTHEW 5:10, NIV

Benjamin Franklin once said, "In this world nothing can be said to be certain, except death and taxes." Christians can add another item to that list of certainties: persecution.

There aren't many guarantees in life. But here's one of them: if you love Jesus, you will be persecuted. No question about it.

To persecute someone means to treat them cruelly for their beliefs. Persecution comes in many forms. It can be as simple as people teasing you when you tell them about Jesus. Or in some countries that outlaw Christianity, it can be as serious as imprisonment, torture, or death.

Maybe you've never been mistreated for your faith before. But persecution is a very real danger today. There are people all over the world who are being jailed, beaten, or killed because they love Jesus. God calls these dear saints—and anyone else who is persecuted for proclaiming the name of Jesus—"blessed."

And when you're persecuted, you'll never guess what Jesus says your response should be. He says you should . . . rejoice!

Say *WHAT*?!

WHAT'S IT MEAN?

Look at Jesus' exact words from Matthew 5:11-12: "Blessed are you when people insult you, persecute you and falsely say all kinds of evil against you because of me. Rejoice and be glad, because great is your reward in heaven, for in the same way they persecuted the prophets who were before you" (NIV).

Seems pretty strange at first, huh? Rejoicing when bad things happen doesn't come naturally to us. Our first inclination is to avoid pain and suffering.

Let's be clear: Jesus isn't telling us to love pain. He's telling us that persecution says something about our faith. It's a mark of a true believer. If you go through life and are never persecuted for your faith, maybe it's not obvious to others that you're a follower of Jesus. Maybe you're not different enough from the world. Jesus calls his followers to stand up for their faith, regardless of what anyone thinks or does to them.

To rejoice at persecution, you need an eternal perspective. You can remain joyful when people mistreat you by remembering that Jesus, too, was persecuted and that he promises a great reward for those who stay faithful to him. The heavenly prize that awaits true believers far outweighs any pain we'll experience on earth.

And that's as certain as death and taxes.

NOW WHAT?

Pray that God will strengthen you to stand firm in your faith when persecution comes.

DID YOU KNOW?

The famous "Hall of Faith" in Hebrews 11 (especially verses 32-40) talks about what some ancient believers suffered for the sake of Christ.

You are the salt of the earth. MATTHEW 5:13

We know, we know—you've been anxiously awaiting a history lesson about ancient minerals and their uses, haven't you? Well, good news: the wait is over. It's time to talk about salt.

In Jesus' day, salt was a very valuable commodity. In fact, some ancient cultures used to pay workers and buy slaves with salt. That's where the phrase "He's worth his salt" comes from.

Back then, salt was widely used as a food preservative, since mechanical refrigeration wouldn't be invented for another 1,800 years. Salt draws out moisture and helps to kill bacteria, which are both helpful in making food last longer. It was also used as a food seasoning and an antiseptic (something that fights infections)—same as today. (You've probably sprinkled it on corn on the cob or gargled saltwater for a sore throat.) Finally, historians believe that Dead Sea salt—which was contaminated with other minerals and not fit for consumption—was thrown on the ground to keep vegetation from growing on footpaths.

Why the history lesson on salt? Because early in the Sermon on the Mount, Jesus told his listeners the following: "You are the salt of the earth. But what good is salt if it has lost its flavor? Can you make it salty again? It will be thrown out and trampled underfoot as worthless" (Matthew 5:13).

WHAT'S IT MEAN?

Jesus loved using examples from everyday life to make a point. So he talked about salt to teach an important lesson to his followers, both then and now.

Why did Jesus call Christians salt? Because people who truly follow Jesus are similar to this helpful mineral. They flavor the earth. They make it a better place. But they can do so only by remaining different from the world. A Christian who is not distinct from the evil around him is not worth much, just like unsalty salt. A foolish Christian has no influence—and adds no flavor—in the world.

Christlike people also act as a preservative. Many sinners are saved, or preserved, from God's wrath because of the faithful witness of Christians. And just like salt acts as an antiseptic, followers of Jesus help fight off the infectious, destructive nature of sin by being agents of God's truth, goodness, and love.

Flavor the earth by being different from the world around you, and preserve others by sharing the gospel of Christ. In doing so, you'll be worth your salt!

NOW WHAT?

Pray that God will help you be different from the world around you.

DID YOU KNOW?

Salt was so valuable in medieval Africa, the Moors used to trade it straight up for gold!

FEBRUARY 22

You are the light of the world. MATTHEW 5:14

Imagine living without lightbulbs.

This is the world that Jesus lived in while on earth. People in the first century AD had no electricity or artificial light. Without the sun, moon, or some type of fire present, everything was dark.

In ancient times, people would often work from sunup to sundown because after sunset, activities were limited to what you could do by candlelight, oil lamp, or torch, especially if you lived in rural areas. However dark it was inside the house, it was often even darker outside, unless the moon was out. Because roads were not well lit, most travel was restricted to daytime.

Flashlights? Light switches? Ceiling lights? Lightbulbs? The ancients never heard of 'em. (Thank goodness for Thomas Edison!)

So Jesus' words in Matthew 5:14-16 probably made sense to the people listening during the Sermon on the Mount: "You are the light of the world— like a city on a hilltop that cannot be hidden. No one lights a lamp and then puts it under a basket. Instead, a lamp is placed on a stand, where it gives light to everyone in the house. In the same way, let your good deeds shine out for all to see, so that everyone will praise your heavenly Father."

WHAT'S IT MEAN?

The world is a dark, evil place, filled with sin and corruption. But Christians have a great light to shine into the gloom. This light—the one that Jesus refers to in today's verse—is the message of hope for lost sinners through faith in Christ. This light should be shared with others.

A secret disciple is of no more use than a hidden light. Jesus wants us to stand out like a city on a hill, burning brightly with the gospel in the midst of a dark, wicked world. In all you do, through your actions and words, shine a bright light for Christ!

NOW WHAT?

Ask your parents how you can shine the light of Jesus to others. Maybe it's sponsoring a child in a developing country, helping at a soup kitchen, or performing volunteer service in the community.

DID YOU KNOW?

Jesus used the light/dark idea in John 12:46, too: "I have come as a light to shine in this dark world, so that all who put their trust in me will no longer remain in the dark."

Don't misunderstand why I have come. I did not come to abolish the law of Moses or the writings of the prophets. No, I came to accomplish their purpose. MATTHEW 5:17

Fulfilling predictions is a tough business. The sports world is littered with examples of athletes who failed to live up to expectations.

For every LeBron James (NBA), Peyton Manning (NFL), and Ken Griffey Jr. (MLB)—all former number one draft picks who became superstars—there's a Kwame Brown (Washington Wizards' number one overall pick in 2001), Tim Couch (Cleveland Browns, 1999), and Bryan Bullington (Pittsburgh Pirates, 2002). If you're not familiar with those last three names, that's exactly the point.

We're not trying to pick on those guys. It just goes to show that lofty predictions are often difficult to live up to.

That said, here's an amazing truth: when it comes to the Bible's predictions about Jesus, he fulfilled every single one of them.

WHAT'S IT MEAN?

During the Sermon on the Mount, Jesus made an interesting statement. He told the people that he did not come to get rid of the law and the prophets but to fulfill them (see today's verse). In other words, he came to complete the entire Old Testament.

This is remarkable. Many biblical scholars believe the Old Testament contains more than three hundred prophecies about God's promised Messiah. These predictions span more than a thousand years. And Jesus fulfilled every single one!

He was the "offspring" of Eve who would crush Satan (Genesis 3:15), "the prophet" Moses spoke of in Deuteronomy 18:15, the Suffering Servant from Isaiah 53, the Son of Man in Daniel 7:13, and the "righteous Branch" in Jeremiah 23:5 (NIV). He was born in Bethlehem (Micah 5:2), pierced for sin (Zechariah 12:10), and resurrected from the dead (Psalm 16:9-11). The list goes on and on.

Jesus also fulfilled the Old Testament law. In fact, he was greater than the law. By remaining sinless on earth, Jesus perfectly kept all of God's commands in Exodus, Leviticus, Numbers, and Deuteronomy (Romans 10:4). He secured for us the salvation that we could never earn on our own.

The law and the prophets—all thirty-nine books of the Old Testament—point to Jesus. He fulfilled it all!

NOW WHAT?

The next time you're reading in the Old Testament, look for hints of Jesus' coming. There are plenty!

DID YOU KNOW?

Genesis 3:15 is the first prophecy about Jesus (see the January 8 devotion), while the last in the Old Testament is found in its final verse—Malachi 4:6. Check it out!

Human anger does not produce the righteousness God desires.
JAMES 1:20

Murder.

We all know it's wrong. Taking the life of someone who is created in God's image is one of the most heinous sins possible. Murder is outlawed in the Ten Commandments (Exodus 20:13), and Old Testament law demanded the death penalty for all premeditated killing (Numbers 35:31).

But during the Sermon on the Mount, Jesus said something shocking to his audience: "You have heard that our ancestors were told, 'You must not murder. If you commit murder, you are subject to judgment.' But I say, if you are even angry with someone, you are subject to judgment! If you call someone an idiot, you are in danger of being brought before the court. And if you curse someone, you are in danger of the fires of hell" (Matthew 5:21-22).

In other words, at the heart level, Jesus equated anger with murder. That means, in some respects, we are all guilty of murder.

Gulp.

WHAT'S IT MEAN?

Israel's first-century religious leaders had terribly misinterpreted the Old Testament and misled the people. They loved rule keeping, but they rarely addressed heart issues. Truly pleasing God, though, is always a matter of the heart. So Jesus used much of his Sermon on the Mount to accurately interpret God's laws for the people.

Take anger, for instance. Most people don't murder (an example of rule keeping), but everyone gets angry (a heart issue). So Jesus warned that, in some respects, anger toward someone is like murderous thoughts in the heart. After all, at the root of all murder is anger.

Acting in anger toward someone is an attack on someone who is made in God's image. Not good. If left unchecked, anger is a dangerous sin that can destroy relationships, or worse.

James 2:10 says if we break one part of the law, we're guilty of breaking it all. When we fail to keep God's laws on anger, we are guilty of breaking all his laws, including the prohibition against murder.

That sounds like grim news. But don't fear! There is hope in Christ! Jesus fulfilled the law for us (see yesterday's devotion) to cover us in his righteousness. He will forgive our sins of anger and help us avoid hateful thoughts toward others if we follow him.

So fight anger. Work hard to love and forgive others, even when they wrong you. In doing so, you'll reflect the righteousness of Christ.

NOW WHAT?

If you have harbored any anger toward someone, ask for forgiveness and make things right today.

DID YOU KNOW?

Galatians 5:19-23; Ephesians 4:31-32; and Colossians 3:8 are good Scripture passages about avoiding anger.

FEBRUARY 25

See that no one pays back evil for evil, but always try to do good to each other and to all people. I THESSALONIANS 5:15

The Major League Baseball rulebook is a thick document of more than one hundred pages with instructions on how to play America's grand old game. But baseball players also abide by an infamous, sometimes dangerous, set of "unwritten rules."

Perhaps the most well known is the unofficial law of retribution. If a hitter "shows up" an opposing pitcher by admiring a home run too long, that hitter or a teammate can expect a ninety-miles-per-hour fastball to the ribs later in the game. Ouch! It's baseball's version of the age-old principle of "eye for an eye, tooth for a tooth"—if you do something to someone else, you deserve equal payback.

Believe it or not, the Old Testament commands this principle multiple times (Exodus 21:22-25; Leviticus 24:17-22; and Deuteronomy 19:21). But these are also some of history's most misinterpreted portions of Scripture.

WHAT'S IT MEAN?

By Jesus' day, the Israelites had developed a bad misunderstanding of the "eye for an eye" principle. So Jesus corrected the people's thinking during the Sermon on the Mount. "You have heard the law that says the punishment must match the injury: 'An eye for an eye, and a tooth for a tooth,'" he said. "But I say, do not resist an evil person! If someone slaps you on the right cheek, offer the other cheek also." You can read the whole principle in Matthew 5:38-42.

Was Jesus saying you should let others bully you? No! He was exaggerating to make this important point: revenge is not an option for us.

God never intended the "eye for an eye" principle to be carried out by individuals. It was for Israel's leaders as they sought to promote justice in court cases.

Only God has the right to bring vengeance (Romans 12:19). He alone is the Judge (James 4:12). When someone wrongs you, don't retaliate. Repay evil with good. Jesus calls for you to show great love and patience that will be a witness to others.

So put that ninety-miles-per-hour fastball of vengeance away, and turn the other cheek!

NOW WHAT?

Talk to your parents about a godly way to respond when someone wrongs you.

DID YOU KNOW?

Long before the Old Testament was written, the ancient Babylonian king Hammurabi mentioned the "eye for an eye" rule in his famous "Hammurabi Code," a set of 282 laws from the eighteenth century BC.

Watch out! Don't do your good deeds publicly, to be admired by others, for you will lose the reward from your Father in heaven.
MATTHEW 6:1

Late in the evening on April 18, 1775, Paul Revere mounted a horse in Boston, Massachusetts, and galloped into history. His midnight ride to nearby Lexington alerted colonial leaders Samuel Adams, John Hancock, and many others along the way that the British were coming. Eighty-five years later, Henry Wadsworth Longfellow immortalized Revere's journey in his famous poem "Paul Revere's Ride."

Revere's journey was one of the most important announcements in American history. Announcements are usually a good thing. They give helpful information.

But it's not always good to publicize news. Take, for instance, the things you do to serve God. In Matthew 6:1-4, Jesus said this:

Watch out! Don't do your good deeds publicly, to be admired by others, for you will lose the reward from your Father in heaven. When you give to someone in need, don't do as the hypocrites do— blowing trumpets in the synagogues and streets to call attention to their acts of charity! I tell you the truth, they have received all the reward they will ever get. But when you give to someone in need, don't let your left hand know what your right hand is doing. Give your gifts in private, and your Father, who sees everything, will reward you.

WHAT'S IT MEAN?

Doing good deeds is a good thing. Scripture is full of exhortations for us to give to the poor, serve others, etc.

But announcing your good deeds is a bad idea. That's what the hypocritical leaders of Jesus' day did. The Pharisees, scribes, and other religious officials often made a show of their prayers and acts of charity. They wanted others to think highly of them.

God doesn't share that view. Jesus said if we care more about human recognition than divine approval, the praise we receive from others is all the reward we'll ever get.

Jesus calls us to give and serve in secret. When you give to others, in fact, Jesus said, "Don't let your left hand know what your right hand is doing." That's a way of telling us to be humble and quiet about serving.

Don't trumpet your acts of service. Make sure they are for God's glory, not your own.

NOW WHAT?

Pick an area to serve in your church or community that rarely receives public recognition.

DID YOU KNOW?

Paul Revere did not make his famous midnight ride alone as Longfellow's poem says. He also probably didn't loudly yell, "The British are coming!" His ride likely would have been shrouded in secrecy to avoid detection.

Never stop praying.   I THESSALONIANS 5:17

We humans tend to talk a lot.

In her 2006 book, *The Female Brain*, author Louann Brizendine claimed that females speak about twenty thousand words a day, while men use about seven thousand words. A year later, a study published in the *Science* journal suggested a different finding—that both genders speak roughly sixteen thousand words a day. Either way, that's a lot of words.

When it comes to the words *you* speak, how many of them are directed to God in prayer?

Prayer is an essential part of the Christian life. But many people don't really understand what prayer is. That's why Jesus addressed prayer extensively during the Sermon on the Mount in Matthew 6:5-13.

WHAT'S IT MEAN?

Prayer is simply talking to God. It's having a conversation with our Creator. It's offering him our praises, shortcomings, thoughts, and desires. And it's a huge privilege! Nothing else in creation can talk with the Lord God Almighty, but humans can.

Prayer is not for God's benefit. When you praise him, it doesn't make God feel better about himself. He is eternal and unchanging (James 1:17). When you ask him for something, your request isn't a surprise to him. He has always known what you need (Matthew 6:8).

Prayer is for *our* benefit. It drives us to our knees in dependence on God, which is a good place to be.

Prayer is so important, in fact, that Jesus himself prayed. Bible verses such as Mark 1:35; Luke 5:16; and Hebrews 5:7 show us that God's Son, although perfect, prayed to the Father constantly. If prayer was important to Jesus, it should be important to us!

Tomorrow's devotion will discuss more specifics of prayer. But as today's verse says, we should always be in prayer. Colossians 4:2 exhorts us in similar fashion: "Devote yourselves to prayer with an alert mind and a thankful heart."

Don't give God the silent treatment. You speak thousands of words a day. Use many of them to communicate with the God who created you and dearly loves you!

NOW WHAT?

Develop a plan to make prayer—and Scripture reading—a daily part of your life. These are essential parts of the Christian life.

DID YOU KNOW?

The Bible never specifically commands us to say, "In Jesus' name, amen," like many Christians do at the end of a prayer. But this phrase can be a helpful reminder that sinful humans can approach a holy God only through the salvation that Jesus offers in his name (Acts 4:12).

This, then, is how you should pray: "Our Father in heaven, hallowed be your name." MATTHEW 6:9, NIV

Here's a small, incomplete list of things that are difficult in life:

- getting straight As
- running a marathon
- sending someone to the moon
- keeping your bedroom clean

You can certainly think of other things to add. Prayer, however, should not be on that list.

Lots of people struggle to pray because they don't know what to say. But it's not difficult. Prayer is simply talking to God. And in Matthew 6:9-13, Jesus gave us specific instructions on how to pray. It's often called the Lord's Prayer. Here's what Jesus said:

This, then, is how you should pray: "Our Father in heaven, hallowed be your name, your kingdom come, your will be done, on earth as it is in heaven. Give us today our daily bread. And forgive us our debts, as we also have forgiven our debtors. And lead us not into temptation, but deliver us from the evil one" (NIV).

WHAT'S IT MEAN?

Jesus intended the Lord's Prayer to be a model for us. Let's take a closer look at it, phrase by phrase:

"Our Father in heaven"—When we pray, we should remember that we're talking to the only true God, who sovereignly rules the universe from heaven but also tenderly loves us as our "Father."

"Hallowed be your name"—The word *hallowed* means "honored" or "holy." We are to give God the honor and respect that his holiness deserves.

"Your kingdom come, your will be done, on earth as it is in heaven"—God's will is always accomplished in his perfect, heavenly dwelling place. We should seek to advance his purposes on earth, too, through Christlike living.

"Give us today our daily bread"—Through prayer, we should acknowledge our need for God's provision in every area of life.

"And forgive us our debts, as we also have forgiven our debtors"—We should confess our sins to God when we fall short of his holy standard and ask for his help to forgive those who have wronged us.

"And lead us not into temptation, but deliver us from the evil one"—God never tempts us to do evil, but we should ask for his help to overcome the devil's schemes and all temptations to sin.

NOW WHAT?

Memorize the Lord's Prayer.

DID YOU KNOW?

While the oldest Greek manuscripts of the New Testament omit it, some later texts add the following line to the end of the Lord's Prayer: "For yours is the kingdom and the power and the glory forever. Amen."

I tell you, keep on asking, and you will receive what you ask for.
Keep on seeking, and you will find. Keep on knocking, and the door
will be opened to you. LUKE 11:9

"Are we there yet?"

"Are we there yet?"

"Are we there yet?"

It's the classic question that all little kids, at some point in their lives, ask during the car ride to an exciting summer destination. But asking over and over for something doesn't always produce immediate results, as any vacation-bound child knows. Disney World isn't always right around the corner.

It's interesting, then, to read Jesus' parable about prayer in Luke 11:5-13. Jesus told his disciples a story about a man who persistently knocked on his neighbor's door at midnight to ask for some food to give to a weary traveling guest. Annoyed, the sleepy neighbor refused at first. Finally, though, the neighbor relented because of the man's persistent knocking and gave him some food.

Jesus compared this story to prayer. So does that mean if we—like the annoying, foodless man—pester God enough for whatever we want, he'll give it to us, just to get rid of us?

No, not exactly.

WHAT'S IT MEAN?

Jesus was *not* saying that God will always give us whatever we ask for if we harass him enough. God is not a genie in a bottle. He doesn't exist to do our bidding. He is the Lord God Almighty, the Creator and Ruler of the universe. We serve him, not vice versa.

So when we come to him in prayer, our requests should be for things that please *him* and bring honor to *his* name. Our lives—and our prayers—should be all about God's Kingdom coming and God's will being done (Matthew 6:10).

Here's Jesus' point: if a sinful human will answer someone's persistent request (albeit reluctantly), how much more will our loving heavenly Father give us good things if we ask according to his will? The blessings that God wants to pour out on us are beyond our imaginations (1 Corinthians 2:9)!

So as you pray, avoid selfish requests. Rather, ask, seek, and knock for things that would please God, and watch in wonder as he showers you with blessings that you never expected!

NOW WHAT?

Read James 5:16 and 1 John 5:14-15. These Scripture passages are helpful for learning how to pray according to God's will.

DID YOU KNOW?

The story of Aladdin and the genie in the bottle comes from *The Arabian Nights*, also known as *One Thousand and One Nights*, a large collection of Middle Eastern tales compiled sometime around the fourteenth century.

MARCH 2

For the love of money is the root of all kinds of evil.
1 TIMOTHY 6:10

Yarrrr, mateys! Ahoy, off the starboard bow—it's the *Queen Anne's Revenge*!

In 1995, maritime archaeologists working off the coast of North Carolina found a remarkable artifact of buried pirate treasure—the sunken flagship of Blackbeard, history's most famous buccaneer. Since the discovery, scientists have been carefully removing valuable pieces from the nearly three-hundred-year-old ship, which currently sits about twenty-five feet under the ocean's surface near Beaufort, North Carolina.

Blackbeard was once the terror of the seas. From 1716 to 1718, he plundered merchant vessels through intimidation and force in the Atlantic and Caribbean waters. Upon seeing *Queen Anne's Revenge*, most ships surrendered without a fight. Those that didn't got a rude welcome from *Queen Anne's* forty cannons and a merciless boarding party of scurvy sea dogs, including Blackbeard himself. Legend says the infamous pirate wore all black, covered himself in guns and blades, and even stuffed burning fuses under his hat to strike fear into his victims. Shiver me timbers!

Why did Blackbeard go to such lengths? Because he loved money.

WHAT'S IT MEAN?

Like Blackbeard, many people today spend their whole lives trying to get rich. But in Matthew 6:19-21, Jesus gave this warning: "Don't store up treasures here on earth, where moths eat them and rust destroys them, and where thieves break in and steal. Store your treasures in heaven, where moths and rust cannot destroy, and thieves do not break in and steal. Wherever your treasure is, there the desires of your heart will also be."

Money is a good thing. We need it to pay for important things like a home, food, clothing, school, doctor appointments, and lots more. Having money isn't sinful. But loving money is (see today's verse).

Jesus wants us to think correctly about the stuff we have. Everything that you own here on earth will one day break, get lost, or stop being interesting to you. And when you die, you can't take anything with you anyway. Material possessions aren't worth loving.

Jesus created us to worship him, not earthly treasures. We don't have enough room in our hearts for both. As Jesus said in Matthew 6:24, "You cannot serve both God and money" (NIV).

Treasure Jesus above all else, and tell the love of money to walk the plank. *Yarrrr!*

NOW WHAT?

With your parents' help, make a plan to regularly give some of your money to your church (this is called tithing). It's a great way to demonstrate that you treasure Jesus, not money.

DID YOU KNOW?

The *Queen Anne's Revenge* shipwreck site has yielded some amazing historical treasures. In October 2013, divers recovered five original cannons!

I tell you, do not worry about your life, what you will eat or drink; or about your body, what you will wear. Is not life more than food, and the body more than clothes? MATTHEW 6:25, NIV

The Jews of first-century Israel had plenty to worry about. Or so they thought.

The New Testament–era Judeans lived in a mostly agricultural society. If it didn't rain, the local economy suffered greatly, and people went hungry. Many families were poor. Disease and afflictions were rampant.

Then, of course, there were the hated Romans. Judea's foreign rulers heavily taxed the people, disregarded Jewish religious practices (Luke 13:1), and ruled with a heavy, often vicious, hand (Matthew 2:16). Life was hard.

Then along came a man from Nazareth who astounded the people with miracles, opposed the powerful religious leaders, and spoke authoritative words that the people had never heard before. Among his many stunning statements during the Sermon on the Mount, Jesus said this: no worrying allowed.

WHAT'S IT MEAN?

Jesus' discussion of worrying in Matthew 6:25-34—mainly his statement "do not worry about your life" in verse 25—wasn't merely a suggestion or a nice idea. It was a command.

Worry, or anxiety, means you are afraid or nervous about something. But worrying is a sin, according to the Bible. Worrying shows a lack of trust in God. It's like saying, "God, I know you're powerful, but I'm not sure you can handle *this* situation. So I'm going to go ahead and worry about how I'm going to fix it." And that's not right.

Jesus told his mountainside audience to consider simple things such as birds and flowers. God feeds and clothes them, and if he takes care of the relatively unimportant parts of his creation, he will certainly care for humans, the only creatures on earth that are made in his image!

Whatever is troubling you, don't worry about it—literally! God promises to provide for all the needs of those who love him (Matthew 6:33). Bring your concerns to God in prayer and trust him for the outcome.

NOW WHAT?
Memorize Philippians 4:6-7: "Do not be anxious about anything, but in every situation, by prayer and petition, with thanksgiving, present your requests to God. And the peace of God, which transcends all understanding, will guard your hearts and your minds in Christ Jesus" (NIV). It is one of Scripture's greatest passages about avoiding worry.

DID YOU KNOW?
Medical studies have shown that excessive worrying can lead to physical illness in some cases. That's not what God intended for his children!

Do not judge others, and you will not be judged. For you will be treated as you treat others. The standard you use in judging is the standard by which you will be judged.
MATTHEW 7:1-2

Sitting at 1 First Street NE in Washington, DC, is a grand, ornate building that represents one of the most powerful entities in the world: the Supreme Court of the United States.

The Supreme Court consists of one chief justice and eight associate justices who decide some of America's most important legal cases. These nine individuals have the authority to make certain rules for lower courts to follow, and there is no higher US court to which a case can be appealed. They are the most powerful judges in the country.

While some of their decisions are controversial, the Supreme Court justices have the responsibility to promote fairness and equality for all American citizens. In this respect, being a judge is a good thing. But during the Sermon on the Mount, Jesus gave a very specific command to the people. He said, "Do not judge others."

Does that mean we should shut down the Supreme Court and all other courts of law?

WHAT'S IT MEAN?

Jesus' command wasn't referring to professional judges. Courts of law are good and necessary to help society function properly. Jesus was referring to our heart attitudes toward others.

To judge someone, as the Bible defines it, is to form a negative opinion of that person to the point where sinful pride affects how you think of or act toward him or her. Wrongful judging means looking down on someone who messes up as if you are better than he or she is.

Rather than worrying about other people's faults, it's better to try to improve your own. That's what Jesus meant when he said, "Why worry about a speck in your friend's eye when you have a log in your own?" (Matthew 7:3). The desire to fix other people's problems before your own is hypocritical.

Judging other people's hearts and motives is not what God has called us to do. He has called us to show love, kindness, and forgiveness toward others.

When it comes to the final judgment on everyone's life, there is only one true Judge: the Lord God Almighty. As James 4:12 says, "God alone, who gave the law, is the Judge. He alone has the power to save or to destroy. So what right do you have to judge your neighbor?"

NOW WHAT?

Have you sinfully judged someone? Ask forgiveness from both God and that person.

DID YOU KNOW?

US Supreme Court justices are appointed by the president, approved by the Senate, and serve for life.

MARCH 5

In everything, do to others what you would have them do to you, for this sums up the Law and the Prophets.   MATTHEW 7:12, NIV

There's no denying it: during his time on earth, Jesus said some stuff that was difficult to understand.

At various points in his ministry, some of his teachings left people scratching their heads in confusion. Even his own disciples—his twelve closest friends—were often left blinking their eyes in bewilderment at Jesus' words. He spoke like this to separate his true followers from imposters.

But sometimes Jesus took difficult things and made them beautifully simple. Matthew 7:12 is a perfect example. During his Sermon on the Mount, Jesus summed up the entire Old Testament's teaching on how to treat others in one famous sentence: "Do to others what you would have them do to you."

We call this the Golden Rule.

WHAT'S IT MEAN?

The ancient Jews of Jesus' day had a lot of Old Testament rules to follow. It was impossible for them to remember—let alone perfectly obey—all of them.

Maybe you feel the same way. Does your head ever spin at the thought of recalling everything the Bible tells you to do? Don't worry—here comes Jesus to the rescue!

When it comes to how to act toward others, Jesus tells you to ask yourself one question: "How do I want to be treated?" Then you are to do the same to others.

Do you want to be hit, ignored, made fun of, yelled at, or lied to? No, of course not. Then don't do those things to others.

Do you want others to love you, show kindness to you, speak well of you, tell you the truth, and consider you important? Of course you do! Then do those things to others.

It's that simple.

The Bible says that Christians are to be marked by their love for one another (John 13:34-35). You want others to love you, right? So show the love of Christ to them, too. That's the Golden Rule.

It's so simple, it's brilliant!

NOW WHAT?

Memorize Matthew 7:12 to help you obey the Golden Rule.

DID YOU KNOW?

When Jesus refers to "the Law and the Prophets," he's referring to all thirty-nine books of the Old Testament. "The Law" is the first five books (Genesis, Exodus, Leviticus, Numbers, and Deuteronomy) and "the Prophets" are the other thirty-four books (although some of these books are also classified as poetry or history).

You can enter God's Kingdom only through the narrow gate. The highway to hell is broad, and its gate is wide for the many who choose that way. But the gateway to life is very narrow and the road is difficult, and only a few ever find it. MATTHEW 7:13-14

In 1979, a popular rock-and-roll band from Australia called AC/DC released a hit album called *Highway to Hell*. The title song's lyrics celebrate sinful living and treat hell flippantly, as if the very idea of a place of eternal punishment is a big joke. Some of the song's lyrics include the following:

Ain't nothin' that I'd rather do
Goin' down
Party time
My friends are gonna be there too

The lyrics are shockingly dismissive of such a serious subject.

In Matthew 7:13, Jesus mentions "the highway to hell." But hell was no laughing matter to Jesus. During the Sermon on the Mount, he warned his listeners that there are only two paths you can travel in life: the narrow road that leads to heaven or the wide road that leads to hell.

WHAT'S IT MEAN?

Heaven and hell are very real places. Heaven is the dwelling place of God and the future hope of all true believers. Hell, meanwhile, is the final destination of judgment for everyone who rejects God's plan of salvation through Jesus. (For a fuller description of heaven and hell, see the January 9 and December 26 devotions.)

Hell's highway is wide because it's easy to travel, and tragically, most of humanity is on it. Most of the world either doesn't know or doesn't care about living for Jesus. According to the Bible, that kind of lifestyle puts you smack-dab in the middle of the road to destruction.

Heaven's gate, on the other hand, is narrow because access is possible only through Jesus (John 14:6; Acts 4:12). It's also not a very popular path. Being a Christian will not win you a bunch of friends. The choice to follow Christ will eventually bring ridicule and persecution.

But it's absolutely the road worth taking! At some point in life, you will face peer pressure to hop on the highway to hell. Resist it and choose the narrow gate that leads to salvation through Jesus.

NOW WHAT?

If you've never turned from your sins and put your faith in Jesus as your Savior, do so today!

DID YOU KNOW?

City gates were major hubs of activity in Jesus' day. That's why he used the analogy of narrow and wide roads and gates to illustrate the two paths we can travel in life.

You will recognize them by their fruits. MATTHEW 7:20, ESV

Poor Little Red Riding Hood.

She should've listened to her mother's warnings about staying on the path in the woods. Then she never would've gotten mixed up with that nasty wolf and all that crazy "Grandmother, what big teeth you have!" business.

You know the story of Little Red Riding Hood, right? It's an old fairy tale about a girl who goes to visit her sick grandmother. Along the way, she meets a wolf, who learns of Little Red Riding Hood's plans, runs ahead, and gobbles up Grandma before the girl reaches the cottage. Then the wolf puts on Grandma's clothing and hops into her bed, impersonating her so he can have Little Red for dessert.

Long before this fable gained popularity, Jesus told his audience in first-century Israel a story about wolves in Matthew 7:15-20 (ESV):

> *Beware of false prophets, who come to you in sheep's clothing but inwardly are ravenous wolves. You will recognize them by their fruits. Are grapes gathered from thornbushes, or figs from thistles? So, every healthy tree bears good fruit, but the diseased tree bears bad fruit. A healthy tree cannot bear bad fruit, nor can a diseased tree bear good fruit. Every tree that does not bear good fruit is cut down and thrown into the fire. Thus you will recognize them by their fruits.*

WHAT'S IT MEAN?

Jesus' words weren't a fairy tale. They were a warning against real-life "false prophets."

In Jesus' day, these tricksters were the Pharisees and other religious leaders who sounded righteous in their words but whose hearts were far from God. Jesus compared them to hungry wolves that disguised themselves as sheep to gain access to the shepherd's flock (the people of Israel), where they could prey on unsuspecting victims.

There are plenty of false prophets out there today—supposed Christians who talk a good game but actually have no interest in God's purposes or your welfare. Beware of them. Jesus says you'll recognize them "by their fruits." In other words, don't only listen to what people say; watch what they do, too. Just like you can tell whether a tree is good or bad by the quality of its fruit, you can know people's hearts by their actions.

Take a cue from Jesus (and Little Red Riding Hood), and choose those you listen to in life carefully.

NOW WHAT?

Ask God and your parents to help you figure out whom you should trust and be friends with.

DID YOU KNOW?

Jesus also used the wolf and sheep symbols in John 10:1-18 when he called himself the Good Shepherd.

*Not everyone who calls out to me, "Lord! Lord!" will enter the
Kingdom of Heaven. Only those who actually do the will of my
Father in heaven will enter.* MATTHEW 7:21

Here's a shocking figure: according to a 2011 Pew Research Center study,
there are 2.18 billion Christians in the world—almost a third of the total
estimated global population of 7 billion people.

That's a lot of Christians.

Unfortunately, it's probably not factual. Here's why: the study also
revealed that some of those 2.18 billion professing "Christians" are Mormons,
Jehovah's Witnesses, or other religious groups that theologically do not line
up with true Christianity. In other words, many of those people have views
about God, Jesus, the Bible, and salvation that contradict what Scripture
teaches.

There has always been a difference between the number of people who
claim to know Jesus and those who actually do. Jesus himself mentioned this
in today's verse. "Only those who actually do the will of my Father," Jesus
said, will enter heaven.

WHAT'S IT MEAN?

The will of God is to draw sinful humanity back into a right relationship
with him. But this amazing gift of salvation doesn't come to everyone. And
it doesn't come through merely going to church, living a good life, being
baptized, confessing your sins to a priest, or performing certain religious
rituals. Scripture is very clear on all this.

Salvation comes only one way: through faith in Jesus Christ.

True salvation is not a matter of words or deeds but of the heart. It comes
only through repentance and faith in God's Son, the perfect sacrifice for sins.
Once that heart change takes place, the true believer will live for Jesus—not
perfectly but obediently.

This is true Christianity. All the other religions of the world fail in some way to acknowledge Jesus as the only Lord and Savior for the fallen human race.

Remember, as we discussed in the March 6 devotion, heaven's gate is narrow. Sadly, some of those 2.18 billion people are probably on the wide road to destruction.

When he returns, Jesus will turn away those who spoke his name on earth but failed to believe Scripture's truth about him. But true Christians—those who trust in God's Son for the forgiveness of their sins and choose to live according to his Word—will enter into eternal paradise with their Savior!

NOW WHAT?

In your pursuit of knowledge about God, Jesus, and salvation, be careful to go to Scripture first and foremost.

DID YOU KNOW?

True believers were first called Christians (meaning "Christ followers") around AD 45 in the ancient city of Antioch (Acts 11:26).

Anyone who listens to my teaching and follows it is wise, like a person who builds a house on solid rock. MATTHEW 7:24

On August 29, 2005, Hurricane Katrina made landfall near Grand Isle, Louisiana. The Category 3 storm with 127-miles-per-hour winds devastated the southeastern United States, becoming the single most catastrophic natural disaster and the costliest hurricane in US history, according to the Federal Emergency Management Agency (FEMA). Katrina's treacherous winds and floodwaters, FEMA reported, were responsible for 1,833 lives lost in five different states and an estimated $108 billion worth of damage.

Among all the unfathomable wreckage, though, at least one house stood strong. The home of Scott and Caroline Sundberg in Harrison County, Mississippi, survived 28-foot-high floodwaters and crushing winds, despite being only about 350 feet from the Gulf of Mexico. That's because the Sundberg home was made almost entirely from concrete. It had a rock-solid foundation.

The Sundbergs' construction marvel is a good example of Jesus' final words during his Sermon on the Mount. As he finished his long, mountaintop discourse, Jesus compared the people's varying responses to his teachings to two types of house-building techniques.

WHAT'S IT MEAN?

Jesus often spoke in difficult parables. But this one is pretty straightforward. Here's what he told the crowds in Matthew 7:24-27:

> *Anyone who listens to my teaching and follows it is wise, like a person who builds a house on solid rock. Though the rain comes in torrents and the floodwaters rise and the winds beat against that house, it won't collapse because it is built on bedrock. But anyone who hears my teaching and doesn't obey it is foolish, like a person who builds a house on sand. When the rains and floods come and the winds beat against that house, it will collapse with a mighty crash.*

Life is filled with storms. If you aren't going through a difficult situation now, you will soon enough. That's just the nature of a fallen, sin-stained world.

Your response to Jesus will dictate the outcomes of your life's trials. If you trust and faithfully obey him, the challenges of life won't overcome you. But if you try to live without Jesus, watch out—disaster lies ahead!

God's Son created you and loves you, and he died and rose again to save you. He has all power and knows all things. Build your life on the rock-solid foundation of Jesus Christ!

NOW WHAT?

Building your life on Jesus means knowing his Word. How are you doing with your Bible reading and Scripture memory plans from January 14? It's never too late to start or to get back on track!

DID YOU KNOW?

Hurricane Sandy was another whopper. The 2012 storm was responsible for 186 deaths in the United States, Canada, and the Caribbean combined.

MARCH 10

This Good News tells us how God makes us right in his sight. This is accomplished from start to finish by faith. As the Scriptures say, "It is through faith that a righteous person has life." ROMANS 1:17

After Jesus finished the Sermon on the Mount, he entered Capernaum, where a Roman centurion (a commander of one hundred soldiers) begged Jesus to heal his servant, who was deathly ill.

Normally, the Romans wouldn't ask their Jewish subordinates for help, nor would the Jews be willing to do so. But this centurion was different. He believed in the one true God of the Bible (not the Roman pantheon of false gods) and respected Jewish customs.

Jesus agreed to go to the centurion's home. But the Roman official humbly acknowledged that he wasn't worthy of Jesus' presence in his home, but he still believed Jesus could heal his servant from a distance.

The Roman centurion understood authority. As a military officer, he could give a command wherever he was located, and his soldiers would obey. He knew Jesus had even greater authority than that. So he asked that Jesus just give the command for his servant to be healed before reaching his house.

Jesus was amazed by the Roman officer's faith. Jesus gave the word, and the centurion's servant was instantly healed. (Read the whole story in Matthew 8.)

WHAT'S IT MEAN?

The Roman centurion is a remarkable example of life-changing faith. When it comes to faith, the Bible is very clear about two things: faith is necessary to be a child of God (Hebrews 11:6), and Jesus will reward the faith of his true followers.

Faith, simply defined, is believing without seeing (Hebrews 11:1). The Gospels are filled with examples of Jesus healing people because of their faith, but there were also some times when Jesus withheld miracles because the people didn't believe.

Faith isn't always easy. As weak, sinful humans, we often have short memories and a hard time believing what we can't see with our own eyes. But Jesus calls us to trust in him in all circumstances, without excuse. Faith is necessary for salvation and for continued blessings in life (see today's verse).

Take a cue from the Roman centurion, and put your full, unreserved faith in Jesus. He deserves it, and he'll reward it!

NOW WHAT?

We need God's help to have great faith. Cry out to him to give you more faith in his life-giving Son!

DID YOU KNOW?

John 4:46-54 records a similar, but different, healing miracle that Jesus did from afar.

The disciples were amazed. "Who is this man?" they asked. "Even the winds and waves obey him!" MATTHEW 8:27

Peter, Andrew, James, and John were grizzled, veteran fishermen. These four disciples knew every inch of the Sea of Galilee. They had cast their nets into those waters countless times, as the hot Middle Eastern sun tanned their skin like leather. They certainly must have had their fair share of maritime tales to tell their future grandchildren.

But they had never seen anything like the miracles that Jesus performed on the Sea of Galilee.

Matthew 8:23-27 tells the well-known story of Jesus calming the sea. One day, Jesus and his disciples were in a boat when a dangerous storm suddenly came upon them. The wind and waves were so violent, the disciples feared for their lives. But with a simple word of rebuke from Jesus—*poof!*—the storm instantly disappeared.

In Matthew 14:22-33, we read another story about Jesus and the sea. This time, the disciples were sailing without Jesus in the middle of the night. Suddenly, in the distance, they saw a figure walking toward them on the water. It was Jesus. No optical illusion, no water skis, and no life vest—just Jesus. Once he got in the boat, the wind stopped.

A third watery wonder is found in John 21:1-11, which describes one of Jesus' post-resurrection appearances to his disciples. Seven of them had been fishing all night without even a single guppy to show for it. Jesus, who was on the shore, shouted for them to throw their nets on the other side of the boat. When they did, they caught so many fish (153), they had trouble hauling the net in.

WHAT'S IT MEAN?

These three separate miracles on the Sea of Galilee prove that Jesus has power over storms, wind, water, sea creatures, and gravity, to name a few. Of course, that's just the beginning. Jesus has total authority over all creation.

If Jesus created the universe (as discussed in the January 2 devotion), that means he controls everything in it. Everything in nature—from thundering tempests to schools of small fish—falls under his dominion.

When we consider this amazing truth, it should lead us to awe, worship, and faith. And, like the disciples in Matthew 14:33, we should exclaim to Jesus, "You really are the Son of God!"

NOW WHAT?

Take some time to consider all that Jesus reigns over in the universe. Then praise him for it!

DID YOU KNOW?

Jesus' rebuke of the storm in Matthew 8:26 is another example of his divinity, since verses like 2 Samuel 22:16 and Psalm 18:15 mention God commanding the sea.

MARCH 12

Brothers, listen! We are here to proclaim that through this man Jesus there is forgiveness for your sins.   ACTS 13:38

Shortly into Jesus' public ministry, huge crowds started following him. Word about his amazing powers was spreading all over the country. The people were fascinated with Jesus' miracles, but now he wanted to teach them that he was someone much greater than just another Old Testament–style prophet who could perform wonders through God's power.

One day, as Jesus was teaching a large crowd in a house, some men broke a hole in the roof. The men lowered to the ground a paralyzed man lying on a mat. They had been unable to carry him on foot to Jesus because of all the people.

Jesus was impressed by their faith, but he didn't immediately heal the man. Instead, he simply said, "Friend, your sins are forgiven" (Luke 5:20, NIV).

This angered the religious leaders who were present. They accused Jesus of the serious crime of blasphemy, which is falsely claiming to be God or to do things that only God can do. You could feel the tension in the air.

Jesus looked directly at the religious leaders and said, "Which is easier: to say, 'Your sins are forgiven,' or to say, 'Get up and walk'? But I want you to know that the Son of Man has authority on earth to forgive sins." Then he said to the paralyzed man, "I tell you, get up, take your mat and go home" (Luke 5:23-24, NIV).

Immediately, the man stood up as if nothing had ever been wrong. Another astonishing miracle performed by Jesus!

WHAT'S IT MEAN?

Do you know the answer to Jesus' question? The easiest statement to make is "Your sins are forgiven." That's because no one can prove if someone has the power to forgive sins. Forgiveness happens spiritually, in the heart. But if Jesus had said, "Get up and walk!" and the man stayed paralyzed, Jesus would be revealed as a fake.

But Jesus is no fake. He proved he can forgive sins by doing something visibly miraculous that only God can do. By healing the paralytic man, Jesus confirmed that not only is he God, but he also has the power to forgive sins.

Jesus never did miracles just to show off. He always did them to prove who he was. Jesus has the power to forgive sins because he is God.

NOW WHAT?

The ancient Jewish religious leaders did not believe Jesus and God were one. Do you? Put your faith in Jesus as the second person of the triune (three-in-one) God!

DID YOU KNOW?

Old Testament law called for a blasphemer to receive the death penalty by stoning (Leviticus 24:13-16).

Jesus knew what they were thinking, so he asked them, "Why do you question this in your hearts?" LUKE 5:22

Reading the Bible is like prospecting during the California gold rush of the mid-1800s, except for one big difference: gold miners never knew when they were going to strike it rich. But there are golden nuggets of godly wisdom to be found every time you dig into Scripture. Sometimes, in fact, there are multiple truths contained in a single story—a mother lode of spiritual riches.

The story of Jesus and the paralytic man is a perfect example. While the main point is Jesus' authority to forgive sins, there's a stunning tidbit of information hidden within.

When Jesus forgave the man's sins before healing him (see yesterday's devotion), Luke 5:21 says, "But the Pharisees and teachers of religious law said to themselves, 'Who does he think he is? That's blasphemy! Only God can forgive sins!'" In other words, these men questioned Jesus silently in their hearts without opening their mouths.

The next verse says, "Jesus knew what they were thinking, so he asked them, 'Why do you question this in your hearts?'" Even though the religious leaders hadn't said a word, Jesus knew exactly what they were thinking.

Whoa.

WHAT'S IT MEAN?

This story is one of many that prove that Jesus is omniscient, or all-knowing. In John 1:43-51, Jesus told Nathanael, a future apostle, what Nathanael was doing before he met Jesus for the first time. In John 4:1-26, Jesus told a Samaritan woman things about her personal life that no one else could've known upon first meeting her. In John 21:17, Peter confessed, "Lord, you know everything." And John 2:25 states it plainly: "No one needed to tell him about human nature, for he knew what was in each person's heart."

If you truly believe that Jesus is God, his omniscience shouldn't come as a surprise. Because God knows all things (Job 31:4; 1 John 3:20), so does God's Son.

Jesus created the universe, upholds it with his unlimited power, provided salvation for sinful humans, and knows all things. He is worthy of worship and praise!

NOW WHAT?

Take a few moments to reflect on what it means that the Lord knows everything about you. Allow this amazing truth to comfort you and build your faith!

DID YOU KNOW?

The NFL's San Francisco 49ers got their nickname from the thousands of gold diggers who flocked to California in 1849, hoping to strike it rich.

I want you to show love, not offer sacrifices. I want you to know me more than I want burnt offerings.   HOSEA 6:6

Rules, rules, rules! Life is filled with rules. . . .

- "Obey your parents."
- "Obey your teacher."
- "Don't cheat."
- "Don't lie."
- "Don't steal."
- "Clean up your room before you go outside."
- "Cross the street at the crosswalk."
- "Be quiet in the library."
- "Be quiet in church."
- "Be quiet at bedtime."
- "And don't forget to eat all your veggies."

Certainly you've heard some of those before. Most rules are good. They protect us, help us mature, and keep order in society. But too many rules isn't always a good thing.

Take the Pharisees, for example. These religious leaders of Jesus' day loved rules. They mistakenly thought the way to earn God's favor was to be a good, moral Jew who tried his or her best to keep the Old Testament law. But in their rule-keeping zeal, they often neglected to show love and mercy toward others.

One day, the Pharisees saw Jesus eating with tax collectors and other so-called sinners—people who didn't meet the Pharisees' misguided standard of righteousness. The Pharisees arrogantly argued that Jesus shouldn't associate with such folks.

Jesus responded by saying, "Go and learn the meaning of this Scripture: 'I want you to show mercy, not offer sacrifices.' For I have come to call not those who think they are righteous, but those who know they are sinners" (Matthew 9:13).

WHAT'S IT MEAN?

Jesus was quoting a nearly eight-hundred-year-old Old Testament passage from Hosea (see today's verse). He wanted the Pharisees to know—from the very pages of the Old Testament that they claimed to follow—that God cares much more about showing mercy and love than he does about the old sacrificial system or any other set of rules. God gave the law to the Israelites to show them how much they needed a Savior, not for the law to *become* their savior (Romans 3:20).

God isn't impressed with rule keeping. Yes, he wants you to obey the rules of his Word, your parents, and your teachers. But what pleases God most is a heart that loves him, trusts in his Son, and shows love, mercy, and compassion to others.

Rules are good, but love is even better!

NOW WHAT?

Read Romans 3 and Hebrews 10 for a clearer understanding of how faith in Jesus more than fulfills the Old Testament law (or rule keeping).

DID YOU KNOW?

The Pharisees were so fussy about rule keeping, some of them actually thought that accidentally swallowing a gnat that had landed in their cup would make them ceremonially "unclean."

MARCH 15

He will not crush the weakest reed or put out a flickering candle.
ISAIAH 42:3

Time was running out, and Jairus knew it. His only child—his precious little girl—was about to die.

Jairus, the leader of a synagogue (a Jewish place of worship) in Galilee, had heard about Jesus' miraculous powers. So when Jairus found Jesus, he pleaded with Jesus to come to his house and save his dying daughter.

A huge crowd followed as Jesus traveled with Jairus. People were pressing against him on all sides. Suddenly, he felt someone touch his cloak. Jesus knew this wasn't just a random person bumping into him. It was someone who needed his help. So he stopped and turned around.

Jairus certainly didn't want to stop. His daughter was on her deathbed. Jesus' disciples were confused by his pause, and the crowd probably was too.

But Jesus knew someone was in desperate need. It was a woman who had suffered a terrible bleeding disease for twelve years. When she touched Jesus, his healing power immediately surged into her body and cured her.

In the midst of the commotion, Jesus gently told the woman, "Daughter," he said to her, "your faith has made you well. Go in peace" (Luke 8:48). It was a beautiful display of Jesus' compassion.

WHAT'S IT MEAN?

Compassion is defined as "a feeling of wanting to help someone who is sick, hungry, in trouble, etc." That perfectly describes Jesus. He is history's greatest compassion giver.

Scripture is full of other stories illustrating Jesus' compassion. He fed huge crowds (Matthew 14:13-21), gave sight to blind beggars (Mark 10:46-52), healed people with lifelong disabilities (John 5:1-9), and cleansed leprous outcasts (Luke 17:11-19). And that's just a tiny sampling.

Matthew, an eyewitness of Jesus' compassion, described the Savior by quoting the prophecy in Isaiah 42: "He will not crush the weakest reed or put out a flickering candle" (Matthew 12:20). In other words, Jesus cares greatly for and deals gently with those who are deeply hurting.

Are you hurting? Are life's troubles piling up on you? Take heart! There is a compassionate Savior who loves you, died to save you, and wants to help you. May Jesus' compassion not only encourage you but also provoke you to show similar concern to those in need around you.

NOW WHAT?

There are millions of people hurting all over the world. Ask your parents to help you find a charity to invest in, perhaps one where you can write letters and provide financial support to needy orphans in a developing country.

DID YOU KNOW?

If you're wondering, Jesus didn't forget about Jairus's daughter. Although the girl died before Jesus arrived, the Lord miraculously brought her back to life!

*When he saw the crowds, he had compassion on them because they
were confused and helpless, like sheep without a shepherd.*
MATTHEW 9:36

Jesus performed some spectacular miracles on earth. But he wasn't some sort
of traveling magician or flamboyant attention seeker.

Jesus was in the business of saving lives. He was a wonderful spiritual
doctor, perfectly diagnosing the life-threatening sin in people's hearts and
offering a remedy not available in any pharmacy.

When he "traveled through all the towns and villages" of Israel and
"healed every kind of disease and illness," as Matthew 9:35 says, it wasn't
to make money or gain popularity. So what drove him to do this? Why did
he temporarily leave perfect heavenly fellowship with God the Father and
the Holy Spirit to enter a wicked world filled with hate and violence? What
spurred him to take on human flesh and all of its frailties? What caused
him to endure long days, sleepless nights, endless persecution, and eventual
torture and death?

Today's verse tells us. It was compassion.

WHAT'S IT MEAN?

The March 15 devotion discussed how Jesus' perfect compassion prompted
him to help the hurting and needy. But it's also important to understand that
compassion fueled Jesus' evangelism.

Along with Jesus' healing miracles, Matthew 9:35 says he was consistently "teaching in the synagogues and announcing the Good News about
the Kingdom" everywhere he went. That "Good News" was that God's eternal rescue plan for lost sinners was now fully coming to fruition through
Jesus' perfect life, sacrificial death, and miraculous resurrection.

It hurt Jesus to see the people wandering through life "confused and helpless,
like sheep without a shepherd" (today's verse). The Jewish religious leaders were
leading the people away from God, not to him, with their human-centered

legalism. So Jesus compassionately offered good news that forgiveness, peace, hope, and eternal life are all possible through repentance and faith in him.

That good news is still needed today. Billions—yes, billions—of people worldwide live in darkness, wandering around "confused and helpless," just like in Jesus' day. Let compassion drive you to share the Good News of Jesus with them!

NOW WHAT?

Jesus told his disciples at the end of Matthew 9, "The harvest is great, but the workers are few. So pray to the Lord who is in charge of the harvest; ask him to send more workers into his fields" (Matthew 9:37-38). May this be your prayer too!

DID YOU KNOW?

The analogy of the Lord being a shepherd to his people is used all throughout Scripture. Perhaps the most famous example is Psalm 23, written by King David.

MARCH 17

Believe in the Lord Jesus and you will be saved.   ACTS 16:31

Imagine if your brother started healing the sick. Or if a neighborhood boy you've known since childhood started preaching to thousands on a mountainside. Or if one of your longtime friends stood up during a church service and began claiming that he was the fulfillment of ancient prophecies.

Would you believe in him?

This was the question facing the residents of Nazareth one day when Jesus spoke to them during a synagogue service. Small and unimportant Nazareth was Jesus' hometown. He spent most of his first thirty years living there quietly—no miracles, no shocking sermons, and no heated debates with the religious leaders. His neighbors knew him best as a local carpenter, one of at least seven children raised by Joseph and Mary (Mark 6:3).

But at the synagogue that day, Jesus stood in front of the assembly and read Isaiah 61:1-2, a seven-hundred-year-old passage that predicted the coming of a messiah to save Israel. Looking out at his captive audience, Jesus said, "The Scripture you've just heard has been fulfilled this very day!" (Luke 4:21).

The people were stunned. When Jesus scolded them for their lack of faith in him, they became furious and tried (unsuccessfully, of course) to throw him off a nearby cliff.

WHAT'S IT MEAN?

Somehow, Jesus' true nature of being both fully God and fully human had been hidden from Nazareth's residents for all those years. The people thought they knew Jesus, but they really didn't. They had become too familiar with the kind, mild-mannered carpenter to step out in faith and believe that he really was God's Son—the promised Messiah who came to earth to rescue lost sinners.

Maybe you've been familiar with Jesus for most of your life too. Maybe you've been raised in church or you go to a Christian school where the stories of Jesus feel like just another history lesson.

Here's a word of encouragement and caution: don't fall into the Nazareth trap. Don't dismiss Jesus as a fraud because you think you know better. And don't believe that familiarity with Jesus is enough.

It isn't good enough to have knowledge *about* Jesus. Salvation requires faith *in* Jesus, as today's verse says.

Jesus really is the Son of God, the promised Messiah, and the only Savior for our sins. Believe in him!

NOW WHAT?

As you read through Scripture, compile a list of verses and details about Jesus' true nature to help you understand who he truly is.

DID YOU KNOW?

Even Jesus' own family had trouble believing in Jesus' divinity at first (Mark 3:21; John 7:3-5).

MARCH 18

Don't be afraid of those who want to kill your body; they cannot touch your soul. Fear only God, who can destroy both soul and body in hell. MATTHEW 10:28

In Matthew 10, Jesus did something quite interesting. After traveling throughout Israel teaching and healing people, he granted similar authority to his twelve disciples. Matthew 10:1 says he "gave them authority to cast out evil spirits and to heal every kind of disease and illness." Jesus sent his disciples into the towns of Galilee to further advance God's Kingdom. What a cool mission!

But Jesus knew the disciples would encounter some resistance from the hard-hearted religious leaders, so before they left, he gave them a pep talk that included today's verse. Take a moment to read it again.

Yikes! That sounds pretty harsh. What's up with that?

WHAT'S IT MEAN?

From the moment a child enters Sunday school at church, chances are he or she will hear all about God's love, kindness, and goodness—and with good reason. God perfectly possesses all those characteristics.

So why did Jesus tell his disciples to "fear" God, "who can destroy both soul and body in hell"? Sounds pretty severe.

First, we need to understand the definition of the word *fear* as Jesus uses it. The fear of God that Jesus spoke of is not fright or terror, but reverence and respect that God deserves as the all-powerful Creator of the universe and Judge over our souls. Yes, God is holy and must punish sins. But true followers of Jesus have been completely forgiven by God (1 John 1:9). Christians don't need to be frightened of God, because they'll never be condemned (Romans 8:1).

This should provide great comfort when people mistreat you for your faith. Any human persecutor has limited power. He might make your life miserable for a little while, but God rules over all things, physical and spiritual. He controls life and death—and life *after* death. He loves us and doesn't hold our sins against us if we come to him in faith.

God deserves our honor, respect, and obedience before anyone else. In that respect, God is to be greatly "feared" above all other names and powers!

NOW WHAT?

The threat of suffering bodily harm at the hands of the religious leaders was a real danger in Jesus' day. Unfortunately, that's a reality for many Christians around the world today, too. Pray for God to strengthen and protect these dear believers.

DID YOU KNOW?

According to a 2014 report by the Pew Research Center's Forum on Religion & Public Life, in 2012, Christians in at least 110 countries around the world were harassed for their faith.

MARCH 19

The very hairs on your head are all numbered. MATTHEW 10:30

Imagine if you had been taught all your life that 1 + 1 = 3. And then one day, someone comes along and tells you, "No, actually 1 + 1 = 2." Life would make much more sense, right? Life is always better when you know the truth.

During Jesus' time on earth, the people of Israel had been taught lies for many years. Although the Pharisees and other religious leaders professed to know God, they had no idea what it meant to truly love him or how to please him. They had misled the people into believing that God was a harsh, distant deity who demanded strict obedience to countless laws.

Jesus wanted to change that mind-set. So as he prepared to send his disciples into the Galilean towns and villages to preach and heal (see yesterday's devotion), Jesus reminded them of who God really is.

Jesus told them, "What is the price of two sparrows—one copper coin? But not a single sparrow can fall to the ground without your Father knowing it. And the very hairs on your head are all numbered. So don't be afraid; you are more valuable to God than a whole flock of sparrows" (Matthew 10:29-31).

WHAT'S IT MEAN?

No offense to sparrows, but they're pretty worthless. They are common throughout the world, and they don't do anything special. Even in Jesus' day, they could be bought for a penny. And yet God knows every time one of these insignificant birds dies.

Jesus' point was this: if God cares that much about the most unimportant things in his creation, think about how much he cares about humans, who are made in his own image (Genesis 1:27)!

You (and every other human) are more valuable to God than anything else on earth. God loves you dearly and intimately knows every detail about you, even the exact number of hairs on your head.

That's why he sent Jesus to earth. If God didn't love you so much, do you think he would've sacrificed his own Son for your rebellion against him? No way!

God's great love for you is endless. In fact, Psalm 103:11 says, "His unfailing love toward those who fear him is as great as the height of the heavens above the earth." He never said that about sparrows!

NOW WHAT?

Read Psalm 139. It's a wonderful song all about God's tender, intimate love and care for his children.

DID YOU KNOW?

The common house sparrow was first introduced to America in New York City in 1851. Today, the species covers most of North America.

MARCH 20

God knew his people in advance, and he chose them to become like his Son.   ROMANS 8:29

Have you ever anticipated something for what feels like an eternity, only to be disappointed when you get it? Perhaps a Christmas present that turned out to be pretty corny or a birthday party that was a complete flop?

Believe it or not, the people in first-century Israel felt the same way about Jesus. For thousands of years, the Jews had waited for God's promised Messiah. Ever since God first foretold the Savior's coming in Genesis 3:15, the people had heard many times of how great life would be when he showed up.

When Jesus finally arrived and claimed to be the promised one, many folks laughed, others walked away confused, and some downright refused to accept it. Some even wanted to kill him.

Most people thought the Messiah would be a political savior who would free them from Roman oppression and start a wonderful new kingdom on earth (mistake number one). They struggled to believe that a humble, seemingly ordinary carpenter from Nazareth was their great hope (mistake number two).

So one day, Jesus responded by saying, "To what can I compare this generation? It is like children playing a game in the public square. They complain to their friends, 'We played wedding songs, and you didn't dance, so we played funeral songs, and you didn't mourn'" (Matthew 11:16-17).

WHAT'S IT MEAN?

Were the Israelites disappointed that Jesus didn't dance or cry more? No. Jesus was using a figure of speech. His meaning was this: "No matter what I do, you aren't satisfied."

Jesus didn't meet the people's expectations. But that wasn't Jesus' fault. It was the people who misunderstood the Messiah's true mission (to free people from sin, not Roman oppression).

Jesus doesn't have to meet our expectations. We need to meet his. True Christians mold themselves into Jesus' image rather than trying to mold Jesus to fit their expectations. Jesus is the eternal, all-powerful Son of God. He doesn't change. So ask Jesus to help mold you into his glorious image. As today's verse says, God specifically chose believers "to become like his Son."

Jesus is perfect the way he is. It's up to us to conform to him, not the other way around.

NOW WHAT?

Conforming to Jesus means speaking and acting in love like he did. Find ways you can do that today.

DID YOU KNOW?

To learn more about God knowing and choosing his people in advance, check out the June 12 devotion.

My Father has entrusted everything to me. No one truly knows the Son except the Father, and no one truly knows the Father except the Son and those to whom the Son chooses to reveal him.

MATTHEW 11:27

What baffles you more than anything else? Algebra? Biology? How planes fly? How rain falls? How the moon's gravitational pull affects ocean tides? How anyone can enjoy eating liverwurst?

There are many puzzling mysteries in this world. But nothing is more inexplicable than God.

God is a spirit (John 4:24) whom no one has ever seen (John 1:18). He was never created (Psalm 90:2) or taught (Isaiah 40:13-14). He rules the universe in absolute, perfect power and wisdom, yet many of his ways and thoughts are beyond human comprehension (Isaiah 55:9).

But here's the amazing thing: God wants you to know him. Not just random facts about him like you'd read in a trivia book. He wants you to know him on a personal level. There's one person—and only one person—who can reveal God to you. Know who it is? (Hint: Look at today's verse.)

WHAT'S IT MEAN?

As funny as it sounds, it's a good thing we can't know everything about God. After all, a God that can be completely figured out by small, weak humans like us wouldn't be a very impressive God, would he?

We can know God—to a point. The Bible tells us plenty about him, and everything it says reveals an awesome God! But if we don't have a personal relationship with God, these are just cold, hard facts. Plenty of people know stuff *about* God, but far fewer people know him as their heavenly Father.

That's why we need Jesus. He reveals to us who God is. As it says in 1 John 5:20, "We know that the Son of God has come, and he has given us understanding so that we can know the true God."

When we trust in God's Son, he forgives our sins, changes our hearts, and brings us into a personal relationship with God. The Lord God Almighty becomes our Heavenly Father, ready to pour out his unlimited love and blessings on us. Faith in Jesus illuminates our minds to the truth about God, turning Bible facts into life-changing truth.

If you want to know God in a personal way, put your faith in his Son. You'll never regret it!

NOW WHAT?

To go deeper with your personal knowledge of God, read *Knowing God*, the classic Christian book by J. I. Packer.

DID YOU KNOW?

You can't separate knowing God from knowing Jesus. As John 17:3 says, "This is the way to have eternal life—to know you, the only true God, and Jesus Christ, the one you sent to earth."

*Jesus said, "Come to me, all of you who are weary and carry heavy
burdens, and I will give you rest. Take my yoke upon you. Let me
teach you, because I am humble and gentle at heart, and you will
find rest for your souls. For my yoke is easy to bear, and the burden
I give you is light."* MATTHEW 11:28-30

If you don't read Matthew 11:28-30 carefully, you might walk away wondering, *Did Jesus really tell me to crack an egg over my head?*

Fear not. Your head is safe from egg goop. Jesus was talking about a *yoke*, not a *yolk*.

If you're not a farmer, you might still be confused. A yoke was a large, wooden beam with two attached loops or holes in it. Farmers in ancient times would hitch two oxen together by putting their heads through the yoke's holes. Then the farmers would attach a plow behind the oxen and lead them through a field to till the earth before planting crops. Thanks to the yoke, the animals bore the plow's burden and did the difficult work of churning up the ground.

Like in so many of his stories, Jesus used familiar examples from everyday life to teach his first-century listeners an important point.

WHAT'S IT MEAN?

Jesus' original listeners were like the oxen in this analogy. The religious leaders had burdened the people with the heavy load of trying to earn favor with God through good works and law keeping. Aware of all their shortcomings, many people felt crushed by the weight of their sin.

Have you ever felt like that? Do you think you have to earn God's forgiveness by being good enough? Do you sometimes feel sad when you think of all your sins?

If so, cheer up! The words Jesus spoke to the crowd two thousand years ago apply to you, too. Jesus provides rest and comfort for weary human souls. Jesus lightened our burden by bearing the massive weight of our sins on the cross to free us from guilt and make us righteous before God.

So be encouraged, and hitch yourself to Jesus. His yoke is indeed easy and light!

NOW WHAT?

Ask Jesus to lift whatever burdens you're carrying and give your soul rest through his grace.

DID YOU KNOW?

In 2 Corinthians 6:14 (NIV), the apostle Paul used the yoking analogy to make sure the Christians in Corinth weren't being influenced by evil men when he wrote, "Do not be yoked together with unbelievers" (see the October 18 devotion).

MARCH 23

Unless you are born again, you cannot see the Kingdom of God.
JOHN 3:3

The rich man crept through the dark streets, looking over his shoulder at every turn. He scurried quickly past street lanterns, hoping no one noticed him as he went to talk to the controversial man from Nazareth. Few, if any, of his peers would approve of such a meeting, so Nicodemus came to Jesus secretly at night.

Nicodemus was a Pharisee and a member of the Sanhedrin, the seventy-member ruling group that had significant power and authority over all religious matters in Israel. But Nicodemus was different from most of the Pharisees. His heart wasn't hardened toward Jesus. He wanted to hear more from this man who claimed to be the Messiah.

"Rabbi," he said as he greeted Jesus that night, "we all know that God has sent you to teach us. Your miraculous signs are evidence that God is with you" (John 3:2). Nicodemus was on the right path, but he didn't fully understand who Jesus was yet. Instead of calling him "Rabbi" ("teacher"), he should have called him "Lord." Jesus got right to the point. "Unless you are born again," Jesus said in today's verse, "you cannot see the Kingdom of God."

Nicodemus scratched his head. "What do you mean?" he asked. "How can an old man go back into his mother's womb and be born again?" (John 3:4).

WHAT'S IT MEAN?

Maybe you share Nicodemus's confusion about the phrase "born again." Don't worry. Jesus wasn't talking about a second physical birth. You'll never again have to drink from a baby bottle, get a diaper change, or endure your Aunt Gertrude's habit of tickling you under your chin and saying, "Cootchy-cootchy-coo!" That's not what "born again" means.

Jesus was referring to a *spiritual* rebirth—a changed heart.

All humans are sinful (Romans 3:23). Our hearts are diseased with sin, and we deserve death (Romans 6:23). But in his mercy, God lovingly reaches out and changes people's hearts to help them recognize their desperate need for a Savior. This is what it means to be born again. It's a spiritual transformation performed by a God who loves you more than you can imagine.

That's good news! Now you just need to figure out what to do with dear Aunt Gertrude.

NOW WHAT?

To understand the concept of being born again, ask God to give you his wisdom . . . and make sure to read tomorrow's entry! This topic is so important, it's been split into two days' worth of devotions.

DID YOU KNOW?

It seems Nicodemus eventually trusted in Jesus. He rebuked his fellow Pharisees for their treatment of Jesus (John 7:50-51), and he helped bury the Savior after the Crucifixion (John 19:39-40).

I will give you a new heart, and I will put a new spirit in you.
I will take out your stony, stubborn heart and give you a tender,
responsive heart. EZEKIEL 36:26

The animal kingdom is filled with regenerative wonders.

Regenerators are animals that can regrow lost body parts. For instance, a deer can grow back its antlers. If a predator grabs a lizard's tail, the lizard can shed it and later produce a new one. A starfish can grow new arms. And then there's the Mexican axolotl salamander. This odd sea creature, which looks like a rejected Muppet, can regenerate a limb, its tail, and even parts of its brain, heart, and lower jaw. Because, hey, everybody needs a new lower jaw now and then. . . .

Anyway, the Bible talks about regeneration too. In fact, another way to say someone has been born again is to say that person has been regenerated. But don't worry—when you become a Christian, you don't grow new limbs, tails, or antlers. Spiritual regeneration is about heart change, as today's verse from Ezekiel says.

Today's devotion continues our study on what it means to be born again, or regenerated.

WHAT'S IT MEAN?

When Jesus told Nicodemus that no one can enter heaven without being born again (John 3:3), he was talking about regeneration.

According to Scripture, regeneration is a onetime, life-changing event that is completely God's initiative. This is important to understand.

When we talk about becoming a Christian or "being saved," we often discuss how a person needs to put their faith in Jesus. And that's certainly true. But that faith isn't possible without God first doing a miraculous work of regeneration inside that person. If it weren't for God mercifully positioning our sinful hearts to receive the gospel, we wouldn't even *know* we need to be saved, and we'd remain lost in our sins forever.

In other words, while we play an important role by putting our faith in Christ, it is God who brings us to that point. Salvation is totally a work of God.

Every time Scripture mentions being born again, it attributes this act to God, not us. As today's verse says, it is God who removes our "stony, stubborn" (in other words, sinful) hearts and gives us "tender, responsive" hearts that can respond to the gospel of Jesus with faith.

Praise God for regenerating our lost, rebellious hearts to receive his love, mercy, and forgiveness!

NOW WHAT?

Check out some of the Bible's other verses about regeneration, such as John 1:13; Acts 16:14; Colossians 2:13; and 1 Peter 1:3.

DID YOU KNOW?

Worms that are cut in half can regenerate a new tail section. Creepy!

For God so loved the world that he gave his one and only Son, that whoever believes in him shall not perish but have eternal life.
JOHN 3:16, NIV

It's the most famous verse in the Bible. It's been featured on car bumper stickers, highlighted on roadside billboards, and even displayed on homemade posters by fans at major sporting events.

The verse is John 3:16, today's Scripture passage. It's perhaps the best summary of the gospel message in the entire Bible.

As Jesus spoke to Nicodemus during their secret meeting (see March 23 and 24), Jesus wanted this sincere but confused Pharisee to understand true salvation. John 3:16 was at the heart of his message.

The verse is so simple yet so profound. Those twenty-six words are packed with as much meaning as any other twenty-six words in Scripture. Let's take a closer look by breaking it into smaller parts.

WHAT'S IT MEAN?

"For God so loved the world"—Look at the main subject of the verse. It's not people; it's God. John 3:16 doesn't say, "For the world so loved God." It says, "For God so loved the world." Salvation only happens thanks to God's initiative and his great love for us. We (sinful humans) weren't looking for God. He came looking for *us*. Also notice that God's love is not just for certain people, but for the whole world.

"That he gave his one and only Son"—This short phrase summarizes Jesus' entire earthly life, death, and resurrection, all of which happened to offer God's forgiveness to lost sinners. What a great sacrifice by God, in sending us his only Son, and what a great sacrifice by Jesus, in following through with God's plan!

"That whoever believes in him"—While God starts and completes the salvation process for all Christians, we have a responsibility to trust in Jesus and his work on the cross.

"Shall not perish but have eternal life"—Faith in Jesus saves us from eternal punishment and separation from God in hell and provides us a place in heaven, forever enjoying the presence of our Savior!

NOW WHAT?

Memorize John 3:16. It's definitely one verse that you need to commit to memory.

DID YOU KNOW?

Tim Tebow, a former star quarterback, used to inscribe his eye black with "John 3:16" while playing for the University of Florida. In a 2011 play-off game against the Pittsburgh Steelers, he passed for 316 yards, leading the Denver Broncos to a surprise win. He also averaged 31.6 yards per pass that game, which came to be known as the "316 game."

MARCH 26

*God did not send his Son into the world to condemn the world, but
to save the world through him.* JOHN 3:17, NIV

On September 21, 1776, less than three months after America declared freedom from Great Britain with the Declaration of Independence, Captain
Nathan Hale was captured in New York as he returned from an intelligence-
gathering mission for General George Washington.

Because British soldiers found incriminating papers hidden in Hale's shoe
soles, there was no trial. British General William Howe immediately condemned Hale to death as a spy.

The next morning, Hale, who was only twenty-one years old, was taken
to a nearby orchard. Asked if he had anything to say, Hale supposedly uttered
these now-famous words: "I only regret that I have but one life to lose for my
country." Then he was hanged from an apple tree.

Most people who are condemned to die don't face it with as much courage
as Nathan Hale. Death, no matter how patriotic, is a terrible thing.

Did you know that all humans are condemned to die? It's true. The
Bible says that we are condemned—or pronounced guilty and sentenced to
punishment—because of our sins against God.

WHAT'S IT MEAN?

Perhaps you're thinking, *Wait a minute. Why am I condemned to die? I'm not
a bad person. I don't lie, cheat, or steal, and I certainly haven't killed anyone.*

That's good. But it's not good enough. God's Word clearly says that
everyone is born into sin because we are descendants of Adam, the original sinner (Romans 5:12). No matter what you have or haven't done, you still haven't
lived up to God's standard of holiness (Romans 3:23). Therefore, without any
outside help, you are condemned to die apart from him (Romans 6:23).

But, praise God, the story doesn't end there! God's holy justice is perfectly
balanced by his great love. So he provided a way for us to escape our death
sentence. Jesus came to save us from the condemnation our sin deserves,

169

as Jesus himself told Nicodemus in today's verse. Romans 5:18 agrees: "Consequently, just as one trespass [Adam's] resulted in condemnation for all people, so also one righteous act [Jesus' death on the cross] resulted in justification and life for all people" (NIV).

Now we can rejoice in the truth of Romans 8:1: "So now there is no condemnation for those who belong to Christ Jesus"!

NOW WHAT?

Pray to God, and thank him that he condemned Jesus, not you, to bear the punishment for your sins.

DID YOU KNOW?

On his spy mission, Nathan Hale disguised himself as a Dutch schoolmaster to cross behind British lines. No one knows how he was discovered.

He must become greater; I must become less.   JOHN 3:30, NIV

Have you ever been upstaged by someone?

The word *upstage* is a term that comes from the world of the theater. When one actor positions himself onstage in a way that takes the audience's attention away from other actors and focuses it onto himself, it's called "upstaging."

Over the years, *upstage* has become a general term that means "to draw attention away from someone else." It's like slamming home a monster dunk to give your basketball team the lead, only to watch an opposing player nail a three-pointer at the other end to go back on top.

Early in his earthly ministry, Jesus upstaged John the Baptist. Not in a bad or arrogant way—it was just the way things were meant to be.

Shortly after speaking with Nicodemus, Jesus took his disciples to the Judean countryside, where they began baptizing people. When John's disciples found out, they got jealous and told John. They didn't want John to be upstaged.

John's response is one of the coolest statements in the Bible. John said, "He must become greater; I must become less."

WHAT'S IT MEAN?

When Jesus started his ministry, John was already quite a local celebrity with a large following of people. It seems like John's disciples had begun to enjoy the attention.

But John knew his place. He understood his chief mission was not his own fame; it was to point people to someone far more important than himself. So John basically told his followers, "Jesus must get more of your attention, and I must get less. Jesus is the one you should be following."

Is that your attitude? Do you treat Jesus as the most important person in your life? Are you making Jesus greater and yourself lesser, or vice versa?

Don't try to upstage Jesus. He is the eternal Lord and Savior who died and rose again so you could be saved. Live your life in a way that puts Jesus at the forefront and you in the background.

NOW WHAT?

One way to make Jesus greater in your life is to give adequate time to reading his Word and praying to him each day.

DID YOU KNOW?

Interestingly, the upstage area in a theater is actually the part of the stage furthest from the audience. When an actor goes there, any other actor onstage has to turn his or her back on the audience to interact with the first actor, so the audience's attention turns to the upstage actor, whose face they can see.

MARCH 28

People judge by outward appearance, but the LORD looks at the heart. I SAMUEL 16:7

Sadly, racism was alive and well during Jesus' time. We see that clearly in John 4, which tells the story of Jesus meeting a Samaritan woman.

The Samaritans came from half-Jewish, half-Gentile ancestry. They descended from mixed marriages that occurred after the Assyrian Empire conquered Israel in 722 BC and resettled many other idol-worshiping, non-Jewish people groups in Israel (2 Kings 17:24-31). Believing (incorrectly) that God loved only true Israelites, most Jews despised the Samaritans, and vice versa. By Jesus' day, some Jews wouldn't even set foot in so-called "unclean" Samaria, which was located between the Jewish regions of Galilee (north) and Judea (south).

But Jesus wasn't like that. Wanting to get from Judea to Galilee as quickly as possible, he walked straight through Samaria. Around midday, he stopped for a drink at a water well and began chatting with a Samaritan woman. The Jewish religious leaders would've labeled her a "sinner" and frowned upon anyone talking to her. Even the woman was shocked that Jesus spoke to her (John 4:9).

Jesus didn't care about the woman's ethnic background. He wanted to share the gospel with her. News of Jesus' presence quickly spread. By the time he left two days later, "many Samaritans from the village believed in Jesus" (John 4:39).

WHAT'S IT MEAN?

Racism is a serious problem in today's world, just like it was in Jesus' time. Open up a national newspaper any day of the week and you'll likely find stories of how discrimination toward others of different skin color or ancestry causes people to do terrible things.

But Jesus does not discriminate. He doesn't care about people's heritage, birthplace, skin color, or anything like that, as today's verse says. He loved

Samaritans and Jews alike. Even now, he loves all humans equally, no matter who they are or what they look like.

Remember, John 3:16 says, "For God so loved the *world*," not just certain races or people groups (emphasis added). Romans 3:22 tells us salvation through Jesus "is true for everyone who believes, no matter who we are." And Revelation 7:9 promises that heaven will be filled with believers "from every nation and tribe and people and language."

Praise Jesus for his love for all people!

NOW WHAT?

Befriend someone of a different race or culture. You'll surely learn something new about other cultures, and you'll have a great opportunity to show the love of Jesus to them.

DID YOU KNOW?

After Jesus' ascension to heaven, God reaffirmed to the apostle Peter and the early church that the gospel was for all people. Check it out in Acts 10–11 and the September 12 devotion.

*Anyone who does not honor the Son is certainly not honoring the
Father who sent him.*   JOHN 5:23

To start today's devotion, let's travel back in time.

Pretend you're living in Jerusalem around AD 30. Each time you pass
through the Sheep Gate on the north side of the city, you notice a crippled
man lying on a mat near what's known as the Bethesda pool. The man has
been unable to use his legs for nearly four decades. All he does every day is
lie by the pool, begging for money.

Then one Saturday, Jesus arrives. He sees the disabled man and says,
"Stand up, pick up your mat, and walk." Immediately, the man jumps up
completely healed!

If you saw that miracle, what would you do? Would you praise Jesus,
or would you start planning how to kill him? The question sounds utterly
ridiculous. You would praise him, of course!

Not the Pharisees. They hated that Jesus healed on the Sabbath, a day
when they said no work was to be done, according to God's law. And when
Jesus told them, "My Father is always working, and so am I" (John 5:17)—in
essence, equating himself with God—they thought he was blaspheming. So
their wicked hearts began scheming about how to destroy him.

Knowing their hearts, Jesus responded with today's verse: "Anyone who
does not honor the Son is certainly not honoring the Father who sent him."

WHAT'S IT MEAN?

Those must have been shocking words to the Pharisees. They thought they
knew God and were obeying his Word. That's why (in their misguided way of
thinking) they tried so hard to honor the Sabbath. But they were so caught up
in trying to follow religious rules and please God on their own terms that they
missed what Scripture actually says about the Savior they desperately needed.

Sadly, the same thing is true today. Countless people from many different religions worldwide claim to know God. But you can't truly know God

without believing in Jesus. You can't honor and obey God without honoring and obeying Jesus. And you can't love God without loving and trusting in Jesus. Why? Because Jesus is God's Son—the center of God's entire rescue plan to save sinful humanity. To reject Jesus is to reject God.

To truly be a child of God, you must submit to the lordship of his Son.

NOW WHAT?

Ask God to reveal more of his Son to you so you can give both of them the honor they deserve.

DID YOU KNOW?

Apparently, God gave the Bethesda pool miraculous healing powers at specific moments (John 5:6-7). But the disabled man never could get into the waters in time. Jesus solved that problem!

You search the Scriptures because you think they give you eternal life. But the Scriptures point to me! Yet you refuse to come to me to receive this life. JOHN 5:39-40

It's time for a little lesson on the Pharisees. Since the New Testament mentions them dozens of times and they often argued with Jesus, it would be helpful to know who they were.

By Jesus' time, the Jewish religious system had experienced some major changes since the days of Moses, David, and Hezekiah. The focus had shifted from priests, prophets, and the Temple to weekly services at the local synagogue, where the Pharisees and scribes would teach.

The Pharisees were self-proclaimed Old Testament experts, and they took it upon themselves to interpret God's laws for the people. For instance, the fourth commandment in Exodus 20 prohibited the people from doing work on the Sabbath. But it didn't specifically define what "work" was. So the Pharisees created a long list of daily activities that the people were to avoid on the Sabbath. The Pharisees piled up their man-made rules by the hundreds.

While the Pharisees knew the words of the Old Testament very well, their head knowledge didn't translate to heart change. So when Jesus rebuked them in John 5, he pointed out that their knowledge of Scripture and their lack of faith in him didn't match up (see today's verse).

WHAT'S IT MEAN?

How well do you know your Bible? Can you name all sixty-six books in order? Do you read it every day? A few times a week? Several times a month? Do you have five verses memorized? Ten? Twenty or more?

Whatever your knowledge of the Bible is, understand this: knowing God's Word is wonderful, but it does you no good if you don't believe what it says about Jesus.

The Pharisees are a prime example of this. They were Old Testament experts who could quote large portions of Scripture. But ironically, they didn't believe in the Savior whom the Old Testament points to!

The entire Bible is ultimately about Jesus (see the February 23 devotion). If you read the whole Bible but don't put your faith in Christ, you've completely missed the point! From Genesis to Revelation, the Bible is one big story about God's great plan of salvation for lost sinners through his Son.

As you read God's Word, keep in mind that what matters most is what you believe about Jesus.

NOW WHAT?

Have a contest with some friends: see who can find the most references to Jesus in the Old Testament in five minutes!

DID YOU KNOW?

The apostle Paul, history's greatest missionary, started out as a Pharisee (Philippians 3:5).

MARCH 31

Anyone with ears to hear should listen and understand.
MATTHEW 13:9

Jesus loved speaking in parables.

Parables are simply stories with spiritual meanings. In Matthew 13, Jesus taught the people an important lesson about their response to God's Word using a farming parable.

In Jesus' story, a farmer sowed seeds in his field to grow crops. The seeds fell in four different locations and produced different results:

- Seeds that fell on a footpath were gobbled up by hungry birds.
- Seeds that fell on shallow, rocky soil sprouted up quickly but soon died in the hot sun because they lacked roots.
- Seeds that fell among thorns were choked and died.
- Seeds that fell on good, fertile soil grew well and multiplied into a bountiful crop.

WHAT'S IT MEAN?

Later, Jesus took his disciples aside and explained the parable. The seeds represent the "message about the Kingdom" (Matthew 13:19)—in other words, the gospel message about salvation through Christ—while the farmer could be anyone who spreads this good news.

Here's Jesus' explanation of the parable:

- The seeds that were eaten by birds represent people who hear the gospel but don't understand it, allowing Satan—like a flock of hungry birds— to snatch away any truth that could otherwise change someone's heart.
- The seeds that fell on shallow, rocky soil represent people who joyfully accept the gospel initially but fail to grow spiritually. When any sort of trouble or persecution comes (the hot sun in the parable), their shallow faith withers away.

- The seeds that fell among thorns represent people who show initial interest in the gospel but quickly fall prey to worldly temptations, which choke out any chance of true growth.
- The seeds that fell in good soil represent people who receive the gospel with life-changing faith.

So which illustration best represents you? Has the gospel message of Jesus failed to take root in your heart for various reasons? Or is your heart like good, deep soil where the seeds of God's Word can flourish?

As Jesus says in Matthew 13:9, we should listen and seek to understand Scripture's message about him. Pray that God would soften your heart like rich, rain-drenched soil to joyfully receive the Bible's words about Jesus and produce a bountiful spiritual harvest in you!

NOW WHAT?

Plant God's Word deep in your heart through frequent reading, memorization, and meditation (prayerfully thinking through what you've read).

DID YOU KNOW?

Matthew's Gospel records many other farming and agricultural illustrations from Jesus. Here are some other examples: Matthew 12:1-8; 13:24-43; 20:1-16; 21:33-46; and 24:32-35.

APRIL 1

Everything else is worthless when compared with the infinite value of knowing Christ Jesus my Lord. PHILIPPIANS 3:8

Hidden deep within the Smithsonian Institution's National Museum of Natural History in Washington, DC—stored behind thick glass and constantly monitored by security cameras—is a priceless gem that's believed to have been discovered about 350 years ago. Once owned by King Louis XIV of France, the jewel sparkles with mesmerizing blue radiance and has been viewed by more than 100 million gawking visitors.

It's the famous Hope Diamond.

At 45.52 carats, the Hope Diamond is the world's largest deep blue diamond. (A carat is a weight measurement for precious stones, with one carat equal to 200 milligrams. The average diamond size for a woman's engagement ring is about one carat.)

Yet incredibly, the Hope Diamond might not even be the world's most expensive diamond. In 2013, the 59.6-carat Pink Star diamond was sold at auction for a record $83.2 million.

Kind of makes your baseball card collection seem pretty trivial, huh?

In Matthew 13:44-46, Jesus described a treasure that's infinitely more valuable than any diamond. Here's what he said:

> *The Kingdom of Heaven is like a treasure that a man discovered hidden in a field. In his excitement, he hid it again and sold everything he owned to get enough money to buy the field. Again, the Kingdom of Heaven is like a merchant on the lookout for choice pearls. When he discovered a pearl of great value, he sold everything he owned and bought it!*

WHAT'S IT MEAN?

In Jesus' parables, the man who found the precious jewels (representing the "Kingdom of Heaven") gave up everything else to keep them. The connection is clear: the Christian life is priceless.

As today's verse says, nothing is more valuable than a relationship with Jesus. Why? Because salvation through Christ brings countless blessings for this life and the life to come. Jewels and other earthly treasures might bring temporary pleasure, but only Jesus can provide the righteousness that God requires for eternal life in heaven. Worldly riches will fade away, but faith in Jesus brings blessings that last forever.

Forget Pink Stars, Hope Diamonds, and other earthly treasures. Set your hope on the "pearl of great value"—a life devoted to the Savior!

NOW WHAT?

Make sure you hold your earthly belongings loosely. In other words, don't place too much importance on whatever your favorite earthly possessions are—things such as money, video games, clothes, and jewelry. They can vanish in an instant.

DID YOU KNOW?

In 2014, a 122.5-carat uncut blue diamond was discovered in a South African mine. Gemology experts believe that, once it's cut, it could become the most valuable gem in the world.

APRIL 2

Jesus saw the huge crowd as he stepped from the boat, and he had compassion on them and healed their sick. MATTHEW 14:14

Have you ever needed a break from humanity? A time away from everyone else? An escape-behind-your-headphones day? An evening locked away in your bedroom?

If there was ever someone who needed a vacation from people, it was Jesus. From the moment he started his public ministry, huge crowds followed him everywhere. Jesus rarely got time to himself, even during moments of great personal grief.

In Matthew 14, we read about how wicked King Herod beheaded John the Baptist. The news devastated Jesus. So he sailed across the Sea of Galilee to find a "remote area to be alone" (Matthew 14:13). That peaceful solitude lasted for, oh, about a nanosecond. When the crowds learned where Jesus was, they caught up to him before he even stepped out of the boat.

What would you have done in that moment? Would you have rolled your eyes? Gotten back in the boat and set sail for privacy? Shouted out, "C'mon, people! Can't I get a minute by myself?"

Here's what Jesus did: "He had compassion on them and healed their sick" (today's verse).

Despite being sad and tired, Jesus spent the entire day with the crowds. When dinnertime came, Jesus' disciples told him to shoo everyone away. But Jesus looked at the huge crowd surrounding him—people who were both physically and spiritually hungry—and felt love for them. So he performed one of his most famous miracles, the feeding of the five thousand with five loaves and two fish (Matthew 14:15-21).

WHAT'S IT MEAN?

Jesus was never too busy to help others. It didn't matter if he was hungry, tired, sad, or having a bad day. He always made time for other people and met their needs.

Nothing was more important to Jesus than people. We are why he temporarily gave up heaven's glory to come to a fallen world. We are why he died on the cross. Jesus loves you more than you can imagine.

Be encouraged by Jesus' love for people (and you!). But also let it motivate you to show the same love and concern toward others. Never be too busy or tired to help someone else and meet their needs. Look for ways you can love others, just like the Savior!

NOW WHAT?

With your parents' help, find a way to volunteer your time to a charitable cause through your church or community. There are many needs to be filled around you!

DID YOU KNOW?

Some Bible scholars estimate that, including women and children, the crowd that Jesus fed with the loaves and fish actually numbered around ten thousand!

APRIL 3

I am the true bread that came down from heaven.   JOHN 6:58

The day after Jesus miraculously fed the multitude with five loaves of bread and two fish, the crowd caught up with him again in Capernaum. They loved being around Jesus. Not only were they awed by his miracles, but he kept their bellies full too!

Jesus, though, hadn't come to earth to be the world's most powerful food caterer. He came to save souls. So he told the people, "Don't be so concerned about perishable things like food. Spend your energy seeking the eternal life that the Son of Man can give you. For God the Father has given me the seal of his approval" (John 6:27). Confused, the crowd asked him for a sign to prove that he was sent from God, mentioning how God used Moses to miraculously provide manna to the Old Testament Israelites (Exodus 16).

Wow, talk about short memories! The people had either completely forgotten or disregarded Jesus' fish-and-loaves miracle from twenty-four hours earlier.

Jesus chastised them for their lack of faith and replied, "I am the true bread that came down from heaven. Anyone who eats this bread will not die as your ancestors did (even though they ate the manna) but will live forever" (John 6:58).

Sadly, many of Jesus' followers left him that day. They didn't believe that he was God's Son.

WHAT'S IT MEAN?

The people that day were more concerned with their stomachs than their hearts. They also didn't realize that the Old Testament story of the manna foreshadowed (or looked ahead to) much greater things to come.

When God provided bread from heaven to satisfy Israel's physical needs in the desert, it pointed ahead to God's provision of his Son—"the true bread from heaven"—to satisfy his people's spiritual needs. Jesus is infinitely better than floating flakes of bread!

After much of the crowd left, Jesus asked his twelve disciples if they wanted to leave too. Peter answered, "Lord, to whom would we go? You have the words that give eternal life. We believe, and we know you are the Holy One of God" (John 6:68-69). It was a beautiful moment of faith!

So who will you be? Will you be like the disbelieving crowd who dismissed Jesus, or like Peter and the disciples who put their faith in Jesus as the true, life-giving bread from heaven?

NOW WHAT?

The next time you eat a piece of toast, an English muffin, or a sandwich, remember that Jesus is the true bread from heaven who gives eternal life!

DID YOU KNOW?

Jesus also used bread to illustrate his sacrificial death (Matthew 26:26).

APRIL 4

Those the Father has given me will come to me, and I will never reject them. JOHN 6:37

On October 6, 1945, Billy Sianis arrived at Wrigley Field excited to attend Game 4 of the World Series. The hometown Chicago Cubs had built a 2–1 series lead over the Detroit Tigers, only two wins away from their first world championship since 1908.

Sianis, the owner of the local Billy Goat Tavern, wasn't like most of the other forty-three thousand fans that day, though. He had brought his pet goat, Murphy, to the game.

Sianis bought two tickets, but when Wrigley's gate ushers denied entrance to Murphy, Sianis supposedly left in a rage, proclaiming, "The Cubs ain't gonna win no more. The Cubs will never win a World Series so long as the goat is not allowed in Wrigley Field!"

The infamous "Curse of the Billy Goat" was born.

Chicago eventually lost that World Series. Since then, the "Lovable Losers"—as the Cubs are now called—have made the play-offs only six times and have never returned to the World Series (through the 2014 season). Many Cubs fans blame Sianis's alleged curse for the team's lack of success.

What's the moral of the story? You can go with "Don't ever reject a baseball-loving billy goat" if you want. But we'll choose something slightly different. It's found in today's verse.

As Jesus was talking with the crowd the day after he miraculously fed the five thousand, he said these beautiful words: "Those the Father has given me will come to me, and I will never reject them."

WHAT'S IT MEAN?

Major league ballparks might turn away billy goats, but Jesus never rejects anyone who comes to him in faith. In a world full of rejections, this is a wonderful, comforting truth.

At some point in life, you will be rejected—guaranteed. It might be by a friend or classmate, at a sports tryout or music audition, or during a job search or school admissions process.

But Jesus never rejects those who come to him with humble hearts. If you turn from your sins and approach Jesus in faith (Mark 1:15), he will forgive you, clothe you in his righteousness, and welcome you into God's eternal family. Guaranteed!

If only poor Murphy had it so good.

NOW WHAT?

If you've never done so, turn to Jesus today. You will experience his amazing love and blessings!

DID YOU KNOW?

Bill Sianis's nephew, Sam, has brought many different goats to Wrigley Field over the years to try to break the supposed curse.

There is no judgment against anyone who believes in him. But anyone who does not believe in him has already been judged for not believing in God's one and only Son. JOHN 3:18

Jesus had a big earthly family.

From Matthew 13:55-56, we learn that Joseph and Mary had four sons and at least two daughters after Jesus was born. But it seems Jesus' siblings initially had no idea that their older brother was actually the incarnate Son of God.

Early in Jesus' ministry, his family tried to bring him home, thinking he was "out of his mind" (Mark 3:21). Another time, Jesus' brothers encouraged him to leave Galilee and take his miraculous powers to the larger region of Judea. "You can't become famous if you hide like this!" they said. "If you can do such wonderful things, show yourself to the world!" (John 7:4). They had no idea who Jesus really was or why he performed miracles.

Jesus' response was telling: "Now is not the right time for me to go, but you can go anytime. The world can't hate you, but it does hate me because I accuse it of doing evil" (John 7:6-7).

That last part bears repeating: the world hates Jesus because he points out its sins.

WHAT'S IT MEAN?

Nobody likes being told they're doing something wrong. It's human nature. Most people don't like to think about things such as sin, judgment, and hell. And they certainly don't like being told that there's a God in heaven who will punish them eternally if they don't repent of their sins and turn to him. The world thinks that's crazy talk.

God's Word says otherwise. There *is* right and wrong in the world, and there *is* a God whose Son has the power to judge between the two (Romans 2:16; 2 Timothy 4:1).

But Jesus doesn't point out our sins to be unkind. Quite the opposite! He does it out of love, to make us aware of our great need for a Savior.

To trust in Jesus is to accept the hard truth of the gospel: God will judge all humans one day, and only faith in his Son can save them from everlasting punishment. But this isn't bad news. It's good news—if you have the faith to believe!

NOW WHAT?

Read Romans 1–3 to understand more about God's righteous judgment and salvation.

DID YOU KNOW?

It seems like most, if not all, of Jesus' earthly family members eventually put their faith in him. Acts 1:14 says that his mother and brothers joined the disciples in prayer after Jesus' ascension. Plus, two of his brothers, James and Jude, wrote self-named New Testament books.

APRIL 6

The people who walk in darkness will see a great light. For those who live in a land of deep darkness, a light will shine.   ISAIAH 9:2

If you happen to be shopping for a going-away gift to give someone who is moving to Barrow, Alaska, consider buying *a lot* of flashlights.

Barrow (population 4,373) is located on the northern tip of Alaska. Because of its location 330 miles above the Arctic Circle, the sun doesn't rise in Barrow for more than two months in the winter. From November 18 to January 23, Barrow is in complete darkness. (The lightbulb industry must be making a fortune there!)

The good people of Barrow live in a place of extreme physical darkness, but that temporary sunless existence is nothing compared to the spiritual darkness of sin-marred creation. The world we live in is a dark, wicked place. All you have to do is watch the evening news to see that.

Ever since Adam and Eve rebelled against the Creator in the Garden of Eden, sin has cast a terrible, gloomy shadow over God's once-perfect creation. The world desperately needs the light of hope.

Enter Jesus.

In John 8:12, Jesus told the crowd around him, "I am the light of the world. If you follow me, you won't have to walk in darkness, because you will have the light that leads to life."

WHAT'S IT MEAN?

The spiritual darkness of the world is the grim effect of sin and the death it brings, but Jesus' "great light" (today's verse) is the hope and salvation he offers. His light is far greater than the darkness and will ultimately be victorious (John 1:5). The Son of God's perfect sacrifice on the cross provides everything that a dim, dying world needs:

- Sinners can be made right with a holy God through faith in Jesus.
- Hope, joy, peace, and purpose in life are available to those who submit to Jesus' lordship.

- Jesus will one day return to defeat evil, sweep away all the darkness, and inaugurate his eternal kingdom of light and purity.

As Isaiah 60:2 says, "Darkness as black as night covers all the nations of the earth, but the glory of the Lord rises and appears over you." Jesus pierces sin's horrible blackness with his loving light. That's great news for the people of Barrow—and the rest of us!

NOW WHAT?

Read Psalm 119:105. Allow the risen Savior and his Word to illuminate the way you live.

DID YOU KNOW?

In the summer, Barrow gets more than eighty days of nonstop sunlight.

Jesus said to the people who believed in him, "You are truly my disciples if you remain faithful to my teachings. And you will know the truth, and the truth will set you free." JOHN 8:31-32

When it comes to lies, there have been some whoppers throughout history:

- During World War II, the Nazis in Germany spread terrible anti-Semitic lies through a massive propaganda campaign in order to win support for their horrific efforts to completely exterminate all Jews.
- On November 17, 1973, US President Richard Nixon claimed innocence in the Watergate political scandal and declared, "I'm not a crook." Turns out he was. Less than a year later, after his misconduct was revealed, Nixon resigned from office.
- Remember that surprise gift the ancient Greeks gave the city of Troy during the Trojan War? Yeah, that was a lie in the form of a huge, hollow, wooden horse filled with soldiers waiting to attack.

Of course, the greatest lie of all came from Satan, who twisted God's words and tricked Adam and Eve into eating the forbidden fruit in the Garden of Eden (Genesis 3:4-5), bringing sin and death into the world. The devil is "the father of lies" (John 8:44), and his mission to destroy God's creation is based completely on deceit and falsehoods.

Jesus, however, is "the way, the truth, and the life" (John 14:6). He is a complete contrast to Satan. There are no lies or trickery with Jesus. As today's verse says, Jesus brings life-giving truth that "will set you free."

WHAT'S IT MEAN?

As fallen humans, we are slaves to sin and death (see the July 26 devotion). This slavery is what Jesus came to set us free from (Romans 6:16-18), and he does it by bringing us truth. He shows us the way to be saved and the right way to live.

God's Word is truth (John 17:17). Everything the Bible says about Jesus—and everything Jesus says in the Bible—is true. He really is the sinless Son of God who died, rose again, and provides the only way to heaven for sinners like us.

Don't believe Satan's lies that you don't need God. Don't believe the world's lies that money, fame, and pleasure are the best things to live for. Believe in the Savior who is the very essence of truth.

You don't have to be a slave to sin and death any longer. Trust in Christ, live in obedience to him, and experience the amazing freedom that his truth brings!

NOW WHAT?

Read Psalm 119. It's a great psalm about loving the truth of God's Word.

DID YOU KNOW?

Richard Nixon is the only US president in history to resign from office.

Jesus answered, "I tell you the truth, before Abraham was even born, I AM!" JOHN 8:58

Faces were getting red, voices were rising, and tempers were flaring. The Pharisees were arguing with Jesus again.

In John 8, some of Jesus' listeners took offense when he said that his truth would set them free. "But we are descendants of Abraham," they replied. "We have never been slaves to anyone. What do you mean, 'You will be set free'?" (John 8:33).

Jesus explained that they were slaves to sin. Then he mentioned that even Abraham, Israel's great patriarch, "rejoiced as he looked forward to my coming. He saw it and was glad" (John 8:56).

The crowd was confused and angry. Abraham had lived more than two thousand years before Jesus came. "How can you say you have seen Abraham?" the people asked (John 8:57). Jesus replied, "I tell you the truth, before Abraham was even born, I AM!"

WHAT'S IT MEAN?

Jesus' "I AM" statement stunned the crowd—and with good reason. It was a claim of deity.

Jesus' use of the title "I AM" was a reference to Exodus 3:13-14, when God told Moses that he was "I AM WHO I AM" before sending Moses to free Israel from Egypt. The name speaks to God's eternal nature, self-existent power, and immutability (the fact that he doesn't change or improve).

By saying he was "I AM," Jesus was claiming all that for himself, too. Jesus was claiming to be God.

Jesus is indeed God (see the January 3 devotion). But this begs the question: Why does this matter so much? What if Jesus was nothing more than a great prophet, or a good man, as many people have argued? Is it really that important that Jesus is God?

Yes, it is.

If Jesus was merely human, he would have had sin. Heroes like Abraham, Moses, David, and Paul were great men too, but none of them could have removed our sins because they, too, were sinners.

God the Son, though, was sinless. Jesus is the perfect, and only, Savior for our sins because nobody else could fulfill that role. Only Jesus could satisfy God's wrath toward sin and earn our forgiveness on the cross.

Yes, Jesus is God—and thank God for that!

NOW WHAT?

Read the following verses that all prove Jesus' deity: Matthew 28:19; John 5:17-18 and 10:30; 2 Corinthians 13:14; and Colossians 1:19.

DID YOU KNOW?

The people's claim in John 8:33 that they had never been slaves was flat-out wrong. By Jesus' day, Israel had been subject to foreign rule for most of the preceding six hundred years, not to mention their earlier four-hundred-year period of Egyptian slavery!

It is clear that no one can be made right with God by trying to keep the law. For the Scriptures say, "It is through faith that a righteous person has life." GALATIANS 3:11

Imagine it's your birthday and your family excitedly gathers around you. Your mom hands you a gigantic gift-wrapped box—the biggest present you've ever seen. Everyone smiles at you as they await the grand opening.

But then you pause and say, "Thanks, Mom, but let me go wash the dishes before I open this."

Your family just stares at you, stunned and silent. Then you say, "I don't think I deserve this yet. I'd better take out the trash, sweep the porch, and mow the grass first."

As everyone else struggles to understand your response, your mom says, "This is a gift. You don't have to work for it. It's free. Just open it."

"No," you reply, "it just doesn't feel right. This is really something I've got to earn first. I'll come in and open it as soon as I dust the dining room, weed the backyard, unclog that troublesome toilet downstairs, and reshingle the roof. See you soon!" And off you go. . . .

Crazy story, right? Well, that's kind of what legalism is like.

WHAT'S IT MEAN?

Legalism is trying to earn your salvation by works. This perfectly describes the Pharisees. In Matthew 15, they noticed that Jesus' disciples didn't wash their hands before eating, a violation of one of their countless ceremonial laws. So they pestered Jesus about it.

Jesus replied, "These people honor me with their lips, but their hearts are far from me" (Matthew 15:8).

The Pharisees thought if they piled up enough good deeds, God would *have* to welcome them into heaven. But that's not the way it works. As sinners, there's nothing we can do to earn God's favor. We have fallen far short of his holy standard (Romans 3:23).

Like a birthday present, salvation is a free gift that is to be received, not a wage to be earned (Ephesians 2:8-9). Jesus has already accomplished everything we need through the cross. We just have to believe, as today's verse says.

So leave the roof shingles and troublesome toilets for another day, and accept God's gracious gift of salvation with faith!

NOW WHAT?

Take a few moments to consider if you're trying to earn God's favor by the things you do. If so, repent and remember that salvation is a gift to be received through faith.

DID YOU KNOW?

Jesus' statement in Matthew 15:8 was a quote from Isaiah 29:13.

APRIL 10

*What goes into someone's mouth does not defile them, but what
comes out of their mouth, that is what defiles them.*

MATTHEW 15:11, NIV

What did your parents teach you to always do before sitting down at the
dinner table?

Wash your hands.

It's sound advice to avoid germs. But did your parents ever tell you that
if you failed to wash your hands before a meal, you'd be spiritually unclean
and would need a priest to perform a ritual cleansing before you could re-
enter normal society?

Doubt it.

But that's what the Pharisees believed. Food and personal-hygiene rules
were very important to them. But they completely missed the point of the
Old Testament's dietary laws (like those in Leviticus 11). God didn't intend
for those laws to burden people but to teach them about his holiness and how
they needed something more than rule keeping to be righteous before him.

So when the Pharisees started nitpicking about Jesus' disciples not washing their hands, Jesus said, "Anything you eat passes through the stomach and
then goes into the sewer. But the words you speak come from the heart—
that's what defiles you. For from the heart come evil thoughts, murder, . . .
theft, lying, and slander. These are what defile you. Eating with unwashed
hands will never defile you" (Matthew 15:17-20).

WHAT'S IT MEAN?

Unlike what the Pharisees believed, people are defiled—or made spiritually unclean—not by what they put *into* their bodies (certain foods, things
touched by unwashed hands) but by what is *already* inside of them.

The human heart is wicked and bent against God from birth (Psalm
51:5). As Jeremiah 17:9 says, "The heart is deceitful above all things and
beyond cure" (NIV). The bad things we do—like lying, cheating, stealing, and
speaking unkindly—are simply outward signs of the sinful hearts within us.

This is important to understand. Some people say, "I'm generally a good person. I don't commit any big sins, and I try to be nice to people, so I think God will let me into heaven."

Other people think, *I'm a terrible person. I've done so many bad things. God could never love me.*

Both mind-sets are wrong. Like the Pharisees, each of those people are too concerned about how their deeds affect their standing before God, instead of focusing on their hearts.

Our hearts are the problem. But praise the Lord that Jesus can cleanse sinful hearts!

NOW WHAT?

Read Romans 3:10-18 to learn more about the inherent evil of the human heart.

DID YOU KNOW?

Thanks to Jesus, we are no longer under Old Testament food laws (Mark 7:19 and Acts 10–11). So eat up . . . in moderation, of course!

Peter answered, "You are the Messiah, the Son of the living God."
MATTHEW 16:16

In comic books and movies, superheroes go to great lengths to hide their true identities. But just for kicks, let's blow their covers. See if you can guess each superhero's true identity based on what their real name rhymes with:

- Superman: Shark Scent
- Batman: Juice Stain
- Wonder Woman: Banana Rinse
- Iron Man: Bony Mark
- Spider-Man: Eater Barker (sounds like a description of a dog!)

Unlike these fictional characters, Jesus is a real person who did *not* try to conceal his true identity. He wanted everyone to know who he was, and he made it very clear through his words and miracles.

But few people actually believed. Matthew 16:14 tells us that some people mistakenly thought he was an Old Testament prophet such as Elijah or Jeremiah who had returned from the dead, or even John the Baptist (by this time, King Herod had beheaded John).

Certain people said Jesus was "the Prophet," the Moses-like figure predicted in Deuteronomy 18:15. Some thought he was merely a good teacher (Mark 10:17), while others called him demon possessed (John 8:48).

So one day, Jesus asked his disciples, "But who do you say I am?" With one of the greatest statements in Scripture, Peter replied in today's verse, "You are the Messiah, the Son of the living God."

WHAT'S IT MEAN?

What, though, if Peter was wrong? What if Jesus *wasn't* the Messiah and *wasn't* the Son of God? Could he still have been a great teacher or a powerful prophet— someone who was still sent from God, who we should imitate and listen to?

No.

Jesus claimed that he exists eternally (John 8:58), came from heaven (John 6:58), is God (John 10:30), and is the only way sinners can be made right with God (John 14:6). Either Jesus really was who he claimed to be or he was a huge phony and the worst liar who ever lived.

With Jesus, it's all or nothing. No one else in history made the claims that he made. You have to either completely believe him or totally reject him. There is no middle ground.

Peter got it right. Choose to believe that, yes, Jesus is indeed "the Messiah, the Son of the living God"!

NOW WHAT?

Pray for the faith to believe that Jesus is everything he claimed to be.

DID YOU KNOW?

Here are the true identities of the superheroes listed earlier:

- Superman: Clark Kent (Shark Scent)
- Batman: Bruce Wayne (Juice Stain)
- Wonder Woman: Diana Prince (Banana Rinse)
- Iron Man: Tony Stark (Bony Mark)
- Spider-Man: Peter Parker (Eater Barker)

How did you score?

APRIL 12

As Jesus was going up to Jerusalem, he took the twelve disciples aside privately and told them what was going to happen to him.

MATTHEW 20:17

Swimming in a pool of man-eating sharks isn't very smart. Neither is skydiving without a parachute, having a picnic lunch on the highway, or using a hornet's nest as a football.

You'd never do those things, because you would get hurt. As humans, we are really good at self-preservation. We generally avoid things that are guaranteed to cause pain.

It's interesting, then, to read in the Gospels how Jesus predicted his own death many times. He knew what awaited him, yet he didn't shy away from it. Matthew 20:17-19 says,

> *As Jesus was going up to Jerusalem, he took the twelve disciples aside privately and told them what was going to happen to him. "Listen," he said, "we're going up to Jerusalem, where the Son of Man will be betrayed to the leading priests and the teachers of religious law. They will sentence him to die. Then they will hand him over to the Romans to be mocked, flogged with a whip, and crucified. But on the third day he will be raised from the dead."*

Jesus' arrest and death didn't surprise him. As God, he fully knew what was in store for him in Jerusalem. Yet he still went. In fact, Luke 9:51 says Jesus "set his face to go to Jerusalem" (ESV). In other words, Jesus traveled to the place of ultimate suffering with determination. Jesus knew his purpose. Nothing was going to stop him from reaching Jerusalem.

WHAT'S IT MEAN?

If you knew that torture and death awaited you if you entered a certain city, would you still go? No, of course not. You'd avoid that place at all costs!

But Jesus wasn't interested in self-preservation. He was interested in self-sacrifice. He courageously marched toward Jerusalem because of the mission that he and God the Father had planned before time began (Ephesians 1:4-5).

Love for you propelled Jesus toward Jerusalem. Love for you helped him endure unspeakable pain and shame. Love for you sent him to the cross, where he suffered God's terrible wrath toward your sins. Revelation 1:5 describes Jesus as the one "who loves us and has freed us from our sins by shedding his blood for us."

Never forget Jesus' amazing, self-sacrificing love for you!

NOW WHAT?

Read Jesus' other predictions about his death in Matthew's Gospel: Matthew 12:40; 16:21; 17:22-23; 20:17-19; and 26:2.

DID YOU KNOW?

Just because Jesus is God doesn't mean he didn't struggle with his coming death (Matthew 26:36-38). But he remained true to his mission out of love for us.

Jesus said, "Whoever has ears to hear, let them hear."
MARK 4:9, NIV

Peter couldn't believe his ears.

He had just made his great confession, proclaiming his faith that Jesus was "the Messiah, the Son of the living God" (Matthew 16:16). But now Jesus was predicting his own arrest, torture, and death in Jerusalem—the very city where he and the disciples were headed!

Peter was deeply troubled. He couldn't fathom that God's long-awaited Savior had to die. He hadn't realized yet that the Old Testament prophecies about a suffering Messiah—such as Psalm 22; Isaiah 53; and Zechariah 12:10—were actually speaking of Jesus.

So Peter, being the most outspoken of Jesus' disciples, actually began to reprimand Jesus for these gloomy predictions. "Heaven forbid, Lord," he said. "This will never happen to you" (Matthew 16:22).

This wasn't one of Peter's best decisions. It's never a good idea to scold the eternal, all-powerful Son of God. Jesus turned to Peter and said, "Get behind me, Satan! You are a stumbling block to me; you do not have in mind the concerns of God, but merely human concerns" (Matthew 16:23, NIV).

Yikes!

WHAT'S IT MEAN?

Have your parents ever told you to "put on your listening ears"? What they're really saying is, "Please pay attention. Don't let what I'm saying go in one ear and out the other."

Well, Peter hadn't put on his listening ears. If he had, he would've realized that Jesus' true mission was the cross. He spent several years with Jesus, yet it took him a while to fully grasp Jesus' real purpose. So in a moment of spiritual weakness, Peter succumbed to Satan's evil influence and tried to distract Jesus from his God-given task. (The good news is, Peter eventually got it right and became one of the early church's greatest leaders.)

When Jesus spoke to the crowds, he often ended by saying, "Whoever has ears to hear, let them hear" (today's verse). We all, of course, have ears on either side of our heads, but not everyone has "ears to hear" and believe what Jesus says.

Do you have ears to hear Jesus? Do you accept what you read about him in Scripture? Do you believe that he is God's perfect Son who died and rose again to save you from your sins?

Put on your listening ears and let the gospel truth about Jesus radically change your life!

NOW WHAT?

For a similar "ears to hear" passage, read James 1:22-25. Those who truly hear God's Word do what it says.

DID YOU KNOW?

The human ear is not just the organ that allows us to hear sound. It is also responsible for a person's overall balance, head positioning, and eye movement.

APRIL 14

Everyone who wants to live a godly life in Christ Jesus will suffer persecution. 2 TIMOTHY 3:12

Ancient Roman crucifixions were possibly the worst kind of executions in history. They were horrifically painful and utterly humiliating. Roman soldiers forced the condemned prisoner to carry his own cross through public streets to the place of his execution. It was Rome's way of saying, "You might have broken our laws before, but now you are literally under our rule at the end of your life," as evidenced by the heavy wooden cross on the criminal's back.

So you can imagine the disciples' shock when Jesus told them, "Whoever wants to be my disciple must deny themselves and take up their cross and follow me" (Matthew 16:24, NIV). It must have taken the disciples a moment to pick up their jaws off the ground. They had to be thinking, "Jesus, did you really just compare following you to the Roman death penalty?"

Why in the world did Jesus use the Roman cross—a historic symbol of shame, suffering, and death—as a way to describe the attitude he expects from all his followers?

WHAT'S IT MEAN?

To understand Scripture's teachings, we must always consider the context— or the other things happening at the time—of what we're reading.

Before Jesus mentioned taking up one's cross, Peter had rebuked Jesus for predicting his own death (see yesterday's devotion). Peter didn't understand Jesus' mission yet. He was expecting Jesus to overthrow the Romans and inaugurate an earthly kingdom. Maybe he was even secretly hoping for a high-ranking position in the Messiah's future reign. So Jesus corrected him with shocking words.

Jesus used the image of the Roman cross, a symbol of death and submission, to explain that true believers must "die" to themselves and submit their lives to Christ. It's a vivid picture of crucifying our own selfishness and personal desires to a cross, so to speak. Following Jesus means making him the complete Lord of our lives.

Jesus also wanted us to know that following him involves a great cost. Being a Christian isn't always easy. Godliness brings persecution, as today's verse says. We must be willing to "lose" our lives (Matthew 16:25), meaning we should be ready to sacrifice anything for our Savior.

Of course, we should be more than willing to do that. After all, our Savior sacrificed everything for us.

NOW WHAT?

Ask Jesus in prayer to reveal any areas in your life where you need to "deny yourself" to better follow him.

DID YOU KNOW?

Philippians 1:29 says it's a "privilege" to suffer for Jesus.

As the men watched, Jesus' appearance was transformed so that his face shone like the sun, and his clothes became as white as light.
MATTHEW 17:2

Everybody loves a good movie trailer. The best previews show just enough clips from the film to leave you saying, "Wow, I've *got* to see that movie when it comes out!"

In Matthew 17, a few of the disciples got a fascinating preview of Jesus' glory. We call this event the Transfiguration.

One day, Jesus took his three closest disciples—Peter, James, and John— up a high mountain. There, Jesus was "transfigured"—or transformed— before their eyes. His physical appearance became so bright, it was impossible to look directly at him.

If that wasn't cool enough, suddenly Moses and Elijah—Old Testament heroes who had both been dead for centuries—appeared and spoke with Jesus. Eventually, God's voice spoke from a huge cloud covering the mountain: "This is my dearly loved Son, who brings me great joy. Listen to him" (Matthew 17:5). Peter, James, and John "were terrified and fell face down on the ground" (Matthew 17:6).

When the disciples finally looked up, the cloud was gone. So were Moses and Elijah. They saw only Jesus.

Just like that, the preview was over.

WHAT'S IT MEAN?

The Transfiguration was a preview of Jesus' full glory. Little by little—through teaching, miracles, and the Transfiguration itself—Jesus was revealing his true identity to his disciples.

Here's the cool part: the awesome, indescribable, knock-you-over glory that Peter, James, and John witnessed on the mountain is the way Jesus looks right now! This is clear from the remarkable story of Jesus' post-resurrection appearance to Saul on the Damascus Road (Acts 9:3; 26:13).

Remember, Jesus didn't always have a human body. He took on flesh when he came to earth (John 1:14). Jesus' human body temporarily shrouded the eternal glory that he had before Creation (John 17:5). The Transfiguration was a sneak peek at Jesus' full, unrestrained magnificence.

One day, humanity will behold Jesus in all his majesty and splendor when he returns to earth to destroy evil forever and set up his eternal heavenly kingdom. For believers, this will be a beautiful sight. For unbelievers, it will be terrifying.

Let the Transfiguration transform your faith in our great Savior!

NOW WHAT?
Read Revelation 1:12-18 and 19:11-16 to learn additional, vivid details of Jesus' glory and breathtaking appearance.

DID YOU KNOW?
Many Bible scholars believe the Transfiguration occurred on Mount Hermon (on the border of modern Lebanon and Syria), which has an elevation of 9,232 feet.

Jesus rebuked the demon in the boy, and it left him. From that moment the boy was well. MATTHEW 17:18

As Jesus descended the mountain following the Transfiguration, a desperate father ran up to him. The man pleaded frantically with Jesus to heal his son, who was suffering demonic attacks that led to life-threatening epileptic seizures.

The man had come to the right person. As today's verse says, Jesus rebuked the demon, and it left the boy, never to return. Bam! Just like that, the problem was solved.

This was just one of many instances when Jesus freed someone from demonic oppression. The Gospels are filled with stories of Jesus defeating the unseen forces of evil with great power. Take, for instance, Matthew 8:16, which says, "That evening they brought to him many who were oppressed by demons, and he cast out the spirits with a word and healed all who were sick" (ESV). All it took was a single command from Jesus, and evil spirits scattered like scared jackrabbits.

WHAT'S IT MEAN?

Demons aren't just an ancient phenomenon. There are dark spiritual forces in the world today, too. Ephesians 6:12 says, "We are not fighting against flesh-and-blood enemies, but against evil rulers and authorities of the unseen world, against mighty powers in this dark world, and against evil spirits in the heavenly places."

Demons are fallen angels who rebelled against God long ago. Their leader is Satan himself, the "prince of demons" (Matthew 9:34), and their mission is to turn people away from God through lies, temptation, fear, doubt, guilt, sickness, and so on.

We are to be aware of our enemies and how they work (2 Corinthians 2:11), but there is no need to fear them. Satan and his demons are already defeated, and they know it (Revelation 12:12). One day, they will be thrown into hell forever (Matthew 25:41).

Who is to thank for this amazing triumph over evil? Jesus! Colossians 2:15 says that he "disarmed the spiritual rulers and authorities" and "shamed them publicly by his victory over them on the cross." Jesus' death and resurrection authenticated him as God's perfect Savior and destroyed the power of Satan, sin, and death (Hebrews 2:14).

Don't fear the forces of evil. Take heart that there's a mighty Savior who rules over all powers in the world, both seen and unseen!

NOW WHAT?

Read the following passages to learn more about the power that Jesus has—and we have through him—over the spiritual realm: Ephesians 6:16; James 4:7; 1 John 3:8; 4:4; 5:18.

DID YOU KNOW?

Jesus once forced a "legion" (a lot!) of demons out of a man and into a herd of pigs (Luke 8:26-39).

APRIL 17

The father instantly cried out, "I do believe, but help me overcome my unbelief!" MARK 9:24

Oftentimes, multiple Gospels tell the same story of Jesus but provide different details. Such is the case with the story of the boy who suffered demon-related seizures.

Mark 9 sheds more light than Matthew 17 does on the interaction between Jesus and the boy's father. As the boy fell to the ground, convulsing violently and foaming at the mouth, the boy's father cried out to Jesus, "Have mercy on us and help us, if you can" (Mark 9:22).

At that, Jesus paused. "What do you mean, '*If* I can'?" he asked. "Anything is possible if a person believes" (Mark 9:23, emphasis added). Despite his desperation for a miracle, the father recognized that his heart was struggling for faith. So he immediately responded, "I do believe, but help me overcome my unbelief!"

With great compassion and power, Jesus threw out the demon and gave the boy, completely healed, back to his father. While the crowd gasped in awe, huge tears of joy must have been streaming down the man's cheeks. His little boy—his only child—had been saved.

WHAT'S IT MEAN?

Mark's account of this miracle is a helpful reminder of a wonderful truth: Jesus is patient with growing faith.

The Bible is full of stories about faith-filled heroes, such as Abraham, Moses, Gideon, and David. But if you're honest, your faith doesn't always feel that heroic, does it? Sometimes, your faith wavers and belief is hard to come by. Have you ever had a day like that?

If so, be encouraged by today's story. When the father asked Jesus for a miracle, he said, "*If* you can," not "I *know* you can." Yet Jesus didn't rebuke or refuse him. He patiently helped the man's faith along and healed his son.

The fact is, none of the Bible's greatest heroes had perfect faith. Abraham sure didn't (Genesis 17:15-18). Neither did Moses (Exodus 3:1–4:17), Gideon (Judges 6), or David (Psalm 13:1-4).

Faith *is* required to please God (Hebrews 11:6), but God doesn't expect perfect faith. He knows that we are weak and need his help. As his Son did on earth, our heavenly Father gently helps us grow in our faith through the Holy Spirit.

Trust in Jesus. He knows you won't always do it perfectly, but do it faithfully and he will answer you.

NOW WHAT?

Memorize Hebrews 11:1 and Hebrews 11:6, two great verses on faith.

DID YOU KNOW?

Jesus had earlier given his disciples authority to cast out demons (Matthew 10:1), but they apparently didn't pray enough or have the faith to conquer this stronger demon (Mark 9:18, 29).

He said, "I tell you the truth, unless you turn from your sins and become like little children, you will never get into the Kingdom of Heaven." MATTHEW 18:3

To start today's devotion, consider your age.

If you're ten, you probably want to be twelve. If you're twelve, you probably want to be thirteen—a teenager! If you're thirteen, you probably want to jump to sixteen and start driving. If you're sixteen, you're probably thinking, *Next stop, adulthood!*

Of course, a lot of thirty-year-olds still wish they were twenty-one, and forty-year-olds wish they were thirty. And if you're fifty? Well . . . good luck with that.

We never seem to be satisfied with our age. Of course, the one thing people never say is, "Man, I sure wish I were back in preschool."

But in today's verse, Jesus said something interesting. He told his disciples to "become like little children."

Jesus was responding to a question from the disciples. They had asked him, "Who is greatest in the Kingdom of Heaven?" (Matthew 18:1). The disciples wrongly believed that Jesus was about to overthrow the Romans and set up an earthly kingdom. They coveted positions of power and prestige. They were concerned about the wrong things.

So Jesus called over a little kid and told his disciples—twelve grown men—to act more like the child.

WHAT'S IT MEAN?

Don't worry. Jesus isn't encouraging you to rekindle your love for pacifiers, Pull-Ups, and strained peas. He's not saying we should go back to a childish maturity level.

Jesus was correcting the disciples' self-centered, worldly thinking. They were too concerned about human achievement and not concerned enough about what matters to God.

By telling the disciples they must become like little children to enter heaven, Jesus was calling them to childlike humility and faith. Young children have an innocence that older people often lack. Children don't think too highly of themselves. They haven't learned arrogance or pride like adolescents and adults have. Young children also believe whatever their parents tell them.

Jesus is calling you to childlike faith and humility too. Trust God's Word and believe in Jesus. Be more concerned about others and less concerned about yourself. In your faith and actions, strive for the God-glorifying innocence of a child. This is one case where it's okay not to act your age!

NOW WHAT?

Memorize 1 Peter 5:5-6. It's a great passage on godly, childlike humility.

DID YOU KNOW?

Jesus loves children so much, he gave a stern warning to anyone who would even think about harming a child. Read it in Matthew 18:6.

APRIL 19

If another believer sins against you, go privately and point out the offense. If the other person listens and confesses it, you have won that person back. MATTHEW 18:15

What do you do when people hurt you? Do you react to the person in any of the following ways?

- yell at them
- call them names
- give them the silent treatment
- gossip about them
- tattle on them
- throw punches
- strap them to a rocket and blast them to the moon

We've all reacted in at least one of those ways (except, hopefully, the last one). The truth is, it's difficult to respond kindly when someone wrongs you.

Jesus knows this, so he taught his disciples an important lesson on reconciliation, which means restoring peace between two people who are in disagreement. Check it out in Matthew 18:15-17 (including today's verse). It's great advice, but what he says might surprise you.

WHAT'S IT MEAN?

From the time you were little, your parents probably taught you to apologize and ask forgiveness whenever you sinned against someone. But in Matthew 18:15, Jesus puts the responsibility of reconciliation on the person who's been sinned *against*. In other words, if someone has wronged you, Jesus says you should avoid anger, swallow your pride, and gently approach the other person to make things right.

This takes lots of humility, prayer, and God's grace. But it's always better to pursue reconciliation than to let the problem fester and get worse.

If you want to be like Jesus, don't return evil for evil. Seek out people who wrong you. Show them Christ's love by forgiving them and being a friend to them. Even if they don't respond well, you've been faithful to obey the Savior.

NOW WHAT?

Has someone wronged you? Apply what Jesus taught in Matthew 18:15 and try to make it right with them today!

DID YOU KNOW?

During the Sermon on the Mount, Jesus addressed reconciliation from the opposite viewpoint. At that time, he gave instructions for the people who know they've sinned against others but haven't yet asked for forgiveness. His command? Stop whatever you're doing and go reconcile with the other person. (Check out Jesus' exact words in Matthew 5:23-24.)

Matthew 5:23-24 and 18:15-17 are equally important. Jesus' point is this: no matter who starts the problem, it's the responsibility of both people to reconcile. Don't wait for the other person to approach you. Be the first one to try to make things right!

APRIL 20

Instead, be kind to each other, tenderhearted, forgiving one another, just as God through Christ has forgiven you. EPHESIANS 4:32

Admit it: there's someone in your life who really gets on your nerves, isn't there?

Maybe it's a neighborhood bully. Or a younger sibling who likes to tattle. Or that classmate named Bert who's fond of giving people wet willies.

You know the Bible says to forgive people when they sin against you. But sheesh, isn't there some sort of forgiveness limit?

The apostle Peter wondered the same thing. In Matthew 18, he tried to figure out when he could stop forgiving and start throwing punches. The Pharisees taught that forgiving a person three times was enough. So Peter, thinking he was pretty righteous, asked if seven times would do the trick.

"No," Jesus replied, "not seven times, but seventy times seven!" (Matthew 18:22).

Does that mean 490 is the magic forgiveness number? When Bert gives you wet willie number 491, can you sock him in the teeth?

No! Jesus was exaggerating to make a point. He picked a crazy-high number to show that our forgiveness should never end.

To illustrate this, Jesus told a parable about a powerful king and his servant. The servant owed the king an enormous amount of money, but when he pleaded for mercy, the king lovingly forgave the entire debt. Shortly thereafter, the man found one of his own servants who owed him a very small amount and treated him harshly. When the king heard about it, he threw the wicked servant in prison for life. (Read the whole story in Matthew 18:21-35.)

WHAT'S IT MEAN?

In Jesus' parable, God is the king and we are like the servant who owes the huge debt, which is our sin. On our own, we can never repay God for all our rebellion against him.

However, through Jesus' sacrifice on the cross, God completely cancels our debt! And because God has forgiven us for far more wrongs than anyone will commit against us, we have no right to withhold forgiveness from others.

We are sinners saved by grace—God's undeserved favor toward us. This truth should humble us and shape our attitudes toward those who have wronged us. We must forgive others because God forgives us.

The next time someone sins against you, remember how much God has forgiven you, and forgive that person . . . even if it's Bert and his nasty wet willies.

NOW WHAT?

Memorize today's verse and apply it to any situation where you might be withholding forgiveness from someone.

DID YOU KNOW?

The Pharisees' idea of a person needing to forgive someone else only three times might have come from a misunderstanding of Job 33:29 (NIV) or Amos 1:3 (NIV).

Gently instruct those who oppose the truth. Perhaps God will change those people's hearts, and they will learn the truth.

2 TIMOTHY 2:25

At some point during his earthly ministry, Jesus nicknamed James and John the "Sons of Thunder." And for good reason, too! These two brothers had really bad tempers. Like a thunderstorm, James and John's anger could flare up quickly and cause great damage.

Luke 9 gives a vivid example of this. One day, Jesus and his disciples came to a Samaritan village whose residents refused to show Jesus hospitality. James and John were furious. So they asked Jesus, "Lord, should we call down fire from heaven to burn them up?" (Luke 9:54).

(A word of advice: never, ever do anything to upset any brothers nicknamed the Sons of Thunder.)

James and John thought their anger was justified. Because the Samaritans had rejected Jesus, the brothers arrogantly assumed those people weren't fit to live.

Jesus rebuked the Sons of Thunder. He never condones that type of hateful, dismissive attitude toward anyone, even those who reject him.

WHAT'S IT MEAN?

In a perfect world, everyone who hears about Jesus would put their faith in him. But it's not a perfect world. There are countless people who treat Jesus like the Samaritans of Luke 9 did. One day, everyone who rejects Jesus will be judged. But that's Jesus' role, not ours.

As you go through life, Jesus wants you to tell other people about him (Matthew 28:19). Some people will believe, some won't, and others might even aggressively disagree with you or persecute you. But as today's verse says, no matter how people respond, you are to speak "gently" to them and pray that "God will change those people's hearts."

Don't hate or judge others who disagree with you. That would be a poor witness for Jesus. After all, if you weren't a Christian, would you want to become one if the person telling you about Jesus got mad at you when you didn't immediately believe? No, of course not. However, if people see Jesus' love from you regardless of their response, that's a powerful witness that the Holy Spirit can use to convict them.

If someone disagrees with your faith, be respectful, pray for that person, and above all, keep showing them the love of Jesus!

NOW WHAT?

Check out Colossians 4:6. It's another great verse about how to respectfully share your faith with others.

DID YOU KNOW?

The Sons of Thunder turned out okay. James became a key leader in the Jerusalem church who was martyred for his faith, and John wrote five books of the Bible.

*I say, love your enemies! Pray for those who persecute you! In that
way, you will be acting as true children of your Father in heaven.*
MATTHEW 5:44-45

Israel's religious leaders during Jesus' day were always probing, prodding, and
looking for ways to attack him.

One such time came in Luke 10, when an "expert in religious law" tested
Jesus by asking, "Teacher, what should I do to inherit eternal life?" When
Jesus told him to fulfill the Old Testament's two most important laws—love
God and love your neighbor—the man tested Jesus further. "And who is my
neighbor?" he asked (Luke 10:25, 29). In other words, "Tell me who I have
to be nice to." Knowing the man's insincere heart, Jesus told him the parable
of the Good Samaritan.

In Jesus' story, a Jewish man who was traveling from Jerusalem to Jericho
was assaulted and badly injured by bandits, who left him half dead on the road.
Before long, a priest and a Levite—two highly respected religious officials in
ancient Judaism—walked by at separate times, but neither stopped to help.

Finally, a man from Samaria came by. Jews and Samaritans hated each
other in those days (see the March 28 devotion). But the Samaritan bandaged
the man's wounds, took him to a local inn, and paid for all the man's expenses
until he recovered.

The real neighbor in the story was the reviled Samaritan.

WHAT'S IT MEAN?

The point of Jesus' parable is clear: we shouldn't regard anyone as an enemy.
It doesn't matter who people are, where they're from, or even how they treat
you. A true Christian shows Jesus' love to everyone. After all, others are made
in God's image, just like you.

Today's verse, which comes from Jesus' Sermon on the Mount, echoes
this truth. To be "true children of your Father in heaven," you must "love
your enemies."

Jesus is the ultimate example of this. He loved Samaritans (John 4:1-42) and Romans (Matthew 8:5-13) and even gave the hard-hearted religious leaders every opportunity to trust in him. And when he was dying on the cross, as people scoffed at him and soldiers gambled for his clothes, Jesus said, "Father, forgive them, for they don't know what they are doing" (Luke 23:34).

If you want to be like Jesus, love everyone and regard no one as an enemy.

NOW WHAT?

Have you been fighting with someone? Seek out that person, ask forgiveness, and make things right.

DID YOU KNOW?

In Jesus' day, the road from Jerusalem to Jericho was an eighteen-mile stretch of rocky terrain perfect for bandits to hide in.

APRIL 23

I will study your commandments and reflect on your ways.
PSALM 119:15

Weekends are good for chores.

When Saturday morning rolls around, your parents probably give a list of household jobs to you and any brothers or sisters you might have. Maybe it's taking out the trash, tidying up your bedroom, emptying the dishwasher, vacuuming, folding laundry, or (*gaaaaack!*) cleaning the bathroom.

Whatever your chores are, how do you think your siblings would react if you were lounging on the sofa while everyone else was working hard? They'd be pretty upset, wouldn't they?

That's how Martha felt.

Martha and Mary were sisters who were good friends of Jesus. During one of Jesus' visits to their home in Bethany, Martha was scurrying around the house, trying to make Jesus and his disciples comfortable and make preparations for their evening meal together. Meanwhile, Mary was doing nothing but listening to Jesus talk.

Annoyed, Martha complained to Jesus, "Lord, doesn't it seem unfair to you that my sister just sits here while I do all the work? Tell her to come and help me" (Luke 10:40). Jesus' answer probably surprised her. He said, "My dear Martha, you are worried and upset over all these details! There is only one thing worth being concerned about. Mary has discovered it, and it will not be taken away from her" (Luke 10:41-42).

WHAT'S IT MEAN?

Before you start doing celebratory cartwheels, let's be clear: Jesus is *not* saying that chores are unimportant. So if your parents are telling you right now to scrub the toilets, get to it!

But here's Jesus' point: while Martha was worrying about her to-do list, Mary realized that spending time with Jesus was the most important thing she could be doing at that moment.

It's easy to let the busyness of lives or our own desires eat up our time. But don't neglect spending time with the Lord. You obviously can't do it in person like Martha and Mary did. But you can spend time in Jesus' presence today by praying and reading his Word.

Make time for Jesus, like Mary did. Sit at his feet and listen to his voice. His words echo as loudly in Scripture today as they did in person two thousand years ago (Hebrews 4:12). Soak them up, think and pray about them, and believe them. In doing so, you will please the Savior!

NOW WHAT?

As today's verse says, make it a daily habit to study God's Word and reflect on Jesus' life and teachings. They are the "one thing worth being concerned about"!

DID YOU KNOW?

Martha and Mary's brother was Lazarus, whom Jesus raised from the dead (John 11:1-43).

APRIL 24

He may come in the middle of the night or just before dawn. But whenever he comes, he will reward the servants who are ready.
LUKE 12:38

Remember *The Cat in the Hat*?

The classic Dr. Seuss book tells the story of two bored children who are stuck indoors on a rainy day while their parents are out. A mischievous cat and his two destructive sidekicks—Thing 1 and Thing 2—come over and trash the house, causing the children (and a persnickety goldfish) great angst. When the kids look outside and see their mom returning, a mad scramble ensues to get the house back to normal, like nothing ever happened.

Although it's a great children's book, *The Cat in the Hat* would never work as an allegory for Jesus' return. Unlike the Dr. Seuss tale, there won't be any chance to "tidy up the place," so to speak, before Jesus returns, since no one knows his timing (Matthew 24:36).

Jesus wants his followers to be fully prepared for his second coming. So in Luke 12:35-48, he told a parable about a master who left his servants in charge of his house while he was away.

Jesus said, "Be dressed for service and keep your lamps burning, as though you were waiting for your master to return from the wedding feast. Then you will be ready to open the door and let him in the moment he arrives and knocks. The servants who are ready and waiting for his return will be rewarded" (verses 35-37).

But for those who aren't ready for the master's return, Jesus said, "He will cut the servant in pieces and banish him with the unfaithful" (verse 46). Yikes!

WHAT'S IT MEAN?

Jesus' first visit to earth was to offer salvation. His final, future visit will be for judgment. At his second coming, he will carry the righteous to heaven but punish the wicked (2 Thessalonians 1:7-10). For the believer, Jesus' return is to be greatly anticipated. But for the unbeliever, it promises nothing but terrible punishment.

Jesus' parable in Luke 12 was meant to encourage us to be ready for his return. Let the anticipation of his second coming affect the way you live now.

The first step toward readiness is to trust in Jesus. Then live to glorify him. Obey God's Word. Honor your parents. Show love to others. Spread the gospel.

If you do these things, you'll be a faithful, "ready" servant who will receive eternal blessings at Jesus' second coming!

NOW WHAT?

To learn more about being prepared for Jesus' second coming, read 1 Thessalonians 5:1-11; 1 Peter 4:1-11; and 2 Peter 3:1-18.

DID YOU KNOW?

Dr. Seuss's real name was Theodor Seuss Geisel.

Those who exalt themselves will be humbled, and those who humble themselves will be exalted. LUKE 14:11

These days, it seems like some professional athletes are more narcissistic than ever.

Watch any sporting event—whether it's football, baseball, basketball, soccer, or virtually anything else—and you'll likely see athletes preen and pose in blatant displays of self-centeredness after big plays. Football players flex after quarterback sacks, basketball players thump their chests after hitting a clutch shot, soccer players slide on their knees with arms outstretched after scoring a big goal—the list goes on and on.

Most sports fans might not mind the excessive vanity, but the Bible has a lot to say about drawing attention to yourself. Luke 14:7-14 tells about the time Jesus visited a Pharisee's house. Before dinner was served, Jesus noticed many of the guests jockeying for seats of honor near the head of the table. They wanted to look important, kind of like many athletes do today. Jesus encouraged his fellow guests to humbly offer the best seats to others. Then he said, "Those who exalt themselves will be humbled, and those who humble themselves will be exalted" (today's verse).

WHAT'S IT MEAN?

God hates pride. Simply put, pride is thinking too highly of yourself. And if left unchecked, it's a deadly sin. It's first on the list of "seven things [God] detests" in Proverbs 6:16-19. According to Proverbs 16:18, "Pride goes before destruction." And pride, it seems, led to the downfall of Satan himself (Isaiah 14:13-14).

Humans have no reason for pride. We are created beings, helpless apart from our Creator and doomed without his grace. Any skills and abilities we have are gifts from our Maker.

God wants his children to be humble, not calling attention to ourselves but rather being fully aware of our need for him. Humility is having a proper, God-honoring view of ourselves. This is what today's verse is talking about.

Likewise, Isaiah 66:2 says that God favors "those who are humble and contrite in spirit, and who tremble at my word" (NIV).

Those who are prideful will eventually be brought low. But if you humbly admit you are a sinner in need of the Savior, God will greatly exalt you to enjoy life in his presence forever!

NOW WHAT?

Make a list of all the things you do well. Then one by one, humbly give God credit for them in prayer.

DID YOU KNOW?

The greatest example of today's verse is found in Jesus. Check it out in Philippians 2:3-11.

If you do not carry your own cross and follow me, you cannot be my disciple. But don't begin until you count the cost. LUKE 14:27-28

Jesus said some pretty shocking things during his three years of earthly ministry. Listen to this doozy from Luke 14:26: "If anyone comes to me and does not hate father and mother, wife and children, brothers and sisters—yes, even their own life—such a person cannot be my disciple" (NIV).

Uh, okaaayyy . . .

Did Jesus really tell us that we have to hate our families and ourselves before we follow him? What happened to all that talk about loving others?

First, let's consider the context of the story. One verse earlier, Luke 14:25 says, "A large crowd was following Jesus." The multitude—probably thousands of people—was mesmerized by Jesus' radical teachings and incredible miracles.

But Jesus wasn't interested in winning a popularity contest. He didn't want groupies; he wanted true believers. So he used hyperbole—purposefully exaggerating to make a point. Jesus wasn't supporting hatred. What he meant was, "If you truly want to follow me, you have to love me above everything else, even the things dearest to you." To follow Jesus well, we must first count the cost.

WHAT'S IT MEAN?

Financially, following Jesus doesn't cost a penny. But it does require 100 percent commitment.

Becoming a Christian—a Christ follower—means you are willing to give up everything for Jesus. It might cost you popularity (John 15:19) or even physical comfort (Luke 9:58). It means you must give up your selfish, worldly desire for things like money, power, and fame to live in God-pleasing ways. Following Jesus might cost a close relationship with friends and family members. For some Christians around the world, it might cost even their lives.

But what it costs to follow Jesus is nothing compared to what it cost him to save you. Your salvation required Jesus to endure rejection, torture, God's wrath toward sins, and ultimately, death. That's how much Jesus loves you.

The Christian life is so much richer than anything you have to give up. Nothing in this world can offer you the peace, joy, love, forgiveness, and eternal life that Jesus can. Whatever the cost, following Christ is well worth it!

NOW WHAT?
Read Luke 9:57-62 and 14:25-33. Then make a list of the things that matter most to you in life, and ask God to help you count Christ as more important than each of them.

DID YOU KNOW?
The apostle Paul is a great example of someone who gave up lots of worldly benefits to follow Christ. You can read about his attitude toward living for Christ in Philippians 3:3-11.

APRIL 27

Since it is through God's kindness, then it is not by their good works. For in that case, God's grace would not be what it really is—free and undeserved.   ROMANS 11:6

One day, as told in Luke 15, some Pharisees were grumbling about a group of tax collectors and "sinners" who were crowding around Jesus to listen to his teaching. The self-righteous Pharisees didn't approve of Jesus welcoming these supposedly "unclean" people to be near him. So to illustrate God's love for lost sinners, Jesus told them the now-famous parable of the Prodigal Son.

In Jesus' story, a young man foolishly asked his father for his share of the family inheritance, left home for a faraway country, and "wasted all his money in wild living" (Luke 15:13). Penniless and desperate for food, the man took a job feeding pigs and even longed to eat the swine's dirty slop. The young man had hit rock bottom.

Eventually, he realized that even being a lowly servant in his father's house was better than his current situation. So with a humble, repentant heart, he returned home, ready to beg for his father's forgiveness.

While the son was still quite a way away, "his father saw him coming. Filled with love and compassion, he ran to his son, embraced him, and kissed him" (verse 20). His father dressed his son in fine clothing, gathered his entire household together, and exclaimed, "We must celebrate with a feast, for this son of mine was dead and has now returned to life. He was lost, but now he is found" (verses 23-24).

WHAT'S IT MEAN?

Jesus' parable is a beautiful example of God's mercy and grace. Mercy is when deserved punishment is withheld. Grace is undeserved favor. God is wonderfully rich in both.

The father in this parable represents God, and the Prodigal Son represents sinful humans. Like the son, we have chosen to rebel against our heavenly Father and deserve nothing but punishment.

When the son came home, he had nothing to offer. He was completely destitute and worthless. He simply returned in humble repentance and faith, and his father enthusiastically welcomed him back into the family and poured out great love and blessings on him.

What a wonderful picture of what God does for us through repentance and faith in Jesus, as today's verse describes. God loves welcoming prodigal sons and daughters into his heavenly family and showering them with undeserved mercy and grace!

NOW WHAT?

Read the whole parable of the Prodigal Son in Luke 15:11-31.

DID YOU KNOW?

The word *prodigal* means "reckless, wasteful, or wayward."

APRIL 28

The human heart is the most deceitful of all things, and desperately wicked. Who really knows how bad it is? JEREMIAH 17:9

Here's a quick quiz, probably the easiest you've ever taken. If you had the choice, which would you pick?

- A million dollars or utter poverty?
- A Lamborghini or a tricycle with a broken front wheel?
- A vacation in Hawaii or at the local trash dump?
- A royal feast every night for dinner or bread crumbs?
- A Beverly Hills mansion or a pigpen?

The answers seem blatantly obvious, don't they? In each example, the first choice is clearly the best. And yet millions of people in life choose the latter. Today's devotion is all about picking the pigpen.

In the parable of the Prodigal Son, the young man had it made. He lived on a nice estate with a loving family, servants, and good food. He lacked nothing. Yet he recklessly threw it all away so he could follow his heart's wicked desires and indulge in sinful living. He traded love and blessings for life in a pigpen.

WHAT'S IT MEAN?

It's important to understand that the Prodigal Son describes us all. You don't have to run away from home and squander a fortune on wild living to be prodigal. Because of your sinful nature, you were born with a wayward heart that naturally rebels against God.

As today's verse says, your heart is corrupted by sin, which is disobedience toward God. Sin lies, tricks, and deceives. It tells you that you don't need God. It tries to convince you that you will find happiness in worldly pleasure. The Prodigal Son believed these lies, and look where it got him.

Sin promises everything but ultimately delivers only emptiness. If left unchecked, sin will always lead you away from God's grace and into hopelessness and spiritual bankruptcy.

This parable is a vivid picture of what happens if you choose a life of sin over God. It's utter foolishness, like choosing a dirty pigpen over a beautiful mansion.

The parable also wonderfully illustrates God's glorious grace and forgiveness, which are available to you through Christ. God is rich in mercy and patience. Like the loving father in the parable, he is ready to pour out immeasurable blessings of love, joy, and forgiveness on lost sinners who come to him in repentance and faith in Jesus.

Don't forfeit God's blessings for lies. Choose God over the pigsty of sin!

NOW WHAT?

To better understand our struggle with sin and the solution for it, read Romans 7:14-25.

DID YOU KNOW?

For ancient Jews, pigs were "unclean" animals under Old Testament law (Deuteronomy 14:8). The Prodigal Son couldn't stoop any lower than to feed swine.

APRIL 29

There is joy in the presence of God's angels when even one sinner repents. LUKE 15:10

On March 25, 2014, the National Football League tightened up one of its "excessive celebration" sportsmanship rules when it announced it would start penalizing players who dunk over the goalpost crossbar after scoring a touchdown.

Tony Gonzalez, for one, didn't like the decision. Gonzalez, a star tight end who retired after the 2013 season, performed crossbar dunks after many of his 111 career touchdowns. "Looks like I got out just in time," he tweeted afterward.

As football players have invented more ways to draw attention to themselves after big plays, the league has cracked down on some of the extreme displays. For instance, players can't taunt opponents, perform choreographed dances, or use any items that aren't part of their uniform as a celebratory prop.

Good thing the Prodigal Son's father in Jesus' parable wasn't an NFL player. He might've been flagged for fifteen yards.

When the young man's father saw his son a long way off, he sprinted out to welcome him back, wrapped him in a huge bear hug, and kissed him. Then he told his servants, "'Quick! Bring the finest robe in the house and put it on him. Get a ring for his finger and sandals for his feet. And kill the calf we have been fattening. We must celebrate with a feast, for this son of mine was dead and has now returned to life. He was lost, but now he is found.' So the party began" (Luke 15:22-24).

WHAT'S IT MEAN?

Heaven is a place of excessive celebration. When a person becomes a Christian, God's angels throw a big party! Don't believe it? See today's verse, which gives us a brief but fascinating glimpse into what happens in God's holy dwelling place when someone comes to Christ.

God's love for us is beyond comprehension. It's so great, in fact, that it affects the angels in his presence. As they witness his affection for us, they can't help but get excited and cheer when someone trusts in Jesus.

God's greatest desire is to receive glory as people worship him through faith in Jesus. As 2 Peter 3:9 says, "He does not want anyone to be destroyed, but wants everyone to repent."

Praise God that he's a God who celebrates our salvation!

NOW WHAT?

If you've never trusted in Jesus to save you from your sins, give heaven's angels a reason to celebrate today!

DID YOU KNOW?

Angels are powerful spiritual beings that God created, but one day, believers will rule over them (1 Corinthians 6:3).

*Abraham said to him, "Son, remember that during your lifetime
you had everything you wanted, and Lazarus had nothing. So now
he is here being comforted, and you are in anguish."* LUKE 16:25

Have you ever heard the term *carpe diem*?

It's an ancient Latin phrase that translates to "seize the day." Some people make it their life motto, trying to squeeze the most out of every moment because life is short. But the phrase also carries a negative meaning of enjoying momentary pleasures without a concern for the future. Jesus addressed this shortsighted perspective in the parable in Luke 16:19-31.

Jesus' story was about two men—a very rich man and a penniless beggar named Lazarus. Every day, the rich man wore the finest clothes and feasted on delicacies. Meanwhile, Lazarus sat outside the rich man's large estate, hoping for the crumbs from the man's table. As Lazarus sat there, stray dogs came and licked his wounds. It was a miserable existence. Yet the rich man didn't lift a finger to help Lazarus.

When both men died, their roles were reversed. For Lazarus's faith, God brought him to heaven. But the rich man's selfish living and godlessness doomed him to hell.

WHAT'S IT MEAN?

Jesus' parable contains many important lessons for us. But perhaps the greatest is this: the decisions you make on earth will affect your eternal destiny.

There's nothing wrong with "carpe diem" in terms of enjoying life's present moments. But there's a difference between living each day to its fullest and pursuing the wrong goals in life.

The rich man in Jesus' parable had rejected God. This is clear from his self-absorbed lifestyle. He ignored the needs of others, pursued worldly riches, and seized each day for himself, thinking his actions wouldn't affect his future. He scoffed at the notion that God rewards the righteous but punishes the wicked (Ezekiel 18:20). In the end, he paid a terrible price for his decisions. His life is a reminder of Jesus' words in Mark 8:36: "What do you benefit if you gain the whole world but lose your own soul?"

Lazarus, though, was different. It seems that despite his poverty, he honored God. His reward was eternal life in God's presence.

The things you do in this life matter. So love God, trust in his Son, pursue righteousness, and put others before yourself. Go ahead and seize the day, but seize it for the Lord!

NOW WHAT?

Make a commitment to study God's Word. It's the best way to learn how to make good decisions in this life.

DID YOU KNOW?

The Lazarus in today's parable is different from the real-life Lazarus whom Jesus raised from the dead in John 11.

MAY 1

There is a great chasm separating us. No one can cross over to you from here, and no one can cross over to us from there.
LUKE 16:26

You'd think Jesus' parable of Lazarus and the rich man in Luke 16 would end after he revealed the eternal destinations of the two individuals. But actually, that's when the story really gets interesting!

After the rich man died, his soul "went to the place of the dead," where he was "in torment" (Luke 16:23). Somehow, he was able to see Lazarus and Abraham in heaven, so he begged them for relief, hoping for even a single drop of water to soothe his "anguish in these flames" (verse 24).

Abraham told him that hell was his fair sentence for the self-centered, ungodly life he had lived. "And besides," Abraham said, "there is a great chasm separating us. No one can cross over to you from here, and no one can cross over to us from there" (verse 26).

WHAT'S IT MEAN?

When reading this parable, it's refreshing to see that Lazarus's earthly suffering turned into eternal rest in heaven. But the story ends on a sobering note. After dying, the rich man was doomed to spend the rest of eternity in hell, with no hope of relief or escape.

Death brings finality. The Bible is very clear on this: when a person dies, he or she will spend eternity in either heaven or hell, based upon that person's relationship with Jesus (Matthew 25:31-46).

Heaven is the perfect, wonderful-beyond-words dwelling place of God. Hell is a horrible place of punishment and separation from God. There is no other option. And for unbelievers, there are no second chances after death. Sadly, anyone who rejects Jesus in this life will suffer apart from him forever.

This underscores the importance of trusting in Jesus as your Lord and Savior today if you never have! None of us knows when we'll die, and when we do, it will be too late—your eternal fate has already been determined. As Hebrews 9:27 says, "Each person is destined to die once and after that comes judgment."

NOW WHAT?

There's no better time to trust in Jesus than today! In 2 Corinthians 6:2 we read, "Now is the time of God's favor, now is the day of salvation" (NIV).

DID YOU KNOW?

In Mark 9:48, Jesus gave a frightening description of hell as a place "where the maggots never die and the fire never goes out." He was quoting the last verse in the book of Isaiah (66:24).

MAY 2

Let us come to him with thanksgiving. Let us sing psalms of praise to him.   PSALM 95:2

As Jesus was heading to Jerusalem shortly before his death, he met ten lepers. Leprosy is a terrible skin disease that can cause great discomfort and sometimes disfiguration.

Even worse, lepers were social outcasts in ancient Israel. According to Old Testament law, people with leprosy were considered ceremonially unclean, and so was anyone who touched them (Numbers 5:2-4). Lepers had to live away from the general public, wear torn clothing, let their hair grow long, cover their faces, and shout, "Unclean!" whenever they approached anyone (Leviticus 13:45-46). Being a leper was awful.

So when these ten lepers saw Jesus, they knew he could make everything better. They cried out, "Jesus, Master, have mercy on us!" (Luke 17:13). Full of compassion, Jesus told them to go and show themselves to the local priest (for a ritual cleansing, according to the law), and as they walked away, he healed them.

One man, a Samaritan, came back shouting and praising Jesus. Sadly, the other nine did not. Jesus was disappointed. "Didn't I heal ten men?" he asked. "Where are the other nine? Has no one returned to give glory to God except this foreigner?" Then Jesus said to the man, "Stand up and go. Your faith has healed you" (Luke 17:17-19).

WHAT'S IT MEAN?

It's so important to have a heart of thankfulness toward our Savior. The Bible is packed with examples of godly people praising the Lord for all his blessings. Other than today's verse, here are a few examples:

- "Devote yourselves to prayer with an alert mind and a thankful heart" (Colossians 4:2).
- "Be thankful in all circumstances, for this is God's will for you who belong to Christ Jesus" (1 Thessalonians 5:18).

- "Since we are receiving a Kingdom that is unshakable, let us be thankful and please God by worshiping him with holy fear and awe" (Hebrews 12:28).

A thankful heart directs our focus to where it should be—on God. Thankfulness helps us stay humble and remember that God is responsible for all our blessings (James 1:17). He has provided for all our physical needs (a family, home, clothes, food) and our spiritual needs too (providing Jesus for our salvation, his Word, his Spirit).

God is worthy of all our praise and thanksgiving!

NOW WHAT?

Make a long list of God's blessings toward you. Then take time over the next few weeks to prayerfully thank him for a few each day.

DID YOU KNOW?

Three whole chapters in Leviticus are devoted to Old Testament laws about leprosy.

We know that a person is not justified by works of the law but through faith in Jesus Christ. GALATIANS 2:16, ESV

One of the coolest parables that Jesus told is found in Luke 18. It's only six verses long, but it illustrates a critical truth of Scripture: the doctrine of justification.

Jesus' parable focused on a Pharisee and a tax collector who both went to the Temple in Jerusalem to pray. The Pharisee, a self-righteous religious leader who built his life on following rules, puffed out his chest and said, "I thank you, God, that I am not a sinner like everyone else." Then he proudly listed all the good things he did. Meanwhile, the tax collector, who was despised for being dishonest in his job as well as working for the Roman oppressors, humbly bowed his head, beat his chest (a sign of sorrow in those days), and said, "O God, be merciful to me, for I am a sinner" (Luke 18:13).

Jesus then shocked his audience by saying, "I tell you, this sinner, not the Pharisee, returned home justified before God" (Luke 18:14).

WHAT'S IT MEAN?

The word *justified* means to be made right with God, which is something each of us greatly needs since our sins separate us from him. *Justification* is a legal term. It's when God, the Almighty Judge, declares a guilty sinner innocent, removing the person's blame and withholding the punishment he or she deserves.

Sounds great! But . . . how does it happen?

As Jesus' parable explains, it's not through human effort. The Pharisee thought he could impress God with his good works. We can fall into this trap too. It's easy to think we can earn God's favor through being obedient, going to church, being a "good" person, or doing other deeds.

But no amount of human goodness can erase our sinful nature. Trying to earn justification is like tying a pretty ribbon on a bag of smelly trash. The bag might look a little nicer, but it's still smelly trash.

As today's verse says, justification comes through Jesus alone. He makes us right before God by giving us *his* righteousness. He did this by paying for all our sins and guilt on the cross.

Now, as the tax collector demonstrated, the only thing that's left is for us to humbly repent before God and ask for his mercy. When we trust in Jesus' sacrifice for us, God declares us righteous!

NOW WHAT?

Understanding the doctrine of justification is crucial to becoming a Christian. To learn more about it, read Romans chapters 3–4.

DID YOU KNOW?

To justify us, God imputes (or transfers) our sin-guilt to Jesus, and Jesus' righteousness to us. What a bargain!

MAY 4

He said to them, "Let the little children come to me, and do not hinder them, for the kingdom of God belongs to such as these."
MARK 10:14 (NIV)

Jesus loves me! This I know,
For the Bible tells me so.
Little ones to him belong;
They are weak, but he is strong.

Yes, Jesus loves me!
Yes, Jesus loves me!
Yes, Jesus loves me!
The Bible tells me so.

You've probably sung these words before. They are the lyrics to "Jesus Loves Me," one of the most beloved Christian hymns of all time. The song was first published in a novel titled *Say and Seal*, written by sisters Susan and Anna Warner in 1860. About a year later, a man named William Bradbury added the refrain of "Yes, Jesus loves me" and the song's tune.

The song is so simple but so true. Mark 10:13-16 gives us a beautiful example of this. One day, people brought little children and infants to Jesus so he could bless them. Jesus' disciples tried to shoo the children away. They considered the children a bother.

Jesus sharply rebuked his disciples, then spoke some of the most wonderful words in Scripture: "Let the little children come to me, and do not hinder them, for the kingdom of God belongs to such as these" (today's verse). Then he took the children in his arms and blessed them.

WHAT'S IT MEAN?

Jesus dearly loves children and places a high value on them. His heart toward children reflects the intimate care God the Father shows for each individual life (Psalm 139:13-16).

Jesus fully embraced Old Testament passages such as Deuteronomy 6:6-7 and Psalm 78:1-6, which highlight the importance of training the next generation in godliness. And he issued stern warnings to anyone who would harm a child (Matthew 18:6). As discussed in the April 18 devotion, he even used a child's humility and trusting nature as examples for adults to follow (Matthew 18:3).

Jesus is the eternal Son of God, the Creator and Sustainer of the universe, the Savior of the world, and the coming King. Yet despite all his glory, majesty, and power, he has a tender heart for the little ones in the world.

Aren't you glad we have a Savior who loves children?

NOW WHAT?

If you're old enough, get involved in the children's ministry in your church and share Jesus' love with little kids.

DID YOU KNOW?

When Jesus said, "The kingdom of God belongs to such as these," he meant that all who come to him with simple, childlike faith will go to heaven.

MAY 5

The love of money is a root of all kinds of evil.
1 TIMOTHY 6:10, NIV

One day, a rich young man asked Jesus an important question.

"Teacher," he said in Matthew 19:16, "what good deed must I do to have eternal life?" He thought he could earn salvation through human achievement.

Wanting to help the man see his mistake, Jesus told him that reaching God's holy standard meant perfectly obeying the law. So Jesus rattled off a bunch of the Ten Commandments. "All these I have kept," the man replied. "What do I still lack?" (verse 20, NIV). (The man didn't get it. But boy, he sure had a high opinion of himself!)

Jesus could see into the man's heart. He knew the man loved his wealth, so he told the man to sell all his worldly possessions, give the money to the poor, and "then come, follow me." Then, he'd have true riches—"treasure in heaven" (Matthew 19:21).

The rich man loved his possessions too much to do a thing like that. So he turned his back on Jesus and "went away sad" (verse 22).

WHAT'S IT MEAN?

Earthly treasures are deceitful. They promise pleasure and fulfillment—and may even provide them temporarily—but they never truly satisfy us.

Let's be clear: money isn't the problem. The love of money is. Loving worldly possessions is a dangerous idol of the human heart—a violation of the first commandment (Exodus 20:3). It's impossible to worship both God and money (Luke 16:13), and choosing money over God leads to disastrous results (Luke 12:13-21).

Today's verse is part of a wonderful Scripture passage in 1 Timothy 6:9-10, where the apostle Paul warns us about the trap of worldly riches:

People who long to be rich fall into temptation and are trapped by many foolish and harmful desires that plunge them into ruin and destruction. For the love of money is the root of all kinds of evil. And some people, craving money, have wandered from the true faith and pierced themselves with many sorrows.

Don't be like the rich young man in this story. True riches aren't found in a bank account; they're found in the Son of God!

NOW WHAT?

Sell some of your favorite stuff, and give the money to a Christian charity. It's a great way to demonstrate that you love Jesus more than earthly treasure.

DID YOU KNOW?

The cure for a love of money is contentment—being satisfied with what God has given you. In 1 Timothy 6:6-8 we read, "Godliness with contentment is great gain. For we brought nothing into the world, and we can take nothing out of it. But if we have food and clothing, we will be content with that" (NIV).

Jesus looked at them intently and said, "Humanly speaking, it is impossible. But with God everything is possible."
MATTHEW 19:26

Camels are big creatures. A dromedary (one-hump) camel stands about seven feet tall and weighs up to 1,600 pounds. As the largest animal in ancient Israel, it was a perfect illustration for an important spiritual lesson that Jesus wanted to teach.

After the wealthy young man refused to give up his money and follow Jesus in Matthew 19, the Lord turned to his disciples and told them, "It is very hard for a rich person to enter the Kingdom of Heaven. I'll say it again—it is easier for a camel to go through the eye of a needle than for a rich person to enter the Kingdom of God" (Matthew 19:23-24).

In case sewing isn't your thing, the eye of a needle is the small hole at the top of a needle that the thread goes into. It's the tiniest of openings—physically impossible for a camel to fit through.

As he often did, Jesus was speaking in hyperbole (exaggeration to make a point) to show how difficult it is for rich people to love him more than money. But the disciples were confused. They apparently considered the rich man to be a great man since he was a "ruler" (Luke 18:18, ESV), a follower of Old Testament law (Matthew 19:20), and very wealthy, which they probably viewed as God's favor on him. They were impressed with the wrong things.

"Astounded" at Jesus' statement, the disciples asked, "Then who in the world can be saved?" (Matthew 19:25). Jesus answered, "Humanly speaking, it is impossible. But with God everything is possible."

WHAT'S IT MEAN?

When Jesus said, "Humanly speaking, it is impossible," he wasn't just referring to rich people being saved. He was talking about salvation in general. Salvation is nothing short of a miraculous work of God. It's a spiritual process in which God calls us to believe, regenerates our hearts to accept his truth, makes us right before him, and helps us become more like him (see Romans 8:30 for more on this incredible process).

Yes, there is human responsibility involved. We must "repent and believe in the gospel" (Mark 1:15, ESV). But without God, we wouldn't even *know* we needed to be saved because of our spiritually "dead" condition (Ephesians 2:1).

Salvation is impossible without God. Thank God that he does the impossible in our sinful hearts!

NOW WHAT?
Memorize Romans 8:30. It's a great verse to remember about the process of salvation.

DID YOU KNOW?
A dromedary camel can travel up to one hundred miles in the desert without drinking water.

Everyone who has given up houses or brothers or sisters or father or mother or children or property, for my sake, will receive a hundred times as much in return and will inherit eternal life.
MATTHEW 19:29

You've got to love Peter.

This disciple of Jesus was as blunt as they come. He usually said whatever was on his mind, for better or worse. Such was the case in the story of Jesus and the rich young man in Matthew 19.

After the rich man left, Peter started thinking. He had heard Jesus tell the man to "sell all your possessions and give the money to the poor . . . then come, follow me" (Matthew 19:21). He had watched the man walk away, unwisely choosing earthly riches over Jesus.

So being Peter, he decided to remind Jesus that, unlike the rich man, he *had* made the right choice. "We've given up everything to follow you," Peter boasted. "What will we get?" (Matthew 19:27).

Good ol' straightforward Peter. No beating around the bush with him.

In Matthew 19:28-29, Jesus replied as follows:

I assure you that when the world is made new and the Son of Man sits upon his glorious throne, you who have been my followers will also sit on twelve thrones, judging the twelve tribes of Israel. And everyone who has given up houses or brothers or sisters or father or mother or children or property, for my sake, will receive a hundred times as much in return and will inherit eternal life.

WHAT'S IT MEAN?

One day, Jesus will return to earth a final time, destroy all evil, and inaugurate an eternal, heavenly Kingdom. Jesus' apostles apparently will have special ruling privileges. (Pretty sweet deal for them!) But as today's verse says, Jesus made a wonderful promise for the rest of us too.

If receiving eternal life wasn't amazing enough, Jesus also assured us of many other blessings. All true believers will receive far greater spiritual rewards—in this life and the life to come—than anything this sinful world can offer.

It's hard to imagine what our heavenly rewards will be, and that's the point. They are too marvelous for our limited human minds to comprehend now.

But one day, if we're faithful to our Savior, he will shower us with indescribable heavenly rewards. Now *that's* worth living for!

NOW WHAT?

Ask your parents if there's anything you need to give up to grow in your walk with Jesus. If they mention something, take steps to make the necessary changes.

DID YOU KNOW?

While good deeds don't save us, Jesus will reward in heaven the acts of kindness and obedience that we did on earth (Matthew 16:27 and Revelation 22:12).

MAY 8

Work willingly at whatever you do, as though you were working for the Lord rather than for people. Remember that the Lord will give you an inheritance as your reward, and that the Master you are serving is Christ. COLOSSIANS 3:23-24

Imagine you did chores from 9:00 a.m. to 5:00 p.m. on a Saturday and received a ten-dollar allowance, only to see your parents give your sibling a ten-dollar bill for one hour's worth of work. You'd be pretty upset, wouldn't you?

That was the situation in a parable Jesus told in Matthew 20. Prompted by Peter's selfish question about rewards in Matthew 19, Jesus told his disciples a story about a wealthy landowner who had a vineyard. Early in the morning, he agreed to pay some laborers a fair day's wage to work in his vineyard. Throughout the day, the man hired additional workers, at 9:00 a.m., noon, 3:00 p.m., and even 5:00 p.m.

When the sun was setting, he called everyone in for their pay. Starting with the laborers who worked the least, he gave everyone a denarius (a coin representing one day's wage). When the laborers who worked a twelve-hour day received the same amount, they started grumbling. They thought they deserved more.

But the landowner replied, "I haven't been unfair! Didn't you agree to work all day for the usual wage? Take your money and go. I wanted to pay this last worker the same as you. Is it against the law for me to do what I want with my money? Should you be jealous because I am kind to others?" (Matthew 20:13-16).

WHAT'S IT MEAN?

God, represented by the landowner in this parable, is the Creator and Ruler of the universe. He made us and bestowed various gifts and abilities on each person. He gives more to some people, less to others. Abilities, blessings, and rewards are entirely up to him. Who are we, the created, to argue with the Creator?

Our responsibility is to use the gifts and abilities God has given to us with hearts of gratitude and be thankful for any heavenly rewards. After all, God owes us nothing. Rather than comparing ourselves to others or complaining about our lot in life, we should serve the Lord with joy, remembering the eternal blessings that await everyone who faithfully serves him.

NOW WHAT?

As you do chores, quietly give prayers of thanksgiving to God for his many blessings to you.

DID YOU KNOW?

The disciples would've been quite familiar with vineyards because grapes were an important crop in ancient Israel.

Whoever wants to be a leader among you must be your servant,
and whoever wants to be first among you must become your slave.
MATTHEW 20:26-27

James and John, the "Sons of Thunder" siblings, couldn't get heavenly thrones out of their heads.

When Peter brazenly asked Jesus how the disciples would be rewarded for giving up everything to follow him, the Lord promised them an amazing reward. "You who have been my followers will also sit on twelve thrones, judging the twelve tribes of Israel," he said (see the May 7 devotion).

Those words stuck with James and John. But apparently, not even that incredible privilege was enough. The brothers, it seems, convinced their mother to make a bold, selfish request—perhaps because they were too scared to do it themselves.

"In your Kingdom," she said to Jesus in Matthew 20:21, "please let my two sons sit in places of honor next to you, one on your right and the other on your left."

(C'mon, fellas! You got *your mom* to say that to Jesus? Shame on you!)

When the other disciples heard about the request, "they were indignant" (verse 24). But Jesus quickly stepped in and said in verses 25-28:

> *You know that the rulers in this world lord it over their people, and*
> *officials flaunt their authority over those under them. But among*
> *you it will be different. Whoever wants to be a leader among you*
> *must be your servant, and whoever wants to be first among you*
> *must become your slave. For even the Son of Man came not to be*
> *served but to serve others and to give his life as a ransom for many.*

WHAT'S IT MEAN?

The disciples still had a lot to learn about greatness. They thought of greatness in worldly terms: position, power, and prestige. But Jesus adjusted their thinking. True greatness, he said, is found in a humble heart that seeks to serve others.

The Savior is the ultimate example of this. He sacrificed his very life for sinful rebels like us. If humility is greatness, you can't get any greater than that.

Where's your heart? Do you crave human recognition and authority? Do you seek worldly status and fame? Or do you put others' needs first and seek God's honor instead of your own?

Follow Jesus' example, and you will be truly great in God's eyes!

NOW WHAT?

Offer to help someone in an unexpected way today. It's a great way to humble yourself and be a servant.

DID YOU KNOW?

Some Bible scholars believe that James and John's mother was Jesus' earthly aunt (compare Matthew 27:56; Mark 15:40; and John 19:25), making James and John his cousins.

Even the Son of Man came not to be served but to serve others and to give his life as a ransom for many. MARK 10:45

Jesus' disciples were a rowdy bunch.

As discussed in the February 7 devotion, Jesus' closest friends were often dishonest, impatient, self-centered, argumentative, angry, arrogant, and faithless. They were big ol' sinners, like the rest of us.

They also had a lot to learn about true greatness. So as the disciples began to bicker with one another about who would sit in positions of highest honor in Jesus' heavenly Kingdom, the Lord taught them a lesson that those who are truly great in God's eyes are humble servants. As the ultimate example of this, he pointed to himself: "Even the Son of Man came not to be served but to serve others and to give his life as a ransom for many" (today's verse).

Jesus wasn't being prideful. He was just stating the facts. But his choice of words is interesting. Why did he say his death was a "ransom for many"?

WHAT'S IT MEAN?

A ransom is a payment for the release of someone held captive. Ransoms are often demanded in kidnappings—when a criminal abducts another person and holds that person hostage, demanding a large sum of money in exchange for the captive's freedom. In ancient times, ransoms were also paid to free slaves.

Did you know that you were born a captive and a slave? It's true. In John 8:34, Jesus said, "I tell you the truth, everyone who sins is a slave of sin." That means all of us are slaves, for all have sinned (Romans 3:23). In Luke 4:18, Jesus said, "He [God] has sent me to proclaim that captives will be released, that the blind will see, that the oppressed will be set free" (a nod to the messianic prophecy in Isaiah 61:1).

From the moment we're born, we are held captive by our sins, which carry the steep price of death (Romans 6:23) and can be forgiven only by a great sacrifice (Hebrews 9:22). Jesus sacrificed his life on the cross to become our ransom! He bought our freedom at a great cost—not with money but with his own blood.

The ransom has been paid. Jesus' sacrifice satisfied God's wrath toward sin. Now we can have freedom from sin and death if we trust in Jesus. Praise the Lord!

NOW WHAT?

Many people are held captive by sin. Offer someone freedom by sharing the love of Jesus today!

DID YOU KNOW?

Romans 5–7 is a great passage for learning more about how Jesus ransoms us from being slaves to sin and death.

MAY 11

The Son of Man came to seek and save those who are lost.
LUKE 19:10

The little man frantically raced through the crowd, searching for even a small opening in the wall of bodies that lined the streets of ancient Jericho. As he ran, he hiked up his long, luxurious robe to avoid tripping and face-planting on the dusty road. His fellow Jews already despised him for working as a tax collector for the hated Romans. He certainly didn't want to give them a reason to laugh at him.

But the mob of spectators was too thick. What the man boasted in riches, he lacked in height. So as a last resort, he climbed up a sycamore tree. There, he could catch at least a passing glimpse of the miraculous man everybody was talking about.

Zacchaeus *had* to see Jesus.

When Jesus approached, he looked into the tree and said, "Zacchaeus! Quick, come down! I must be a guest in your home today" (Luke 19:5).

This shocked the crowd. No one could believe that Jesus chose to spend time with a dishonest tax collector, who had become rich by overcharging his own countrymen. "He has gone to be the guest of a notorious sinner," the people grumbled (Luke 19:7).

WHAT'S IT MEAN?

The people didn't understand Jesus' true heart. The Messiah didn't come to earth to socialize with the "in" crowd or to hang out with those who thought they were already holy, such as the Pharisees. No, as today's verse says, Jesus came to seek and save the lost.

While most people of Jesus' day turned their backs on tax collectors, lepers, beggars, the disabled, and other social outcasts, Jesus welcomed them with open arms. He healed them, ate with them, taught them, and showed them unconditional love. He wasn't snobbish, and he didn't play favorites.

Jesus' heart for lost people and outcasts led to a wonderful change in

Zacchaeus. The little tax collector trusted in Jesus, repented from his deceitful, greedy ways, and gave away much of his riches to help others (Luke 19:8-9).

Jesus' heart should inform our thinking too. Do you play favorites? Do you shun those who aren't considered "cool"? Those actions don't please Jesus. To be like the Savior, show love to people whom others reject.

NOW WHAT?

Do you know someone who is ignored by others? Strike up a conversation and be a friend to him or her.

DID YOU KNOW?

Scripture never says that Jesus and Zacchaeus had ever met before. Yet Jesus called him by name. By doing this, Jesus demonstrated that he knew everything about Zacchaeus and could see that his heart was ready for faith.

The kind of sorrow God wants us to experience leads us away from sin and results in salvation. There's no regret for that kind of sorrow. But worldly sorrow, which lacks repentance, results in spiritual death.

2 CORINTHIANS 7:10

Climbing that sycamore tree in Jericho was the best decision Zacchaeus ever made. Instead of simply catching a glimpse of Jesus, the undersized tax collector received an unexpected, life-changing visit from the Son of God.

What did Jesus and Zacchaeus talk about that day? The weather? The current price of camels in Israel? How the tax collection business was going? What it was like to be so short?

Probably not.

The Bible doesn't say exactly what they discussed. But it's clear that Jesus confronted Zacchaeus with the gospel, because Zacchaeus repented and placed his faith in Jesus. That's evident by what Luke 19:8 says: "Zacchaeus stood before the Lord and said, 'I will give half my wealth to the poor, Lord, and if I have cheated people on their taxes, I will give them back four times as much!'"

Zacchaeus had truly repented.

WHAT'S IT MEAN?

Repentance is a frequently misunderstood term. True repentance is more than just saying "I'm sorry" after you do something wrong. Biblical repentance means turning from sinful patterns and choosing to live in a way that pleases God (see today's verse).

Zacchaeus did that. Old Testament law required a thief to repay the full amount he stole plus an additional one-fifth of the value (Leviticus 6:5). But Zacchaeus promised to give back four times the amount he stole. In other words, if Zacchaeus stole $100 from someone, the law required him to pay back $120. But Zacchaeus said, "I'll pay back $400!" He also willingly offered half his riches to the poor.

Thanks to Jesus, Zacchaeus experienced a radical heart change. He realized how great his sins were and how much he had been forgiven. His good works didn't save him, but they were evidence of his genuine turnaround.

Repentance, along with faith in Jesus, is necessary for salvation (Mark 1:15). But throughout our lives, we need to continue to repent whenever we sin, asking God's forgiveness and his help to obey.

God loves a repentant heart!

NOW WHAT?

Do you have any unconfessed sin? Bring it to the Lord, and ask him to forgive you and help you change.

DID YOU KNOW?

Judas Iscariot is a tragic example of feeling bad about something but *not* repenting. After betraying Jesus for thirty pieces of silver, Judas "was seized with remorse" and returned the money (Matthew 27:3, NIV). Then he went out to a field and hanged himself. That's worldly sorrow, not true repentance.

I am the good shepherd. The good shepherd sacrifices his life for the sheep. JOHN 10:11

In John 9, Jesus lovingly healed a man who had been blind since birth. As the people were marveling at the miracle, the Pharisees became upset. They disagreed with Jesus healing on the Sabbath, their holy day. They argued with Jesus and eventually threw the healed man out of the local synagogue. They wrongly chose worthless rules over mercy and compassion.

Sadly, these were the men in charge of Israel's spiritual health. These religious leaders were supposed to be wise shepherds, guiding their flock toward proper worship of God. Instead, they were self-righteous hypocrites who led the people astray.

Wanting to show the people a better way, Jesus told the crowd, "I am the good shepherd; I know my sheep and my sheep know me—just as the Father knows me and I know the Father—and I lay down my life for the sheep" (John 10:14-15, NIV).

WHAT'S IT MEAN?

Throughout Scripture, the image of a shepherd is used to describe Israel's leaders, such as Moses (Isaiah 63:11) and David (2 Samuel 5:2). Old Testament prophets frequently used the shepherd analogy to criticize Israel's wicked leaders at the time of the Assyrian and Babylonian captivities (Jeremiah 10:21).

Yet where all of Israel's human leaders (shepherds) failed, Jesus succeeded. The book of 1 Peter calls Jesus "your Shepherd, the Guardian of your souls" (2:25) and "the Great Shepherd" (5:4). Hebrews 13:20 refers to Jesus as "the great Shepherd of the sheep."

A shepherd is someone who loves, watches over, and protects those in his care. He provides for the needs of his flock and sacrifices himself for their safety.

This perfectly describes Jesus. On the cross, he sacrificed his life for his sheep. Micah 5:4 says, "He will stand and shepherd his flock in the strength of the LORD, in the majesty of the name of the LORD his God" (NIV). Jesus is also described as "the gate for the sheep" (John 10:7). Only through him can we enter God's heavenly Kingdom.

Unfortunately, not everyone hears the Good Shepherd's call. Only Jesus' true followers "recognize his voice and come to him" (John 10:3). Are you one of Jesus' sheep?

NOW WHAT?

No one can recognize the Good Shepherd's voice, as John 10:3 says, without believing that he is God's Son, who was sent to save us from our sins. Believe in Jesus today!

DID YOU KNOW?

The Bible often refers to God the Father as a shepherd too. Psalm 80:1 calls God the "Shepherd of Israel," and the most famous psalm—Psalm 23—starts with these words: "The LORD is my shepherd; I shall not want" (ESV).

MAY 14

I have come that they may have life, and have it to the full.

JOHN 10:10, NIV

Ask ten people on the street what a good life is, and you'll probably get ten different answers. Some might say a long, healthy existence filled with family and friends. Others might say a life of riches and comfort, not ever worrying about basic necessities like food, clothing, and shelter. Still others may say pursuing their dreams and goals—another thrill around every corner.

In John 10, as Jesus was describing himself as the "Good Shepherd," he told the people, "I have come that they may have life, and have it to the full" (today's verse).

So that begs the question: What, exactly, is this full life that Jesus is promising?

WHAT'S IT MEAN?

First, it's important to understand the context of Jesus' statement. It came during a rebuke of the Pharisees. While these hypocritical leaders loaded the people down with worthless man-made rules in an effort to please God, Jesus offered a life free of such heavy religious burdens.

Similarly, the full life Jesus offers has nothing to do with other empty worldly pursuits like money, power, fame, or pleasure. It doesn't have anything to do with health or longevity, either.

No, the full life Jesus offers is all about rich spiritual blessings that can be found only in one Person. As the Good Shepherd, Jesus leads us to "good pastures" (John 10:9) of heaven-sent abundance, both in this life and eternity.

A truly full life involves forgiveness of sin, peace with God, and eternal hope. It involves a loving heavenly Father taking care of your every need. It involves the joy of being God's child and knowing his favor rests on you.

Jesus can offer us life to the fullest because he created us and knows what's best for us. We were made to worship him, so when we submit our lives to the Good Shepherd's lordship, we experience the fullness of everything he intended for us.

All this is possible because "the good shepherd sacrifices his life for the sheep" (John 10:11). But this full life is available only to the sheep of Jesus' pasture.

Trust in Jesus, the Good Shepherd, and experience life to the fullest!

NOW WHAT?

To have the "full" life that Jesus promises, believe in him, follow his voice, and obey his Word.

DID YOU KNOW?

Jesus, who knew the Scriptures perfectly as the all-knowing Son of God, probably had Ezekiel 34:12-15, 25-31 in mind when he described himself as the "Good Shepherd." Check out this wonderful Old Testament passage.

MAY 15

No one can snatch them from the Father's hand. JOHN 10:29

One day, Jesus was walking through the Temple area in Jerusalem when the religious leaders confronted him. With hateful eyes and faithless hearts, they said, "How long are you going to keep us in suspense? If you are the Messiah, tell us plainly" (John 10:24).

Jesus knew these men were too hard hearted to be his true followers, so he said, "My sheep listen to my voice; I know them, and they follow me. I give them eternal life, and they will never perish. No one can snatch them away from me, for my Father has given them to me, and he is more powerful than anyone else. No one can snatch them from the Father's hand" (John 10:27-29).

This was a profound statement. In fact, for the last two thousand years, that declaration—"No one can snatch them from the Father's hand"—has both comforted and confused Christians. Those words raise a very important question: Can Christians lose their salvation?

WHAT'S IT MEAN?

First, let's define the phrase "lose your salvation." Some people believe that a Christian can somehow forfeit his or her righteous standing with God by falling into sinful patterns and drifting away from the faith. In other words, they believe a person's actions can cause him or her to go from saved child of God back to hell-bound sinner.

But today's Scripture refutes that idea. To lose your salvation would mean the following:

- Certain portions of Scripture (such as Romans 8) are false.
- Jesus' death was not powerful enough to defeat all sin.
- Salvation depends on Jesus' sacrifice *plus* human effort.
- Christians must constantly worry about avoiding that final, fateful sin that cancels out their salvation.

Of course, not one of those points is true.

Jesus clearly teaches in John 10—and other Bible passages agree—that true Christians cannot lose their salvation. Once God saves a person from their sins, they are eternally secure in Jesus' righteousness.

How do we know this? Because salvation is all about God, not us. True believers can't lose their salvation, because they didn't earn it in the first place. When it comes to our salvation, God initiates it, accomplishes it, and preserves it (Ephesians 1:1-14). God doesn't make mistakes. His plan of salvation through Jesus was fully sufficient for our needs.

When God saves, he saves completely!

NOW WHAT?

To learn more about this important subject, read John 6:37; John 17:2; and Romans 8:1, 28-39.

DID YOU KNOW?

Jesus spoke the words of John 10:27-29 during the annual Festival of Dedication, which today is referred to as Hanukkah.

MAY 16

Live as people who are free, not using your freedom as a cover-up for evil, but living as servants of God.   1 PETER 2:16, ESV

The doctrine of eternal security (also called "the perseverance of the saints") that was discussed in yesterday's devotion is a wonderful truth that provides great comfort to Christians.

Because salvation depends on God's power and Jesus' righteousness—and *not* on human achievement—true believers can rest assured that they cannot lose their salvation. As Romans 8:39 so beautifully proclaims, "Nothing in all creation will ever be able to separate us from the love of God that is revealed in Christ Jesus our Lord."

However, we must be very careful, because this doctrine raises an interesting question: If we as Christians can't lose our salvation, why does it matter how we live? In other words, once we trust in Jesus and our eternal destiny is secured, can't we do whatever we want without any consequences?

The answer is a resounding NO!

WHAT'S IT MEAN?

It's true that Christians cannot lose their salvation. But salvation doesn't give us the freedom to do whatever we want. The person who views God's grace like that might not be saved at all. It's like he or she is spitting on the precious cross of Christ (Hebrews 10:26-29).

You see, Christianity is not just a one-time prayer or an emotional decision that may or may not last. It's not some sort of golden ticket to heaven that you cash in when you die, regardless of how you live.

No, Christianity is a lifetime commitment to love, trust, and obey Jesus as your Lord and Savior. It involves daily dying to yourself and following Christ (Mark 8:34). A genuine follower of Jesus continually becomes more like him, not less (2 Corinthians 3:18).

True believers don't wipe sinful feet on God's grace like it's a doormat. Rather, they cherish that grace and understand that sin is a destructive enemy (Psalm 106:43), not a friend to hang out with.

As today's verse says, we must not use our "freedom" in Christ "as a cover-up for evil." Rather, we are to live "as servants of God." Galatians 5:13 echoes that thought when it says, "You have been called to live in freedom, my brothers and sisters. But don't use your freedom to satisfy your sinful nature. Instead, use your freedom to serve one another in love."

True Christians are eternally secure—and continually growing—in Jesus!

NOW WHAT?

Memorize today's verse to help you remember this important truth.

DID YOU KNOW?

Hebrews 10:26-29 contains a sobering warning for people who call themselves Christians but live without caring about their actions. Check it out.

MAY 17

Jesus said to her, "I am the resurrection and the life."
JOHN 11:25, NIV

Lazarus was dead. Deceased. Departed. Done. Kaput. No more.

He had been in a tomb four days. His time had come and gone.

Or had it?

The story of Lazarus in John 11 represents Jesus' greatest miracle, other than his own resurrection. Jesus' friend, Lazarus, had become gravely ill. But before Jesus came to him, Lazarus died.

When Jesus finally arrived, Lazarus's sisters, Mary and Martha, were devastated that Jesus hadn't come earlier and healed their brother. Jesus promised Martha that Lazarus would rise again. When it was clear that Martha didn't fully understand what he was saying, Jesus proclaimed, "I am the resurrection and the life. The one who believes in me will live, even though they die; and whoever lives by believing in me will never die. Do you believe this?" (John 11:25-26, NIV).

"Yes, Lord," she told him. "I have always believed you are the Messiah, the Son of God" (verse 27).

Once he reached Lazarus's tomb, Jesus ordered the large stone blocking the entrance to be removed. The people there were puzzled. Then Jesus shouted, "Lazarus, come out!" (verse 43). Within death's deep darkness, life began to stir. Moments later, to the crowd's astonishment, a man wrapped in grave clothes emerged into the light of day.

Lazarus was alive!

WHAT'S IT MEAN?

Jesus possesses all power—even resurrection power. But notice the interesting thing he said to Martha in John 11:25. He didn't say, "I *can* resurrect people and give life" or "I *have* the power of resurrection and life" (although both of these are true). He said, "I *am* the resurrection and the life" (emphasis added). Resurrection and life exist because of Jesus. As the eternal, incarnate

Word of God who spoke all life into existence (John 1:1-4), the very essence of life and resurrection are part of Christ's being (John 5:26).

This is why, after dying on the cross, Jesus returned to life by his own power (John 10:18). It's also why he has the power to give eternal life to all who call on him (John 17:2) and resurrect all believers to live forever with him in heaven one day (1 Thessalonians 4:16-17).

The same question Jesus asked Martha in John 11:26 now comes to you: "Do you believe this?"

NOW WHAT?

Take a little time to meditate on (think and pray about) the apostle Paul's words in Philippians 3:10: "I want to know Christ and experience the mighty power that raised him from the dead."

DID YOU KNOW?

The Bible records four separate resurrection miracles performed by Jesus: Jairus's daughter (Matthew 9:18-26), the widow's son from Nain (Luke 7:11-17), Lazarus, and, of course, himself!

MAY 18

When Jesus heard about it he said, "Lazarus's sickness will not end in death. No, it happened for the glory of God so that the Son of God will receive glory from this." JOHN 11:4

What would you do if you heard a dear friend was on his or her deathbed? Would you wait a couple of days before going to visit? No, of course not!

But that's exactly what Jesus did.

In John 11, when Jesus heard that his good friend Lazarus was terribly ill, he didn't lace up his running sandals, hop on a turbocharged camel, or rent the fastest chariot in Israel. No, he stayed exactly where he was for two more days. When Jesus finally arrived in Lazarus's hometown, his friend was dead.

Even Lazarus's sisters, Mary and Martha, voiced their disappointment. Both of them said, "Lord, if only you had been here, my brother would not have died" (John 11:21, 32).

If Jesus knew Lazarus would die (because Jesus is God and knows everything), why did he wait to go to Lazarus? Was he uncaring? Indifferent? Heartless?

Not at all. Jesus purposefully timed his arrival after Lazarus's death so he could display his resurrection power and bring God praise. As today's verse says, "It happened for the glory of God so that the Son of God will receive glory from this."

WHAT'S IT MEAN?

God sometimes lets bad things happen in our lives so he can receive greater glory through these situations. None of Lazarus's family or friends wanted him to die. But Jesus allowed it to happen to reveal his true identity as the Messiah and to bring more glory to God through a remarkable miracle.

We don't always understand why God allows difficulties in our lives. And that's okay. He is God, and we are not. As Isaiah 55:9 says, "Just as the heavens are higher than the earth, so my ways are higher than your ways and my thoughts higher than your thoughts."

Your life is not all about you and your plans. You exist to bring glory to God (Isaiah 43:7). And sometimes, that happens through trials. But even in those situations, you can rest assured that God uses them for your good (Romans 8:28). (Make sure to check out tomorrow's devotion, which discusses Jesus' response to our suffering.)

The God of all glory loves you more than you can imagine. Trust him during trials, and live to glorify him!

NOW WHAT?

When trouble comes, your job is to follow the words of 1 Peter 4:19: "So then, those who suffer according to God's will should commit themselves to their faithful Creator and continue to do good" (NIV).

DID YOU KNOW?

See John 9 and 2 Corinthians 12:1-10 for more examples of God using human trials for his glory.

MAY 19

Jesus wept. JOHN 11:35, NIV

Today's verse is one of the shortest in the entire Bible. It's only two words long and contains nine letters total. It has a noun and a verb and nothing else—the bare minimum for a sentence. And yet, those two words pack a wonderful wallop of truth about Jesus.

The verse is found within the story of Lazarus's resurrection. When Lazarus's sister Mary heard that Jesus had arrived in Bethany, she rushed to see him. With tears flowing down her cheeks, she cried out, "Lord, if only you had been here, my brother would not have died" (John 11:32).

When Jesus saw Mary's sorrow and everyone else mourning around her, he felt "a deep anger" and "was deeply troubled" (John 11:33). He asked the crowd to take him to Lazarus's tomb.

Then Jesus wept.

WHAT'S IT MEAN?

Why did Jesus cry? And why did he get angry? The Bible doesn't tell us exactly.

Jesus knew he was about to raise Lazarus, so it's unlikely that his tears were *only* tears of mourning. Perhaps Jesus was upset over the pain Lazarus endured before he died.

Jesus' tears most likely came from the genuine sorrow he felt as he watched Mary and Martha endure the terrible realities of a sinful, fallen world. Perhaps his anger was directed at Satan, whose lies and treachery in the Garden of Eden resulted in the arrival of sin and death (Hebrews 2:14-15). Jesus hates sin and death and the sadness and pain they produce. None of these things was part of God's original creation in Genesis 1.

Jesus experienced all these emotions that day because he is both fully God and fully man (Colossians 2:9). He felt everything we do—joy, excitement, sadness, anger, frustration, and loss (all without sin, of course).

Jesus shed many tears during his time on earth. He wept over Jerusalem's future destruction (Luke 19:41-44) and often prayed to God "with loud cries and tears" (Hebrews 5:7, ESV).

The point is, Jesus—the eternal Son of God, the Creator and Ruler of the universe—cares about us deeply. He's not a far-off god. He's near, and he cares. He hurts when we hurt. He empathizes with our weaknesses and sufferings (Hebrews 4:15).

As verses go, "Jesus wept" is short . . . but it's also oh-so-sweet!

NOW WHAT?

When you are struggling or feeling down, cry out to the Savior, who understands human weakness. He will listen and help you!

DID YOU KNOW?

John 11:35 is short, but depending on the translation you're using, Job 3:2 might be the shortest verse in the Bible. In some versions, the verse simply reads: "He said." (Others read, "And Job said.")

MAY 20

You must not forget this one thing, dear friends: A day is like a thousand years to the Lord, and a thousand years is like a day.
2 PETER 3:8

Tick, tock, tick, tock . . .

The seconds crept by slowly, followed by the minutes, then the hours. When Jesus heard that his good friend Lazarus was sick, he waited two whole days to leave for Bethany, the town where Lazarus lived. The trip took another couple of days. By the time Jesus arrived, Lazarus had been dead for four days. Jesus' disciples probably didn't understand why Jesus waited. Neither did Lazarus's sisters, Mary and Martha.

As discussed in the May 18 devotion, Jesus delayed his trip so long in order to perform a greater miracle, reveal his true identity, and bring God more glory (John 11:4). God often allows us to go through difficult times in order to display even greater power and love.

The story of Lazarus's resurrection, though, can also teach us another important lesson about God: his timing is not like ours.

WHAT'S IT MEAN?

There is no grandfather clock in heaven. The Lord God Almighty does not wear a watch. He does not work by human time.

God is eternal and all-knowing. He never had a beginning, and he'll never have an end. Today's verse, 2 Peter 3:8, provides a fascinating glimpse into how God tells time. He doesn't view it from a limited human perspective. He sees the whole course of history—past, present, and future—at once. So what might seem like an eternity to us (or to Mary and Martha as they waited for Jesus' arrival) is only an infinitesimal blip on God's everlasting timeline.

This is important to understand, since life won't always happen according to your schedule. Often, good times end too quickly, while difficulties drag on and on. It doesn't mean God has forgotten about you or doesn't love you. His timing is just different from ours.

God knows what's going to happen every day of your life. In fact, he planned them all (Psalm 139:16). The long waits and lengthy trials in your life are all part of his perfect design for you.

Through it all, your job is to trust God "with all your heart," submit to his will (Proverbs 3:5-6, NIV), and patiently persevere (James 1:4, NIV). God's timing and plan are not only different from yours, they're infinitely better! Just ask Lazarus.

NOW WHAT?

Memorize 1 Peter 5:6. It's a great verse to keep in mind when thinking about God's timing.

DID YOU KNOW?

The apostle Peter might have had Psalm 90:4 in mind when he wrote today's verse. Check it out.

I love God's law with all my heart. But there is another power within me that is at war with my mind. This power makes me a slave to the sin that is still within me. ROMANS 7:22-23

Lazarus was alive!

Those who witnessed Jesus' miraculous resurrection of Lazarus were awestruck. Jesus had returned life to a four-day-old corpse. It was the Messiah's greatest miracle to date.

As eyewitnesses were marveling at Jesus' power, though, some people reported what happened to the Pharisees. For them, this miracle represented a red-alert crisis. They immediately called a meeting of the Sanhedrin, the powerful, seventy-one-member religious ruling body in Israel.

The Sanhedrin was concerned about Jesus' growing popularity. They viewed him as a threat to their power, wealth, and prestige. They worried that Jesus would start a revolt and cause Rome to attack Israel and destroy the Jews (John 11:47-48). In reality, they had no idea about Jesus' true identity or his real mission.

Eventually, the Sanhedrin reached a dreadful decision. "From that time on," John 11:53 says, "the Jewish leaders began to plot Jesus' death."

WHAT'S IT MEAN?

Yes, you read that right. Jesus had just performed his greatest miracle yet, and the wicked leaders responded by scheming to kill him.

The religious leaders should have been worshiping Jesus and rejoicing with him. Instead, these wicked, hard-hearted men wanted to destroy him.

That's how sin works. Sin lies, deceives, and blinds people to the truth. Sin causes us to think and act irrationally. Ancient Israel's religious leaders are a prime example of this.

God created us to worship him (Ephesians 1:12). But sin, which is disobeying God's laws, is the exact opposite of worship. It's rebellion and defiance. Sin was never in God's perfect plan for us. It causes us to act the complete opposite way of how God intended us to live. Worst of all, it eventually leads to death (Romans 6:23). As today's verse says, sin is a powerful enemy that every Christian must continually fight against.

But here's the good news: through his atoning death on the cross, Jesus broke the power of sin (Romans 6:10)! We don't have to give in to sin's lies and deceit anymore.

Don't be like the Pharisees and let sin cloud your judgment. Trust in Jesus as your Lord and Savior, and fulfill God's plan for your life.

NOW WHAT?

Read Romans 7:14-25 to help you understand the inner spiritual battle with sin that every Christian faces.

DID YOU KNOW?

The evil religious leaders even considered killing Lazarus, too, in order to wipe out any evidence of Jesus' miracle (John 12:10).

MAY 22

The one who endures to the end will be saved.   MATTHEW 24:13

Have you ever heard someone say, "He jumped on the bandwagon"? The phrase is often used to describe a sports fan who starts rooting for a team only because the team is winning. To be a "bandwagon fan" means your support is based solely on a team's success.

Jesus had lots of bandwagon fans. This is clear from the story of his Triumphal Entry, which is recorded in all four Gospels.

On the Sunday before he was crucified, Jesus climbed onto a donkey and rode into Jerusalem, fulfilling a five-hundred-year-old prophecy about the Messiah, found in Zechariah 9:9. Word spread like wildfire about Jesus' arrival, and soon a great crowd surrounded him.

The people spread their cloaks and palm tree branches on the dusty road ahead of him (demonstrating their reverence to him and their Jewish patriotism). They shouted, "Hosanna to the Son of David!" (Matthew 21:9, NIV) and "Blessed is the king who comes in the name of the Lord!" (Luke 19:38, NIV), showing that they believed he was God's long-awaited Messiah (Isaiah 9:1-7; 11:1-16; and Jeremiah 23:1-8). And the fact that Jesus entered Jerusalem at the start of Passover—the weeklong festival that celebrated God's deliverance of Israel from Egyptian slavery—fueled the crowd's belief that Jesus would deliver them from Roman oppression.

Jesus' popularity had never been higher. As Matthew 21:10 says, "The entire city of Jerusalem was in an uproar as he entered."

But five days later, it was an entirely different scene. Instead of shouting "Hosanna," the people of Jerusalem were screaming, "Crucify him!"

What happened?

WHAT'S IT MEAN?

Sadly, many who praised Jesus when he entered Jerusalem quickly turned against him. They weren't fully devoted to him. They were bandwagon fans. When things looked good, they loved Jesus. But when they realized he wasn't the Roman-conquering warrior they had hoped for, they turned on him.

When it comes to Jesus, don't be a bandwagon fan. As today's verse says, true devotion to Christ involves a lifetime of faith, through good times and bad times. Believe what the Bible says about Jesus' true identity, and let it shape your life.

Avoid the bandwagon, and jump into a life that's fully devoted to the Savior!

NOW WHAT?

To be truly devoted to Christ, spend time with him often in his Word and in prayer.

DID YOU KNOW?

The term *jump on the bandwagon* has its roots in nineteenth-century America, when people would literally jump onto horse-drawn bandwagons—large, colorfully decorated carts used by political candidates to campaign through city streets—to show their support.

*Jews demand signs and Greeks look for wisdom, but we preach
Christ crucified: a stumbling block to Jews and foolishness to
Gentiles, but to those whom God has called, both Jews and Greeks,
Christ the power of God and the wisdom of God.*

I CORINTHIANS 1:22-24 (NIV)

What a difference five days can make.

In less than a week, the huge Passover crowds in Jerusalem went from greeting Jesus with shouts of "Hosanna!" (Hebrew for "Oh, save!") to screams of "Crucify him!" Somehow, between his Triumphal Entry on Sunday and the Crucifixion on Friday, the joyful, praise-filled crowd had transformed into a vicious, bloodthirsty mob.

What happened?

It seems like the people lost faith when Jesus didn't meet their expectations. The crowd that enthusiastically welcomed Jesus into Jerusalem expected the Messiah to be a political and military Savior, someone who would win Israel's freedom by force. So when Jesus was arrested and put on trial by the very Romans he was expected to defeat, the crowd quickly abandoned him.

The people's assumptions about the Messiah were badly mistaken.

WHAT'S IT MEAN?

Jesus is indeed God's promised Messiah. But his mission was far different from what the Jews expected. They were looking for the Messiah to set up an immediate earthly kingdom.

As today's verses show, the idea of a crucified Messiah was utterly ridiculous to people in the first century AD. The Jews were offended by the thought of the Messiah being executed by the hated Romans. And the rest of the Gentile (non-Jewish) world thought it was utter nonsense to trust in a deity who was killed by humans.

But God's plans are not like human plans. What is foolishness to man is wisdom to God. And honestly, who knows best: God or man?

God's plan all along was to sacrifice his Son, the Messiah, as a payment for human sin. Jesus didn't come to set up an earthly rule by saving his people from the Romans (John 18:36). He came to rule people's hearts by saving them from their sins.

Jesus is the eternal, all-powerful Son of God. He doesn't need to meet our expectations; we need to meet his. And his expectations are simple: repent of our sins and trust in him for salvation.

Let your thoughts of Jesus be informed by his Word, not by human expectations.

NOW WHAT?

Take some time to think and pray about your beliefs about Jesus. Do they come from the Bible or from your own ideas? Make sure your thoughts of the Messiah align with Scripture.

DID YOU KNOW?

Even Jesus' disciples thought he had come to set up an earthly kingdom (Acts 1:6).

Come, let us worship and bow down. Let us kneel before the LORD our maker, for he is our God. PSALM 95:6-7

Jerusalem was bursting at the seams.

The week that Jesus died was Passover week—the busiest time of the year in Israel's capital. Each spring, Jews from all over the Roman Empire flocked to Jerusalem for the weeklong festival celebrating God's deliverance of his people from Egyptian slavery.

Thousands of people came to the Temple that week to offer animal sacrifices. The atmosphere there, though, was anything but worshipful.

Within the Temple grounds, merchants sold animals to Jewish pilgrims for sacrificial use but overcharged their customers to make a profit. Plus, all adult Jewish males had to pay an annual Temple tax (Exodus 30:13-14), and greedy money changers charged extra fees to anyone who needed to exchange their Greek or Roman coins for the required Temple currency.

Sadly, all this happened in God's special dwelling place. What was meant to be a distinctive, holy place of worship had become a noisy, money-hungry marketplace.

So Jesus did something shocking. On Monday of that week, one day after his Triumphal Entry, Jesus entered the Temple in righteous anger. In front of the huge Passover crowds, he flipped over the money changers' tables and drove out those who sold animals. Then he said, "The Scriptures declare, 'My Temple will be called a house of prayer,' but you have turned it into a den of thieves!" (Matthew 21:13). At this point, the religious leaders renewed their plots to kill him (Luke 19:47).

WHAT'S IT MEAN?

The people of Israel during Jesus' time didn't understand how to truly worship the Lord. This is clear from their rejection of Jesus and their misuse of the Temple.

As today's verse says, worship involves bowing our hearts before God and acknowledging his rule over us. Because God is holy, we should approach him in reverence and awe (Hebrews 12:28, NIV), meaning we should recognize that he has every right to destroy us for our sins but has mercifully offered salvation through Jesus.

True worship is possible only through faith in God's Son. To worship God, we must realize our desperate need for Jesus. Without him, the perfect sin-sacrifice, we cannot approach a holy God.

Proper worship of God clearly was important to Jesus. May it be important to us, too!

NOW WHAT?

Make a plan to read the entire book of Psalms, which is all about worship. The book features 150 psalms, so reading one a day means you'll finish in five months.

DID YOU KNOW?

Jesus may have cleared the Temple twice. A similar, but somewhat different, account is found in John 2:13-22.

MAY 25

As we pray to our God and Father about you, we think of your faithful work, your loving deeds, and the enduring hope you have because of our Lord Jesus Christ. 1 THESSALONIANS 1:3

The Jerusalem Temple during Jesus' time on earth wasn't officially considered one of the seven wonders of the ancient world. But it could've been.

The building was actually the second Jewish Temple, built after the Babylonians destroyed King Solomon's original structure in 586 BC. The second Temple was built between 536 and 516 BC by the Jews who had returned to Israel after the Babylonian exile.

Starting around 20 BC, Herod the Great, the Roman-appointed king of Judea, began a vast expansion project on it, enlarging the structure itself and constructing many other buildings around it. By the early 30s AD (during Jesus' earthly ministry), the entire Temple Mount covered about 1.5 million square feet. The Temple itself was about one hundred feet long, roughly the same width, and stood at least sixteen stories tall.

For the ancient Jews, the Temple was a national identity symbol. Many of the people placed their religious hope in the Temple, the Old Testament law, and their ancestry from Abraham, thinking these three things proved that they had received God's salvation.

Even Jesus' disciples were impressed with the Temple. A day after Jesus cleared the Temple, one of them said, "Teacher, look at these magnificent buildings! Look at the impressive stones in the walls" (Mark 13:1). Jesus gave a spine-tingling reply: "Do you see all these buildings?" he said. "I tell you the truth, they will be completely demolished. Not one stone will be left on top of another" (Matthew 24:2).

WHAT'S IT MEAN?

Forty years later, in AD 70, the Romans stormed into Jerusalem and destroyed the Temple, fulfilling Jesus' prophecy and ending the nation's sacrificial system. To this day, the Temple has never been rebuilt.

Those who had put their hope in the Temple misplaced their trust. Today, many people do the same. Some people worship false gods. Others put their hope in good behavior, church attendance, or following certain religious rituals to earn God's favor.

Our hope should be only in Jesus. Hope in anything other than the Son of God's saving work on the cross is bound to fail. Christ is our only hope, because only he can make sinners right with a holy God. And as today's verse says, Jesus provides an "enduring hope" because he offers salvation and eternal life.

Now *that's* real hope!

NOW WHAT?

Share the "enduring hope" of Jesus with someone today.

DID YOU KNOW?

Today in Jerusalem, you can still see the "Western Wall," the only remaining part of the ancient Jewish Temple.

Jesus replied, "You must love the Lord your God with all your heart, all your soul, and all your mind." This is the first and greatest commandment. A second is equally important: "Love your neighbor as yourself." MATTHEW 22:37-39

Have you ever read the entire Old Testament? It's fascinating, diverse . . . and really long!

The Old Testament contains thirty-nine books written by more than thirty authors who lived over a span of approximately one thousand years. The actual historical period covered in the Old Testament is much longer, spanning the creation of the universe (Genesis 1–2) to the resettling of Israel in the 400s BC (Ezra, Nehemiah) after the Jewish exiles returned from Babylon.

The Old Testament is filled with historical narratives, religious laws, songs of praise and lament, proverbs, prophecies, and poetry. It can be challenging to understand how it all fits together and what the central message is.

Leave it up to God's Son to perfectly and concisely explain it!

On Tuesday of Holy Week, three days before Jesus died on the cross, a Pharisee tested him by asking what the most important commandment in the "law of Moses" was (Matthew 22:36). The "law of Moses" refers to the first five books of the Bible, called the Pentateuch or Torah.

Jesus answered by beautifully summarizing the entire Old Testament in about thirty-five words with today's Scripture passage. He said the message is essentially this: love God and love others.

WHAT'S IT MEAN?

The Old Testament accomplishes many things. It explains God's creative power and total sovereign rule over everything in the universe. It gave the ancient Israelites a moral code to live by and to help them avoid the wickedness of the nations around them. It showed them God's holiness and how far they fell short of his perfect standard. Most of all, it reveals humanity's desperate need for a Savior.

But amidst all the rules and regulations, the Pentateuch really boils down to a simple message: love God and love others. In fact, Jesus said, "The entire law [Pentateuch] and all the demands of the prophets [the rest of the Old Testament] are based on these two commandments" (Matthew 22:40).

You love God by obeying his commands (1 John 5:3) and trusting in his Son (1 John 4:15). You love others by putting their needs above your own (1 John 3:16).

It's so simple, it's profound!

NOW WHAT?

Plan to read the entire Pentateuch—Genesis, Exodus, Leviticus, Numbers, and Deuteronomy. It's not all easy to read, but it's God's holy and inspired Word, so it will be well worth it!

DID YOU KNOW?

Most evangelical Bible scholars credit Moses with writing most of the Pentateuch.

MAY 27

This is what the LORD of Heaven's Armies says: Judge fairly, and show mercy and kindness to one another.   ZECHARIAH 7:9

Imagine you and a friend are rolling down the highway in the backseat of your friend's dad's car. All of a sudden, you hear four loud pops, and the car starts skidding uncontrollably. Other vehicles have to brake sharply and swerve to avoid a collision. Eventually, the car slams into the roadside guardrail and comes to a halt. Incredibly, all four tires had blown out at once.

Shaken but unhurt, your friend's dad gets out of the driver's seat, inspects the car thoroughly, and says, "Whoa, this car is filthy! I'd better wash it when we get home!"

That's what's called having your priorities out of whack. The car owner was so concerned about a minor issue that he completely ignored the major one.

This perfectly describes Israel's leaders during Jesus' day. Three days before his death, Jesus delivered some very harsh criticisms of the Pharisees and other key religious figures.

Matthew 23 records seven woes (words of judgment) against these hypocritical men. In the fourth woe, Jesus said, "You are careful to tithe even the tiniest income from your herb gardens, but you ignore the more important aspects of the law—justice, mercy, and faith. You should tithe, yes, but do not neglect the more important things" (Matthew 23:23).

WHAT'S IT MEAN?

In an effort to please God, the Pharisees tried to follow the Old Testament law perfectly, even down to tithing (or giving to the Lord one tenth of) the smallest plants in their home gardens (Leviticus 27:30-33). But they failed to show love and mercy. They had become so obsessed with what was less important to God that they ignored what was most important (see today's verse).

As you grow in your Christian walk, it's critical to know God's Word and obey his commands. But never let knowledge and obedience snuff out love and kindness.

You can be the best rule keeper in the world, but it doesn't mean anything if you don't share God's compassion for people. Consider others better than yourself. Forgive when others wrong you. Be a friend in good times and bad. Help those who are hurting.

Focus on what's most important in life—loving God and others—without neglecting your other spiritual responsibilities, and you will fulfill the words of Jesus!

NOW WHAT?

Show someone an unexpected kindness by sending a card, giving a gift, or telling that person you're praying for him or her.

DID YOU KNOW?

The Pharisees strained liquids before drinking in order to avoid potentially becoming ceremonially unclean by swallowing any tiny insects that might have flown into the liquid (Matthew 23:24; Leviticus 11:23).

Woe to you, teachers of the law and Pharisees, you hypocrites!
MATTHEW 23:13, NIV

"Don't call other people names."

You've heard this before, right? Ever since you were a little kid, your parents have probably told you this countless times. It's good advice. Calling someone names is unkind and prideful.

But here's something that might surprise you: Jesus called people names. Honest. If you don't believe it, check out Matthew 23.

Here's the difference, though: unlike when we call people names, Jesus didn't do it out of spite, cruelty, or sinful anger. As the sinless Son of God, his name-calling was an important, final warning to some wicked men who needed to make drastic changes.

With his crucifixion only a few days away, Jesus brought the hammer down on the Pharisees and religious teachers with a series of seven woes (or words of judgment). Jesus condemned their leadership of the nation by calling them "child[ren] of hell" (verse 15), "blind guides" (verse 16), "blind fools" (verse 17), "whitewashed tombs" (verse 27), "snakes" (verse 33), and "sons of vipers" (verse 33).

Ka-boom!

Why did Jesus condemn the Pharisees and religious teachers so severely? Because they were hypocrites. That's what he called them every time he spoke a woe against them.

WHAT'S IT MEAN?

A hypocrite is someone who says one thing but does something else. In other words, hypocrites don't practice what they preach.

This perfectly described ancient Israel's religious leaders (Matthew 23:3). In Luke 16:15, Jesus denounced the Pharisees' hypocrisy by saying, "You like to appear righteous in public, but God knows your hearts. What this world honors is detestable in the sight of God."

The Pharisees said they loved God, but they didn't show it. They liked to look good to others, but their sinful hearts were filled with pride and self-righteousness. They loved money and boasted about their own deeds, yet they cared little about helping people. Ultimately, their hypocrisy stemmed from their rejection of Jesus. True righteousness doesn't come from law keeping but through faith in Christ (Romans 3:22).

God hates hypocrisy (Psalm 26:4). Christians are to live authentic, genuine lives. What we are in public, we should also be in private. We should care far more about our relationship with God than about what others think of us.

Don't be a hypocrite. That's a name you never want to be called!

NOW WHAT?

Read Matthew 23 to see what the Pharisees' hypocrisy looked like and to read about the heart attitudes you should avoid.

DID YOU KNOW?

The English term *hypocrite* has its roots in the ancient Greek word *hypokrites*, which meant "play-actor." It was used for stage performers who played characters that were different from their real identities.

"He is the stone that makes people stumble, the rock that makes them fall." They stumble because they do not obey God's word, and so they meet the fate that was planned for them. 1 PETER 2:8

When it came to the Pharisees and Israel's other religious leaders, Jesus didn't mince words. As discussed in yesterday's devotion, Jesus harshly rebuked their hypocrisy and unbelief with seven "woes."

But this begs the question: Why did these men reject the Son of God? Many of them knew the Old Testament inside and out. Why didn't they connect the Bible's prophecies about the Messiah to Jesus and realize that he was indeed God's promised Savior? Why didn't they let his astounding miracles inform them of his true identity? Why didn't they believe in him after his resurrection?

Here's why: because as today's verse and 1 Corinthians 1:23 (NIV) say, Jesus was a "stumbling block" to them. While trying to earn God's favor through keeping the Old Testament law, they kept tripping, so to speak, over God's Son. They refused to acknowledge Jesus as the Messiah and the central figure of God's salvation plan. The fact that salvation focused exclusively on Jesus left them flat on their faces.

WHAT'S IT MEAN?

Even today, two thousand years later, Jesus is a stumbling block to many people.

Some people "stumble" over Jesus because they love money (Matthew 19:16-22) or because they refuse to give up their sinful, pleasure-seeking lifestyles (2 Timothy 4:10). For others, Jesus is a stumbling block for religious reasons. They deny his deity or his claim that he is the only way to heaven.

These people "stumble because they do not obey God's word," according to today's verse. To truly be a Christian, you must accept everything the Bible says about Jesus as truth.

In 1 Peter 2:6, the apostle Peter calls Jesus "a chosen and precious cornerstone" (NIV). He is the perfect foundation on which the Christian faith is built. But stumbling over him endangers your eternal soul. Whoever rejects Jesus as Lord and Savior in this life will be rejected by him at the final judgment (John 3:36).

Don't stumble over Jesus! Accept him, embrace him, and worship him exactly as Scripture presents him. Repent of your sins and believe the gospel—the good news that Jesus came to earth as God's incarnate Son, lived a perfect life, died for your sins, and rose again to give you new life.

NOW WHAT?

Remember that Jesus will be a stumbling block for many people you meet. Love them, patiently share Christ with them, and pray for them.

DID YOU KNOW?

In today's verse, Peter is quoting a prophecy from Isaiah 8:14.

God loves a person who gives cheerfully.   2 CORINTHIANS 9:7

Are you on social media?

If so, here's a fun fact for you: at the start of 2015, Facebook's cofounder, chairman, and chief executive officer Mark Zuckerberg's net worth was an estimated $34 billion, according to *Forbes*. Yes, that's right—34 *billion* dollars. *Cha-ching!*

But if Zuckerberg gave $33 billion of his fortune to a church offering one Sunday, it still would be less in God's eyes than the two small copper coins that a poor widow gave in the Temple, according to Mark 12:41-44.

Sound like bad math? I'd better explain.

On Tuesday of Holy Week, Jesus was watching Passover pilgrims deposit money in the Temple offering. Many rich people gave large amounts. Then a widow dropped in two little coins. It was all she had.

Jesus turned to his disciples and said, "I tell you the truth, this poor widow has given more than all the others who are making contributions. For they gave a tiny part of their surplus, but she, poor as she is, has given everything she had to live on" (Mark 12:43-44).

WHAT'S IT MEAN?

The widow's offering was a tiny fraction of what others gave. Yet Jesus could say she had "given more than all the others," because when we give to the Lord, he looks at our hearts, not at how much money our gift is worth. The widow offered everything she had to God and entrusted her well-being to him.

Our giving doesn't impress God. As the Creator and Ruler of the entire universe, he owns everything. His heavenly riches are beyond compare. He doesn't need anything from us, including our money.

Giving to God is for our benefit, not his. He calls us to give, or tithe (Leviticus 27:30-32; Deuteronomy 14:22), to build our trust in his perfect goodness and in his heart to provide for us.

When we give, it should be with a cheerful heart (see today's verse), not from a feeling of obligation. Our hearts should say, "God, everything I have is yours. I'm simply giving you a portion of what you've already given me, to show my love for you. I know you'll take care of me." And he will, because Philippians 4:19 promises: "God will meet all your needs according to the riches of his glory in Christ Jesus" (NIV).

NOW WHAT?

Before you tithe at church, offer a quick prayer of thanks to God for his amazing provision for you.

DID YOU KNOW?

The widow's "two small copper coins" (Mark 12:42, NIV) were called *lepta*, the smallest ancient Jewish coin, worth only 1/64th of a normal day's wage for a Roman laborer. In other words, the widow's offering wasn't even enough to get lunch at McDonald's.

MAY 31

*Heaven and earth will pass away, but my words will never
pass away.* MATTHEW 24:35, NIV

Three days before his death—after spending most of the day speaking in the Temple—Jesus climbed the Mount of Olives outside Jerusalem. There, in a private conversation with the twelve disciples, he described the spectacular and distressing events that would precede his second coming and the end of life on earth as we know it.

He talked about famines, earthquakes, and wars. He foretold the Romans' future destruction of the Temple in AD 70. He prophesied about his return from heaven, the final judgment on evil, and the cataclysmic events that would mark the end of this fallen world and the beginning of a new, eternal one. (You can read about it all in Matthew 24.)

Then, as a guarantee of all his predictions, Jesus spoke these marvelous words: "Heaven and earth will pass away, but my words will never pass away."

WHAT'S IT MEAN?

Nothing lasts forever in this life. Most of the current best-selling electronic gadgets and technology will soon be outdated. A brand-new car today will be in a scrap heap in twenty years.

Have you ever heard of rotary phones, cassette tapes, floppy disks, DeLoreans, or the Atari 2600? Several decades ago, they were the latest in technology. Now, they're completely obsolete.

As today's verse says, even heaven and earth—the oldest things in existence—will disappear one day. But not Jesus' words. They are more durable than creation itself.

This shouldn't surprise us. After all, Jesus existed before the universe was created (Colossians 1:15), and he'll exist for all eternity—long after this world ends (Luke 1:33).

Through his words, Jesus created heaven and earth. In fact, John 1:1 says Jesus *is* the Word. He speaks, and it happens. He commands, and creation obeys. With a word, he can give life (John 11:43-44), heal disease (Matthew 8:3), calm storms (Mark 4:39), and destroy evil (Revelation 19:15).

What does all this mean? It means we can trust every word the Savior spoke in Scripture. Jesus never told a lie, bent the truth, or accidentally said something in error. Every single word he spoke is completely reliable. We can build our lives on Jesus' words. They are the words of eternal life (John 6:68).

Trust the words of the eternal Word! They will never let you down.

NOW WHAT?

Use your words to tell someone about Jesus, the living Word, today.

DID YOU KNOW?

Other examples of the eternal nature of God's (and Jesus') words are found in Psalm 119:89; Isaiah 40:8; and Matthew 5:18.

JUNE 1

His master said to him, "Well done, good and faithful servant. You have been faithful over a little; I will set you over much. Enter into the joy of your master." MATTHEW 25:21, ESV

One day, if you haven't already, you'll get a job. In that job, you'll have certain responsibilities. If you excel in those responsibilities, you'll probably get a promotion and make more money. But if you're lazy and brush off those responsibilities, you could get demoted, receive a pay cut, or even get fired. In other words, faithfulness in your job brings rewards, while unfaithfulness brings discipline.

The same is true in our spiritual lives. This was the point of the parable that Jesus told his disciples in Matthew 25:14-30.

In Jesus' story, a wealthy man took a long journey and left three servants in charge of his money while he was gone. The first servant took his share of the money and doubled it through wise investments. So did the second servant. But the third servant dug a hole in the ground and hid his share for safekeeping.

When the wealthy man returned, he praised the first two men, gave them more responsibilities, and celebrated with them (see today's verse). But the master punished the third servant, calling him "wicked" and "lazy" (verse 26, NIV), and commanded his other servants to "throw that worthless servant outside, into the darkness, where there will be weeping and gnashing of teeth" (verse 30, NIV).

WHAT'S IT MEAN?

The wealthy man in the parable represents Jesus himself, while the trip he took symbolizes the age we're living in now—the time between Jesus' ascension and his second coming. That means the three servants represent us!

Every Christian has been given a job to do. Until Jesus returns, we must be faithful with what he has given us—not just money, but all the talents and abilities he has blessed us with.

The first two servants got this right and were greatly rewarded. The third servant wasn't a believer in the first place. He lacked faith and godly wisdom. He rejected his master's will and was punished forever in hell.

Whatever you are good at—math, science, writing, music, art, sports—use it to serve Jesus faithfully, and you will be richly rewarded. For a lifetime of faithfulness, you'll receive an eternity of blessings. Now *that's* a good deal!

NOW WHAT?

Identify things you enjoy doing, and pray about how you can do them to serve Christ.

DID YOU KNOW?

"The joy of your master" in today's verse probably represents the spiritual blessings that await Jesus' faithful followers both here on earth and in heaven.

The King will reply, "Truly I tell you, whatever you did for one of the least of these brothers and sisters of mine, you did for me."
MATTHEW 25:40, NIV

The Golden Rule—"Do to others what you would have them do to you" (Matthew 7:12, NIV)—is probably the Bible's best-known verse on how to treat others. But what Jesus taught his disciples on the Mount of Olives in Matthew 25:31-46 takes this principle to a whole new level.

One day, Jesus said, he will sit on his heavenly throne during the final judgment of all humanity and separate "the sheep" (the righteous) from "the goats" (the wicked). To the righteous, Jesus will say, "Come, you who are blessed by my Father, inherit the Kingdom prepared for you from the creation of the world. For I was hungry, and you fed me. I was thirsty, and you gave me a drink. I was a stranger, and you invited me into your home. I was naked, and you gave me clothing. I was sick, and you cared for me. I was in prison, and you visited me" (verses 34-36).

To the wicked, Jesus will say, "Away with you, you cursed ones, into the eternal fire prepared for the devil and his demons. For I was hungry, and you didn't feed me. . . ." and so forth (verses 41-42).

Both the righteous and the wicked will respond similarly: "When did we do [or not do] this, Lord?"

Jesus' response will be startling: "Whatever you did for one of the least of these brothers and sisters of mine, you did for me."

WHAT'S IT MEAN?

If Jesus stood right next to you, would you ignore him? Laugh at him? Lie to him? Call him names? Hit him?

No, of course not! But Jesus said when we do anything to "the least of these brothers and sisters of mine," it's like we're actually doing it to Jesus. Kind of makes you want to stop hitting your sibling on the head, huh?

When we love others, we're loving Jesus; when we mistreat others, we're mistreating Jesus. That's how closely Jesus identifies with his people.

This puts a whole new perspective on the way we behave toward others. If you love the Savior, show the Savior's love to everyone else!

NOW WHAT?

Read Matthew 25:31-46 to get the full picture of Jesus' teaching on this matter.

DID YOU KNOW?

Jesus' close association with his followers is vividly seen in the account of Saul's (Paul's) conversion (see Acts 9:1-5 in particular; also see the September 8 devotion).

JUNE 3

Every time you eat this bread and drink this cup, you are
announcing the Lord's death until he comes again.
1 CORINTHIANS 11:26

On the night before his death, Jesus observed the Passover meal with his twelve disciples in an upper room in Jerusalem. Passover is a beautifully symbolic event that Jews have celebrated annually for more than three thousand years to commemorate God's deliverance of Israel from Egypt.

But in the middle of the meal, Jesus surprised the disciples. First, he distributed pieces of bread among his friends and said, "Take this and eat it, for this is my body" (Matthew 26:26).

Then he took a cup of wine and passed it around the table, saying, "Each of you drink from it, for this is my blood, which confirms the covenant between God and his people. It is poured out as a sacrifice to forgive the sins of many" (Matthew 26:27-28).

The Savior had turned the Passover meal into the Lord's Supper. Two thousand years later, Jesus still calls his followers to observe this wonderful sacrament.

WHAT'S IT MEAN?

A sacrament is simply a religious ceremony that symbolizes a spiritual truth. Jesus has commanded all Christians to observe two sacraments: the Lord's Supper and baptism.

Jesus' command for believers to be baptized is found in Matthew 28:19. His command about the Lord's Supper is found in Luke 22:19-20 and 1 Corinthians 11:23-26, among other places.

Baptism and the Lord's Supper, which are usually done in a church setting, are only for true believers in Jesus. A Christian needs to be baptized only once, but the Lord's Supper should be observed regularly.

Neither of these sacraments saves us from our sins. Only Jesus can do that. They are simply ceremonies that outwardly proclaim our salvation.

The act of baptism—when someone is either lowered underwater and brought up again or has water poured over his or her head—represents Jesus' death, burial, and resurrection (Romans 6:3-4). It's a public statement that says, "I believe in the Savior who died and rose again for me, and I am set apart for God!" The water of baptism also symbolizes how Jesus washes away our sins (Acts 22:16).

The Lord's Supper is a reminder and a declaration that Jesus made the ultimate sacrifice on our behalf (see today's verse). It's also a wonderful foretaste of the heavenly "wedding feast of the Lamb" (Revelation 19:7) that Jesus promised in Matthew 26:29.

Christians can find great joy in baptism and the Lord's Supper!

NOW WHAT?

If you have trusted in Christ but haven't been baptized or don't actively participate in the Lord's Supper at your church, ask your parents about doing both of these.

DID YOU KNOW?

The Lord's Supper is often referred to as Communion.

JUNE 4

Jesus, our High Priest, has been given a ministry that is far superior to the old priesthood, for he is the one who mediates for us a far better covenant with God, based on better promises.

HEBREWS 8:6

The Lord's Supper wasn't the only amazing new thing that Jesus introduced during his final Passover meal with the disciples.

As he passed around the cup of wine, Jesus announced another major change that was coming. "This cup," he said, "is the new covenant in my blood, which is poured out for you" (Luke 22:20, NIV).

The "new covenant" Jesus mentioned referred to a six-hundred-year-old Old Testament prophecy in the book of Jeremiah. During his lifetime in the sixth and seventh centuries BC, Jeremiah spoke against the southern kingdom of Judah's wickedness and witnessed the Babylonian invasions that left the nation in ruins.

One day, in the midst of all the turmoil and rebellion, God told Jeremiah to speak these beautiful words: "'The day is coming,' says the Lord, 'when I will make a new covenant with the people of Israel and Judah'" (Jeremiah 31:31).

This is what Jesus was referring to during his final Passover meal. God's Son was ready to establish the long-awaited new covenant.

WHAT'S IT MEAN?

A covenant is a promise or a binding agreement. Throughout history, God has made many wonderful covenants to bless his people. None, though, is better than the new covenant.

The old covenant was the Old Testament law that God gave to Moses and the Israelites after leading them out of Egypt. But all the rule keeping and animal sacrifices within the old covenant were never intended to remove people's sins. They were temporary solutions to show how much the people needed a true Savior (Hebrews 10:3-4).

Jesus is that Savior. As today's verse says, Jesus fulfilled Jeremiah's promise of a new covenant through his death and resurrection. As the perfect Lamb of God (John 1:29), he defeated sin and purchased forgiveness for us once and for all.

We are now the beneficiaries of the new covenant! God's new covenant with us is about heart change (Jeremiah 31:33). It's a promise that he will completely transform and heal the sinful hearts of all who trust in his Son.

Good-bye, priests, altars, and dead sheep . . . hello, mercy, forgiveness, and grace! Through his death and resurrection, Jesus has accomplished what the old covenant could never achieve!

NOW WHAT?

Read the full prophecy about the new covenant in Jeremiah 31:31-34, and then check out Hebrews 10:1-18, which elaborates on it.

DID YOU KNOW?

Jeremiah was once lowered into a muddy well as punishment for speaking God's words against wicked Judah (Jeremiah 38:1-13).

JUNE 5

You must have the same attitude that Christ Jesus had. Though
he was God, he did not think of equality with God as something
to cling to. Instead, he gave up his divine privileges; he took the
humble position of a slave.   PHILIPPIANS 2:5-7

Be honest: Do you have smelly feet?

Don't feel bad if you do. Everybody's feet get dirty and smelly. That's just the way feet are. And hey, look on the bright side: your feet certainly aren't as repulsive as those of Jesus' disciples.

Life in ancient Israel involved a lot of walking in sandals on dusty roads. Israel was predominantly a farming nation, so animals like sheep, goats, mules, and oxen often shared the roads with people. And you know what animals leave behind. . . .

Anyway, it all added up to dirty, smelly feet. In that society, when a traveler entered someone's house, a slave would often wash the person's feet.

That's why Jesus' action at the Last Supper was so astonishing. After finishing the Passover meal, the Lord took a towel and a basin of water, and he went around the table washing each disciple's feet.

Jesus' friends were stunned. In fact, Peter initially objected, thinking it absurd that the Messiah should stoop to the level of a slave. But Jesus insisted.

When Jesus was done, he said to his friends, "Do you understand what I was doing? You call me 'Teacher' and 'Lord,' and you are right, because that's what I am. And since I, your Lord and Teacher, have washed your feet, you ought to wash each other's feet. I have given you an example to follow. Do as I have done to you" (John 13:12-15).

WHAT'S IT MEAN?

Jesus washing the disciples' feet is one of the most beautiful examples of humility and servanthood in Scripture. But this is completely within Jesus' character. As today's verse says, he willingly laid aside his divine rights to show us how to love and serve others. Jesus' perfect humility is most vividly seen in his sacrificial death for lost sinners like us (Philippians 2:8).

We should follow Jesus' example. If the eternal Son of God was willing to temporarily lay aside his majesty, power, and authority for us, we should gladly be willing to humble ourselves and serve others.

You don't have to touch anyone's funky feet. But make sure to model your life after the Savior and humbly put others first.

NOW WHAT?

Read Philippians 2, and pray about a way to consider someone else better than yourself today.

DID YOU KNOW?

Amazingly, Jesus even washed Judas Iscariot's feet, even though he knew Judas was about to betray him (John 13:1-30).

JUNE 6

This is my commandment: Love each other in the same way I have loved you. JOHN 15:12

Jesus must've been exhausted.

It had been a long week, and it was getting late. Jesus had just finished eating the Passover meal and washing his disciples' feet in the upper room. Meanwhile, Judas Iscariot had slipped away into the darkness, his wicked heart full of treachery.

Jesus knew his arrest was imminent. In less than twenty-four hours, he would be unjustly condemned, mocked, tortured, and finally, crucified.

And yet, there was much to teach his disciples. So despite his looming suffering, Jesus sacrificed his own interests to instruct his disciples.

Jesus began by talking to them about love. "So now I am giving you a new commandment: Love each other," he said. "Just as I have loved you, you should love each other" (John 13:34).

How did Jesus love his disciples? He loved them by

- calling them to follow him,
- teaching them the saving news of the gospel,
- patiently bearing with their shortcomings,
- instructing them how to love others,
- dying on the cross for their sins,
- sending the Holy Spirit to guide them,
- and much more!

WHAT'S IT MEAN?

Jesus certainly had great love for his disciples. But guess what? He has the same love for you!

Jesus showed he loves you by

- calling *you* to follow him,
- teaching *you* the saving news of the gospel,

- patiently bearing with *your* shortcomings,
- instructing *you* how to love others,
- dying on the cross for *your* sins,
- sending the Holy Spirit to guide *you,*
- and much more!

When the Bible speaks of love, especially Jesus' love, it's not talking about romantic feelings. Biblically defined, love is sacrificing yourself for the good of someone else (John 15:13).

This is exactly what Jesus did for his disciples—and you—through his life and death. And as today's verse says, he wants you to show that same love to others.

This love should be sacrificial. Like he modeled while on earth, Jesus wants you to put others before yourself. Your love should be kind, patient, forgiving, and—above all—unconditional.

The Savior greatly loves you. Now go show his love to others!

NOW WHAT?

Sometime today, drop what you're doing and show an unexpected act of love to a family member or friend.

DID YOU KNOW?

The verses about love mentioned in today's devotion are part of a long discussion Jesus had with his disciples that's often called the "Farewell Discourse." It's found in John chapters 13–17, but the other Gospels don't mention it.

JUNE 7

By this everyone will know that you are my disciples, if you love one another. JOHN 13:35, NIV

Jesus had amazing knowledge of the future. Being the eternal, all-knowing Son of God will do that for you.

As Jesus spoke to his disciples during the Farewell Discourse, he wanted to prepare them for the years ahead. Jesus knew that after he ascended into heaven, his disciples (minus Judas Iscariot) would spread the gospel message about him and start what we call "the church"—groups of believers all over the world who worship Jesus. He also knew that the world would despise his followers, who came to be known as Christians (Acts 11:26).

Jesus knew that to effectively be a gospel witness to others, his followers would have to be different from the wicked world around them, which was filled with hate, anger, jealousy, selfishness, and strife.

So on the night before his death, Jesus told his disciples, "By this everyone will know that you are my disciples, if you love one another" (today's verse).

WHAT'S IT MEAN?

Jesus' words are so simple, yet so profound. No one's going to say that loving one another is a bad thing. And yet, because every human has a sinful heart, showing love is often easier said than done.

Look around you. The world can be an awful, loveless place. Each day brings fresh news of individuals, groups, or even entire countries doing hateful, violent things to others.

Jesus calls his followers to be different. If you say you love Jesus but don't show love to others, no one will be able to tell that you're a Christian. You'll be a hypocrite who doesn't look different from anyone else.

That's not how Jesus wants us to live. Our lives should be marked by love, a continual self-sacrifice for the good of others—both believers and unbelievers. Love is like a business card for Christians: it tells people who we are and what we're about.

As you show love, be careful not to do it with a haughty attitude, as if you're better than others. That's not true love. We should love others because our Savior commands it—and because people desperately need it.

Be someone who shows others that kind of love!

NOW WHAT?

When you consistently show love, people will naturally wonder why you're different. Look for these opportunities. What a great chance to share the love of Jesus with others!

DID YOU KNOW?

The apostle John, who wrote the Gospel of John, took to heart Jesus' teaching on loving others. John devotes much space in his Gospel and one of his letters, 1 John, to discussing Christian love.

Jesus told him, "I am the way, the truth, and the life. No one can come to the Father except through me." JOHN 14:6

The mood was somber in the upper room that fateful Passover night. The disciples had no idea what was about to happen, but they could feel that something bad was coming.

After all, Jesus had been foretelling his death for months. And on this evening, he had already predicted that Judas would betray him, the rest of the disciples would desert him, Peter would deny him, and he would leave them.

Talk about a downer.

To comfort his visibly disturbed friends, Jesus told them he was going to prepare a place for them in heaven (John 14:2). "When everything is ready," Jesus said, "I will come and get you, so that you will always be with me where I am. And you know the way to where I am going" (John 14:3-4).

This confused the disciples even more. "No, we don't know, Lord," said Thomas, one of the disciples. "We have no idea where you are going, so how can we know the way?" (John 14:5).

Then Jesus spoke these remarkable words: "I am the way, the truth, and the life. No one can come to the Father except through me" (today's verse).

WHAT'S IT MEAN?

This is a bold claim. In essence, Jesus was saying, "I am the only way to get to heaven. No other person, religion, belief system, or code of ethics can grant you access to God."

But it's not a surprising claim. Access to God has always been exclusive because of God's holiness and majesty. To approach God, sinners need a mediator, someone whom God approves to represent them.

Under Old Testament law, the Jewish priests temporarily accomplished this by offering sacrifices at the Temple for the people's sins. But when Jesus died, he took care of sin once for all, providing a far better sacrifice (Hebrews 10:1-18).

This is one reason why Jesus is "the way." But he's also the way *because* he is the truth and the life. Jesus is the truth because he is the Word sent from God (John 1:1; 20:21), and all God's words are true (Psalm 119:160). Jesus is the life because he created life (John 1:3) and has power over death itself, as his resurrection proves.

Jesus truly is the only way to God. He is worthy of all our worship and praise!

NOW WHAT?

If you didn't know the *way* to God before, believe the *truth* about Jesus and receive eternal *life* today!

DID YOU KNOW?

First-century believers often referred to Christianity as "the Way" (Acts 9:2; 19:9; and 24:14).

When the Spirit of truth comes, he will guide you into all truth.
JOHN 16:13

The disciples were scared and confused. As they listened to Jesus during the Farewell Discourse, they began to realize that Jesus was leaving them. But they didn't know exactly when he was departing, where he was going, or how long he'd be gone.

Knowing their fears, Jesus gave them a wonderful promise: "I will ask the Father, and he will give you another Advocate, who will never leave you. He is the Holy Spirit, who leads into all truth. The world cannot receive him, because it isn't looking for him and doesn't recognize him. But you know him, because he lives with you now and later will be in you" (John 14:16-17).

A little later, Jesus made an even more astonishing statement: "It is best for you that I go away, because if I don't, the Advocate won't come. If I do go away, then I will send him to you. And when he comes, he will convict the world of its sin, and of God's righteousness, and of the coming judgment" (John 16:7-8).

Even though the disciples desperately wanted Jesus to stay, he promised them something even greater than his own physical presence.

The Holy Spirit was coming.

WHAT'S IT MEAN?

The Holy Spirit is the third person of the Holy Trinity, along with the Father and the Son. As a spirit, he is a real being but doesn't have a physical body. He is not limited to time and space like humans. He can be everywhere at once.

This is one of the reasons why Jesus told his disciples it was better for him to return to heaven and send the Spirit. When he took human form on earth, Jesus could be in only one place at a time. But the Holy Spirit works in the hearts and minds of every Christian worldwide at the same time. Amazing!

This makes the Holy Spirit a perfect "Advocate" (John 14:16) for believers. An advocate helps others and supports their cause. This is exactly what the Holy Spirit does for Christians. As today's verse says, the Spirit reveals God's truth to us by convicting us of right and wrong and making God's Word come alive in our hearts.

It is indeed good that the Holy Spirit has come!

NOW WHAT?

To learn more about the Holy Spirit's work, skip ahead to the August 16 and 17 devotions about Pentecost.

DID YOU KNOW?

The Bible refers to the Holy Trinity in Matthew 3:16-17; Matthew 28:19; 2 Corinthians 13:14; 1 Peter 1:2; and many other places.

JUNE 10

Let the peace that comes from Christ rule in your hearts.

COLOSSIANS 3:15

A deep darkness had descended on Jerusalem.

Jesus and his disciples were finished with the Passover meal, and Judas Iscariot, the betrayer, had already slithered away to initiate his diabolical plan. In a few hours, Jesus would be dead. God's long-awaited Messiah was not going to fight Rome and restore Israel's freedom, as many people had hoped. Instead, he would be double-crossed by his own traitorous friend and unjustly arrested by a bloodthirsty mob. In the great cosmic battle between good and evil, Satan now appeared to have the upper hand.

Worry and fear washed over the disciples as Jesus spoke of his imminent departure. Aware of their restless hearts, Jesus promised to send the Holy Spirit to them (see yesterday's devotion). Then he said this: "Peace I leave with you; my peace I give you. I do not give to you as the world gives. Do not let your hearts be troubled and do not be afraid" (John 14:27, NIV).

How could Jesus talk about peace at a time like this?

WHAT'S IT MEAN?

Unlike the disciples, Jesus could see into the future. He understood that his crucifixion would ultimately end in a glorious resurrection and the defeat of sin, death, and the devil. And he knew that his wonderful peace would now be available to anyone who trusts in him.

This peace is like nothing else in life. Philippians 4:7 says it "transcends all understanding" (NIV). But it's not available through worldly things like money, fame, power, or pleasure. It comes only through Jesus.

The peace Jesus provides has to do with our relationship to God. Through his sacrifice, the Savior reconciles (or restores harmony between) sinners and a holy God (Romans 5:1) and saves us from his eternal wrath.

This amazing reconciliation then provides additional peace to our souls. We can experience great comfort knowing that Jesus has taken care of our greatest need (forgiveness of sins) and secured our eternal salvation. If God loved us enough to do this, surely he will take care of all our other needs in life (Romans 8:31-32). This kind of peace is impossible to find apart from Christ.

Don't misunderstand: life won't always be rosy. Trials and sadness will still come. But true, lasting peace is available to you through Jesus because of what he did on the cross!

NOW WHAT?

Meditate on (or think prayerfully about) Philippians 4:6-7. It tells you how to consistently experience "the peace of God, which transcends all understanding" (NIV).

DID YOU KNOW?

Isaiah 9:6 calls Jesus the "Prince of Peace."

JUNE 11

I am the vine; you are the branches. JOHN 15:5

Jesus loved metaphors.

A metaphor is a figure of speech where one thing is used to symbolize something else. For instance, in John 10:7, Jesus said, "I am the gate for the sheep." Is Jesus really a swinging door on a barnyard fence? No, of course not. He was using a metaphor to describe how he is the only way into heaven.

Jesus spoke seven "I am" metaphors in the Gospel of John. Each beautifully describes an aspect of his character. Jesus' seventh and final "I am" statement came the night before his crucifixion as he and his disciples traveled from the upper room in Jerusalem to the nearby garden of Gethsemane.

As they walked, Jesus said this (John 15:5-8):

> *Yes, I am the vine; you are the branches. Those who remain in me,*
> *and I in them, will produce much fruit. For apart from me you can*
> *do nothing. Anyone who does not remain in me is thrown away*
> *like a useless branch and withers. Such branches are gathered into*
> *a pile to be burned. But if you remain in me and my words remain*
> *in you, you may ask for anything you want, and it will be granted!*
> *When you produce much fruit, you are my true disciples. This brings*
> *great glory to my Father.*

WHAT'S IT MEAN?

Jesus' final "I am" statement used a grapevine metaphor. Grapes were a common crop in ancient Israel. Like many fruits, they grow on branches that extend from a main vine.

This metaphor perfectly describes a Christian's relationship to Jesus. Just like grapes draw nourishment from a vine, believers draw their spiritual nourishment from Jesus. He is the source of godly growth and strength. Those who are connected to him through faith, obedience, prayer, and

Scripture will grow strong. Those who aren't will shrivel up into weak, worthless branches (John 15:6).

Without Jesus, we can do "nothing" (verse 5) of any spiritual significance. But if we are rooted in Jesus, we will "produce much fruit" (verse 5) for God's glory (verse 8)!

NOW WHAT?

Ask your parents if you can visit a local vineyard or a plant nursery to increase your knowledge of Jesus' grapevine metaphor.

DID YOU KNOW?

Jesus' six other "I am" statements in the Gospel of John are as follows:

- "I am the bread of life" (6:35).
- "I am the light of the world" (8:12).
- "I am the gate for the sheep" (10:7).
- "I am the good shepherd" (10:11).
- "I am the resurrection and the life" (11:25).
- "I am the way, the truth, and the life" (14:6).

JUNE 12

Even before he made the world, God loved us and chose us in
Christ to be holy and without fault in his eyes.

EPHESIANS 1:4

One of the coolest things about the four Gospels is how much spiritual richness and godly truth are found in Jesus' teachings. The Savior's words really
pack a spiritual punch! He was the master of saying a lot with a little.

A great example is when Jesus and his disciples traveled to the garden of
Gethsemane on the night before his death. As they walked, Jesus told them,
"You didn't choose me. I chose you. I appointed you to go and produce last-
ing fruit" (John 15:16).

"I chose you."

Those three words carry profound theological implications. They point
to the doctrine of God's election.

WHAT'S IT MEAN?

The Bible says God chose *all* believers before the world began (see today's
verse). This divine choosing is often referred to as the doctrine of election.
It's an essential Christian doctrine that is as mysterious as it is marvelous.

Here's what it means: if you are a Christian, at some point in eternity
past (the time period prior to Genesis 1:1), God elected you to receive salvation. In other words, long before he created anything, God chose to place
his love on you. He chose you to be a recipient of his undeserved grace, an
act of divine mercy that many others don't receive. He "predestined" you
(Romans 8:29, NIV)—or mapped out the details of your life—so that you
would come to saving faith in his Son, Jesus Christ.

Why did he do this? It certainly wasn't because of anything you did to
earn it—you weren't even born yet! It was simply out of God's good pleasure
and sovereign will.

It staggers the mind, doesn't it?

God's sovereign plan of election is difficult to understand, and it has caused much debate among Christians over the centuries. But Scripture is filled with references to this important truth. Here are some examples:

- Acts 13:48
- Romans 8:28-30, 33
- Romans 9:6-29
- Ephesians 1:4-12
- 1 Thessalonians 1:4-5
- 2 Thessalonians 2:13
- 2 Timothy 1:9
- Revelation 13:7-8

Because the Bible teaches the doctrine of God's election, we must believe it. What's more, it should cause us to worship God for choosing to place his love on lost sinners. He is worthy of all honor and praise!

NOW WHAT?

Look up the Scripture references listed above and marvel at God's wonderful, mysterious plan of election.

DID YOU KNOW?

God did not choose you just for salvation. As John 15:16 says, you were chosen to "produce lasting fruit"—or to live righteously for God!

A person's steps are directed by the LORD. How then can anyone understand their own way? PROVERBS 20:24, NIV

Jesus' statement of "I chose you" to his disciples highlights one of the most difficult concepts to grasp in the entire Bible: the doctrine of election. (See yesterday's devotion.)

The truth that God chose those who will be saved before Creation itself poses some big questions, such as these:

1. If God elected people to be saved before they are born, do our choices really make a difference?

2. If God predestined certain people to be saved, does that mean he also predestined others to be condemned?

Those questions are whoppers, huh? Today's devotion will discuss the first. Tomorrow's entry will discuss the second.

Put on your swimming caps and goggles. We're about to dive in to the deep end of the theological pool!

WHAT'S IT MEAN?

If God already determined who would be saved and mapped out our lives before Creation itself, do the choices we make matter?

Absolutely!

Humans must respond to God's calling. Some Bible scholars call this "free will"—our ability to react positively or negatively to the gospel.

Scripture tells us to *"have faith* in God" (Mark 11:22, emphasis added), *"repent and believe* the good news" (Mark 1:15, NIV, emphasis added), and *"openly declare* that Jesus is Lord" (Romans 10:9, emphasis added). These are all action verbs commanding us to do certain things. Human actions do matter in God's divine plan.

So how does our free will jibe with God's sovereign election? This is a mystery that the Bible doesn't fully answer. And that's okay.

As imperfect beings with limited knowledge, we'll never be able to fully comprehend all of God's ways and plans. There are some things in God's universe that only he understands. (See today's verse, as well as Psalm 139:6; Isaiah 40:28; Isaiah 55:9; and 1 Corinthians 2:16.)

Do you understand how planets stay in perfect orbit? Do you know where the wind comes from? Do you fully grasp the miracle of human birth? No, but they all still happen, don't they? It's the same thing with divine election and human responsibility. We don't fully understand how it all works, but it's still true.

God elects those who will be saved through Jesus, and we must respond in faith. Even if you don't understand all the details, believe the truth of God's Word!

NOW WHAT?

Ask God for the faith to believe his Word even when you don't understand everything in it.

DID YOU KNOW?

Although our faith plays a part in the salvation process, it's God who guides our sinful hearts to the place of belief (see the March 24 devotion).

God chooses to show mercy to some, and he chooses to harden the hearts of others so they refuse to listen.   ROMANS 9:18

"Because I said so."

You've no doubt heard this phrase before, as frustrating as it sometimes seems. When your mom or dad says, "Because I said so," they are telling you to do (or not do) something with no reason or explanation other than their parental authority over you.

Sometimes God does this too. Sometimes in the Bible, he says, "This is the way it is . . . because I said so." The doctrine of election is one of those things. But this wonderful truth that God chose all who would receive salvation long before he created the world also raises a very difficult question: If God predestined some people to be saved, does that mean he also predestined others to be condemned?

As today's verse shows, the answer is yes. And the Bible doesn't really give a reason or explanation.

WHAT'S IT MEAN?

The fact that God predestines some people to experience his righteous wrath—called the doctrine of reprobation—is difficult to swallow. At first, it seems unfair that God sovereignly chose *not* to save many people. It makes you wonder: Did God even give them a chance to believe?

He did. But many of the details remain a deep spiritual mystery. The Bible doesn't explain why sinners are responsible for something they were predestined for, but God's Word clearly teaches that humans are accountable to God if they reject Jesus and choose a life of sin (John 3:18-19; Romans 3:19; 6:23). The Bible also affirms that God "wants everyone to repent" (2 Peter 3:9) and is always just in his judgments (Deuteronomy 32:4).

This whole topic boils down to a fundamental question: Do you believe God has the right to do as he pleases?

He does. As the eternal, holy, all-knowing, and all-powerful Creator, God sets the rules. He mercifully saves many but also justly punishes sin. And he's not obligated to explain all his ways, which are always perfect (Psalm 18:30).

When it comes to election and reprobation, our attitudes and thoughts should not be, *How can God be so cruel to condemn certain people?* Rather, they should be, *Why is God so kind to save* any *rebellious sinners at all?* These doctrines, while mysterious, should cause us to praise God, not accuse him. And when the Lord God Almighty says, "Because I said so," that should be good enough for us.

NOW WHAT?

Read Romans 9. It's the apostle Paul's explanation of the doctrine of election.

DID YOU KNOW?

Reprobation is discussed in Romans 9:17-22; 1 Peter 2:8; and Jude 1:4. Check them out.

JUNE 15

Who are you, a mere human being, to argue with God? Should the thing that was created say to the one who created it, "Why have you made me like this?" ROMANS 9:20

Have you survived our headfirst dive into the deep end of the theological pool (see June 12–14)? Is your head swimming—no pun intended—by all the complex talk of divine election and reprobation?

If you're still confused, don't worry. Even the smartest theologians don't fully understand this stuff.

But election and reprobation are just two examples of how God chooses to not fully explain to us some of life's most difficult questions. Here are some others:

- How is the Holy Trinity (one God in three distinct persons) possible?
- Why did God allow evil to enter the world?
- How was Jesus fully God *and* fully man?

Why doesn't God make all of life's profound mysteries clear to us? It's a question worth asking.

WHAT'S IT MEAN?

When it comes to the tough questions of life, it's important to remember this: God is too big, awesome, and holy for humans to fully comprehend. He has graciously chosen to reveal much to us in his Word about his character and plan of salvation through Jesus. But he hasn't revealed everything. There are "deep secrets" of God (1 Corinthians 2:10) that will always elude human understanding.

And that's okay. Just because we don't fully understand certain doctrines and mysteries of God doesn't mean they're not true. Human comprehension is not the final measuring stick of truth in God's creation. Besides, a God who could be completely understood wouldn't be a very impressive God, would he?

We must swallow our pride and believe all the words of Scripture, even the difficult ones. To think we know better than the Lord God Almighty is both foolish and wicked. As today's verse says, who are we to argue with the Creator about the way he runs his universe?

The apostle Paul is a great example of a proper attitude in the midst of hard-to-understand subjects. After pondering election and reprobation in Romans chapters 9–11, Paul didn't come away frustrated or lose his faith. Instead, he praised his Creator *even more*. "Oh, how great are God's riches and wisdom and knowledge!" he wrote in Romans 11:33. "How impossible it is for us to understand his decisions and his ways!"

May we respond likewise!

NOW WHAT?

Take a few moments to worship God for being too wonderful and awesome to be fully known!

DID YOU KNOW?

Job (whose story of suffering is told in the Old Testament book named for him) is another good example of today's topic. God never explained why Job suffered so much. His answer was simply "Who is this that questions my wisdom?" (Job 38:2).

JUNE 16

*I am praying not only for these disciples but also for all
who will ever believe in me through their message.*

JOHN 17:20

The Bible is filled with many wonderful prayers. Some examples include David's prayer of praise (2 Samuel 7:18-29), Solomon's magnificent Temple dedication prayer (1 Kings 8:22-53), Daniel's prayer for God's mercy (Daniel 9:1-9), and, of course, the Lord's Prayer (Matthew 6:9-13).

On the night before his death, Jesus prayed a wonderful prayer too. Recorded in John chapter 17, it's often called the "High Priestly Prayer" because of Jesus' role as our great High Priest who represents us before God the Father.

Jesus had a lot on his mind that evening. In his prayer, he discussed his successful earthly ministry, asked for the Father to be glorified in his death, and requested God's blessings of protection, unity, and spiritual growth for the disciples after he returned to heaven. And then—believe it or not—Jesus prayed specifically for you!

WHAT'S IT MEAN?

Let that soak in for a moment. Two thousand years ago, on the worst night of his earthly life, Jesus was thinking of you. That's incredible!

Only a few hours after his prayer, Jesus would be betrayed by a friend, arrested unjustly by a wicked mob, and found guilty in a bogus, middle-of-the-night trial. He would then be mocked, humiliated, tortured, and ultimately crucified by ruthless soldiers.

Jesus knew all this was coming. His distress must have been unimaginable as he offered up his prayer. And yet in his darkest hours, you were on his mind. As he finished praying for his disciples and their future gospel witness, he turned his attention toward "all who will ever believe in me through their message" (today's verse). That includes you!

Here's what he specifically prayed about for you:

- spiritual unity between you and other Christians (John 17:21-23)
- a desire for you to be in heaven with him (verse 24)
- a promise to help you grow in godliness (verse 26)
- that you would be filled with his love (verse 26)

Jesus' prayers for you didn't end there, though. Even now, he is "sitting in the place of honor at God's right hand, pleading for us" (Romans 8:34).

Be encouraged! You are always on the Savior's mind!

NOW WHAT?

Pray through the list above and ask God to bless you with the things that Jesus prayed about for you.

DID YOU KNOW?

As Jesus mentioned in his High Priestly Prayer, he fully accomplished his saving mission on earth (John 17:4). There's nothing he left undone!

Sanctify them by the truth; your word is truth.   JOHN 17:17, NIV

Life moves pretty fast these days. We don't like to wait for much anymore. Consider these examples:

- Why wait to eat? Hit the drive-through at the local fast-food joint and be on your way!
- Why wait to receive that package? Just select overnight shipping.
- Need some information pronto? Forget the library. Just hop on your computer and surf the Internet.
- Tired of waiting in long lines? Try the carpool lanes on your local highway, the self-checkout lane at the grocery store, and the FastPass lines at Disney World.
- Need to lose one hundred pounds? Say good-bye to traditional exercise and nutrition plans and say hello to weight-loss surgery, where a doctor can remove part of your stomach to shed those unwanted pounds!

Yes, we certainly like things fast in the twenty-first century. But not everything in life can be done quickly. In his High Priestly Prayer in John 17, Jesus mentioned a process that's beautiful in its slowness. It's called sanctification.

WHAT'S IT MEAN?

Sanctification is a spiritual maturing process that all Christians go through as they become more like Jesus. Sanctification starts the moment you are spiritually born again and continues until you die. It's possible only through Jesus and the Holy Spirit working in your heart (1 Corinthians 6:11, NIV), but you play an important part too. As today's verse says, sanctification comes through knowing and obeying the truth of God's holy Word.

God directly inspired all sixty-six books of the Bible, from Genesis to Revelation (2 Timothy 3:16). Because of its divine origins, Scripture is completely trustworthy. In fact, today's verse says the Bible isn't just *true*, as if it only meets another, higher standard of truth. No, God's Word is *truth*. It's the very *definition* of what's true.

The more we read and obey God's Word, the more we will become like Jesus. And that's what sanctification is all about.

God's Word sanctifies us because it's like a huge truth burger, stacked with scrumptious toppings. It's our job to keep biting off more mouthfuls. They will never run out. There's always more juicy, delicious truth to swallow from God's Word.

There are no shortcuts to sanctification. It's a lifelong process that takes hard work, dedication, and lots of prayer. But it's worth it. To become more like Jesus, open God's Word and start gobbling truth!

NOW WHAT?

Commit to a one-year Bible reading plan and feed yourself the sanctifying truth of God's Word! Have your parents help you find the right one online or at your local Christian bookstore.

DID YOU KNOW?

The sanctification process will be truly complete when God clothes us with new, Christlike bodies in heaven (1 Corinthians 15:49; 2 Corinthians 5:2-3).

While Jesus was here on earth, he offered prayers and pleadings, with a loud cry and tears, to the one who could rescue him from death. And God heard his prayers because of his deep reverence for God. HEBREWS 5:7

Jesus and eleven disciples made their way across the Kidron Valley east of Jerusalem and up the Mount of Olives. The Last Supper was over, and Jesus had finished the Farewell Discourse and the High Priestly Prayer.

The hour was late, and the night felt evil. Jesus and his friends came to the garden of Gethsemane, a familiar meeting spot for them. Since *Gethsemane* means "oil press," the garden was likely a place where workers produced olive oil for eating, making soap, and other things.

But Jesus hadn't come to the garden to pick olives. He was there to fulfill his earthly mission. As the omniscient (all-knowing) Son of God, he knew that Judas Iscariot would soon arrive in the garden with a hate-filled mob. He knew his disciples would desert him, Peter would deny him, the Jewish authorities would condemn him, and the Romans would brutally torture and crucify him.

It was overwhelming to think about. So Jesus prayed.

WHAT'S IT MEAN?

Does it seem strange to you that Jesus prayed? If Jesus is God (and he is), and he knew that his terrible death would end in glorious resurrection (and he did), why was he in so much distress?

Remember, while Jesus is fully God, he was also fully human. As the perfect Son of God, Jesus never succumbed to sinful cowardice or fear. But he did experience many of the same emotions we do. His impending death weighed heavily on him, just like it would anyone else.

So Jesus fell to his knees and cried out to God the Father. And as today's verse says, "God heard his prayers because of his deep reverence for God." If prayer is good enough for the Savior when hardships come, it should be good enough for us!

God is a heavenly Father who loves you and will help you with all your needs if you come to him in *reverence*, which means "honor" or "respect." When difficulties arise, pray to the Lord for wisdom and help. As 1 Peter 5:7 says, "Give all your worries and cares to God, for he cares about you."

Jesus called out to God in times of trouble. So should you!

NOW WHAT?

When trials come, the book of Psalms is a great place to go for godly encouragement and strength.

DID YOU KNOW?

Jesus' anguish in the garden was so great, God sent an angel to strengthen him (Luke 22:43).

*Going a little farther, he fell with his face to the ground and prayed,
"My Father, if it is possible, may this cup be taken from me. Yet not
as I will, but as you will."* MATTHEW 26:39, NIV

What would it be like to know that one of history's cruelest deaths awaited you in less than twelve hours? How would you respond if the weight of all human sin was being placed on your shoulders? How would you react if you knew God was about to forsake you in his righteous anger?

We will never fully grasp the depths of grief that Jesus experienced that night in the garden of Gethsemane. But the four Gospels provide a revealing glimpse.

As the Savior walked through the garden, the full weight of his impending death came crashing down on him. "My soul is crushed with grief to the point of death," he told Peter, James, and John (Matthew 26:38). Later, Jesus was in such distress as he prayed that "his sweat fell to the ground like great drops of blood" (Luke 22:44).

"My Father," he said, "if it is possible, may this cup be taken from me. Yet not as I will, but as you will" (today's verse).

God's will for his Son might surprise you.

WHAT'S IT MEAN?

Isaiah 53:10 explains God's will for Jesus: "It was the LORD's good plan to crush him and cause him grief."

How is that good? It sounds terrible! Well, yes, it was terrible for Jesus. But not for us.

Instead of God giving us the punishment and death that our sins deserve, his will was to pour out his terrible, holy wrath on his own Son. Jesus bore God's anger toward sin so that all we'd know is God's love, grace, and forgiveness. Jesus took the bad, and we get the good! Simply amazing.

But it came at a great price. That's why, in his humanity, Jesus cried to God through sweat and tears, even asking the Father if there was another way to win our salvation.

There was not. So out of his great love for us, Jesus agreed to fulfill his mission. He ended his Gethsemane prayer with a humble submission to God's great plan: "Yet not as I will, but as you will."

That is how much Jesus loves you.

NOW WHAT?

Thank Jesus in prayer for enduring such terrible suffering on your behalf.

DID YOU KNOW?

The "cup" Jesus mentioned in today's verse is a metaphor for God's wrath against sin. Other instances of this can be found in Isaiah 51:17; Jeremiah 25:15; and Matthew 20:22.

Jesus said, "Judas, would you betray the Son of Man with a kiss?"
LUKE 22:48

Judas Iscariot.

The very name sends shivers down the spine. It has become synonymous with "betrayal" and "traitor." Other than the devil himself, Judas might be Scripture's greatest villain.

As one of the twelve disciples, Judas was specifically called by Jesus and enjoyed the rare privilege of close fellowship with the Son of God. For three years, Judas had a front-row seat to the transformative power and teachings of the Savior.

But Judas's heart was blackened by sin. Greedy and deceitful (John 12:6), he refused to repent and accept the truth about Jesus. Yet his evil was so subtle, none of the other disciples suspected his disloyalty (Luke 22:21-23).

Under satanic influence (Luke 22:3), Judas met with the wicked religious leaders during Passover week and agreed to help them arrest Jesus secretly. When Judas learned during the Last Supper that Jesus would be in the garden of Gethsemane later that night, he slipped away and told the Jewish authorities.

Then, in the darkness of the garden, Judas infamously kissed Jesus' cheek—the ultimate insult—to identify him to the arrest mob. For his treachery, Judas received a measly thirty silver coins. That's how little he thought of Jesus.

But later that morning, Judas's conscience hit him. He got rid of his "blood money," ran off, and hanged himself. Acts 1:18 adds this morbid detail about Judas's death: "Falling headfirst there, his body split open, spilling out all his intestines."

Ewww. It was a wretched end to a wretched man.

WHAT'S IT MEAN?

The story of Judas is a tragic tale of how unbelief, greed, and the love of worldly things can destroy faith. He is an unfortunate example of Jesus' parable in Matthew 13, where the weeds of worldly desires choke out the seeds of gospel truth.

Despite spending so much time with Jesus, Judas rejected the Savior in favor of temporary pleasure. In the end, it cost him his physical life and his eternal soul. John 17:12 calls Judas "the one headed for destruction," and Matthew 26:24 says it would have been better for Judas if he had never been born.

As Judas's life revealed, rejecting Jesus and embracing sin has devastating effects. Don't follow in Judas's footsteps. Say no to the selfish, worldly desires and yes to Christ!

NOW WHAT?

Read Acts 1:12-26 to see what happened in the aftermath of Judas's death.

DID YOU KNOW?

John 12:4-7 and Matthew 26:14-16 provide the best insight into Judas's heart and why he may have made his fateful decision to betray Jesus.

He did not retaliate when he was insulted, nor threaten revenge when he suffered. He left his case in the hands of God, who always judges fairly. 1 PETER 2:23

"Innocent until proven guilty."

This well-known phrase is a wonderful principle of the American legal system. Anyone who is accused of a crime is granted "the presumption of innocence," meaning that in a court of law, the prosecution must prove beyond a reasonable doubt that the defendant committed the offense. Presumption of innocence helps defendants receive a fair trial.

When Jesus was arrested, he received no such privilege. After the soldiers led him away from Gethsemane, Jesus made six different appearances before various Jewish and Roman rulers. None of them was fair.

In fact, the members of the Sanhedrin—the influential Jewish ruling council—entered these trials completely biased against Jesus (Mark 14:1-2). In a hasty middle-of-the-night gathering, they accepted lies, dismissed truth, and even broke their own legal rules—all to find Jesus guilty.

The Romans weren't any better. When the Jewish rulers handed Jesus over to Pontius Pilate, the Roman governor cared more about protecting himself than he did about justice. Pilate believed Jesus was innocent, but he sentenced him to crucifixion to satisfy the bloodthirsty crowd (Matthew 27:22-26).

Just like the Jewish authorities had earlier, the Romans mocked and beat Jesus. They also whipped him mercilessly and forced a painful crown of thorns deep into his head.

Jesus, of course, deserved none of this. Yet he never retaliated.

WHAT'S IT MEAN?

Why didn't Jesus defend himself, either verbally or physically? As the perfect Son of God, he was completely innocent and had all of heaven's angelic power at his disposal (Matthew 26:53). In fact, he created the very men who condemned him. Ponder *that* for a few moments.

Jesus gave up his rights for your sake. He endured wicked, unfair treatment to provide the redemption your sins required. Isaiah 53:7 describes Jesus as follows: "He was oppressed and treated harshly, yet he never said a word. He was led like a lamb to the slaughter. And as a sheep is silent before the shearers, he did not open his mouth."

The Innocent One wasn't proven guilty at all. Yet he willingly suffered greatly—all because of his great love for you.

NOW WHAT?

Follow Jesus' humble example and avoid retaliating when others mistreat you. Remember the words of Romans 12:17: "Never pay back evil with more evil."

DID YOU KNOW?

Under Roman rule, the Sanhedrin could issue a death penalty verdict, but only the Romans could carry out the sentence. That's why the Jewish leaders sent Jesus to Pilate after condemning him.

JUNE 22

If anyone is ashamed of me and my message, the Son of Man will be ashamed of that person when he returns in his glory and in the glory of the Father and the holy angels. LUKE 9:26

Shaken and cold, Peter stretched his trembling hands toward the burning logs. His spirit was as restless as the flickering flames dancing before him.

Earlier that night in Gethsemane, when the mob surged forward to arrest Jesus, Peter had brandished his sword and lopped off the right ear of Malchus, the servant of Caiaphas, the Jewish high priest. When the mob led Jesus away, Peter followed them to—*drum roll, please*—Caiaphas's headquarters! Not exactly the place Peter wanted to be at that moment.

As the Sanhedrin barraged Jesus with questions inside, Peter warmed himself by a fire in the courtyard. Before long, some of those standing nearby started to recognize Peter's face in the fire's glow. Three different times, people told Peter they knew he was one of Jesus' disciples, and three times, he vehemently denied it.

Then, a rooster crowed. Jesus' earlier prophecy about Peter's denials had come true. "Suddenly," Luke 22:61 says, "the Lord's words flashed through Peter's mind: 'Before the rooster crows tomorrow morning, you will deny three times that you even know me.'"

WHAT'S IT MEAN?

This was the low point of Peter's life. After promising to follow Jesus even to death (Luke 22:33), Peter denied him three times.

Maybe you're tempted to think, *How could Peter do such a thing?* It's a valid question. But we must be careful not to think we're better than Peter, because we're not.

In that moment in the high priest's courtyard, Peter feared people more than he feared God. He cared more about what other people would say or do to him if they found out he was a follower of Jesus than he cared about honoring his Lord.

This is a temptation that all Christians face. But fearing (or honoring) God is infinitely more important than fearing people (see the March 18 devotion).

Peter's denials are a powerful reminder to all Christians: we should never be ashamed of Jesus. As today's verse says, if you are ashamed of Jesus on earth, you'll be held responsible for it on Judgment Day.

Admitting you love Jesus might not always be easy. But consider what Jesus did for you. He wasn't ashamed of you when he suffered for your sins. So don't be ashamed of him!

NOW WHAT?

Pray that God would help you love Jesus more than you fear people.

DID YOU KNOW?

After his resurrection, Jesus lovingly forgave Peter and instructed him to care for those who would later become Christians (John 21:15-17).

Pilate sentenced Jesus to die as they demanded. LUKE 23:24

If Judas Iscariot is the Bible's worst human villain, Pontius Pilate might be a close second.

Pilate, the Roman governor of Judea during Jesus' earthly ministry, ruled over a politically tense region. In short, the Romans ruled the Jews, the Jews hated the Romans, and Pilate's goal was to somehow keep the peace. Fun job.

So when the Jewish religious leaders brought Jesus to Pilate, accusing Jesus of treason against Rome because he claimed to be a king (which he was—but not of any earthly kingdom!), Pilate knew he was facing a sticky situation.

But Pilate was no dummy. After briefly questioning Jesus, he realized Jesus was completely innocent. In fact, Luke 23:4 says, "Pilate turned to the leading priests and to the crowd and said, 'I find nothing wrong with this man!'"

Fueled by the leaders' hatred of Jesus, the crowd responded with shouts of "Crucify him! Crucify him!" (Luke 23:21). Pilate tried to reason with the crowd. "Why? What crime has he committed?" he asked (Luke 23:22). But the hate-filled chants only got louder: *"CRUCIFY HIM! CRUCIFY HIM!"*

Pilate's weak-willed attempts at freeing Jesus were going nowhere. Finally, the religious leaders pulled out the trump card: "If you release this man, you are 'no friend of Caesar'" (John 19:12).

This shook Pilate. Sensing the beginnings of a full-out riot, he conceded to the crowd's demands and pronounced Jesus' sentence:

Death by crucifixion.

WHAT'S IT MEAN?

As a regional Roman governor, Pilate had great authority and plenty of well-trained soldiers at his disposal. He could have easily declared Jesus innocent and backed up his verdict with force, if necessary.

Yet when he sensed a threat to his power and position, he retreated into a conceited cocoon of self-preservation. Pilate didn't want word to get back to Tiberius Caesar, the Roman emperor, that he couldn't keep law and order in his district. So he threw all reason, morality, and justice aside and looked out only for himself.

What do you do when you feel the pull of worldly power and prestige? How do you respond when your reputation is at stake? Do you look out for number one, like Pilate, or do you walk in humility and put others first?

Don't be like Pilate. Instead, follow the instruction of Philippians 2:4: "Don't look out only for your own interests, but take an interest in others, too." In doing so, you'll be like the Savior, who endured Pilate's injustice for your good.

NOW WHAT?

Memorize Philippians 2:4. It's quick, easy, and great to know!

DID YOU KNOW?

Pilate was removed from his position for incompetence in AD 36, several years after Jesus' crucifixion.

JUNE 24

He was pierced for our transgressions, he was crushed for our iniquities; the punishment that brought us peace was on him, and by his wounds we are healed. ISAIAH 53:5, NIV

The phony trial was over. Pontius Pilate symbolically washed his hands before the bloodthirsty crowd, trying (unsuccessfully) to remove his responsibility for Jesus' death.

Then the torture of the Son of God truly began.

What Jesus suffered that day was indescribable. He had already been slapped, punched, spat upon, and mocked. A crown of thorns sat on his head—the long, sharp barbs opening deep, bloody wounds all over his scalp.

After Pilate pronounced the death sentence, soldiers "scourged" the Savior (Matthew 27:26, ESV). Roman scourging was a dreadful punishment where the victim was tied to a post and beaten continuously with a multistrapped leather whip containing pieces of bone and metal. Scourging left the person's back ripped open, exposing bones and internal organs. It was often fatal itself.

Jesus survived, but the worst was yet to come. Roman crucifixions were notoriously brutal. They were meant to be lengthy, publicly embarrassing, and unbearably painful.

Long nails were driven through the victim's wrists and feet and into a wooden cross, which was then set upright into the ground. The victim, who sometimes hung there for days, usually died from the sheer physical trauma, dehydration, or suffocation as he gasped for air. Every breath was agonizing as the victim attempted to lift up his battered body so his lungs could suck in precious oxygen. In Jesus' case, he hung on the cross for six long, excruciating hours (Mark 15:25, 34). Then he breathed his last.

WHAT'S IT MEAN?

Today's devotion isn't meant to gross you out. It's just really important to try to fully understand Jesus' remarkable sacrifice. Anything less would dishonor him.

For the next couple of weeks, we're going to focus our attention specifically on Jesus' death and all that it means. Christ suffered greatly for your sins. He endured unthinkable pain so you wouldn't have to. He humbly submitted himself to a torturous death so you could be made right with a holy God.

As today's verse—one of the greatest in the Bible—says, Jesus' pain and suffering brings us amazing, undeserved blessings. What a Savior!

NOW WHAT?

Read all four Gospel accounts of the crucifixion (Matthew 27:32-56; Mark 15:21-41; Luke 23:26-49; and John 19:17-37) to get a better understanding of what Jesus did for you.

DID YOU KNOW?

Long before Jesus' death, Isaiah prophesied about the Messiah's appalling physical appearance during his crucifixion: "His face was so disfigured he seemed hardly human, and from his appearance, one would scarcely know he was a man" (Isaiah 52:14).

The wages of sin is death, but the free gift of God is eternal life through Christ Jesus our Lord.   ROMANS 6:23

"Houston, we've had a problem here."

You've probably heard those words before. Other than Neil Armstrong's famous remark—"That's one small step for man, one giant leap for mankind"—during his historic moon walk in 1969, it's probably the most well-known quote in the history of US space travel.

The man who said it was Jack Swigert, one of three NASA astronauts aboard the Apollo 13 space flight of 1970. "Houston" referred to NASA's mission control room at the Johnson Space Center in Houston, Texas.

Apollo 13's mission was to land in the Fra Mauro area of the moon. But an oxygen tank explosion forced the astronauts to skip the lunar landing and fight for their lives. Six long days later, the crew finally splashed down safely in the Pacific Ocean.

Yes, the Apollo 13 astronauts certainly had a problem. But you have a far worse problem. Your problem is called sin.

WHAT'S IT MEAN?

Maybe you're wondering, *How is my sin a bigger problem than a life-threatening disaster in outer space?* The answer is alarming: while the astronauts survived their harrowing ordeal, sin is a guaranteed killer.

Today's verse says it plainly: "The wages of sin is death." Since we've all sinned (Romans 3:23), that's really bad news.

But wait, there's more. Look at the other terrible effects of sin:

- You were "far away from God" (Colossians 1:21).
- "You were his enemies, separated from him by your evil thoughts and actions" (Colossians 1:21).
- "You were living apart from Christ" (Ephesians 2:12).

- "You lived in this world without God and without hope" (Ephesians 2:12).
- "You were dead because of your sins" (Colossians 2:13).

If our sinful condition sounds bleak to you, that's because it is. But that's not the end of the story! Jesus died to solve our sin problem. On the cross, he paid for our sins and took the punishment we deserved so that we could be forgiven and made right with God.

Now, thanks to Jesus, we can say, "Houston, we *had* a problem. But Jesus took care of it for us." Praise the Lord!

NOW WHAT?

Jesus did his part. But to be saved from your sins, you must repent (turn from your sins) and believe (put your faith in Jesus). See Mark 1:15.

DID YOU KNOW?

We don't sin just by our actions, words, and thoughts. We actually inherited a sinful nature from Adam. In other words, our hearts were infected with sin from the moment we were born (Romans 5:12-21).

JUNE 26

Without the shedding of blood there is no forgiveness of sins.
HEBREWS 9:22, NIV

Have you ever wondered why Jesus had to die?

There's no denying that the perfect Son of God's sacrificial death on the cross for sinners was the greatest act of love in history. But was it necessary? In other words, why did Jesus have to go to all the trouble he did—coming down from heaven, becoming fully man while remaining fully God, living a perfect life, dying a horrible death, rising from the dead?

If God wanted to forgive our sins, why couldn't he just do it? Being all-powerful, why couldn't he just snap his fingers, say, "Abracadabra!" and make all our sins magically disappear—*poof!*—just like that?

WHAT'S IT MEAN?

It's an intriguing question. But sin can't be dismissed so easily.

Sin, which is breaking God's laws, is too terrible to just magically vanish. As today's verse says, it requires a blood sacrifice. To forgive sin, something or someone must die. Sin is that serious. That's why the Israelites sacrificed so many animals in the Old Testament.

There's also the matter of God's character. Because God is holy and just, he cannot tolerate sin. Rebellion against him must be punished.

Fortunately for us, God is both perfectly just *and* perfectly loving. When our situation looked bleakest, God demonstrated his abounding love for us by placing the punishment our sins deserved on his own Son.

By sending Jesus to the cross, God was telling us, "My children, I created you to love and worship me. Instead, you've chosen to sinfully rebel and disobey. Because of my justice, your sin must be punished with death or else I wouldn't be a fair God. However, because of my deep love for you, I'm going to pour out all my wrath on my own Son. I will send him to earth to die the death you deserve. Someone must die for your sins, *but it's not going to be you.*"

That's why Jesus came to earth. Jesus shed *his* blood for the forgiveness of *your* sins.

NOW WHAT?

Read Leviticus 17:11 and consider the connection to today's verse.

DID YOU KNOW?

Today's verse, Hebrews 9:22, has its roots in Old Testament law, specifically in verses like Leviticus 17:11. Even as far back as Moses' day (at least 1300 BC, if not earlier), God was preparing his people to understand Jesus' sacrifice many years later.

Jesus said, "Father, forgive them, for they don't know what they are doing." LUKE 23:34

What's your typical reaction when someone hits you? Or calls you a name? Or lies about you? If you're honest, you probably want to hit the person back, say something nasty in return, or get even somehow, right?

But what if your immediate response was to love and forgive? Wow. That would change the relationship, wouldn't it?

Consider what Jesus did while he hung on the cross. The religious leaders were mocking Jesus and challenging him to miraculously come down from the cross to prove he was the Messiah. Others passing by shook their heads in disappointment and ridicule. The Roman soldiers who drove the nails through his hands gambled for his clothing beneath him. Even the two criminals hanging on either side of him sent taunts his way.

How wicked and insulting.

Jesus, though, looked around at everyone who heartlessly derided him, and through the blinding pain, he said, "Father, forgive them, for they don't know what they are doing."

WHAT'S IT MEAN?

At any point during his crucifixion, Jesus could have freed himself, healed his own wounds, and destroyed everyone who was mistreating him. He could've tied the mockers' tongues, turned the Pharisees into pigs, and caused the earth to swallow up the callous soldiers. That certainly would've gotten people's attention!

But he didn't do that. It wasn't part of his mission of salvation. Instead, he remained on the cross and prayed for his enemies.

The love and forgiveness Jesus showed for lost sinners is astounding. Even as death neared, he prayed for those who despised him most. Even though every breath brought searing pain, he pleaded with God to forgive his attackers.

Jesus answered evil with good, hate with love, jeering with mercy, and cruelty with kindness. He wanted even his worst enemies to turn from their sins and experience God's grace and forgiveness.

Not only was this good news for the scoffers surrounding Jesus' cross that day, but it gives us hope too. After all, our sins sent him to the cross as well (Isaiah 53:6).

Rejoice in the Savior who shows amazing love and forgiveness to all sinners!

NOW WHAT?

Follow Jesus' example and show love and forgiveness immediately to those who mistreat you.

DID YOU KNOW?

One of the criminals crucified next to Jesus had a change of heart and put his faith in the Lord before he died. Jesus told him, "Today you will be with me in paradise" (Luke 23:43).

He had done no wrong and had never deceived anyone.

ISAIAH 53:9

Don Larsen was a good pitcher. He pitched for fourteen Major League Baseball seasons, had a lifetime 3.78 earned-run average, and helped the New York Yankees win World Series titles in 1956 and 1958.

But he wasn't *that* good. The six-foot-four right-hander once led the American League in losses (a 3–21 record in 1954), and he never made an All-Star team. His career mark stands at 81-91.

But on one magical day in October 1956, Larsen was perfect. In Game 5 of a riveting, all–New York World Series that lasted a full seven games, Larsen threw a perfect game as the Yankees beat the Brooklyn Dodgers, 2–0.

In front of 64,519 fans at old Yankee Stadium, Larsen struck out seven and was in complete control the entire contest. His gem is the most famous of the major leagues' twenty-three perfect games because it's the only one that's ever happened in the World Series.

For one glorious day, Larsen experienced perfection. Jesus, on the other hand, has been perfect forever. He died a sinner's death, but he was completely sinless.

WHAT'S IT MEAN?

Imagine never doing a single thing wrong your whole life. Ever. No lies. No cheating. No unkind words. No sinful anger. No hatred. No jealousy. No disobeying your parents. That would be amazing.

Well, as today's verse says, Jesus accomplished that. He never sinned in word, deed, or thought (see the February 2 devotion). Incredible!

Jesus' perfection—which was possible because of his divinity and his virgin birth (see the January 16 devotion)—is much more than a nice bedtime story or an inspiring example of godly living for us to follow. His sinless nature is the very reason godly living is possible for us.

Jesus is the only person in history who could die for our sins and make us godly, because only he lived a perfect life. Someone who sins can't remove the sins of others. It's not possible. But Jesus could because he had no sin. As 2 Corinthians 5:21 says, "God made Christ, who never sinned, to be the offering for our sin, so that we could be made right with God through Christ."

As Jesus hung on that cross, unjustly but willingly, he did it as a sinless Savior. And that makes all the difference for us.

NOW WHAT?

Read Hebrews 4:14-16 and rejoice in the grace, salvation, and confidence that Jesus' sinless nature gives us.

DID YOU KNOW?

Although Jesus never sinned, he was tempted to do so (Matthew 4:1-11; Hebrews 4:15), which makes his holiness even more remarkable.

JUNE 29

By the power of the eternal Spirit, Christ offered himself to God as a perfect sacrifice for our sins. HEBREWS 9:14

At some point in your life, someone has probably asked you, "If you were an animal, what would you want to be?" People usually pick lions, tigers, sharks, or something else atop the food chain. Smart move.

But let's flip the script: If you were an animal, which would you *least* want to be? Here are some candidates:

- Slug: You'd leave a trail of shiny slime wherever you crawled. Not good for making new friends.
- Mosquito: You'd drink blood. Disgusting.
- Gnat: Your entire existence would annoy people, and you'd probably end up dying after getting slapped on the back of someone's sweaty neck. No thanks.
- Worm: You'd spend virtually your whole life burrowing underground, eating dirt and hoping to avoid birds and fishermen looking for bait. What a sad life.

Those creatures have unfortunate lives. But livestock animals in ancient Israel had it pretty bad too. When God gave Moses and Israel the Old Testament law on Mount Sinai, he instructed his people to offer animal sacrifices for their sins. For centuries, the Israelites slaughtered millions of sheep, goats, and bulls every year, because blood had to be shed to pay for sins (Leviticus 17:11; Hebrews 9:22).

It doesn't get much worse than being bred to be slaughtered!

WHAT'S IT MEAN?

The Old Testament sacrificial system was bad for livestock but good for the Israelites. It was a wonderful display of God's mercy toward his people. Instead of punishing them for their sins, God offered to accept the death of an animal as a substitute payment.

But this was only a temporary solution. As Hebrews 10:4 says, "It is not possible for the blood of bulls and goats to take away sins." A better sacrifice was needed.

That's where Jesus came in. His sacrifice on the cross made the old sacrificial system obsolete. Because he was completely sinless (see yesterday's devotion), Jesus was the "perfect sacrifice for our sins" (today's verse).

Sheep, goats, and bulls everywhere can relax. No more animal sacrifices are needed to forgive sins. But we can rejoice even more! Jesus' blood covers all our sins through faith in him. He is our perfect sin-sacrifice!

NOW WHAT?

Read Hebrews 9–10 to gain a better understanding of how the temporary Old Testament sacrificial system pointed ahead to the far greater sacrifice of Jesus.

DID YOU KNOW?

In the Old Testament, the Jewish priests burned animal sacrifices on a big bronze altar that was four and a half feet tall and seven and a half feet long and wide (Exodus 27:1-8).

He himself is the sacrifice that atones for our sins—and not only our sins but the sins of all the world.　I JOHN 2:2

The earth is a pretty crowded place.

By the end of 2014, the world's population eclipsed 7.2 billion, according to the US Census Bureau. That's a lot of people.

Currently, the United States ranks third on the list of the most populous countries at 320 million people, but that pales in comparison to the top two—China (1.36 billion) and India (1.25 billion).

Considering massive numbers like that, it's staggering to think about how many human beings have lived since God created the world. Tens of billions? Hundreds of billions? Even a trillion or more? It's impossible to know for sure. Any estimate is a pure guess.

But here's an even more astounding fact: Jesus' death was powerful enough to cover the sins of all humanity—past, present, and future.

WHAT'S IT MEAN?

When Jesus hung on Calvary's cross, he shouldered the horrible weight of our sin. He bore God's terrible wrath for innumerable human rebellions, spanning thousands and thousands of years from the Garden of Eden to today.

Chew on that for a moment. It's hard to believe because of the sheer magnitude of it. But it's true.

Today's verse says Jesus sacrificed himself for "the sins of all the world." And John 3:16 begins with the well-known phrase "For God so loved the world . . ." (NIV). The apostle John, who wrote both of these Scripture passages, wasn't just referring to the first-century "world" of his day. The world he spoke of was all of humanity from Genesis 1:1 to the future return of Christ.

Whoa.

Jesus died for the sins of the whole world. That's how big the scope of God's salvation plan is. That's how powerful and comprehensive the Savior's sacrifice was. That's how much Jesus loves us.

Salvation is offered to all, but not everyone will be saved. To receive God's salvation, we must trust that Jesus is the only possible sacrifice for our sins and live for him.

As you consider the far-reaching scale and power of Jesus' death, remember that he loves you and knows you by name. He died not only for the entire world, but specifically for you. The world doesn't feel so big after all, does it?

NOW WHAT?

Tell someone you know about Jesus' love for him or her. Although Christ died for the whole world, not everyone knows about it.

DID YOU KNOW?

A new baby is born in the United States every eight seconds, according to US Census Bureau statistics.

Christ redeemed us from the curse of the law by becoming a curse for us—for it is written, "Cursed is everyone who is hanged on a tree."
GALATIANS 3:13, ESV

The crown of thorns wasn't the worst of it. Neither were the beatings, the mocking, nor the near-fatal scourging he endured. Not even the crucifixion itself was the most agonizing aspect of Jesus' death.

In fact, none of the Gospels mentions Jesus crying out because of the physical pain he suffered that day. No, what hurt Jesus the most is found in a single phrase he uttered on the cross shortly before he died. Under an eerily darkened afternoon sky, Jesus shouted, *"Eli, Eli, lema sabachthani?"* (Matthew 27:46), an Aramaic phrase meaning, "My God, My God, why have you abandoned me?"

Yes, you read that correctly. As Jesus died, God the Father turned his back on his Son.

WHAT'S IT MEAN?

Jesus' cry represents one of the greatest mysteries in the Bible. We'll never fully understand what it means that God forsook his Son on the cross. But there's a clue in today's verse from Galatians 3. When Jesus became the sin-bearer for all humanity, he actually became a curse.

We don't use the word *curse* much these days. The word dates back to the Garden of Eden. After Adam and Eve committed the original sin by disobeying God and eating the forbidden fruit, the curse of sin entered the world—death, sorrow, pain, and God's wrath (Genesis 3).

Later in the Old Testament, when an Israelite committed a serious sin against God (like idolatry), the penalty was often death by stoning outside the camp (or later, the city's walls), followed by that person's body being displayed on a pole (Deuteronomy 21:22-23). It was the ultimate rejection, a public display that the person was under God's curse against sin.

This is what Jesus suffered for your sake—to shield you from God's wrath toward sin. When Christ became humanity's sin-bearer, he took the horrible curse of sin upon himself, and God, because of his holiness, had to temporarily forsake him. This was the worst punishment Jesus endured. The Father had to cut off their perfect, eternal fellowship and pour out his full wrath against sin on his Son. The dreadfulness of it all caused even the Son of God to cry out in agony.

As today's verse says, he did this "for us." He did this for *you*.

NOW WHAT?

To learn more about God's Old Testament curses against sin, read Deuteronomy 11:26-32; 27–28.

DID YOU KNOW?

Jesus' cry about God forsaking him is actually a direct quote of Psalm 22:1.

JULY 2

No one can take my life from me. I sacrifice it voluntarily. For I have the authority to lay it down when I want to and also to take it up again. For this is what my Father has commanded.

JOHN 10:18

It's time for a quiz. But don't worry! You're not getting graded on this. It's just something to get the brainwaves flowing.

Who was most responsible for Jesus' death?

A. *Judas Iscariot, the disciple who betrayed him*

B. *The Pharisees, chief priests, and other Jewish religious leaders*

C. *Caiaphas, the high priest*

D. *Pontius Pilate, the Roman governor*

E. *The Roman soldiers who tortured him and nailed him to the cross*

Ready for the answer? It might shock you.

While all these men played a significant role in Jesus' death and will be judged for their horrible sins, none of them took Jesus' life from him. Is that hard to believe? It's true. Consider how Matthew 27:50 describes Jesus' death: "Then Jesus shouted out again, and he released his spirit."

Jesus' life wasn't taken from him. He willingly gave it up.

WHAT'S IT MEAN?

Jesus wasn't naive. As the eternal, all-knowing Son of God, he knew how his earthly mission would end (see the April 12 devotion) and was always fully in charge of his circumstances, even during his arrest, torture, and crucifixion. Nothing surprised him on that fateful day. No situation spiraled out of his control.

Today's verse bears this out. So do the Gospels' various descriptions of Jesus' last moments on the cross. When Matthew 27:50 says that Jesus "released his spirit," the emphasis is on what Jesus willingly did, not what others did to him. And Luke 23:46 says, "Then Jesus shouted, 'Father, I entrust my spirit into your hands!' And with those words he breathed his last." Jesus decided what to do and when to do it.

By his own will, Jesus died so that you might live. By his own power, he rose three days later so that you might have eternal life. That's the humility, authority, and love of the Savior!

NOW WHAT?

To marvel at Jesus' sacrifice for you even more, consider this: Jesus didn't speed up his death and avoid more suffering, because as the sin-bearer who died in our place, he had to drink every last drop from the terrible cup of God's righteous wrath.

DID YOU KNOW?

When Jesus "released his spirit," it went to heaven (Luke 23:43). Meanwhile, his physical body stayed on the cross, was placed in a tomb, and eventually reunited with his spirit at his resurrection.

When he had received the drink, Jesus said, "It is finished." With that, he bowed his head and gave up his spirit. JOHN 19:30, NIV

Poor Pheidippides.

Legend has it that, in 490 BC, the ancient Greek messenger excitedly ran twenty-five miles or so from the site of the Battle of Marathon to Athens to announce the news of a victory over the mighty Persians, then collapsed and died from exhaustion.

In 1896, the first modern-era Olympic Games (which were held in Athens) introduced the marathon, a distance-running event at 24.85 miles long, to honor the famous Greek myth. At the 1908 London Games, the marathon was increased to its current length of 26.2 miles.

These days, things are starting to get a little ridiculous. As if the normal marathon length isn't challenging enough, some distance runners now compete in ultramarathons all over the world. There's a 154-mile journey through the 100-degree Sahara Desert in Morocco, a 147-mile trek that climbs 19,000 feet through the Grand Canyon, a 142.6-mile test through the humid, bug-infested Amazon jungle in Peru, and a frigid trip through Canada's northern Yukon Territory to the Arctic Ocean. No matter what kind of marathon it is, it feels awesome to cross the finish line.

Jesus experienced his own grueling marathon on the cross—but it was infinitely worse than a footrace. For six long, torturous hours, he hung from Rome's most sinister instrument of death, bearing the weight of humanity's sins on his bloody shoulders. Finally, around three o'clock in the afternoon, with all the strength he could muster, he declared, "It is finished."

And then the Son of God died.

WHAT'S IT MEAN?

Those three words—"It is finished"—are some of the most beautiful in all of Scripture. They speak of a glorious finality.

With his death, Jesus fully accomplished his salvation mission. He fulfilled everything—*everything!*—he set out to do when he left heaven's glory and came to earth.

Jesus died "once for all" (Hebrews 7:27). His sinless death was all that we needed to make us right with a holy God. It "secured our redemption forever" (Hebrews 9:12).

Now, no more sacrifices are needed—ever. Jesus broke sin's power for good. He did the same to death, Satan, and all the forces of evil.

Yes, "it is finished" indeed!

NOW WHAT?

Enter a local road race or community fun run, and when you cross the finish line, remember Jesus' words: "It is finished."

DID YOU KNOW?

To put it in a biblically historical perspective, the ancient Battle of Marathon occurred between the completion of the second Jewish Temple (Ezra 6:15) and Nehemiah rebuilding Jerusalem's walls (Nehemiah 3).

Anyone who has seen me has seen the Father. JOHN 14:9

Think about all the people you know—family members, friends, classmates, and other acquaintances. If you were to make a list of all their different characteristics, it would probably look something like this:

- kind
- unkind
- loving
- angry
- godly
- foolish
- forgiving
- patient

- impatient
- diligent
- energetic
- lazy
- smart
- athletic
- trustworthy
- forgetful

The list could go on and on. Humans are complex, multifaceted creatures with lots of different traits, emotions, and abilities. That's because we are created in God's image (Genesis 1:27).

God, meanwhile, is holy, eternal, and unchanging. And yet he is also a God of many different attributes. Unlike humans, though, God is perfect in all his ways.

We can never fully know God. He is infinite, and we are not. Our human minds can't comprehend everything about the Almighty Creator. But God has graciously chosen to reveal many things about his nature and character to us. And nothing casts a brighter spotlight on God's major attributes than Jesus' sacrifice.

WHAT'S IT MEAN?

As today's verse says, Jesus reveals the Father. Let's take a look at how the cross shows many of God's wonderful characteristics:

- Truthful—God kept the Old Testament promises he made to send a Savior to redeem his people (Luke 1:69-72).

- Loving—Read John 3:16. Enough said.
- Holy and just—God's perfect purity demanded that a sinless sacrifice had to be made for sin, which can't go unpunished (Romans 3:25-26).
- Wrathful—God poured out his righteous anger and vengeance toward sin on his Son (Romans 5:9).
- Gracious—God showed undeserved kindness to us, seen most vividly in the sacrifice of his own Son for lost sinners (Romans 3:24).
- Merciful—Thanks to Jesus, God didn't punish us for what our sins deserve (1 Peter 1:3).
- Forgiving—Because Jesus took our punishment, God chose to fully pardon our sins and not hold them against us (Acts 13:38).

There's much more that could be said. But this much is clear: Jesus' death provides a front-row seat to God's perfect character. His work on the cross shows just how awesome and loving our heavenly Father is!

NOW WHAT?

Make a list of God's other attributes that the cross reveals, then marvel at the Lord's goodness.

DID YOU KNOW?

The knowledge about God that the cross reveals was something that great Old Testament prophets such as Moses, Elijah, and Isaiah diligently searched for, but didn't always have (1 Peter 1:10-12). You should feel blessed!

JULY 5

The message of the cross is foolish to those who are headed for
destruction! But we who are being saved know it is the very power
of God. 1 CORINTHIANS 1:18

When was the last time you did any of the following?

- brought home a pet rhinoceros
- took a nap in wet cement
- went skydiving without a parachute
- tried to get straight A's without opening any of your schoolbooks

Hopefully, you've never done any of those things. They're all pretty foolish.
Do you know what else is foolish? "The message of the cross," according
to many people. As today's verse says, plenty of folks think the gospel—
the good news of salvation through Jesus, and the very foundation of the
Christian faith—is a bunch of hooey.

Hmmm, we'd better get to the bottom of this.

WHAT'S IT MEAN?

From the first century AD (when the apostle Paul wrote today's verse) until
now, countless people have thought that the message of the cross is pretty
ridiculous. Ancient Jews were "offended" by the thought of God's long-awaited
Messiah being crucified by the hated Romans, while first-century Gentiles
(non-Jews such as Romans and Greeks) thought that the idea of a deity sacrificing himself on a cross was "nonsense" (1 Corinthians 1:23).

Today, it's largely the same. Most of the world either rejects the message
of the cross or flat-out doesn't care. The Bible, though, has a far different
view of Jesus' death. Today's verse says "it is the very power of God." In other
words, Jesus' death reveals God's saving power to us and offers us the chance
to be free from sin and death forever.

The whole issue boils down to this: What will you ultimately trust—human wisdom or God's wisdom? The answer should be obvious. Even the smartest people are no match for the knowledge of God. Human wisdom can't save you from your sins. Not even close. But God's wisdom can. His wonderful plan of salvation through Christ might seem foolish to unbelievers, but it is our only hope for eternal life.

Just say no to the foolishness of pet rhinos. But say yes to the wisdom of the cross!

NOW WHAT?

Read 1 Corinthians 1:18-25 to see how this supposedly "foolish" plan of God's is actually what we should place all our trust in!

DID YOU KNOW?

The apostle Paul was so concerned for his fellow Israelites who rejected the message of the cross that he wished he could trade places with them so they could be saved (Romans 9:1-3).

At that moment the curtain in the sanctuary of the Temple was torn in two, from top to bottom.   MATTHEW 27:51

If you were anywhere near Jerusalem on the day Jesus died, you would have known that something historic had just happened.

When Jesus uttered, "It is finished!" and breathed his last, a series of supernatural events occurred. Here's how Matthew 27:51-52 describes it:

> *At that moment the curtain in the sanctuary of the Temple was torn in two, from top to bottom. The earth shook, rocks split apart, and tombs opened. The bodies of many godly men and women who had died were raised from the dead.*

Crazy!

If you had to guess which of these three events was most amazing, which would it be?

1. A big curtain being torn
2. A major, rock-splitting earthquake
3. Dead people coming back to life

At first glance, choices 2 and 3 seem much more significant. But if you guessed number 1, you'd be correct!

WHAT'S IT MEAN?

The Temple in Jerusalem represented God's presence among his people. But access to God's presence was highly restricted.

While God exists everywhere at once (Jeremiah 23:23-24), he blessed Israel with a special manifestation of his presence above the Ark of the Covenant (Exodus 25:22) within the Temple's Most Holy Place. A huge, ornate curtain separated this sacred room from the rest of the Temple.

Only the high priest was allowed to pass through the curtain, and only on one day each year, the Day of Atonement (Hebrews 9:7), to offer a sacrifice for the sins of the people. The message was clear: without an approved representative shedding atoning blood (or, blood that satisfies God's holy requirements) on their behalf, sinful people cannot approach a holy God.

That's where Jesus comes in! When the Savior died, he became our perfect sin-sacrifice and high priest (Hebrews 9:11-12), abolishing the need for the Temple and the old sacrificial system. The tearing of the Temple curtain was a divinely symbolic event showing that direct access to God is now available through Jesus' sacrifice.

Now sinners can directly approach a holy God for salvation, and Christians can approach him "boldly" (Hebrews 4:16) in prayer, day or night, knowing that he wants to shower us with love, kindness, and heavenly blessings.

That's so much more amazing than an earthquake!

NOW WHAT?
Read Hebrews 7–10 to understand more about Jesus and his relationship to the old Temple system.

DID YOU KNOW?
At sixty feet high and thirty feet wide, the Temple curtain would've been impossible for a human to tear it "from top to bottom," as Matthew 27:51 says. This truly was a miraculous sign from God.

*Don't you know that you yourselves are God's temple and that God's
Spirit dwells in your midst?* I CORINTHIANS 3:16, NIV

Today in Jerusalem, you can see remnants of the ancient Jewish Temple, but
no building itself.

Israel's magnificent second Temple—built by returned Jewish exiles in the
sixth century BC and greatly expanded by Herod the Great starting around
20 BC—was destroyed in AD 70 by the Romans and never rebuilt. These
days, the old Temple site is home to the Dome of the Rock, a seventh-century
AD Muslim shrine.

God never intended for his people to worship him in a man-made temple
forever. The tearing of the Temple curtain when Jesus died (see yesterday's
devotion) proves that.

The Temple, despite its great splendor, was only a symbol of a greater
temple to come. When Jesus came to earth, *he* became the temple (John
2:19)! As the perfect Lamb of God, he fulfilled the requirements of the Old
Testament sacrificial system and made the Temple building itself obsolete.

But since Jesus has returned to heaven, who represents God's temple
today? Christians do! As today's verse says, believers are now God's temple.

WHAT'S IT MEAN?

Are you a believer in Jesus? If so, maybe you're wondering, *How am I a huge,
ancient worship building made of stones?* It's a valid question. For the record,
you are *not* a huge, ancient worship building made of stones.

When the apostle Paul called Christians "God's temple" in 1 Corinthians,
he was using figurative language—kind of like saying, "I'm so hungry I could
eat a horse" or "She's as light as a feather." It's descriptive language to make
a point.

If you trust in Jesus, you are God's temple because God's Spirit lives in
you. This is amazing news! Instead of putting his Spirit in a building, God
has now chosen to put his Spirit in his people!

Being God's temple means we must live for God. We must use our bodies to bring him praise (Romans 12:1). We must worship him with our minds, mouths, eyes, ears, hands, and feet. Our lives should be a reflection of his glory, even more than the old temple was.

The man-made temple is gone, but an even better temple—Spirit-filled believers—is here!

NOW WHAT?

Consider this awesome truth: the same Spirit of God, who was active in creation (Romans 12:1), gave Samson power for mighty deeds (Judges 15:14-15), descended on Jesus at his baptism (John 1:32), and empowered the first Christians at Pentecost (Acts 2:4) now fills the heart of every believer!

DID YOU KNOW?

In 1 Peter 2:4-6, Christians are called "the living stones" of God's new temple, while Jesus is "the cornerstone." He is the firm foundation on which our spiritual lives should be built.

JULY 8

God released him from the horrors of death and raised him back to life, for death could not keep him in its grip. ACTS 2:24

The sun was just beginning to peek above the horizon, casting its soft, welcome light on a new week as several women approached the tomb.

It had been a horrible weekend in ancient Israel. Jesus had died Friday afternoon. Afterward, his disciples and other followers felt lost and alone. The Messiah they had trusted in was gone, mercilessly executed by godless men.

After Jesus died, a Roman soldier drove a spear into his side, just to make sure he was dead. Joseph of Arimathea and Nicodemus—both secret followers of Jesus for fear of the religious leaders—got permission to take his body off the cross so they could prepare it for burial. Then they laid it in a new tomb in a garden not far away from the crucifixion site.

Saturday, the Jewish Sabbath, passed quietly. Then at sunrise on Sunday morning, several women brought more ointment to anoint Jesus' lifeless body.

You know what happened next, don't you? The most glorious event in history! The stone was rolled away. The women marveled. The tomb was empty.

Jesus Christ, the crucified Son of God, had risen from the dead!

WHAT'S IT MEAN?

For the next nine days, we're going to look specifically at Jesus' resurrection and all its implications. Whether you've read about it once or one hundred times, this miracle should never grow old. Jesus' resurrection is a fact, but it's not an average, everyday fact such as 1 + 1 = 2. It's an extraordinary truth that should never cease to amaze you.

Jesus actually beat death. Think about that for a moment. No one else in history has ever done that. Even the people whom Jesus raised from the dead eventually died again. But not Jesus. As he says in Revelation 1:18, "I died, but look—I am alive forever and ever!"

Because the Savior created life, death has no power over him (see today's verse). Sin couldn't keep the Sinless One in the grave. At God's appointed time, Jesus burst forth from the grave in majesty and strength. He "broke the power of death" (2 Timothy 1:10) and defeated "the power of the devil, who had the power of death" (Hebrews 2:14).

How did he do it? Jesus' resurrection is an indescribable miracle, but Romans 6:4 gives us a glimpse into the mystery: "Christ was raised from the dead by the glorious power of the Father."

We serve a mighty, risen Savior!

NOW WHAT?

Read all four Gospel accounts of Jesus' resurrection—Matthew 28:1-15; Mark 16:1-8; Luke 24:1-12; and John 20:1-18.

DID YOU KNOW?

The same heavenly power that raised Jesus from the dead will resurrect all true believers when he returns (2 Corinthians 4:14).

JULY 9

God raised Jesus from the dead, and we are all witnesses of this.
ACTS 2:32

Cinderella is a wonderful fairy tale, one of the most beloved of all time. So are the stories of Beauty and the Beast, King Arthur's Camelot, Snow White, Sleeping Beauty, Rumpelstiltskin . . . the list could go on and on. These legends have been captivating readers for centuries. But they are all fantasies.

The greatest story of all time, however, is not a fairy tale, myth, or fable. It didn't come from the imagination of Aesop, the Brothers Grimm, or Walt Disney screenwriters. It's an authentic, historical event that happened early in the first century AD.

The death and resurrection of Jesus Christ are real!

In fact, Scripture mentions that Jesus made at least twelve different appearances to various people after his resurrection:

1. Mary Magdalene and "the other Mary" (Matthew 28:1, 9)
2. Peter (Luke 24:34)
3. The two followers of Jesus traveling to Emmaus (Luke 24:13-31)
4. The eleven disciples and other believers gathered together, without Thomas (Luke 24:33-49; John 20:19-23)
5. The disciples, including Thomas (John 20:24-29)
6. Seven disciples by the Sea of Galilee (John 21:1-23)
7. The twelve disciples—perhaps including the newly appointed Matthias (Acts 1:6-23; 1 Corinthians 15:5)
8. Five hundred believers at once (1 Corinthians 15:6)
9. James, Jesus' brother (1 Corinthians 15:7)
10. "All the apostles" (1 Corinthians 15:7)
11. Paul (Acts 9:1-9; 1 Corinthians 15:8)

That's a lot of people!

WHAT'S IT MEAN?

Ever since that very first Easter Sunday, people have been questioning, denying, and attacking the authenticity of the resurrection. It started with the ancient Jewish Sanhedrin (Matthew 28:11-15) and continues today. But by rejecting Jesus' resurrection, they are rejecting true history and bringing judgment upon themselves.

More than five hundred eyewitnesses saw the Savior alive after his death. And the majority of the New Testament books, written by at least eight different authors over the course of five decades, mention the risen Lord too. The evidence is overwhelming: Jesus' resurrection really happened.

This was the apostle Peter's message in today's verse when he boldly proclaimed to a huge crowd in Jerusalem: "God raised Jesus from the dead, and we are all witnesses of this."

Thousands believed that day. Now the question comes to you: Do *you* believe in the truth of Jesus' resurrection?

NOW WHAT?

Look up all the different Scripture references listed earlier about Jesus' post-resurrection appearances, and let your faith grow!

DID YOU KNOW?

The first people that Jesus appeared to after his resurrection were Mary Magdalene and another woman named Mary (Matthew 28:1-10).

Christ has been raised from the dead. He is the first of a great harvest of all who have died. I CORINTHIANS 15:20

What are some of the most important events in world history?

Yeah, yeah, it's summertime, and school's out. The last thing you want to do is pretend you're in history class. But this is important!

Here's a sampler to get you started:

- The introduction of Hammurabi's Code of laws (eighteenth century BC)
- Alexander the Great's conquest of the ancient world (fourth century BC)
- English King John's signing of the Magna Carta (AD 1215)
- The introduction of Johannes Gutenberg's printing press (fifteenth century)
- Christopher Columbus's discovery of the New World (1492)
- The signing of the Declaration of Independence (1776)
- World War II (1939–45)

These events, among many others, changed history and shaped the world we live in today. But there's one particular event that is far and away the single most important event in human history: the resurrection of Jesus Christ. Unlike all those other monumental events, Jesus' resurrection has eternal implications for our souls.

WHAT'S IT MEAN?

Billions and billions of people have lived on earth throughout history. Yet Jesus is the only person—*ever!*—who died and returned to life for good.

That's incredible.

But if you've grown up in church, it can be easy to forget just how important Jesus' resurrection is. Sometimes, the more familiar we become with the resurrection story, the less it amazes us. That's unfortunate.

Jesus' resurrection is the most important event in history because:

- It proved Jesus is completely trustworthy and fully God, as he claimed.
- It means he defeated death, sin, and Satan.
- It confirms God's acceptance of Jesus' sacrifice for our sins.
- It ensures that all believers will one day, like their Savior, also rise from the dead to live forever in heaven (see today's verse).

Jesus' death was the greatest sacrificial act of love and humility the world has ever known. But without the resurrection, it wouldn't mean anything. The reality of Jesus' resurrection is critically important to the Christian faith, because a dead savior is really no savior at all.

But Jesus isn't dead. He's alive! Now, thanks to our risen Savior, we have great hope in this life and the life to come!

NOW WHAT?

Make sure to praise Jesus for his resurrection throughout the year, not just at Easter!

DID YOU KNOW?

Jesus' resurrection was so shocking to his disciples, they "were startled and frightened and thought they saw a spirit" when he appeared to them on Resurrection Sunday (Luke 24:37, ESV).

JULY 11

Thank God! He gives us victory over sin and death through our Lord Jesus Christ. 1 CORINTHIANS 15:57

Have you ever played the "What If?" game? It's basically where you wonder what it would be like if something were different in your life, such as:

- What if I were a foot taller?
- What if I were better at sports?
- What if I had a million bucks?
- What if I were president of the United States?
- What if spinach tasted like ice cream?

Interestingly, the apostle Paul played the "What If?" game once too. Apparently, some Christians in the ancient city of Corinth didn't believe in a bodily resurrection of the dead. They thought—contrary to Scripture—that once someone died, that person's body could never be raised to life before the final Day of Judgment. So Paul tackled this issue in his first letter to the Corinthians. First, he warned that doubting human resurrection means doubting Jesus' resurrection. And then he asked the big question: "What if Jesus *hadn't* been raised from the dead?"

The answer is pretty frightening.

WHAT'S IT MEAN?

If Jesus had not been raised, Paul wrote, "then your faith is useless and you are still guilty of your sins. In that case, all who have died believing in Christ are lost! And if our hope in Christ is only for this life, we are more to be pitied than anyone in the world" (1 Corinthians 15:17-19).

Let's summarize Paul's words: if Jesus' resurrection hadn't happened, Christians would be . . .

- believing in a false religion
- wasting their earthly lives on a big sham

383

- without hope of salvation
- lacking anything to look forward to in the afterlife

In other words, we'd be in a nightmare situation. Without the resurrection, we'd have no true purpose, salvation, or hope for eternity.

But we don't have to play the "What If?" game. Jesus' resurrection *did* happen! He really *is* alive and reigning in heaven! And he really *does* offer forgiveness and eternal life to those who believe.

Are you beginning to see how important—and marvelous—Jesus' resurrection is?

Don't play the "What If?" game with Jesus' resurrection. Put your hope in the risen Savior!

NOW WHAT?

Read Paul's great discussion on Jesus' resurrection in 1 Corinthians 15. This chapter is essential to understanding this vital Christian doctrine.

DID YOU KNOW?

Paul references each Christian's bodily resurrection in many other Scripture passages, such as Acts 26:23; Romans 8:29; Philippians 3:21; and 1 Thessalonians 4:13-17.

Jesus came and told his disciples, "I have been given all authority in heaven and on earth." MATTHEW 28:18

The president of the United States is a powerful guy. In fact, some people say that he's the most powerful man in the world. As the leader of the world's most influential nation and commander in chief of the greatest military on earth, he has an impressive amount of authority.

But he doesn't have *all* authority. Nobody on earth does. That privilege belongs solely to the Lord Jesus Christ.

Not long after his resurrection, Jesus told his disciples, "I have been given all authority in heaven and on earth" (today's verse). It's a bold statement. Are you awestruck by Jesus' words? You should be.

WHAT'S IT MEAN?

Authority is the power to give orders, exercise control, and make things happen. And Jesus has all of it.

Jesus controls every square inch of the universe. The fact that he has total authority means he perfectly rules over everything in the material world (kings, armies, nations, animals, individual people, nature) as well as everything in the spiritual world (angels, demons, and even Satan himself). If Jesus commands something to happen, it happens. If he commands something not to happen, it doesn't.

How did Jesus get all this authority? Did he buy it? Inherit it from someone else? Win it in a lottery?

No! The triune (three-in-one) God is unchanging in his nature. When it comes to authority and power, he doesn't collect more over time like bank account interest, and he doesn't earn greater influence like a military officer earning a promotion to a higher ranking.

As the eternal, all-powerful Son of God, Jesus has *always* had all authority. He spoke of this before his death when he said, "My Father has entrusted everything [all power] to me" (Matthew 11:27) and "You [God] have given him [Jesus] authority over everyone" (John 17:2).

Jesus' resurrection proved that he has all authority. If he were still lying dead in a tomb, he wouldn't have any. Corpses don't have power over anything!

But when Jesus rose again, he defeated sin, Satan, the powers of evil, and death itself. There's no enemy left for him to conquer.

The risen Savior has complete authority and reigns over all!

NOW WHAT?

The book of Psalms is filled with songs praising God for his power and rule in the universe. Write a song or poem of your own, praising Jesus for his total authority in heaven and earth.

DID YOU KNOW?

Jesus has defeated sin, Satan, and death, but he hasn't yet destroyed them. That will happen in the future (Revelation 20:10, 14).

JULY 13

As he spoke, he showed them the wounds in his hands and his side.
They were filled with joy when they saw the Lord! JOHN 20:20

Awestruck. Astounded. Dumbfounded. Stunned. Shocked. Stupefied. Flabbergasted.

Pick any word to describe sheer amazement, and it would perfectly describe the reactions of the two women named Mary early on that glorious Sunday morning two thousand years ago.

A few days earlier, Mary Magdalene and "the other Mary" (Matthew 28:1) had seen Jesus' dead body taken off the cross and laid in a nearby garden tomb (John 19:38-42; Matthew 27:61). But now, as dawn broke Sunday morning, their lives were about to change forever. When they came to the tomb, it was empty, and they listened, amazed, as two angels announced Jesus' resurrection.

Matthew 28:8-9 picks up the story: "The women ran quickly from the tomb. They were very frightened but also filled with great joy, and they rushed to give the disciples the angel's message. And as they went, Jesus met them and greeted them. And they ran to him, grasped his feet, and worshiped him."

Everyone who encountered the risen Lord experienced the same ecstatic emotions. Later that evening, when Jesus appeared to his disciples, Luke 24:41 says, "They stood there in disbelief, filled with joy and wonder." Today's verse describes the disciples' reaction in the same way.

WHAT'S IT MEAN?

The people who witnessed Jesus' resurrection reacted with astonishment, exuberance, and worship. Their hearts were filled with praise, joy, and wonder.

Is this your reaction to the risen Savior? It should be!

Sometimes, because we hear about the resurrection so much, we can treat it as routine, like it's not that special. But it is! Jesus' resurrection is the single most important event in history. It means that God's love, forgiveness, and eternal life are available to everyone who trusts in Christ.

You don't have to be an eyewitness of Jesus' resurrection to fully appreciate it and rejoice in it. The resurrection provides the same blessings to Christians today as it did to the first-century disciples.

May their jubilant reactions always be ours, too. Never grow complacent about it or tired of celebrating it. May we continually be "filled with joy," as today's verse says, as we reflect on the risen Savior!

NOW WHAT?

Sing a worship song praising Jesus for the resurrection. If you don't know one already, learn one!

DID YOU KNOW?

Not long after the resurrection, when Jesus appeared to seven of his disciples on the Sea of Galilee's shore, Peter jumped out of a fishing boat and swam one hundred yards to shore (John 21:7). Now *that* is being excited about the resurrection!

We know that the Son of God has come, and he has given us
understanding so that we can know the true God. 1 JOHN 5:20

Have you ever had a "lightbulb moment"? This is when things that were once puzzling suddenly become crystal clear, like someone switching on a light, chasing away the darkness of confusion.

Today's devotion is about a lightbulb moment that happened two thousand years ago.

At first, Resurrection Sunday started with a lot of confusion. Word spread quickly among Jesus' followers that his tomb was empty and that some women had even seen him alive. Some believed; others didn't.

Later that afternoon, two of Jesus' followers were traveling from Jerusalem to a small village called Emmaus, talking about all the recent events involving Jesus. Suddenly, Jesus appeared next to them, but they didn't recognize him.

As they chatted with Jesus, they expressed disappointment that the man they thought was God's long-awaited Messiah had died. They also seemed bewildered at the reports of Jesus' empty tomb. Jesus rebuked their lack of understanding and began explaining how the Old Testament predicted the Messiah's death and resurrection (Luke 24:25-27).

Later that evening as they ate dinner with Jesus . . . *click*! The lightbulb of understanding came on. Luke 24:31-32 says, "Their eyes were opened, and they recognized him. And he vanished from their sight. They said to each other, 'Did not our hearts burn within us while he talked to us on the road, while he opened to us the Scriptures?'" (ESV).

WHAT'S IT MEAN?

Pretty cool story, huh? But there's an important truth that often gets overlooked. It's found in the phrase "Their eyes were opened."

These two individuals didn't come to faith in Jesus on their own. Luke 24:31 doesn't say, "They opened their own eyes." It says, "Their eyes were opened."

Someone else opened their eyes for them. Their lightbulb moment came from Jesus!

God's Son opens our hearts and minds to salvation. Thank goodness, too, because when left to ourselves, our minds are "dark and confused" (Romans 1:21) and our hearts are "hardened" (Ephesians 4:18) in our sin.

Scripture plainly reveals the saving gospel truth. We just need Jesus' help to understand and believe. As today's verse says, he gives us understanding "so that we can know the true God."

Let Jesus turn on the lightbulb of your faith!

NOW WHAT?

Meditate (think about) and pray over Psalm 119:18: "Open my eyes to see the wonderful truths in your instructions."

DID YOU KNOW?

One of the individuals who met Jesus on the Emmaus Road was named Cleopas (Luke 24:18), whom Scripture never mentions again. The other is unnamed.

JULY 15

"My Lord and my God!" Thomas exclaimed. JOHN 20:28

If this was a joke, it wasn't very funny. At least not to Thomas.

When Jesus appeared to his disciples on the evening of Resurrection Sunday, Thomas wasn't present. So when the other disciples saw him later and excitedly told him, "We have seen the Lord," Thomas rejected the idea. He was convinced Jesus was still dead.

Perhaps he thought his friends were just playing a tasteless prank on him. Or maybe he thought they had seen a ghost. After all, that's what the disciples had thought when they witnessed Jesus walking on water (Matthew 14:26).

Either way, Thomas shook his head. He was the very definition of a skeptic—quick to question and slow to trust. He was an "I'll believe it when I see it" type of guy.

"I won't believe it unless I see the nail wounds in his hands, put my fingers into them, and place my hand into the wound in his side," Thomas told the rest of the disciples (John 20:25). He required physical proof. This is where he got his unfortunate nickname—Doubting Thomas.

Soon, however, all his doubts would be blissfully erased. One week later, Jesus appeared again to his disciples, and this time Thomas was present. When Thomas saw Jesus, his heart must've skipped a beat. Turning to Thomas, Jesus said, "Put your finger here, and look at my hands. Put your hand into the wound in my side. Don't be faithless any longer. Believe!" (John 20:26).

Stunned and humbled, Thomas exclaimed, "My Lord and my God!" (John 20:28). They are five of the sweetest words in Scripture.

WHAT'S IT MEAN?

Like Peter's famous confession in Matthew 16:16 ("You are the Messiah, the Son of the living God"), Thomas's statement is one of Scripture's great declarations about Jesus' deity.

Having witnessed Jesus' awesome resurrection power firsthand, Thomas laid aside all his unbelief and fully embraced Jesus as his heavenly master. There were no more doubts about the divinity of the carpenter from Nazareth. Thomas now knew, 100 percent, that Jesus truly was God.

Is that what you believe? Do you accept Jesus' full divinity and rule over your life? Have you embraced him through faith as your Lord and God?

May Thomas's great confession of Christ be yours, as well!

NOW WHAT?

Read Romans 10:9-10. Then, whether it's for the first time or the hundredth, pray to Jesus and confess your faith in him as your Lord and God!

DID YOU KNOW?

Thomas, whose name means "the Twin" (John 11:16), likely had a twin who is unmentioned in Scripture.

Jesus told him, "You believe because you have seen me. Blessed are those who believe without seeing me." JOHN 20:29

It was the greatest day of Thomas's life.

In dramatic fashion, the disciple known as Doubting Thomas had just become Believing Thomas. After seeing the risen Jesus gloriously appear before his eyes, Thomas loudly declared, "My Lord and my God!" The great skeptic had come to saving faith in Christ. What a wonderful moment that must have been for Thomas and the rest of the disciples!

But Jesus' response was interesting. He didn't high-five Thomas or give him a bro hug. He didn't even pat his friend on the back. While Jesus certainly was pleased with Thomas's newfound faith, he replied, "You believe because you have seen me. Blessed are those who believe without seeing me."

Here's the cool thing: what sounded like a mild rebuke of Thomas's prior doubt also provides great news for us today!

WHAT'S IT MEAN?

Read today's verse again. As always, the words of Jesus two thousand years ago contain surprising relevance for us now. If you are a Christian, Jesus was referring directly to you when he said, "Blessed are those who believe without seeing me"!

As discussed in the February 11 devotion, to be "blessed" means to be in a state of peace and well-being with God because your sins are forgiven. That's a good place to be! And as Jesus says in today's verse, this is true of every Christian who has ever lived after Jesus returned to heaven.

No one since the apostle Paul (Acts 9:1-6) has seen the Lord in person—a span of about two thousand years. Sure, it would be awesome to walk and talk with Jesus like Thomas and the disciples did. But Christians today are at no disadvantage to anyone who witnessed the resurrected Savior firsthand. In fact, Jesus says we receive a special blessing if we believe *despite* not seeing him in person!

As 2 Corinthians 5:7 says, "We live by faith, not by sight" (NIV). The apostle Peter spoke of this too, when he wrote, "You love him even though you have never seen him. Though you do not see him now, you trust him; and you rejoice with a glorious, inexpressible joy" (1 Peter 1:8).

God is especially pleased with those who trust in his Son without seeing him!

NOW WHAT?

Read Hebrews 11, the Bible's great chapter on faith without sight.

DID YOU KNOW?

While the Bible doesn't specifically say what happened to Thomas after Jesus ascended, early Christian tradition suggests he became a missionary to India.

These are written so that you may continue to believe that Jesus is the Messiah, the Son of God. JOHN 20:31

The apostle John had just finished writing the account of Doubting Thomas confessing his faith in the resurrected Christ. It was late in the first century AD, and the elderly apostle was nearly finished with his masterpiece, what we now call the Gospel of John.

He had one more story left to tell before ending his work—a beautiful look at Jesus' restoration of Peter—but then he laid down his pen and paused. There was something important he needed to add. So John took up his pen again and wrote these words (John 20:30-31):

> *The disciples saw Jesus do many other miraculous signs in addition to the ones recorded in this book. But these are written so that you may continue to believe that Jesus is the Messiah, the Son of God, and that by believing in him you will have life by the power of his name.*

WHAT'S IT MEAN?

John's decision to interrupt his own narrative with a two-sentence purpose statement was interesting. Normally, you place a purpose statement near the front of a literary work. But John saved it until the end, hoping to powerfully impact readers by telling them about Jesus' life, death, and resurrection *before* sharing his own motivation for the book.

It worked. John's Gospel is a powerful witness to Jesus' incarnation.

But honestly, John's purpose statement could have worked in Matthew, Mark, and Luke, too. All four Gospels—the Bible books we've been studying for the past six months—were written for one purpose: to bear witness to the atoning work of Jesus (reconciling God and people) and to offer salvation to all who believe.

Jesus proved he was God's Son, the saving Messiah, by what he said and did on earth (John 10:25). Four godly men, inspired by the Holy Spirit, felt compelled to record some of these events for all time, so that future generations like us would have a truthful account of the Savior.

So as we near the end of our study of the life and work of Jesus in the Gospels, the question comes to you: Do you believe that he is the Messiah, the Son of God?

NOW WHAT?

As John 20:30-31 encourages us, believe in Jesus and have life!

DID YOU KNOW?

John wrote, "The disciples saw Jesus do many other miraculous signs in addition to the ones recorded in this book" (John 20:30). While John's Gospel records seven miracles, the four Gospels mention thirty-five separate miraculous signs.

O Lord, you are so good, so ready to forgive, so full of unfailing love for all who ask for your help. PSALM 86:5

The veteran fisherman breathed deeply. The salty sea air felt good in his lungs.

Seagulls circled above, speaking in shrill calls. Waves lapped against the creaking hull of his boat. The sun was just waking up, poking its head above the horizon. Peter was back in familiar surroundings—fishing once again on the Sea of Galilee, just like when Jesus had first called him several years earlier.

Yet Peter had no peace. Regret gnawed at his soul. He had seen Jesus a few times since the Resurrection, but he hadn't been reconciled to the Lord for his many failings on the night before the Crucifixion. In Jesus' darkest hours, Peter had fallen asleep, lashed out in violence, scurried away like a coward, and worst of all, denied the Savior three times. His guilt must have felt unbearable.

Then suddenly, Peter and the six other disciples on the boat that morning heard a familiar voice calling from the shore. It was Jesus! Excitedly, Peter dived into the sea and swam a hundred yards to land.

After a bread-and-fish breakfast (*mmmm, yum!*), Jesus looked directly at Peter and shattered the silence: "Simon son of John, do you love me more than these?" (John 21:15).

The words felt like sharp daggers in Peter's heart. Twice more, Jesus asked, "Do you love me?" Peter answered, "Lord, you know everything. You know that I love you" (John 21:17).

Jesus replied, "Then feed my sheep" (John 21:17).

WHAT'S IT MEAN?

The meaning of Jesus' trio of questions wasn't lost on Peter. Just as Peter denied him three times, Jesus asked Peter three times, "Do you love me?" He wanted Peter to confirm his love.

But when Jesus said, "Feed my sheep," it signaled his forgiveness. He was giving Peter a mission—to shepherd the early Christian church. Jesus had forgiven Peter and now had a new calling for him.

What amazing love Jesus has for wayward sinners like Peter—and us! Peter committed some terrible sins, but Jesus didn't reject him. Instead, he offered him love, forgiveness, and purpose.

Jesus does the same for us today. As today's verse says, he is a loving Savior who is "so ready to forgive" those who acknowledge their sins and approach him in humble faith.

We stray, but Jesus strengthens. We stumble, but Jesus restores. We fail, but Jesus forgives. Praise Jesus!

NOW WHAT?

Read John 21 to learn more about what Jesus said to Peter.

DID YOU KNOW?

Jesus performed one of his final miracles that day, helping the disciples catch 153 fish at once (John 21:4-6, 11).

Jesus told him, "Follow me." JOHN 21:19

Peter was forgiven, but Jesus wasn't through with him yet.

In a wonderful display of love and compassion by the Sea of Galilee, the risen Lord had restored Peter after his three cowardly denials and had given him a new mission: Peter was to be a key leader in the early Christian church.

But Jesus had another, more sobering message for Peter. Jesus wanted to show Peter that following him requires total commitment. So he gave Peter a glimpse into the future. "When you are old," Jesus said, "you will stretch out your hands, and others will dress you and take you where you don't want to go" (John 21:18). In other words, one day Peter would be martyred for his faith.

Then, to further emphasize the importance of Peter's devotion, Jesus said bluntly, "Follow me."

WHAT'S IT MEAN?

Jesus' choice of words wasn't accidental. Three years earlier, when the Lord first called Peter to be his disciple, Jesus shouted similar words from the shore as Peter was fishing on the Sea of Galilee. "Follow me," he said, "and I will show you how to fish for people!" (Matthew 4:19).

The irony of the situation was obvious. It was as if Jesus was saying, "Peter, three years ago near this same spot, I called you to follow me. And you have, to a point. But more is required. I'm about to return to heaven, and I need to know if you are truly devoted to me. So I say once more: follow me." Jesus was demanding Peter's complete, unquestioned loyalty.

Jesus requires the same from us today. To be a Christian, you have to follow Christ wholeheartedly.

Jesus is not a fad or a phase. He's not a cool video game that you enjoy for a while but eventually get bored with. Or an outfit you try on but never buy. Or a meal that you leave half-eaten on the kitchen table after having your fill.

Following Jesus requires lifelong commitment. We must be willing to give up everything for him because he gave up everything for us!

We are weak and prone to fail, just like Peter. Jesus knows this. He is patient and forgiving with his children. But he also requires full allegiance. As he told Peter, Jesus is telling you, "Follow me."

Will you?

NOW WHAT?

Following Jesus means knowing and obeying his Word. Commit to reading the Bible daily.

DID YOU KNOW?

Many Bible scholars believe Peter was martyred for his faith around AD 64–67 during Roman emperor Nero's persecution of Christians. In fact, 2 Peter 1:13-14 might imply this.

*Go and make disciples of all the nations, baptizing them in the
name of the Father and the Son and the Holy Spirit.*
MATTHEW 28:19

Jesus' work on earth was done.

The Savior had perfectly carried out the Father's wonderful plan of salvation for sinful humanity. The Son of God came to earth in human form, lived
a sinless life, died a sacrificial death, and rose again in great power to provide
redemption for all who trust in him.

Now, it was time for Jesus to return to heaven. So he gathered his disciples
on the Mount of Olives near Jerusalem one last time. Before ascending, he
told them:

*I have been given all authority in heaven and on earth. Therefore,
go and make disciples of all the nations, baptizing them in the name
of the Father and the Son and the Holy Spirit. Teach these new
disciples to obey all the commands I have given you. And be sure of
this: I am with you always, even to the end of the age.*

This passage, in Matthew 28:18-20, is called the "great commission."

WHAT'S IT MEAN?

A "commission" is a job given to someone to do on another's behalf. Before
returning to heaven, Jesus commissioned every Christian—from the first-
century disciples to current believers—with the following task: we are to tell
others about Jesus.

This is not optional or only meant for people with outgoing personalities.
Jesus didn't say, "Go if you want to," or "Go if you're a talkative person." No,
he said, "Go and make disciples of all the nations." The great commission is
for all believers.

Telling others about Jesus should never be considered a duty or a burden.

It's actually a great privilege! Considering what Jesus has done for you, why *wouldn't* you want to tell others about him?

You don't have to become an overseas missionary to obey the great commission. There are plenty of people around you—in your neighborhood, at school, on your sports teams, maybe even in your own family—who need to hear the gospel.

Maybe you're wondering what exactly to say. Simply share the good news that God loves them and sent Jesus to save them from their sins.

You've been commissioned! Time to tell others about the wonderful love of Jesus Christ.

NOW WHAT?

Make a list of people you know who need to hear about Jesus. But don't stop at just making a list. Share your faith with those on it!

DID YOU KNOW?

Today's verse not only highlights the great commission, but it's also one of the clearest references to the Trinity in Scripture.

JULY 21

Be sure of this: I am with you always, even to the end of the age.
MATTHEW 28:20

The disciples were confused and anxious. They sensed something big was about to happen, but none of them knew what.

For three years, they had spent virtually every day with Jesus, soaking up his teaching, witnessing his miracles, and experiencing his great love. He had changed their lives.

But things were different now. After the resurrection, Jesus appeared to the disciples occasionally, but he no longer hung out with them every day. Questions filled their minds: What would the risen Messiah do next? Would he gather an army to free Israel from Roman oppression? What were his plans for them?

And now, here they stood with Jesus on the Mount of Olives, just outside of Jerusalem. Jesus charged his disciples with spreading the gospel message "to the ends of the earth" (Acts 1:8). He promised to send the Holy Spirit to them. And then he rose off the ground, out of sight, and into heaven. Just like that, Jesus was gone!

Well, sort of. Before he ascended, Jesus spoke these final words: "Be sure of this: I am with you always, even to the end of the age."

WHAT'S IT MEAN?

This beautiful promise is as much for us today as it was for the disciples back then. Jesus left earth physically, but he didn't leave us alone.

Sound strange? Here's the deal: as the eternal, all-powerful Son of God, Jesus' divine, unseen presence remains with all believers even though we can't see him now. He actively and lovingly rules the lives of all Christians from heaven.

How does he do this? Through the Holy Spirit. As Jesus said in John 14:16-17, "I will ask the Father, and he will give you another Advocate, who will never leave you. He is the Holy Spirit, who leads into all truth."

Life in a sinful world can be difficult, even scary at times. You will experience joy, sadness, blessings, and trials. Yet we can rest assured that Jesus hasn't left us alone. He is still very much with us. As Philippians 4:5 says, "The Lord is near" (NIV).

So take heart! Although Jesus is now in heaven, he is close by. His Spirit dwells in all believers. You have a Savior who is always with you!

NOW WHAT?

Pray every day! It's the greatest way to fellowship with Jesus and experience his presence in your life.

DID YOU KNOW?

In Matthew 18:20, Jesus made another promise about his presence when Christians gather to pray: "Where two or three gather in my name, there am I with them" (NIV).

JULY 22

After saying this, he was taken up into a cloud while they were
watching, and they could no longer see him. ACTS 1:9

Three . . . two . . . one . . . blastoff!

Early in the morning on April 12, 1981, astronauts John Young and
Robert Crippen boarded a spaceship called Columbia at NASA's Kennedy
Space Center in Florida and launched into history on the world's first-ever
space shuttle mission.

Over the next three decades, five NASA space shuttles—Columbia,
Challenger, Discovery, Atlantis, and Endeavour—would fly 135 total missions, closing with the final mission in 2011. These remarkable spaceships
represented humanity's first reusable spacecraft. They would take off like
rockets (vertically) and land like airplanes (horizontally).

A space shuttle launch is quite a sight to behold. The amount of scien-
tific research, technology, and sheer power that goes into each space shuttle
launch is staggering.

Every launch takes years of planning. To blast into orbit, the 178,000-
pound shuttle requires a massive external tank that carries 526,000 gallons
of fuel and weighs nearly 1.7 million pounds when full. Two solid rocket
boosters (weighing 1.3 million pounds each when filled with propellant
chemicals), along with three huge shuttle engines, burn the fuel to produce
about 5.3 million pounds of total thrust to lift the shuttle into space. That's
an incredible amount of work to propel humans into outer space!

Jesus, though, did the same thing without any help whatsoever.

WHAT'S IT MEAN?

When the Son of God ascended into heaven, he didn't need rocket boosters, external fuel tanks, or hundreds of NASA scientists flipping switches at
Mission Control. He just rose off the ground, straight through the clouds,
and into heaven by his own power. What a miracle! No wonder Acts 1:10
says the disciples "strained to see him rising into heaven."

This spectacular phenomenon proved that what Jesus had told his disciples a few moments earlier—"I have been given all authority in heaven and on earth" (Matthew 28:18)—was 100 percent true. The risen Savior is truly Lord of heaven and earth. Sin couldn't trap him, death couldn't beat him, and gravity couldn't hold him!

NOW WHAT?

Go outside, look into the sky, and visualize what it must have been like to see Jesus ascending into the clouds. Use this opportunity to praise the ascended Lord!

DID YOU KNOW?

As the disciples watched Jesus ascend, two angels appeared and made a wonderful promise: "Jesus has been taken from you into heaven, but someday he will return from heaven in the same way you saw him go!" (Acts 1:11). Also see 1 Thessalonians 4:17.

JULY 23

*Christ has gone to heaven. He is seated in the place of honor next
to God, and all the angels and authorities and powers accept his
authority.* I PETER 3:22

Have you ever wondered what Jesus is doing now? After all, he ascended into
heaven nearly two thousand years ago. What's he been up to for the last two
millennia?

Has he been lounging poolside in heaven sipping on lemonade? Directing
saintly choir concerts? Shooting hoops with Lazarus and Zacchaeus on
Thursdays? Challenging the angels to weekend Ping-Pong tournaments?

No, of course not!

The Bible doesn't provide many details about Jesus' current activities. But
it does give us a few glimpses, and what it says might surprise you.

WHAT'S IT MEAN?

Today's verse—and others like it—makes it clear that after Jesus ascended, he
sat down at God's right hand in heaven. Because of his mighty triumph over
sin and death, Jesus now reigns over the entire universe from his heavenly
throne. In fact, he literally "holds all creation together" (Colossians 1:17).
He keeps the sun shining, the earth revolving, the grass growing, and gravity
working.

Jesus has dominion over every square inch of creation. Every earthly and
spiritual power—including Satan and his demons—are subject to him (see
today's verse).

But Christ's current activities aren't limited to a grand, universal scale;
he is also intimately involved in the life of every Christian. The risen, reigning Savior constantly has you on his mind! As our great "High Priest"
(Hebrews 4:14), Jesus is always "interceding for us" (Romans 8:34, NIV),
meaning that he stands before God as our sinless representative.

Jesus also makes his presence felt among believers. He is "among" Christians
who gather in his name (Matthew 18:20), and he actively works within his

worldwide church to sanctify (or make holy) all believers (1 Thessalonians 5:23).

And if that isn't enough, he is also preparing a heavenly home for us (John 14:2) beyond our wildest dreams and planning his future return to earth to destroy all evil and set up his eternal kingdom for us to enjoy.

Oh yeah, Jesus is busy right now. But every single thing he's doing is for our good and God's glory!

NOW WHAT?

Take a moment to prayerfully thank Jesus for interceding for you—allowing a sinner to approach a holy God.

DID YOU KNOW?

In ancient times, a king's right hand was a symbol of strength. That's why verses such as Exodus 15:6 say, "Your right hand, O LORD, is glorious in power. Your right hand, O LORD, smashes the enemy." Jesus' heavenly position at God's right hand shows his supreme authority.

We also boast in God through our Lord Jesus Christ, through whom we have now received reconciliation. ROMANS 5:11, NIV

The death and resurrection of Jesus Christ was the pivotal moment in history. When Jesus miraculously rose from the dead, it represented the glorious culmination of God's age-old rescue plan to save lost sinners like us.

After discussing Jesus' death, resurrection, and ascension to heaven for the last four weeks, we now turn our attention to salvation itself. For the next three weeks or so, we'll discuss the salvation that Jesus purchased for us through the cross and empty tomb: Why was this salvation necessary? What did it do? How does it affect us? We'll tackle some big words and tough concepts and try to make sense of it all.

First up: the concept of reconciliation.

WHAT'S IT MEAN?

The word *reconciliation* means restored harmony between two or more people or groups who were at odds with each other. The Bible says we all start life at odds with God. But it's not just a little tiff or a minor disagreement. We were actually God's "enemies" (Romans 5:10).

Maybe you're thinking, *Wait a minute. That sounds a little extreme. I've never felt like an enemy of God.*

This is where a proper perspective on sin is needed. Sin is worse than you think. The Bible says that sin is outright rebellion against God (1 John 3:4), sin completely corrupts us (Ephesians 4:22), and every human sins (Romans 3:23). That means we're all in a heap of trouble.

When Adam and Eve first disobeyed God in the Garden of Eden, sin entered the world and infected every corner of God's creation like a disease, including each human heart. Sin broke Adam and Eve's fellowship with God and forced them to leave God's perfect presence in Eden (Genesis 3:22-24), and it still separates us from our Creator today. Because we are guilty before a holy God and can do nothing to earn his forgiveness on our own, we needed someone else's help to reconcile us—or make us right—with our Creator. Without this intervention, we'd all be headed toward an eternity in hell.

That's where Jesus comes in. His death and resurrection satisfied God's wrath toward our sin. Jesus' sacrifice restores the broken harmony between God and sinners. He took what was separating both parties (sin) and paid for it in full.

Jesus is the Great Reconciler!

NOW WHAT?

Read Romans 5:6-11; 2 Corinthians 5:18-21; and Colossians 1:19-22 to understand more about reconciliation through Christ.

DID YOU KNOW?

Colossians 1:22 says Jesus' reconciliation allows Christians to approach God "holy and blameless as you stand before him without a single fault." Wow!

You were dead because of your sins and because your sinful nature was not yet cut away. Then God made you alive with Christ, for he forgave all our sins.   COLOSSIANS 2:13

Death row is a horrible place to be.

That's the place in prison where criminals who have committed capital offenses (serious crimes punishable by death) are kept, awaiting execution. In America, the death penalty is used only for the most horrible crimes, mostly murders. Most death-row prisoners often wait at least a decade before their execution, which is usually performed by lethal injection but can also be done by electrocution, lethal gas, hanging, or firing squad. Ghastly stuff.

By the end of 2012, there were 3,033 prisoners in thirty-five states facing the death penalty, according to US Department of Justice statistics. In 2013, thirty-nine of them were executed. Without an official pardon by the state governor or the US president or some other intervention, the rest of them will eventually be executed too.

But consider this: we all started out on a spiritual death row. Does that shock you? It shouldn't.

WHAT'S IT MEAN?

Maybe you're thinking, *But I haven't committed any of the "big sins." How could I be on a spiritual death row?*

Don't forget yesterday's devotion. Because of sin, we desperately need reconciliation with God. Sin is a spiritual death sentence (Romans 6:23).

In addition to today's verse, here's how the Bible describes our sinful condition:

- You were "far away from God" (Colossians 1:21).
- "You were his enemies, separated from him by your evil thoughts and actions" (Colossians 1:21).
- "You were living apart from Christ" (Ephesians 2:12).

- "You lived in this world without God and without hope" (Ephesians 2:12).
- "You were full of darkness" (Ephesians 5:8).
- "We were subject to God's anger" (Ephesians 2:3).
- "No one is seeking God" (Romans 3:11).
- "All have turned away; all have become useless" (Romans 3:12).

That's not a rosy outlook.

You see, sin is not a matter of "big" and "little" offenses; it's a matter of the heart. And every human heart is utterly corrupt and rebellious against God. We are guilty as charged.

But our story doesn't have to end on death row. In his great mercy and love, God sacrificed his own Son for us. On the cross, Jesus suffered the death penalty we deserved. Now, if we trust in Christ, God will forgive all our sins. *Every single one.*

Jesus pardons us from death row!

NOW WHAT?

Memorize today's verse. It's a great reminder of our pardon through Christ.

DID YOU KNOW?

In the early 1600s, you could receive the death penalty in Virginia for stealing grapes or killing chickens!

We know that our old sinful selves were crucified with Christ so that sin might lose its power in our lives. We are no longer slaves to sin. For when we died with Christ we were set free from the power of sin. ROMANS 6:6-7

Slavery is a terrible thing.

The United States has had a sad, shameful history of slavery, even from its beginning as a collection of European colonies. The first slaves arrived in 1619 when a Dutch ship carrying twenty Africans arrived at the British settlement in Jamestown, Virginia. With no rights of their own, slaves were treated cruelly and forced to work without pay. They were viewed as property—less than human.

Slave labor grew rapidly in America until the Civil War, when President Abraham Lincoln issued the Emancipation Proclamation in 1863, freeing slaves in Confederate states. The addition of the US Constitution's Thirteenth Amendment in 1865 officially abolished slavery in America.

The evil of slavery makes the following biblical truth all the more stunning: you were born as a "slave to sin."

WHAT'S IT MEAN?

A slave is someone who is controlled by someone (or something) else. Because you were born with a sinful nature, you were born under sin's control.

Think about it: as soon as children can walk and talk, they start throwing tantrums. They hit, scream, and yell, "No!" As we get older, our sins get worse. We intentionally hurt others and disobey our parents. We lie, cheat, and steal. This all comes naturally to us because our hearts are enslaved to sin.

Sin is a wicked master. It tempts but never fully satisfies. It makes great promises but delivers only problems and pain. It controls and eventually kills. Isaiah 42:7 says our sin makes us "captives [in] prison" and like "those who sit in dark dungeons."

But there's hope! God sent Jesus "to proclaim that captives will be released, that the blind will see, that the oppressed will be set free" (Luke 4:18). By living a sin-free life and dying in our place, Jesus broke the power of sin (see today's verse).

When you trust in Jesus, your sins are nailed to the cross (Galatians 5:24) and no longer condemn you. Yes, Christians still sin. But sin won't be your master. God's Spirit lives in you to help you say no to sin and yes to righteousness.

Jesus is our wonderful Emancipator!

NOW WHAT?

Read Romans 6, the Bible's great chapter about the freedom from sin we receive through Christ.

DID YOU KNOW?

Today, you can still see the original Emancipation Proclamation at the National Archives in Washington, DC.

JULY 27

In this is love, not that we have loved God but that he loved us and sent his Son to be the propitiation for our sins.

1 JOHN 4:10, ESV

Have you ever killed an animal?

This isn't about cutting open a worm in science class, stepping on a caterpillar and watching its insides ooze out, or even hunting in the woods. This is about lifting a large bull, sheep, or goat onto a bronze altar, plunging a knife into its heart, and watching as parts of its carcass are consumed by fire.

Just a wild guess here, but chances are you've never done that. It's certainly not for the faint of heart. But this was normal life for an ancient Israelite. It was all part of the sacrificial system—what Old Testament law required when someone committed a sin. You can read God's instructions for these offerings in Leviticus 1 and 4.

Before killing the animal, though, the individual would do something interesting: he'd lay his hands on the animal's head. This act symbolized the transfer of guilt and God's wrath from the sinner to the sacrifice.

The sacrificial animal became propitiation for the sinner.

WHAT'S IT MEAN?

The word *propitiation* means "a wrath-bearing sacrifice." And "wrath" is simply God's righteous anger toward sin. In other words, our sins deserve God's righteous anger and punishment. To avoid suffering this terrible fate, we need propitiation—a sacrifice that bears God's wrath in our place and turns it into a gift.

In the Old Testament, God mercifully provided Israel with a sacrificial system where animals would bear his wrath against the people's sins instead of the people bearing it themselves. But animal sacrifices were never the real answer for sins (Hebrews 10:4). They were simply a sign pointing ahead to the Ultimate Propitiator, Jesus Christ. On the cross, God's Son bore all of humanity's guilt, becoming a wrath-bearing sacrifice.

You see, Jesus wasn't just some nice, unselfish guy who thought his martyrdom might inspire some folks to be better people. Improving on the Old Testament sacrifices before him, Jesus became the perfect, once-for-all sacrifice we needed to avoid God's wrath. Jesus endured all of God's terrible wrath for our sins.

So let your local bull, sheep, or goat graze in peace. They aren't needed anymore. Because of his great love, Jesus provided propitiation for you!

NOW WHAT?

Memorize today's verse. It's a wonderful reminder of what Jesus did for you on the cross.

DID YOU KNOW?

There were five main types of offerings in the Old Testament—burnt, grain, peace, sin, and guilt offerings. Not all involved animals and not all were to propitiate sins (Leviticus 1–7).

God did not appoint us to suffer wrath but to receive salvation through our Lord Jesus Christ. 1 THESSALONIANS 5:9, NIV

Yesterday's devotion explained how Jesus is the propitiation, or the wrath-bearing sacrifice, for our sins. Christ died on the cross to save us from God's anger toward our rebellious hearts.

But this raises another question: What exactly is the wrath that Jesus saves us from? When God pours out his wrath, what happens?

Scripture is filled with stories of God's wrath against sin. And make no mistake: they should send a shudder down your spine. Here are a few examples:

- In Genesis 7, God wiped out the entire human race except for Noah and his family with a worldwide flood because of humanity's corruption.
- In Genesis 19, God completely incinerated two cities, Sodom and Gomorrah, with fire from heaven for their wickedness.
- In Numbers 16, God destroyed more than fifteen thousand rebellious Israelites by causing the earth to swallow them up, consuming some with fire and inflicting many others with a deadly plague.

There are many more stories like these. But this much is clear: the wrath of the Lord God Almighty is terrifying.

WHAT'S IT MEAN?

Although frightening, God's wrath is also often greatly misunderstood. When God punishes people for sin, he is never unfair or vicious. He does not delight in punishment or death but desires for everyone to repent (Ezekiel 18:32, NIV). However, because of his holiness and justice, he must punish wickedness.

When Scripture speaks of "the coming wrath" (1 Thessalonians 1:10, NIV), it's referring to a future, final judgment of humanity's sinful rebellion. One day,

God will punish unbelievers on earth with terrible judgments (Revelation 6; 8–9; 16), purify the universe with destruction and then renewal (2 Peter 3:10, 13), and condemn the wicked to a fiery eternity in hell, where they will be tormented and separated from God's love forever (Revelation 20:15). This horrible, but just, fate is what awaits the ungodly.

Here's the good news: no Christian will ever experience God's wrath—not even one little bit (see today's verse). That's because Jesus endured his Father's wrath for us on the cross. He took sin's punishment so we can enjoy heavenly blessings. This is the miracle of propitiation!

NOW WHAT?

Read the Scripture references above and on the previous page, especially those in Revelation, to learn more about God's wrath.

DID YOU KNOW?

Many people mistakenly think God was different—and more wrathful—in the Old Testament than in the New Testament. But that's not true. God does not change (Malachi 3:6). He has always hated sin and loved righteousness (Psalm 45:7, NIV). Plus, the New Testament specifically mentions God's wrath dozens of times.

JULY 29

Jesus suffered and died outside the city gates to make his people holy by means of his own blood. HEBREWS 13:12

Have you heard the term *scapegoat*?

These days, it refers to someone who takes the blame for others. But the word's origin dates back to at least the fifteenth century BC, when God provided the Book of the Law to ancient Israel so the people would know how to live and worship him properly.

In Leviticus 16, God gave Israel instructions for the Day of Atonement, the most holy date on the Jewish calendar. It was the only day of the year when the high priest was allowed to enter the Most Holy Place—the sacred, innermost room of the Tabernacle—and atone (make amends) for the sins of the people.

One of the high priest's duties was an interesting ceremony with two goats. After killing one goat as a sin offering, the high priest would lay his hands on the head of the other goat—the scapegoat—and confess all of Israel's sins over it. Then he'd send the scapegoat outside Israel's camp and into the wilderness.

There, the goat would likely die of starvation, be killed by a predator, or if he was a plucky little fellow, actually survive and settle down in a retirement community for exiled goats. Just joking on that last one.

WHAT'S IT MEAN?

Why did God command the Israelites to go through this unique scapegoat ritual? It vividly illustrated that, through an innocent sacrifice, God would mercifully forgive sins and banish them far away from his presence. Leviticus 16:22 says, "As the goat goes into the wilderness, it will carry all the people's sins upon itself into a desolate land." The scapegoat symbolically took the people's blame.

Of course, goats can't truly remove sins. The Old Testament scapegoat ritual was only a temporary solution and a foreshadowing (a sign of future things) of what Jesus would ultimately accomplish.

On the cross, Jesus became our perfect, once-and-for-all scapegoat! He took the blame of others as he hung outside Jerusalem's walls (see today's verse) and was temporarily banished from God's presence (Matthew 27:46).

The Old Testament Day of Atonement was a powerful reminder of God's mercy, love, and forgiveness. But the ultimate Day of Atonement, when Jesus became the true scapegoat for our sins, was far better!

NOW WHAT?

When we trust in Jesus, God doesn't just put our sins on a wilderness-bound goat. Read Psalm 103:12 to learn what he does with them.

DID YOU KNOW?

Observant Jews still celebrate the Day of Atonement. It's called Yom Kippur, and it occurs each September or October.

*God presented Christ as a sacrifice of atonement, through
the shedding of his blood—to be received by faith.*

ROMANS 3:25, NIV

Let's say you go over to your friend's house to hang out, and at some point
you notice that he or she owns the newest video game system and some of the
coolest games. Your friend also has a huge flat-screen TV and a sweet surround-
sound stereo system to play it on. Your jaw drops. It's gaming paradise.

You, on the other hand, play *Pac-Man* and *Donkey Kong* at home on a
small TV that your parents bought used in 1992. Envy sets in, and you begin
to covet (or want) your friend's possessions. Uh-oh. You just broke the tenth
commandment. Time to go slaughter the family sheep.

Well, that's what you would've been required to do if you lived in ancient
Israel. According to Leviticus 4, anyone who broke one of God's laws had to go
to the Tabernacle (or later, the Temple) to sacrifice a sin offering to the Lord.

Thankfully, that ritual doesn't apply to Christians today. (Phew!) But the
offering's purpose was clear: sin requires atonement.

WHAT'S IT MEAN?

To atone for something means to make amends for a wrong or to satisfy a
demand. Sin is the ultimate wrong. Unless taken care of, sin will bring spiritual
death and eternal separation from our Creator (Romans 6:23). Not good.

But making amends for sin isn't easy. In fact, it's downright impossible
for humans. There's nothing we can do on our own to get right with God
(Ephesians 2:8-9). We need atonement.

This is where something *amazing* comes into play! The God whom we
offended with our wicked rebellion is the same God who gave up his Son to
atone for our sins. As today's verse says, "God presented Christ as a sacrifice
of atonement." This was a completely voluntary act by a loving Heavenly
Father! But it was necessary for atonement.

For fallen humanity to be reconciled to a holy God, divine wrath had to be satisfied. Heavenly justice had to be met. A sacrifice had to be made. Blood had to be shed. A death had to take place.

Jesus took care of it all! This is what it means when we say Christ atoned for us. Where we failed to make amends for our own sins, Jesus came to the rescue!

NOW WHAT?

Want to learn more about Jesus' atonement? Read Hebrews 9.

DID YOU KNOW?

In the Old Testament system of atonement, the animals presented as sin offerings had to be males without any defects (Leviticus 1:3). This requirement pointed ahead to our sinless Savior!

*[God] canceled the record of the charges against us and took it away
by nailing it to the cross.*   COLOSSIANS 2:14

Mike Tyson was once the greatest boxer in the world.

Nicknamed "Iron Mike" for his devastating power, at age twenty, Tyson
catapulted to international fame and fortune in 1986 by becoming the youngest heavyweight champion in history. By the late 1980s, he was commanding
$30 million per fight, living an extravagant lifestyle, and buying mansions,
exotic vehicles, expensive jewelry, and even pet Siberian tigers. Once, he bought
a gold chain encrusted with 80 carats of diamonds, worth $173,706.

Over the course of his career, Tyson earned approximately $400 million.
That'll buy you a lot of Siberian tigers. Unfortunately, though, wild living
and poor financial choices caught up with him.

In 2003, Tyson filed for bankruptcy, claiming $23 million worth of debts.
Amazingly, even with all his earlier riches, he had come to a place where he
owed more than he earned. He faced a debt he could not pay.

Kind of like us.

WHAT'S IT MEAN?

No, the debt you owe has nothing to do with money. (At least, let's *hope* you
aren't $23 million in the hole.) The debt we're talking about is the account-
ability for sin that everyone faces before God.

Like racking up unpayable bills, all humans have piled up a massive debt
of sin. We have disobeyed our Creator countless times in thought, word,
and deed.

Worse yet, we can't reconcile this debt on our own. We are spiritually bankrupt. Broke. Penniless. Busted. As they say in the financial world, we are "in the
red" of debt. We need someone's help to "get in the black" of the profit column.

That's where the red of Jesus' precious blood comes in! When Jesus sacrificed himself, God nailed the power and guilt of our sins to the cross to die
along with his Son. Jesus paid sin's terrible price (death) for us.

Now, through faith in Christ, our incalculable debt of sin is erased. We owe nothing more to God for our transgressions. Every word of unkindness, act of disobedience, blatant lie, fit of anger—every single sin—is forgiven. Believers are debt free and rich in Christ!

(Just don't buy any Siberian tigers.)

NOW WHAT?

Take a few moments to thank God for canceling the record of charges—sin's debt—against you.

DID YOU KNOW?

Jesus told a parable describing God's forgiveness of the great debt of our sin in Matthew 18:21-35.

AUGUST 1

God made him who had no sin to be sin for us, so that in him we might become the righteousness of God.

2 CORINTHIANS 5:21, NIV

One day, you will drive a car.

The very thought of it probably sets you daydreaming . . . and gives your parents nightmares. But it will happen. Eventually, you will be mobile. Hopefully, you'll stay between the lines, brake for little old ladies, and avoid treating the highway like the Daytona 500. Life will be good.

Then one day, you'll realize that your beloved vehicle has become a money-sucking piece of junk. So you'll sell it, trade it in for another car, or banish it to the junkyard. If you decide to trade it in, the auto dealership will examine your car and pay you fair market value. Then you can use that money toward another car purchase.

Don't expect much for the trade-in, though. As you will learn in life, what you give is usually what you get. You can't trade trash for treasure.

But what if you could? Imagine if you could trade in a broken-down Toyota for a brand-new Lamborghini, or a rusty old Chevy for a shiny, red Ferrari.

That's silly talk. You can't trade your rubbish for riches and your garbage for glory, right?

Wrong. You can through Jesus Christ. It's called the doctrine of imputation.

WHAT'S IT MEAN?

No, no, no, not *amputation* . . . *imputation*! Don't worry. No limbs will be lopped off here.

The doctrine of imputation is both mysterious and magnificent. When we trust in Jesus, God actually imputes our sins to his Son and imputes Jesus' righteousness to us. In other words, God chooses to view our sins as belonging to Christ, while choosing to view Christ's righteousness as ours!

This does *not* mean that Jesus sinned or that God *thinks* Jesus sinned. No, as God's Son, Jesus is perfectly pure. Rather, imputation means that God *considers* our sins as belonging to Jesus.

This is the sweetheart deal of a lifetime! Jesus took our sinful garbage and punishment, and we get his glorious righteousness and salvation.

It sounds almost too good to be true! But it's not. Scripture passages like Galatians 3:13; 1 Peter 2:24; and today's verse clearly teach this remarkable truth. It's all God, and it's all grace.

Ferrari, schmerrari! Through imputation, Jesus gives us the greatest trade-in ever!

NOW WHAT?

Read and think about the three imputation verses mentioned above, and praise God for this glorious truth!

DID YOU KNOW?

Speaking of imputation, want to know how we got into this big sin mess in the first place? Adam's sin was imputed to all humans (Romans 5:18-19).

It is by grace you have been saved, through faith—and this is not from yourselves, it is the gift of God—not by works, so that no one can boast. EPHESIANS 2:8-9, NIV

The storm was raging, clobbering the merchant ship with violent wind and waves. Aboard the endangered vessel, a man who was running from God feared for his life. Death seemed unavoidable, and that was a terrifying concept since he was not right with his Creator.

No, the man was not Jonah. This story happened roughly 2,500 years after the biblical prophet disobeyed God's command to preach in Nineveh. The year was 1748 and the wayward soul was John Newton, a British sailor working aboard a slave-trading ship carrying human cargo from Brazil to Newfoundland.

By age twenty-two, Newton had already lived a terribly wicked lifestyle, but now, with his life in danger, he finally acknowledged the God he had been resisting.

"Lord," he cried, "have mercy on us!"

Newton changed that night. His heart that was hardened by sin and disbelief began to soften. He survived the storm, eventually left the inhumane slavery business, and became a pastor at age thirty-nine. For the next forty-three years, he preached and wrote hymns about the God he once denounced.

The first verse of his most famous song goes like this:

Amazing grace! How sweet the sound
That saved a wretch like me!

I once was lost, but now am found;
Was blind, but now I see.

Have you sung these words before? You probably have. *Amazing Grace*, one of the most famous Christian hymns ever, was written by a onetime slave trader and spiritual rebel.

WHAT'S IT MEAN?

God's grace is amazing indeed. It's remarkable, incredible, astonishing, awesome, overwhelming—pick a word! God's grace can turn a salty, rebellious seaman like John Newton into one of the eighteenth century's most powerful defenders of the faith. God's grace can radically change you, too.

Remember: salvation is completely and thoroughly an act of God's grace—his undeserved kindness toward us. As today's verse says, salvation is a free gift. It's "not from yourselves" and it's "not by works." There's nothing we can do to earn salvation. It starts and ends with God.

Why does God go to such great lengths to save spiritual rebels? It's all because of his great love for us. It's all because of amazing grace!

NOW WHAT?

Read a biography on the fascinating life and faith of John Newton, or ask your parents if you can watch the movie *Amazing Grace*.

DID YOU KNOW?

Newton was a strong influence on British Parliament member William Wilberforce, who helped abolish the nation's slave-trade industry in 1807.

AUGUST 3

God saved us and called us to live a holy life. He did this, not
because we deserved it, but because that was his plan from before
the beginning of time—to show us his grace through Christ Jesus.
2 TIMOTHY 1:9

On July 6, 1957, a fifteen-year-old lad watched in fascination as a band of older teenage boys played skiffle—a fusion of jazz, blues, and folk music popular in that era—during a summer party at St. Peter's Parish Church in Liverpool, England.

As the band, called the Quarry Men, left the stage following its musical set, the boy rushed over and demonstrated his promising guitar abilities to the older boys. He even showed them how to properly tune a guitar, a skill none of them possessed. The Quarry Men were impressed.

Pop-culture history changed forever that day. Two weeks later, John Lennon, the leader of the Quarry Men, invited Paul McCartney, the eager fifteen-year-old, to join his group. The Lennon-McCartney songwriting duo was born. Within four years, the two would bring on guitarist George Harrison and drummer Ringo Starr, change their band name to the Beatles, and eventually become arguably the greatest, most influential rock band in history.

The heart of the Beatles was always Lennon and McCartney. Paired together, the twosome wrote nearly two hundred original songs, and most of the Beatles' whopping twenty-seven number-one singles were Lennon-McCartney compositions. The band broke up in 1970, but by 2012, Beatles albums had sold more than six hundred million copies.

It's amazing what a great duo can achieve. But today's verses speak of a far greater pair than Lennon and McCartney. The two Beatles produced great music, but grace and faith save human souls.

WHAT'S IT MEAN?

As we learned yesterday, salvation is possible only by God's grace. But God, in his infinite wisdom, matched faith with grace to produce lasting change in sinful human hearts through Jesus.

Salvation isn't possible without both. It's a package deal. Unlike the way Lennon and McCartney equally contributed to the Beatles' success, though, we do not equally contribute with God for the final product. As Ephesians 2:8-9 says, our salvation is completely "a gift of God" and that "no one can boast."

Still, we play a part. God's grace changes our hearts to realize our need for a Savior (Jeremiah 24:7), and human faith expresses the trust God requires for salvation (Hebrews 11:6). God's initiative (grace) paired with our response (faith) produces beautiful, life-changing music in the human soul!

NOW WHAT?

For more on grace and faith, read Romans 3:20-26 and Titus 3:4-7.

DID YOU KNOW?

While John Lennon died in 1980, Paul McCartney was still making music and performing when this book was published.

AUGUST 4

God chose him as your ransom long before the world began, but now in these last days he has been revealed for your sake.

1 PETER 1:20

Shortly before 8:00 a.m. on December 7, 1941, everything seemed normal at Pearl Harbor, the United States Navy base near Honolulu, Hawaii. The American flag had been raised during the morning bugle call, the seamen had finished their breakfasts, and the base was stirring to life.

But everything was not normal. At that moment, hundreds of Japanese fighter planes were stealthily zooming toward Pearl Harbor. For the next two hours, bullets, bombs, and torpedoes rained down all over the base, causing massive destruction.

Nearly 2,500 Americans were killed, and another 1,000 were wounded in the attack. Eighteen US ships and almost three hundred airplanes were either damaged or destroyed.

The following day, America entered World War II, leading to four years of bloody, brutal fighting in Europe and the Pacific. And it all started because of a surprise attack.

As we study salvation, our attention turns to another momentous day in history: the day sin entered the world. But unlike America's experience with Pearl Harbor, sin's arrival was not a surprise attack on God. In fact, he knew it was coming and already had a plan in place when it arrived.

WHAT'S IT MEAN?

God has always existed. And at some point during the eons of time before he created the universe (a period we call "eternity past"), he settled on his great plan of salvation for sinful humanity.

Adam and Eve's original sin in the Garden of Eden did not catch God unaware. Being the omniscient (all-knowing) Creator and Ruler of the universe, he foresaw sin's arrival and initiated a marvelous solution: the sacrifice of his own Son, Jesus Christ.

As today's verse says, God appointed Jesus as our "ransom" (or payment for sins) "long before the world began." Likewise, Acts 2:23 mentions God's "prearranged plan [that] was carried out when Jesus was betrayed." And Ephesians 3:11 refers to God's "eternal plan" of salvation through Christ.

In the dark void of eternity past, God was thinking of you! He knew exactly when you'd be born and how your sinful heart would turn against him. And in great love, he offered his own Son so you could be saved. It was all part of God's eternal plan.

Amazing!

NOW WHAT?

Having learned about God's eternal plan of salvation, reread Genesis 1–3. Knowing that God had a plan to save people from their sins even before he made Adam and Eve puts a new, glorious perspective on Creation and the Fall.

DID YOU KNOW?

Today at Pearl Harbor, you can still see the top of the sunken battleship USS *Arizona* in the water and oil from the ship bubbling up to the surface.

Everyone who calls on the name of the LORD will be saved.
ACTS 2:21

Baseball is a humbling game.

One night, a player crushes two home runs. Then next, he's just as likely to strike out three times. The greatest hitters in the game typically have a career batting average slightly above .300. That means they're failing to get a hit more than six out of every ten trips to the plate. On the mound, the greatest starting pitchers win only about 60 percent of their games.

Baseball is a tough game, and nothing's certain in it. But Mariano Rivera was about as reliable as they come.

In a phenomenal career from 1995 to 2013, the New York Yankees' superstar closer was as clutch as they come. Over nineteen seasons, Rivera became Major League Baseball's all-time saves leader. He was the pitcher his team called on late in games to preserve close wins. Rivera saved 652 games in 732 chances, an amazing 89-percent success rate. He was even better in the playoffs, saving 42 postseason games in 45 attempts (93 percent).

When Rivera's name was called, he almost always saved the game. However, there is a much greater man who will always save—100 percent of the time—when called upon.

His name is Jesus.

WHAT'S IT MEAN?

Today's verse says it loud and clear: "Everyone who calls on the name of the Lord will be saved." It's one of the most beautiful promises in the Bible.

Salvation is a free gift from God for all people. It doesn't matter if you're male or female, short or tall, rich or poor. It doesn't matter if you're white, black, brown, red, or green with yellow polka dots! Jesus died to save you from your sins.

But salvation doesn't come to everyone. To receive God's forgiveness, you must call on the name of Jesus. What's that mean? Well, it's not simply singing a Christian song in church or yelling, "Help me, Jesus!" when you're getting attacked by a swarm of bees. To call on Jesus' name means to surrender yourself to him through faith. It's putting your trust in him as the only Savior who can remove the guilt of your sins before God.

Jesus will never turn away anyone who calls on him in this way. That's a save you can count on every single time.

NOW WHAT?

Today's verse originally comes from an Old Testament prophecy in Joel 2:32. Check it out!

DID YOU KNOW?

Interestingly, Rivera began his Hall of Fame career in 1995 by getting demoted to the bullpen as a relief pitcher because he was ineffective as a starting pitcher.

There is one God and one Mediator who can reconcile God and humanity—the man Christ Jesus. He gave his life to purchase freedom for everyone. 1 TIMOTHY 2:5-6

Like a red-hot furnace, God's holy anger smoldered against Israel.

Tired of waiting for Moses to return from meeting with God atop Mount Sinai, the Israelites asked Aaron, Moses' brother, to make gods for them to worship. So Aaron melted their jewelry and crafted the infamous golden calf. No sooner had God given Israel the Ten Commandments than the people broke his first two laws (Exodus 20:3-4).

Up on the mountain, God's anger blazed. "Let me alone," he said in Exodus 32:10 (ESV), "that my wrath may burn hot against them and I may consume them." Yikes! The people were in danger of receiving the righteous punishment they deserved.

Moses, though, bravely pleaded with God to spare Israel. He appealed for love and mercy to prevail. God listened and relented. Atta boy, Big Mo!

Moses was a good mediator. He spoke up for wayward Israel many times, saving the people from similar destruction in Numbers 14 and 16. But he was a flawed, sinful man who eventually died, just like all the Jewish high priests who eventually took his place (Hebrews 7:23). A better mediator was needed.

As today's verse says, the one true Mediator is Jesus.

WHAT'S IT MEAN?

Mediator is a legal term. It's an individual who acts as an intermediary, or a go-between, for two people who are at odds with each other. A mediator comes between the opposing parties and works toward a solution to reconcile them.

This is exactly what Jesus does for us! Like ancient Israel, we start life at odds with God because of our sins. But unlike most human legal cases, this divine conflict was not the result of offenses by both sides. God was not at fault in the least. We were completely wrong, and he was completely right.

Our sins deserve God's righteous wrath. But Jesus, the great Mediator, stepped in to make us right with God by enduring the punishment we deserved on the cross. The reconciliation we needed came at a great price: Jesus' blood.

But it worked! Jesus has mediated "the new covenant between God and people" (Hebrews 12:24). Now, through faith in Jesus' great sacrifice, we can be made right with God.

Case closed!

NOW WHAT?

Has your heart been stubbornly at odds with God? Ask for his forgiveness and help to obey.

DID YOU KNOW?

Moses was so angry at Israel's golden calf idolatry that he smashed the Ten Commandments and then burned the idol, ground it into powder, mixed it with water, and forced the Israelites to drink it (Exodus 32:19-20)!

AUGUST 7

My dear children, I am writing this to you so that you will not sin.
But if anyone does sin, we have an advocate who pleads our case
before the Father. He is Jesus Christ, the one who is truly righteous.

I JOHN 2:1

In the wee hours of the morning on June 3, 1961, someone broke into the Bay Harbor Pool Room in Panama City, Florida. As burglars go, this one wasn't too ambitious. The thief took some beer, wine, soda, and some coins from the old music jukebox—less than fifty bucks in value.

Shortly afterward, police arrested Clarence Earl Gideon and charged him with the crime. All things considered, it was a petty offense, barely worth a headline in the local newspaper.

But then a remarkable chain of events took place. Gideon was convicted and sentenced to five years in state prison after being refused a lawyer. Once behind bars, Gideon wrote a petition letter challenging his imprisonment, and the US Supreme Court took up the case. Two years later, in the landmark case *Gideon v. Wainwright*, the Supreme Court ruled that the Sixth Amendment of the US Constitution guarantees the right to counsel to every defendant in a serious criminal trial.

Gideon was provided a lawyer and received a new trial. This time, he was acquitted. For Gideon, having an advocate to plead his case made all the difference.

Christians have a great Advocate too. As today's verse says, he is Jesus Christ, the Righteous One.

WHAT'S IT MEAN?

Advocate is a legal term referring to someone who represents a defendant in a legal case, such as a lawyer. Without an advocate to defend their cause, it's much easier for people on trial to get into serious legal trouble.

Spiritually speaking, all humans begin life in serious trouble before God, the great Judge. We are all guilty of great rebellion against our Creator (Romans 3:10-23).

But Jesus is every Christian's great Advocate! As today's verse says, Christ "pleads our case before the Father." In other words, when a believer sins, Jesus approaches God's holy throne on the basis of his righteousness and secures God's forgiveness for us. This happens by God imputing, or crediting, Jesus' righteousness to us based on the Savior's acceptable sacrifice (see the August 1 devotion).

When Jesus becomes your Savior, he becomes your Advocate. And when you have an advocate like Jesus, you can't lose!

NOW WHAT?

For more descriptions of Jesus in legal terms, check out John 5:30; Romans 2:15-16; and 2 Timothy 4:1.

DID YOU KNOW?

The Sixth Amendment is part of the Bill of Rights, which James Madison wrote as an addition to the US Constitution in 1791.

AUGUST 8

Thank God! He gives us victory over sin and death through our Lord Jesus Christ. I CORINTHIANS 15:57

On January 9, 1969, quarterback Joe Namath stepped to a microphone at a social gathering in Miami. Super Bowl III, featuring Namath's New York Jets against the highly favored Baltimore Colts, was just three days away.

The Jets were huge underdogs. They had finished the regular season 11–3 in the American Football League, which was far less competitive at the time than the National Football League, where the Colts played. Baltimore, with the NFL's top-ranked defense that year, went 13–1 and destroyed Cleveland, 34–0, to reach the Super Bowl. They entered the game as overwhelming favorites.

As Namath prepared to speak that night, a Colts fan in the crowd shouted about how Baltimore was going to dominate New York. Without hesitating, Namath said, "I've got news for you. We're gonna win the game. I guarantee it." It has since become the most famous victory guarantee in the history of American sports.

Namath made good on his promise. In an MVP performance, he crisply dissected Baltimore's defense for 206 passing yards, directed an offense that racked up 337 total yards, and led the Jets to a stunning 16–7 win. After the game, Namath ran off the field, famously wagging his index finger in the air, letting everyone know who was number one.

While Namath accurately predicted a Super Bowl win, Christians are guaranteed a far greater victory. Salvation through Christ brings victory over humanity's greatest enemies: Satan, the world, sin, and death.

WHAT'S IT MEAN?

Being a winner feels great. Knowing you're going to win before it happens feels even better. This is the privilege of everyone who trusts in Jesus!

With his death and resurrection, Jesus defeated the devil (1 John 3:8) and purchased eternal victory for believers over sin and death (see today's verse) and the world (John 16:33). By living a perfect life, Jesus defeated the power of sin and the false promises that the world offers. By resurrecting from the grave, Jesus got the best of Satan and death. Best yet, he transfers all these victories to his followers!

In Christ, we don't have to follow the wicked ways of the world, we are no longer slaves to sin, and we don't have to fear death. We know that eternal life in heaven awaits us. Salvation through Jesus brings ultimate victory.

Guaranteed.

NOW WHAT?

The next time you watch your favorite sports team, remember the guaranteed victory Jesus brings!

DID YOU KNOW?

Joe Namath was voted into the Pro Football Hall of Fame in 1985 despite having thrown more career interceptions (220) than touchdowns (173).

Whether you eat or drink, or whatever you do, do it all for the glory of God. 1 CORINTHIANS 10:31

"What is the meaning of life?"

This question has puzzled humans since time began. Philosophers have pondered it, scientists have studied it, pastors have preached about it, authors have written books on it, and regular folks like you are left to consider all the opinions and figure out what's true.

Today, you'll find out the truth!

Many people say pleasure is the main goal in life. The phrase "Eat, drink, and be merry, for tomorrow we die" defines them. Some people live for money and material wealth. Others say gaining knowledge is life's chief end, or even trying to earn God's favor. Then there are those who don't believe life has any true meaning. These are just a small sampling of all the theories out there on the meaning of life.

So which of these options is true?

Actually, it's none of them.

WHAT'S IT MEAN?

Despite the various ideas throughout the centuries, the answer to "What is the meaning of life?" is no mystery. We have meaning in life because we are not random beings. The Creator of the universe made us in his image (Genesis 1:27). As such, we have a purpose, which God graciously reveals to us in his Word.

The Bible is very clear: God created us to worship and glorify him. This means he made us to bring him all the praise and honor he deserves. It's that simple.

Today's verse says it quite clearly: we are to glorify God in all we do. In Isaiah 43:7, God says he made us "for [his] glory."

Because God created us for this purpose, nothing else will truly satisfy us—not pleasure, money, knowledge, or anything else. Only in glorifying God will we find true happiness.

Sadly, though, many people don't understand this life-changing truth. As Romans 5:2 says, only faith in Christ brings us to a place of "undeserved privilege where we now stand, and we confidently and joyfully look forward to sharing God's glory."

Salvation through Jesus changes our outlook on life. When God saves us, he gives us a different, better perspective. He helps us focus more on him and less on ourselves. We begin to realize we are needy sinners who serve an awesome God, and we start living for his glory, not ours.

So strive to glorify God in everything. This is the true meaning of life!

NOW WHAT?

Memorize 1 Corinthians 10:31. It's a great verse to remember about glorifying God.

DID YOU KNOW?

Today's devotion is another example of God making "the wisdom of this world look foolish" (1 Corinthians 1:20).

AUGUST 10

You are all children of God through faith in Christ Jesus.
GALATIANS 3:26

You've heard of Babe Ruth, right?

The New York Yankees legend is thought by many to be the greatest baseball player ever. During his Hall of Fame career from 1914 to 1935, the Sultan of Swat hit .342, smashed 714 home runs (a record that stood for thirty-nine years), and won seven World Series.

But did you know Ruth was adopted?

Growing up in Baltimore, Ruth (whose full name was George Herman Ruth Jr.) was an unruly child whose neglectful parents sent him to St. Mary's Industrial School for Boys, a Catholic reform school and orphanage, when he was seven years old. The school assumed official custody of Ruth, who learned to play baseball there. When Ruth was eighteen, Jack Dunn, the owner of the Baltimore Orioles (then a minor league team), legally adopted him so the underage player could legitimately sign with the team.

The rest, as they say, is history.

WHAT'S IT MEAN?

Adoption is when someone who is not a child's biological parent takes legal custody of that child. It's a wonderful, loving act that often helps children who are trapped in difficult situations receive the care they need.

Here's an awesome truth: when we trust in Jesus, God adopts us as *his* children! Maybe you're thinking, *Wait a minute. God created us. Weren't we always his children?*

Actually, we were the opposite. Because of our sin, we start life as God's enemies (Romans 5:10). Without Jesus, we are "children of wrath" (Ephesians 2:3, ESV)—spiritual orphans cut off from God's blessings and in danger of eternal separation from him.

But God loves us so much that he sacrificed his own Son to gain new sons and daughters. Ephesians 1:5 says, "God decided in advance to adopt us into his own family by bringing us to himself through Jesus Christ. This is what he wanted to do, and it gave him great pleasure."

Whether you come from a strong family or a broken home, you have a heavenly Father who loves you, wants to adopt you as his child through faith in Jesus, and showers you with untold spiritual blessings, both in this life and in the one to come.

Adoption by God sounds like a home run!

NOW WHAT?

Lots of great charities provide care for orphans worldwide. Ask your parents if your family can start supporting one of these organizations.

DID YOU KNOW?

Besides Babe Ruth, other famous adoptees include former US president Bill Clinton, country singer Faith Hill, actor Jamie Foxx, and San Francisco 49ers quarterback Colin Kaepernick. Even Moses was adopted (by Pharaoh's daughter)!

AUGUST 11

Since we are his children, we are his heirs. In fact, together with Christ we are heirs of God's glory. ROMANS 8:17

Bill Gates is one rich dude.

At the start of 2015, Gates, the cofounder of computer software giant Microsoft, was the wealthiest man in the world. His estimated net worth, according to *Forbes*, was hovering around $80 billion. Yes, you read that correctly. That's "eighty" with nine zeroes behind it. That's a lot of dough.

Imagine what life must be like for Gates's three children, Rory, Jennifer, and Phoebe. They probably don't have to beg their dad for the latest video game system or a new pair of jeans.

Gates has said that after he dies, he wants his children to live comfortably but not receive an inheritance worth billions. Still, when your dad's net worth exceeds the entire economy of many small nations, you can probably expect a pretty sweet amount.

The Bible speaks of an inheritance that is worth far more than $80 billion— or all the money in the world, for that matter. As today's verse says, those saved by Christ "are heirs of God's glory."

WHAT'S IT MEAN?

When God adopts us as spiritually reborn sons and daughters through faith in Jesus (see yesterday's devotion), he also makes us "heirs" of his glory. If "God's glory" doesn't sound as exciting of an inheritance to you as, say, $80 billion, then—to put it bluntly—your heart needs some work. A better understanding of biblical "inheritance" will help too.

In the Old Testament, God promised the Israelites an inheritance as they came out of Egypt—the Promised Land of Canaan, where his people would have a lasting home in his presence (Genesis 15:18). It's why he created people: to personally fellowship with them and be worshiped by them.

Sin ruined that intimate fellowship. But one day, God will completely restore that relationship. He will fully reveal his glory and dwell in perfect fellowship with all believers for eternity (Revelation 21:3). In heaven, sin, suffering, and death will be replaced with joy, fulfillment, and peace. This is our inheritance through Jesus!

It's hard to describe with human words how great this heavenly inheritance will be. Ephesians 3:8 calls it "endless treasures," and 1 Peter 1:4 calls it a "priceless inheritance . . . that is kept in heaven for you, pure and undefiled, beyond the reach of change and decay."

Not even $80 billion can buy that.

NOW WHAT?

Read Revelation 21:1–22:5 for a small glimpse of every Christian's future inheritance.

DID YOU KNOW?

Before becoming the world's richest man, Bill Gates was a Harvard University dropout.

AUGUST 12

What I received I passed on to you as of first importance: that Christ died for our sins according to the Scriptures.

1 CORINTHIANS 15:3, NIV

"We're number one! We're number one!"

Every sports fan hopes to chant this phrase. It means that your team is ranked at the top, better than all competitors.

Virtually every sport has a ranking system. Rankings are a subjective way to determine the best player or team in a given sport. A number-one ranking is a nice honor, although in most sports it doesn't come with any tangible benefits.

For instance, from June 12, 2005, to October 30, 2010, superstar golfer Tiger Woods set a PGA Tour record for the most consecutive weeks at number one in the Official World Golf Ranking (281). He also holds the record for the most total weeks ranked at the top (683). But being golf's top-ranked athlete didn't get Woods a new car, a trip to Disney World, or even a free burger at McDonald's. All he got was a nice title behind his name: *Tiger Woods, world's best golfer.*

When it comes to Christianity, the most important thing—the number one ranking, so to speak—isn't church attendance, singing in a choir, being kind to others, or even memorizing Scripture. The most important thing in the Christian faith is the gospel.

Without the gospel, there is no Christian faith.

WHAT'S IT MEAN?

As we discuss salvation, it's critical to understand the gospel.

The word *gospel* simply means "good news." The gospel is the wonderful message of salvation that is available to us exclusively through Jesus Christ. The apostle Paul defined the gospel beautifully in 1 Corinthians 15:1-8, and he made sure his readers (including us) knew how important the gospel is by calling it a message of "first importance" (NIV).

447

You can't be a Christian without believing the gospel. You can't please God without accepting the truth of the gospel. You can't spend eternity in heaven without building your life on the foundation of the gospel's message.

The entire Christian faith rests on the good news that Jesus died for our sins and rose from the dead so that we could be saved.

The gospel is indeed of "first importance"!

NOW WHAT?

Read 1 Corinthians 15:1-8 to see Paul's description of the gospel.

DID YOU KNOW?

The earliest mention of "the gospel" in the Bible comes from Jesus in Mark 8:35. Check it out!

I am not ashamed of the gospel, because it is the power of God that brings salvation to everyone who believes. ROMANS 1:16, NIV

"Hahahahahahahahaha!"

Laughter is a sound everyone wants to hear when they tell a joke but no one wants to hear when they're the object of the amusement.

But here's a little secret: if you are a Christian, you will almost certainly be laughed at during your life.

No one knew this better than the apostle Paul. If anyone suffered verbal—and physical—abuse for believing the gospel of Jesus Christ, it was Paul. This amazing first-century believer was hunted by Syrians (2 Corinthians 11:32), dismissed by Greeks (Acts 17:32), insulted by Ephesians (Acts 19:23-41), hated by Jews (Acts 21:27-36), mocked by governors (Acts 26:24), and imprisoned by Romans (Acts 28:16). The man had a tough life.

To stop the hostility, all Paul had to do was renounce the gospel—or at least stop talking about it. But for Paul, that wasn't even an option. After God saved him, Paul never stopped proclaiming the good news of salvation through Jesus. No matter how much opposition he faced, Paul could proclaim—like he wrote in today's verse—that he was not ashamed at all of the gospel.

It's an attitude every Christian should imitate.

WHAT'S IT MEAN?

If you are a Christian, along with countless spiritual blessings you're also guaranteed to experience persecution (2 Timothy 3:12).

At some point, every Christian will be mocked. Some people will laugh at you, belittle you, or exclude you for your faith. Others will wonder how you can possibly believe in a God you can't see, or question why you follow a book that's thousands of years old.

But never be ashamed of the good news that Jesus saves. The gospel that godless people ridicule is the same message that offers eternal life to your soul.

Being ashamed of Jesus as a Christian makes as much sense as someone trying to avoid being seen with the firefighter who rescued him or her from a burning building. Those who are unwilling to side with Jesus will suffer disastrous consequences. As Jesus himself said in Matthew 10:33, "Everyone who denies me here on earth, I will also deny before my Father in heaven."

Never be ashamed of the gospel that speaks of God's power to save! Never be ashamed of the Savior who sacrificed his life for yours!

NOW WHAT?

When people make fun of your faith, pray for them (Matthew 5:44).

DID YOU KNOW?

In 2 Corinthians 11:23-33, Paul details the extreme persecution he faced because of the gospel.

AUGUST 14

We must listen very carefully to the truth we have heard, or we may drift away from it. HEBREWS 2:1

Think for a moment about your last trip to the beach.

If you spent any amount of time floating in the ocean—whether on a boogie board, surfboard, or raft—you know how easy it is to drift from your family's location on the beach. When you're in the water, if you're not careful, the ocean tide will carry you far down the shoreline to places that don't look familiar to you. You have to work hard—constantly paddling against the ocean's unseen currents—to stay in the same spot where you entered the water.

The Christian life is kind of like that too. In this world, there's no shortage of temptations that tug at us like deceptive ocean tides, trying to pull us away from the place God wants us to be.

As we study salvation, it's important to remember the warning of today's verse: we must actively fight against drifting away from the truth of the gospel.

WHAT'S IT MEAN?

No beachgoer ever *means* to float down the coastline and lose his or her way. Similarly, a Christian never means to drift away from the gospel. But it can happen gradually over time if you're not careful.

This fallen world presents all kinds of temptations, enticements, and lies to pull believers away from God's truth. Satan, the "father of lies" (John 8:44), wants nothing more than to distort your understanding of the gospel. He loves leading people down dead-end alleys of false religions or misperceptions about Jesus. And the wicked world around you, generally speaking, wants nothing to do with God's Word or the reality that it is hell bound apart from Christ. These are powerful, persuasive forces we must resist.

But fear not! God has given us everything we need to stand firm against the tide of evil. His Spirit convicts our hearts of right and wrong (John 16:8), and his Word helps all believers to be "thoroughly equipped for every good work" (2 Timothy 3:17, NIV). Meeting together often with other Christians—at church and elsewhere—is also important (Hebrews 10:24-25).

As yesterday's verse proclaims, the gospel is "the power of God that brings salvation to everyone who believes" (Romans 1:16, NIV). Nothing else can make that claim. So stay true to the gospel and remain drift free!

NOW WHAT?

Reading the Bible daily and memorizing key passages often will help you avoid spiritual drifting.

DID YOU KNOW?

Demas, a former coworker of the apostle Paul, is an unfortunate example of someone who drifted from the gospel. Check out Demas's life before (Philemon 1:24) and after (2 Timothy 4:10) he drifted.

He brought [Paul and Silas] out and asked, "Sirs, what must I do to be saved?" ACTS 16:30

The Bible is truly an amazing book.

Holy Scripture vividly describes God's plan of salvation for sinful humanity through his Son, Jesus Christ. It's the only God-inspired book that answers the all-important question in today's verse: "What must I do to be saved?"

But the Bible is not written like an instructional manual for your computer, TV, or video-game system. There's no book or chapter featuring a five-step process entitled "How to Be Saved!" as if salvation were like installing a ceiling fan or changing a flat tire.

God doesn't work like that. He is a loving, personal God who deeply cares about humans. So his Word—all sixty-six books spanning thousands of years of history—explains his salvation plan through the lens of humanity, from the Creation account in Genesis 1 to the apostle John's futuristic visions in Revelation.

Since you probably can't speed-read the entire Bible in the next 5 to 10 minutes, here's a chronological summary of the salvation process.

WHAT'S IT MEAN?

1. **Election**—In his divine wisdom and mercy, God chose in eternity past whom he would save (Ephesians 1:3-5).

2. **The gospel call**—God causes the good news of forgiveness of sins through Jesus to be proclaimed worldwide (Matthew 24:14).

3. **Regeneration**—God's Spirit changes a person's dead, sinful heart to receive the gospel call (Titus 3:5).

4. **Conversion**—A spiritually regenerated person responds to the gospel call with repentance and faith, believing in Jesus' finished work on the cross for salvation (Mark 1:15).

5. **Justification**—God officially declares the converted believer completely forgiven and righteous before him (Romans 5:1).

6. **Adoption**—God welcomes the new believer into his heavenly family, giving the believer the full rights and blessings of a child and heir (Ephesians 1:5).

7. **Sanctification**—Through God's Spirit, the believer gradually becomes more like Jesus throughout the rest of his or her life (1 Thessalonians 5:23).

8. **Perseverance**—A true believer can never lose salvation but will always remain God's child (John 10:28).

9. **Death**—A believer's physical body will eventually perish, bringing that person's soul immediately into God's presence (2 Corinthians 5:8).

10. **Glorification**—The believers will one day inherit a new, perfect resurrection body and enjoy eternity with the Savior in heaven (1 Corinthians 15:53).[1]

What a glorious plan of salvation!

NOW WHAT?

Read the ten Scripture passages in the list above to see how God's Word describes each step of the salvation process.

DID YOU KNOW?

Today's verse records the words of a Philippian jailer to Paul and Silas.

---

[1] This list was adapted from theologian Wayne Grudem's book *Bible Doctrine* (Zondervan, 1999).

After doing all those things, I will pour out my Spirit upon all people.
JOEL 2:28

Imagine this: you're sitting in a room with other people when all of a sudden, your best friend's hair looks like it catches on fire. Then he starts speaking in a foreign language that he didn't know before. You look around the room, and the same thing is happening to everyone else. *They're all crazy!* you think . . . until it happens to you, too!

This is what took place on the Day of Pentecost, one of the most remarkable days in history!

About ten days after Jesus' ascension, the disciples and many other believers were gathered in a room in Jerusalem. They were observing Pentecost, also known as the Festival of the Harvest (Exodus 23:16), an annual Jewish festival celebrating God's provision, while also obeying Jesus' earlier command to "stay here in the city until the Holy Spirit comes and fills you with power from heaven" (Luke 24:49).

Acts 2:2-4 describes what happened next:

> *Suddenly, there was a sound from heaven like the roaring of a mighty windstorm, and it filled the house where they were sitting. Then, what looked like flames or tongues of fire appeared and settled on each of them. And everyone present was filled with the Holy Spirit and began speaking in other languages, as the Holy Spirit gave them this ability.*

Incredible! Jesus had poured out his Spirit on all his followers.

WHAT'S IT MEAN?

The Day of Pentecost was a dazzling display of God's presence and power. It fulfilled Jesus' promise to send the Spirit to believers (Luke 24:49; John 14:16-17), as well as a much older prophecy from the book of Joel (see today's verse).

In Old Testament times, God gave the Spirit to his saints for specific, temporary purposes (for example, Gideon in Judges 6:34, Samson in Judges 14:19, and David in 1 Samuel 16:13). But a better day was coming. Starting with Pentecost and continuing today, God graciously gives his Spirit to all believers for life.

This is fantastic news! In fact, the Spirit's presence in Christians' lives is so great, Jesus said it was better that he departed to make way for the Spirit (John 16:7)!

First, God's Spirit works in our hearts to bring about saving faith (John 6:63). Once that happens, he dwells in us for life. With the Spirit living inside us, we become God's living, breathing temple of worship (1 Corinthians 3:16-17).

That's enough to set your hair on fire!

NOW WHAT?

Want to know more about the Holy Spirit's work? Check out the next page!

DID YOU KNOW?

The Spirit-empowered phenomenon of Christians talking in different languages is called "speaking in tongues."

When you believed in Christ, he identified you as his own by
giving you the Holy Spirit, whom he promised long ago.
EPHESIANS 1:13

The wild, wonderful Day of Pentecost deserves a recap:

One day roughly two thousand years ago, the disciples and other new believers were gathered together in Jerusalem. Suddenly, a great wind rushed through the room, and everyone began speaking in foreign languages they didn't know before. Meanwhile, flames of fire appeared above people's heads. It was the day when Jesus poured out the Holy Spirit on the first Christians!

Sounds pretty wild, huh? But it's completely true because it's in God's Word (Acts 2:1-13).

It's crucial that we believe the Holy Spirit exists and understand what he does, because of his importance in the lives of all believers. Still, understanding the Holy Spirit can be difficult. The idea of an invisible being who is equal in the Godhead to the Father and Son and lives inside all Christians is not an easy concept for our limited human minds to grasp.

So let's talk more about the Holy Spirit.

WHAT'S IT MEAN?

The full scope of the Holy Spirit and all his characteristics can't be adequately described in one day's devotion. He's far too great for that. But here's a look at some of his major roles.

The Holy Spirit:

- inspired all the words of Scripture (2 Peter 1:20-21)
- regenerates our sinful hearts to believe the gospel (John 3:6)
- lives inside all Christians (1 Corinthians 6:19)
- confirms our salvation (see today's verse)
- guarantees all God's promises to us (2 Corinthians 1:22)
- reminds us of Scripture (John 14:26)

- convicts us of sin (John 16:8)
- sanctifies us—or makes us more like Jesus (2 Thessalonians 2:13, NIV)
- gives us different spiritual gifts to serve God (1 Corinthians 12:4-11)

Are you beginning to comprehend the greatness and importance of the Holy Spirit? Faith in Jesus and growth in godliness are simply not possible without him. Knowing that, our hearts should overflow with gladness that God, in his perfect plan of salvation, brought Jesus back to heaven after he completed his work of redemption on earth and sent the Spirit to live inside all believers.

The Lord God Almighty—the Creator of heaven and earth—wants to change our lives and live in our hearts through his Spirit. Amazing!

NOW WHAT?

Look up all the Scripture references above to increase your understanding of the Holy Spirit and his glorious work.

DID YOU KNOW?

Among all the other things he does, the Holy Spirit speaks to God on our behalf when we don't know what to pray (Romans 8:26).

Peter's words pierced their hearts, and they said to him and to the other apostles, "Brothers, what should we do?" ACTS 2:37

Jerusalem was buzzing with activity on the Day of Pentecost.

Thousands of devout Jews had traveled there from all over the Roman Empire to celebrate the annual Festival of the Harvest. Suddenly, dozens of Jesus' followers who had just experienced an outpouring of the Holy Spirit rushed into the streets, loudly praising God in foreign languages!

The crowd was shocked. These early Christians were from Galilee, a district of Israel just north of Jerusalem, yet they were fluently speaking the languages of Parthia, Mesopotamia, Asia, and many other places. "How can this be?" the crowd wondered (Acts 2:7).

With newfound boldness, the apostle Peter—the same guy who had denied Jesus several weeks earlier—raised his voice above all the commotion and preached a powerful sermon. Using various Old Testament passages, Peter proved that Jesus—the man whom the people had killed less than two months earlier—was actually the Messiah. As today's verse says, "Peter's words pierced their hearts."

"Brothers, what should we do?" they asked. Peter replied, "Each of you must repent of your sins and turn to God, and be baptized in the name of Jesus Christ for the forgiveness of your sins" (Acts 2:38).

The Holy Spirit's conviction was beginning to change lives.

WHAT'S IT MEAN?

If you get angry and speak unkindly to a friend, which response best describes true conviction?

1. "No way am I talking to her again!"
2. "I probably shouldn't have said that, but he had it coming."
3. "That was wrong of me. I need to go apologize."

If you guessed number 3, you're correct!

Spiritual conviction is when someone realizes that he or she is a sinner who needs to be made right with God. Conviction comes to unbelievers who realize they need a Savior. Conviction also comes to believers who realize they've sinned and need to repent. Both are possible only through the Holy Spirit, whose role is to "convict the world of its sin, and of God's righteousness, and of the coming judgment" (John 16:8).

Is a voice inside you calling you to trust in Jesus? If you're already a Christian, is that inner voice convicting you of a sin? Don't ignore that voice! It's God's Spirit speaking to you.

Respond to the Spirit's conviction with repentance and faith, just like Peter's listeners did during Pentecost!

NOW WHAT?

Pray that God would soften your heart to always feel the Spirit's conviction when you disobey God.

DID YOU KNOW?

Thanks to Peter's sermon and the Spirit's conviction, about three thousand people became Christians that day (Acts 2:41)!

AUGUST 19

Christ is also the head of the church, which is his body.
COLOSSIANS 1:18

Peter was on fire!

Not literally, of course. Good thing, too, since there were no fire stations in ancient Israel. No, Peter was just preaching a humdinger of a sermon!

The apostle who once denied Jesus was now boldly proclaiming the gospel to thousands in Jerusalem on the Day of Pentecost. He told people, "Repent of your sins and turn to God, and be baptized in the name of Jesus Christ for the forgiveness of your sins" (Acts 2:38).

It was a historic moment. About three thousand people put their faith in Jesus and became Christians that day—a staggering number, considering there had been only about 120 believers before that (Acts 1:15). It was the day the church started.

WHAT'S IT MEAN?

What is "the church"?

Sounds like a simple question, doesn't it? But it trips up many people. This question is so important, we're going to spend the next five days discussing what the church is, how it should work, and why it's essential in the Christian life.

Christians today often refer to "church" and "*the* church." The terms are nearly identical—only distinguished by the article *the* in the second reference—but there's a big difference between the two.

"Church" is a physical building people go to on Sundays to worship God through prayer, singing, and listening to the preaching of Scripture. Going to church is very important.

But when the Bible mentions "*the* church," it's not referring to a building or a religious denomination (such as Baptist, Presbyterian, or Lutheran). The church, as Scripture defines it, is the worldwide community of true believers in Jesus Christ.

461

The Bible also calls this community "the body of Christ" (1 Corinthians 12:27, NIV). The head of this body, as today's verse says, is Jesus. Just like a human body does what the head tells it to do, the worldwide body of Christians (the church) is supposed to obey Christ. That means loving others, living righteously, proclaiming the gospel, and worshiping Jesus.

You see, the church should be all about Jesus. Christians are *the church*— a group of people redeemed by the blood of Jesus—and we gather together *at church* each week to worship our great Redeemer.

Kind of puts a new perspective on Sunday mornings, doesn't it?

NOW WHAT?

Keep this worldwide "body of Christ" perspective in mind the next time you attend worship services at your church.

DID YOU KNOW?

The Bible's first reference to "church" is found in Matthew 16:18, when Jesus prophesies that he will use Peter to build "my church."

AUGUST 20

This mystery is that through the gospel the Gentiles are heirs together with Israel, members together of one body, and sharers together in the promise in Christ Jesus. EPHESIANS 3:6, NIV

Arthur Conan Doyle pushed himself away from his desk and breathed a sigh of relief. It was the fall of 1886, and the twenty-seven-year-old Scottish doctor and part-time author had just finished his first full-length novel.

Little did Doyle know it at the time, but the main character in his story *A Study in Scarlet* would become the most famous crime-solving detective in history. His name was Sherlock Holmes.

With his deerstalker hat, curved pipe, and analytical mind, Sherlock Holmes has been captivating the public's imagination through books, stage plays, radio programs, TV shows, big-budget Hollywood movies, and even video games for well over a century. People love a good mystery.

Today's devotion is about a mystery too. But it doesn't involve any brainy detectives using magnifying glasses to hunt for clues. This biblical mystery is all about the church!

WHAT'S IT MEAN?

When sin entered the world in Genesis 3, God initiated his great salvation plan to redeem sinners through his Son, Jesus Christ. First, God made Abraham into the "great nation" of Israel (Genesis 12:2), which eventually produced the Messiah. But throughout the Old Testament, God hinted at even greater things to come. In Isaiah 49:6, for instance, he promised that Jesus, the Messiah, would "bring my salvation to the ends of the earth," not just to Israel.

God accomplished this through the church! After Peter's Pentecost sermon, God started the church and providentially expanded the gospel's reach beyond Israel to the rest of the world, through the apostles and other early Christians (Acts 22:21; 28:28; and Romans 11:11).

The New Testament writers described all these events as a "mystery" (today's verse) because, quite frankly, no one saw it coming! Not even Jesus' own disciples foresaw God creating a universal body of believers through Christ.

What does this mean for you today? If you're a Christian, it means you are the beneficiary (recipient) of God's amazing plan that was set in motion eons ago, all for your salvation. As today's verse says, the gospel wonderfully unites people of all ethnic backgrounds as "members together of one body, and sharers together in the promise in Christ Jesus."

Mystery solved . . . case closed!

NOW WHAT?

To further understand this "mystery" of Israel, the gospel, and the church, check out Romans 9–11 and Ephesians 2:11–3:6.

DID YOU KNOW?

Arthur Conan Doyle based much of the Sherlock Holmes character on Dr. Joseph Bell, one of his medical professors at the University of Edinburgh in Scotland.

AUGUST 21

Let us think of ways to motivate one another to acts of love and good works. And let us not neglect our meeting together, as some people do, but encourage one another, especially now that the day of his return is drawing near. HEBREWS 10:24-25

Each Sunday, millions of Christians all over the world gather together in various locations to attend church services. They pray, sing worship songs, listen to the preaching of God's Word, baptize new believers, take the Lord's Supper together, and more.

But why?

Over the last few days, we've learned what the church is. It's the world-wide community of people who follow Jesus Christ—called Christians. But why do Christians go to church every Sunday? Is it just out of tradition? Is it to earn God's favor? Is it just because there's nothing better to do on Sunday mornings before NFL games start?

No, no, and no! The answer is something completely different.

WHAT'S IT MEAN?

Perhaps you attend church now because your parents take you. That's good! They are obeying Scripture's command to raise you in godliness (Proverbs 22:6). And there's no better place to be than in God's house (Psalm 84:10).

But as you get older and make your own decisions, consider these reasons why, if you're a Christian, you should go to church:

- **To obey Scripture**—As today's Bible passage says, Christians should meet regularly to "motivate one another to acts of love and good works" as we wait for Jesus to return.
- **To worship God**—Gathering together with other believers is one way (but certainly not the only way) to fulfill our calling to worship our Creator (Psalm 122:1-4).

- **To become more like Jesus**—Joining other Christians in prayer, worship, fellowship, and listening to God's Word helps us "mature in the Lord" (Ephesians 4:13).
- **To avoid false teaching**—There are lots of bogus ideas out there about God, Jesus, and Scripture. Going to a strong, biblically centered church helps Christians avoid falling prey to believing heresy (Ephesians 4:14).
- **To evangelize the world**—Christians are to represent Jesus' love to others in word and deed (Matthew 28:19-20). Gospel-centered churches offer programs to help believers do this.

Going to church to worship our great Savior is not only a necessity for every Christian, but also a huge privilege and blessing!

NOW WHAT?

Ask your parents how you can get more involved at church to grow in your faith and encourage others.

DID YOU KNOW?

The tradition of attending church on Sundays dates back to the book of Acts, when Christians began gathering together on Sundays, which they called "the Lord's day" (Revelation 1:10), because that's when Jesus rose from the dead.

AUGUST 22

This is the church of the living God, which is the pillar and foundation of the truth. 1 TIMOTHY 3:15

Throughout the history of warfare, the biggest, most well-equipped army has often won. But in ancient times, the survival of a kingdom often hinged on the presence and effectiveness of massive, motionless structures. If your chief cities weren't fortified with walls, towers, and other defensive measures, your empire was toast.

Eventually, militaries learned that if you couldn't scale a wall or dig under it, perhaps you could break through it. So they started using battering rams, catapults, siege towers, and other large, wall-busting devices. The Romans, for example, became experts at siege warfare as they expanded their vast empire during New Testament times.

As wall-busting tactics and weaponry advanced, so did wall design. Ancient architects constantly searched for new ways to strengthen city ramparts. It was an endless, high-stakes game of cat-and-mouse between offenses and defenses.

It was against this backdrop that the apostle Paul wrote today's verse.

WHAT'S IT MEAN?

Paul called the church "the pillar and foundation of the truth." In architecture, pillars and foundations are the skeletal system of a structure.

The English Standard Version translation of this verse is slightly different, calling the church "a pillar and buttress of the truth." A buttress is a sturdy stone structure that provides additional support and strength to a wall.

Either way, Paul's image is clear: like an impenetrable fortress wall, the church is meant to defend God's truth. That truth is the gospel, the good news that salvation from sins comes through Jesus alone.

Ever since the early church began and the gospel started to spread throughout the world, the church has been under attack. False teachings started assaulting the church like a band of plundering invaders. Some people questioned Jesus' deity. Some claimed that salvation is not by faith alone, contrary to Scripture. And there were many other false claims.

The same is true today. False religions abound. Some "preach a different Jesus" (2 Corinthians 11:4) than the biblical gospel. Others preach no Jesus at all.

But Scripture calls the church to stand strong. Christians must defend the gospel and protect it from enemy attacks. The threat against the truth is real. But as Jesus promised in Matthew 16:18, God's church will prevail!

NOW WHAT?

It's all-hands-on-deck in the fight to defend the gospel. Pray and ask your parents about how you can be an individual "pillar and foundation of the truth."

DID YOU KNOW?

The Romans employed siege warfare to capture the city of Jerusalem in AD 70, which resulted in the destruction of the sacred Jewish Temple.

AUGUST 23

*Together, we are his house, built on the foundation of the apostles
and the prophets. And the cornerstone is Christ Jesus himself.*

EPHESIANS 2:20

The early church was growing like gangbusters.

After the apostle Peter's history-making sermon on the Day of Pentecost, the small group of early Christians—originally about 120 people—exploded to more than 3,000. Each day afterward, more people were being saved and joining the church (Acts 2:47). It was a remarkable time!

But how did these new Christians grow in their faith? At that time (somewhere between AD 30 and 33), the New Testament didn't exist. The first New Testament book (probably the letter of James) wouldn't appear for more than ten years. No written accounts of Jesus' time on earth existed yet. How did these young believers learn the truth about their Savior?

The first part of Acts 2:42 has the answer: "*All the believers devoted themselves to the apostles' teaching*, and to fellowship, and to sharing in meals (including the Lord's Supper), and to prayer" (emphasis added).

Note the italicized phrase above. As we discuss the church's beginning, it's important to understand this verse. In fact, this truth laid the foundation for Christianity and still benefits us today!

WHAT'S IT MEAN?

The apostles' words carried great weight in the early Christian church—and rightfully so. As eyewitnesses to Jesus' life, death, and resurrection, the eleven remaining disciples, plus Matthias (Acts 1:26), were uniquely qualified to instruct new believers in their faith. This is exactly why Jesus had called these men to be his disciples in the first place. They were God's chosen instruments to start the church and spread the gospel throughout the world.

Eventually, two of them, Matthew and John, wrote Gospel accounts of Jesus' life based on Holy Spirit–inspired memories (John 14:26) of their personal experiences with Christ. John and Peter wrote letters to Christian churches that eventually became New Testament books. So did James and Jude, Jesus' earthly brothers. The other books of the New Testament were written by Mark, Luke, and Paul—all capable men who were either eyewitnesses of Jesus or friends of those who were.

Here's the point: as today's verse says, Christianity was not built on man-made myths or folklore but "on the foundation of the apostles and the prophets," with the cornerstone—the chief building block of the whole structure—being Jesus himself.

The Christian faith, as taught in holy Scripture, is a rock-solid foundation you can build your life on!

NOW WHAT?

Read Acts 2:42-47 for a fuller description of how the early church functioned.

DID YOU KNOW?

The only New Testament book with an unknown author is Hebrews.

AUGUST 24

It was at Antioch that the believers were first called Christians.
ACTS 11:26

Let's start today's devotion with a quiz.

How many times is the word *Christian* used in the Bible?

A. 3

B. 50

C. 115

D. 522

E. 1,040

If you guessed A, you're correct! Ironically, the book that Christians cherish and obey mentions the actual word *Christian* only three times.

In today's world, Christianity is often discussed but frequently misunderstood. Almost a third of the world's population claims to be Christians (see the March 8 devotion). Yet in Matthew 7:14, Jesus said, "The gateway to life is very narrow . . . and only a few ever find it."

After discussing salvation and the church in recent devotions, our attention now broadens to consider the concept of Christianity: What does it mean to be a Christian, and how do you become one? These are vitally important questions.

WHAT'S IT MEAN?

The word *Christian* simply means "follower of Christ." As today's verse says, believers were first called Christians in Antioch, the capital of ancient Syria, in the mid-first century AD.

Over the years, *Christian* has come to mean a lot of different things to a lot of different people. These days, the term is used quite loosely. Many people think they're Christians simply because they grew up in a religious home, go to church regularly, or try to live a moral life.

But those things don't make anyone a Christian. To truly be a Christian, you have to follow Christ with your heart and your life, trusting in Jesus as your Lord and Savior. This involves the following elements:

- humbly acknowledging that your sins separate you from a holy God and deserve punishment (Romans 6:23)
- repenting of your sins (Mark 1:15)
- trusting that Jesus' sinless life, sacrificial death in your place, and glorious resurrection provide the only way to God's forgiveness and a right relationship with him (Romans 3:24-25)
- putting away selfish, sinful desires and choosing to live your life in a way that glorifies the Savior (Matthew 16:24-25)

It's also important to understand that becoming a Christian isn't a matter of human effort or achievement. While faith and repentance are required on our part, salvation is solely by God's grace (Ephesians 2:8-9). He lovingly initiates the entire process and sees it to completion through his Spirit.

This is what it means to be a Christian.

NOW WHAT?

Meditate on (or think prayerfully about) the four points above to make sure you understand what true Christianity is all about.

DID YOU KNOW?

The Bible's references to the word *Christian* are found in Acts 11:26; Acts 26:28; and 1 Peter 4:16.

*He has reconciled you by Christ's physical body through death
to present you holy in his sight, without blemish and free from
accusation—if you continue in your faith, established and firm,
and do not move from the hope held out in the gospel.*

COLOSSIANS 1:22-23, NIV

Let's talk about weddings.

We know, we know . . . all the girls reading this are probably thinking, *Yay!* And all the guys reading this are probably thinking, *Gross!*

Bear with me. There's a point.

At weddings, the groom and bride exchange wedding vows proclaiming their complete, lifelong commitment to each other. Here's an example:

> I, (name), take you, (name), to be my lawfully wedded (wife/
> husband), to have and to hold from this day forward, for better or
> for worse, for richer or for poorer, in sickness and in health, to love
> and to cherish, from this day forward until death do us part.

But imagine if you went to a wedding and heard a vow like this:

> I, Clarence, take you, Bertha, to be my lawfully wedded wife (well,
> at least I think I do), to have and to hold when it's convenient,
> for better and richer, but definitely not for worse or poorer, only
> in great health, to love and to cherish when I'm not doing other
> important stuff, from this day forward until death (and Wednesday
> night poker, Friday night bowling, and Sunday football on TV) do
> us part.

That union would be doomed to failure, wouldn't it? Marriage works only as a total, lifetime commitment.

The same is true with Christianity.

WHAT'S IT MEAN?

Following Jesus is not just a matter of praying a onetime "sinner's prayer," a hand raised during a church service, or a walk down the aisle during an "altar call." Christianity is a lifetime commitment to follow Christ. As today's verse says, God will reconcile you (or make you right with him) and declare you innocent of sins through Jesus "if you continue in your faith."

Christianity is not like a book or video game. You don't do it for a while, but then put it aside when you get tired of it. Following Christ is a total, lifetime commitment. It's a marathon, not a sprint. Jesus himself said in Matthew 24:13, "The one who endures to the end will be saved."

When you say, "I do" to following Christ, it's a commitment that should last forever!

NOW WHAT?

Commitment to Jesus requires God's help. Take a few moments to pray for this lifetime devotion.

DID YOU KNOW?

Today's verse tells believers to "not move from the hope held out in the gospel." Being a Christian means not placing your hope for salvation in anything else except Christ.

AUGUST 26

*If you openly declare that Jesus is Lord and believe in your heart
that God raised him from the dead, you will be saved. For it is
by believing in your heart that you are made right with God,
and it is by openly declaring your faith that you are saved.*

ROMANS 10:9-10

Long ago, in the second century AD, there was a Christian named Polycarp.
Goofy name, yes, but he was a great man.

Polycarp was the bishop, or church leader, of Smyrna, a major coastal city
in the ancient Roman province of Asia (modern-day Turkey). Near the end
of his life, he took a trip to Rome on some church business, but when he
returned, he was arrested for his Christian faith.

The local governor ordered the old man to renounce Jesus and swear by
Caesar's name. To defy this command meant potential execution for treason.
Nevertheless, Polycarp answered, "Eighty and six years have I served him, and
he has never done me wrong; how, then, can I blaspheme my King and my
Savior?" For his declaration, Polycarp was burned at the stake and pierced
with a spear.

Bravo, Polycarp! He is a shining example of today's verse. Even though it
cost him his life, he chose to "openly declare that Jesus is Lord."

WHAT'S IT MEAN?

In our study of salvation and what it means to be a Christian, we've learned
that repentance and faith are absolutely necessary. But today's verse also mentions another mark of true believers: courageous openness about our faith.

Christians aren't meant to be secretive about their beliefs. Faith isn't something we're supposed to lock away in our hearts and hide from everyone. We
should be willing to publicly share our love for Jesus.

Today's verse says salvation requires both faith *and* the willingness to
"openly declare" our trust in the Savior. And in 1 John 4:15 we read: "All
who declare that Jesus is the Son of God have God living in them, and they

live in God." The word *declare* means to state something in a confident, public way. Declaring your faith publicly shows that you trust in Jesus and find your identity in him. It shows that he is your Lord and Master. It shows your highest priority in life is to honor and obey him.

Polycarp was willing to give up everything to openly declare his love for the Savior. May that courageous devotion be ours as well!

NOW WHAT?

If your church or youth group allows people to share their testimonies during worship services, consider sharing yours!

DID YOU KNOW?

Polycarp's death is the oldest recorded Christian martyrdom (circa AD 155) that's mentioned in historical records other than the New Testament.

You have been taught the holy Scriptures from childhood, and they have given you the wisdom to receive the salvation that comes by trusting in Christ Jesus. 2 TIMOTHY 3:15

Virtually every great civilization in human history has prized wisdom in one way or another. For eons, wise men, scholars, and philosophers have written about how to live a sensible, moral, and healthy life.

Among these cultures, none were more renowned for seeking wisdom than the ancient Greeks. The Greeks loved knowledge the way teenage boys love Mountain Dew.

Many Greek philosophers such as Aristotle, Plato, and Socrates spent much of their lives trying to answer questions about society, nature, and the universe. In fact, when the apostle Paul visited Athens in the first century AD, he noticed that many of the city's residents "seemed to spend all their time discussing the latest ideas" (Acts 17:21).

But human wisdom can take you only so far. At some point, humankind's knowledge reaches a limit.

God's wisdom, however, does not. As Isaiah 40:28 says, "No one can measure the depths of his understanding."

Never has God's wisdom been displayed more beautifully than in his great plan of salvation for humanity. And amazingly, this plan is available for us to read anytime in the Bible.

WHAT'S IT MEAN?

Just as a DVD's special features often show how a movie was made, the Bible reveals "behind-the-scenes footage" of God's remarkable plan of salvation to save sinful humanity through his Son, Jesus Christ. Scripture is like the ultimate backstage pass. It shows how God's plan unfolded over thousands of years from the Garden of Eden to the empty tomb and beyond!

This wisdom comes only from God's Word. As we discuss salvation and Christianity, it's critical to understand this. No other book in history offers this life-changing knowledge. Not even Aristotle and his philosophical buddies can compete with holy Scripture.

Aren't you glad that God is a God of love, compassion—and communication? Think about it: when sin threatened to destroy his creation, God not only set in motion his perfect plan of salvation, but he also inspired godly men to write about it along the way so that even today, we could read and believe. As today's verse says, the words of Scripture "have given you the wisdom to receive the salvation that comes by trusting in Christ Jesus."

Praise God for offering us heaven's eternal wisdom through his inspired, inerrant (flawless) Word!

NOW WHAT?

Make sure you're receiving God's wisdom every day by faithfully reading his Word.

DID YOU KNOW?

Acts 17:16-34 details how the people of ancient Athens reacted when Paul preached the gospel of Jesus Christ to them. Check it out!

Anyone who denies the Son doesn't have the Father, either.
But anyone who acknowledges the Son has the Father also.

1 JOHN 2:23

Here's a fun fact for you: as of December 2013, 74 percent of all adults in the United States believed in God, according to a Harris Poll. That's nearly three-fourths of the nation's total population.

Sounds like a lot, doesn't it? But consider this: in the same country where most people believe in God, law enforcement officials made an estimated 11.3 million arrests nationwide that same year, according to FBI crime statistics. That's one arrest every 2.8 seconds. This includes 480,360 arrests for violent crimes; 1,559,284 for property crimes (like burglary, motor vehicle theft, or arson); and 1,501,043 for drug abuse violations. Here's another shocker: in 2013, there were an estimated 14,196 murders in America. That's 39 people *every single day*.

The numbers are staggering. How can a nation where the overwhelming majority of people believe in God struggle so much with sin? Isn't belief in God enough?

No, it's not.

WHAT'S IT MEAN?

Yes, you read that correctly: belief in God is not enough in life.

Now, don't misunderstand. It's absolutely critical to believe in God. One day, all atheists (those who don't believe God exists) will get a rude awakening when they stand before the very God whom they denied.

But by itself, belief in God is not sufficient for salvation. If your religious convictions go no further than admitting there's a God in heaven, you are no better off than one of Satan's demons.

Sound crazy? Read what James 2:19 says: "You say you have faith, for you believe that there is one God. Good for you! Even the demons believe this, and they tremble in terror." James's point was simple: demons acknowledge God's existence, but they're still doomed to hell (Matthew 25:41).

As we study Christianity, it's vitally important to understand this truth: salvation requires full trust in Jesus, not just belief in God. Jesus is God's chosen Savior. He is the key that unlocks heaven's forgiveness. As today's verse says, to reject Jesus is to reject God himself.

If you truly believe in God, you will believe in the saving power of Jesus. If you truly love the Father, you will also love his Son.

NOW WHAT?

Pray that God would strengthen your faith in Jesus. Then pray that those in this country who believe in God would also worship his Son.

DID YOU KNOW?

In that same Harris Poll, 68 percent of Americans expressed belief in Jesus' divinity.

AUGUST 29

Salvation is found in no one else, for there is no other name under heaven given to mankind by which we must be saved.

ACTS 4:12, NIV

In the early days of the church, the apostles Peter and John entered the Jerusalem Temple area and saw a crippled beggar sitting near one of the gates. The man had never been able to walk.

Peter looked at him and said, "In the name of Jesus Christ the Nazarene, get up and walk!" (Acts 3:6). Immediately, the man jumped up, completely healed, while a huge crowd gathered in amazement.

The Jewish religious leaders, however, weren't pleased. They arrested Peter and John for talking about Jesus. (You can read the whole story in Acts 3–4.)

But Peter refused to be silent. So he courageously testified about Jesus before the Sanhedrin (the Jewish religious ruling council), saying, "Salvation is found in no one else, for there is no other name under heaven given to mankind by which we must be saved."

It's one of the boldest statements in Scripture, and it leads to an important question: Is true Christianity right while all other religions are wrong?

WHAT'S IT MEAN?

The world is one big stew of religious groups: Christians, Mormons, Jehovah's Witnesses, Seventh-day Adventists, Christian Scientists, Muslims, Hindus, Buddhists, Jews, Bahá'ís, Jains, Sikhs, Shintoists, Taoists, Wiccans, Zoroastrians, and many others. There are also atheists (people who don't believe in God or an afterlife) and agnostics (people who think it's impossible to know if there's a God or an afterlife). The list could go on and on.

So how do we know Christianity is the right belief? It's a question of eternal significance. Today, we're only dipping our toe into the pool, so to speak. For the next four days, we'll dive headfirst into the details and discuss related questions, such as:

- Do all religions lead to heaven?
- How can we know Christianity is the only true faith?

- Why would a loving God send billions of people to hell?
- How should we react when people are offended by our faith?

In the meantime, let's answer the original question: Is true Christianity—the belief that salvation comes only through Jesus—right, while all other religions are wrong? The answer is . . . yes! God's Word is very clear: "Salvation is found in *no one else*."

Stay tuned—much more to come!

NOW WHAT?

Memorize Acts 4:12. It's short, power packed, and to the point!

DID YOU KNOW?

Nearly six billion people worldwide—or more than 80 percent of earth's total estimated population—claim some sort of religious affiliation, according to a 2012 study by the Pew Research Center's Forum on Religion & Public Life.

AUGUST 30

Salvation is found in no one else, for there is no other name under heaven given to mankind by which we must be saved.

ACTS 4:12, NIV

For the better part of two thousand years, there's been a saying: "All roads lead to Rome."

In ancient times, this wasn't just an old adage; it was true. To protect their vast empire and allow their military to reach faraway destinations swiftly, the Romans cleverly built a huge network of paved roads throughout their kingdom. The meeting point of all the roads, of course, was Rome itself.

Over the centuries, the saying has turned into a proverb that means, "You can take many different paths to reach the same destination."

That might be true for some things in life, but not religion. All roads do *not* lead to heaven.

In today's devotion, we're continuing the discussion of Acts 4:12 and all its implications, specifically the Bible's claim that faith in Jesus is the only way to heaven.

WHAT'S IT MEAN?

Acts 4:12 boldly claims that all faiths in the world except one are wrong. It might sound exclusive or harsh, but logically, it makes sense.

Some people believe that God will let all "good," religiously committed people into heaven regardless of their beliefs, because, well, they tried hard. But that's impossible. Each religion has differing views about what it means to live morally, how to be saved, and how to achieve a good afterlife. Some religions even claim there are multiple gods. To say that all those religious differences will somehow work out in the end just doesn't make sense.

For instance, Hindus believe in many gods and in reincarnation—that after people die, their spirits come to life again in new bodies on earth, depending on how good they were in their former lives. But the Bible teaches that there's one God (Deuteronomy 6:4) and that humans live and die only once (Hebrews 9:27). Both ideas can't be right.

Any god who would welcome into heaven all sorts of people with different beliefs about religions, gods, creation, morality, and salvation would be a very confused deity! No, there can be only one way to heaven.

True salvation, though, isn't just a matter of logic. It's a matter of faith. Eventually, every Christian must say, "I know many people in the world believe many different things, but I believe that repentance and faith in Jesus is the only way I can be made right with God and enter heaven."

NOW WHAT?

Read 1 John 4:1-3. It's a good place to start when thinking about world religions.

DID YOU KNOW?

Today, the remains of many ancient Roman roads can still be seen throughout Europe.

AUGUST 31

Salvation is found in no one else, for there is no other name under heaven given to mankind by which we must be saved.
ACTS 4:12, NIV

As we've studied Acts 4:12 the last few days, we've learned that there are many religions in the world but that not all religious roads lead to heaven. Acts 4:12, in fact, claims that salvation is found through Jesus alone. So to trust in God's Word is to trust that Christianity—the belief that salvation from sins is possible only through faith in Jesus' atoning work on the cross—is the only true faith in the world.

Now it's time for another big question: How can we know *for sure* that Christianity is right and all other religions are wrong? It's a tricky question. Better hold your breath. It's time to dive into the deep end of the spiritual pool!

WHAT'S IT MEAN?

Broadly defined, religion is man's attempt to reach God. It's a human-centered endeavor. All non-Christian belief systems try to explain how sinful humans can somehow earn God's favor (or some sort of ultimate spiritual prize) through a merit-based system. It's the belief that, "If I just do _____ (*fill in the blank*) well enough, I will be spiritually rewarded in the afterlife."

But Christianity says the opposite. Christianity is the belief that man is helplessly sinful before God and needs God's mercy and grace for salvation. Christianity says, "You can't earn God's favor. Salvation comes only as a free gift through faith in Jesus." Christianity correctly takes the focus off human effort and puts it on God's love and Jesus' finished work on the cross.

Why else should you believe that salvation comes only through Jesus? Simply because the Bible says so. God's perfect Word makes many claims that Jesus is the only way to heaven, including John 6:68-69; 8:24; 14:6; 17:3; 1 Timothy 2:5; and 1 John 4:1-3.

Believing all this, of course, takes great faith. The Bible admits as much (Hebrews 11:6). Eventually, you have to say, "Despite all the other religions out there, I believe that spiritual truth is found only in the Bible. I believe Jesus died for my sins and rose again, I trust him as my Lord and Savior, and I'm going to live my life in obedience to his Word. That's the only way I can be saved."

NOW WHAT?

Read the six Bible passages listed on the previous page, and pray to God for wisdom and faith as you seek his truth.

DID YOU KNOW?

In the New Testament's original language, the Greek word for religion (*thréskeia*) is used only four times. Clearly, God cares very little for man-made rituals and beliefs.

SEPTEMBER 1

Salvation is found in no one else, for there is no other name under heaven given to mankind by which we must be saved.

ACTS 4:12, NIV

As we continue to study Acts 4:12, it's time to address one of the biggest problems that people have with Christianity. The question goes something like this: "If Christianity is right and all other religions are wrong, that means that billions of people are going to hell to suffer an eternity of punishment and separation from God. How can a loving God allow that?"

It's a legitimate question, for sure. But here's a better one: "Why did God choose to save anyone at all?"

WHAT'S IT MEAN?

In considering the Bible's teachings about sin, hell, Jesus, and salvation, it's important to have the proper perspective.

God is the all-knowing, all-powerful Creator of the universe. We are his creations. Without him, we wouldn't even exist. God doesn't answer to us; we answer to him. As Romans 9:20 says, "Who are you, a mere human being, to argue with God? Should the thing that was created say to the one who created it, 'Why have you made me like this?'"

God does not owe us anything. When he created humans, he gave us the ability to choose between right and wrong. We chose to rebel. God would have been fully justified to destroy all humans because of our wickedness against him.

Human sin, after all, must be punished. Otherwise, God wouldn't be holy or just. But God does not delight in punishing sinners. As 2 Peter 3:9 says, "He does not want anyone to be destroyed, but wants everyone to repent." That's where Jesus comes in!

Christianity's claim that Jesus is the only way for sinners to be saved should be viewed as a positive, not a negative. Without Jesus, we'd have no hope. Even though God had every right to punish us eternally, he decided to offer us salvation instead. This should cause us to praise him for his mercy and grace!

Again, it's all about perspective. We are not in a position to disagree with God, and understanding that is a step toward salvation. Rather than question God's love because hell is real, we should praise God that heaven is attainable!

NOW WHAT?

The fact that many people are headed for hell shouldn't deter us from believing the gospel. It should motivate us to share Jesus with others. Tell someone about Jesus today!

DID YOU KNOW?

The Bible (especially Psalms) provides many examples of righteous people questioning God and grappling with tough life questions. But when we do, it should be done with respect, not arrogantly as if we know better than God.

SEPTEMBER 2

Salvation is found in no one else, for there is no other name under heaven given to mankind by which we must be saved.

ACTS 4:12, NIV

Being popular is fun. There's no debating that. It feels great to have lots of people think you're cool.

But here's a reality check: being a Christian means that you are going to be distinctly *unpopular* with the world around you.

In our final devotion about Acts 4:12, it's important to understand that being a Christian—especially believing this verse's claim that everyone who doesn't trust in Jesus is subject to eternal punishment—is not a trendy viewpoint. It won't win you any popularity contests.

And you know what? That's okay.

WHAT'S IT MEAN?

Popularity should not be our goal in life. In fact, popularity with the world probably means you have mistaken priorities. James 4:4 is clear about that: "Don't you realize that friendship with the world makes you an enemy of God? I say it again: If you want to be a friend of the world, you make yourself an enemy of God."

If you are a Christian and you believe Acts 4:12, eventually you'll run across people who take offense at your faith. They won't like that you believe they are destined for eternal punishment apart from trusting in Jesus. They'll think you are arrogant and might say, "What makes you so special to think you know the only way to heaven?"

It may not be easy to stand your ground. But do it—in love and gentleness, of course (1 Peter 3:16). Don't ever treat unbelievers as if you're better than they are. Love and respect them. Share the gospel with them, if they'll let you. But stand your ground and hold fast to your faith.

Remember, Jesus said following him is like passing through a "narrow gate" but that the "highway to hell is broad" (Matthew 7:13). Sadly, the majority of people choose the wrong path.

Jesus also said, "If the world hates you, remember that it hated me first. The world would love you as one of its own if you belonged to it, but you are no longer part of the world. I chose you to come out of the world, so it hates you" (John 15:18-19).

God's approval, not the world's, is what matters most. If you believe Acts 4:12, you'll have it.

NOW WHAT?

Do you know people who are not Christians? Pray often that God would save them from their sins.

DID YOU KNOW?

Remember, Jesus said Christians are "blessed" when they are persecuted for believing the truth about him (Matthew 5:10-12, NIV).

*Remember, dear brothers and sisters, that few of you were wise
in the world's eyes or powerful or wealthy when God called you.
Instead, God chose things the world considers foolish in order
to shame those who think they are wise.*

I CORINTHIANS 1:26-27

When Peter and John healed the crippled beggar at the Temple in Jerusalem, it was an astounding miracle. The man had been disabled since birth (Acts 3:2)—more than forty years (Acts 4:22)!

But the hard-hearted Jewish religious leaders were outraged. They hated that Peter and John had healed in Jesus' name (Acts 4:18) and then preached the gospel to hundreds of amazed onlookers.

So they imprisoned the two apostles overnight and brought them before their ruling council, the Sanhedrin, the next day for questioning. Peter didn't flinch. Even amidst threats of violence, he called the religious leaders—many of whom were responsible for Jesus' crucifixion—to repent and believe in Christ.

The Sanhedrin was shocked. Acts 4:13 says, "The members of the council were amazed when they saw the boldness of Peter and John, for they could see that they were ordinary men with no special training in the Scriptures."

WHAT'S IT MEAN?

The well-educated men of the Sanhedrin had no answer for the power and wisdom they saw in the two unschooled fishermen from Galilee. Peter and John's authority came from a source that the Sanhedrin was completely unfamiliar with: Jesus. Peter testified before them that the crippled man "was healed by the powerful name of Jesus Christ" (Acts 4:10).

This story is a wonderful reminder for regular folks like us. You don't need any college degrees or fancy titles behind your name to "be a good Christian." You don't have to be a pastor, theologian, or missionary to accomplish great things for God. You just need to rely on the proper power source. Ordinary people can do extraordinary things through the mighty name of Jesus.

As today's verse says, God rarely calls people who are already really wise, powerful, or special to follow him. Instead, he usually calls normal folks, just like you, to accomplish great things for his name so that he gets the glory.

Remember, every Christian's ability to proclaim the gospel and affect the world for good is found exclusively in the powerful name of Jesus Christ!

NOW WHAT?

Pray for God's boldness to be a strong witness like Peter and John (Acts 4:29).

DID YOU KNOW?

After being released by the Sanhedrin, Peter and John gathered with other Christians to praise God and ask him for continued strength. When they finished, Acts 4:31 says God supernaturally "shook" their meeting place. Cool!

SEPTEMBER 4

Precious in the sight of the LORD is the death of his faithful servants.
PSALM 116:15, NIV

Anger and hatred coursed through the mob's veins like blood. In a fit of fury, they dragged the innocent man outside Jerusalem and picked up their cruel weapons of execution.

The stones, large and small, whistled through the air at breakneck speed, crumpling their victim's body like an empty soda can being kicked down the street. As his life ebbed away, Stephen looked up to heaven and pleaded, "Lord, do not hold this sin against them!" (Acts 7:60, NIV). Then he died.

Stephen had just become the first martyr of the early Christian church.

Stephen was a faithful believer who humbly served others behind the scenes and powerfully preached Christ in public (Acts 6:1-10). But some wicked men concocted false charges against him and dragged him before the Sanhedrin, who listened to his defense until he accused the members of rejecting God's law and claimed to have a vision of Jesus standing next to God in heaven. Enraged at this supposed blasphemy, the Sanhedrin had Stephen stoned to death.

WHAT'S IT MEAN?

Stephen courageously died for his Christian faith, but he was by no means the last person to do so. Throughout history, God's people have endured constant attacks at the hands of the wicked.

In the Old Testament era, "some died by stoning, some were sawed in half, and others were killed with the sword" (Hebrews 11:37). In New Testament times, Paul, Peter, and most of Jesus' disciples were martyred, according to early church tradition. Christians in the Roman Empire were crucified, burned at the stake, and fed to wild beasts for spectacle in large arenas.

Today, Jesus' promise of persecution for his followers (Matthew 24:9) still rings true. Many Christians face great danger in certain parts of Africa, Asia, and the Middle East, among other places.

All Christians will face persecution (2 Timothy 3:12), whether great or small, and are called to endure it (Revelation 13:10). God is pleased with those who remain faithful to him despite mistreatment. These saints are "too good for this world" (Hebrews 11:38). Today's verse says Christian martyrs are "precious in the sight of the LORD."

No matter what persecution comes your way, trust the Lord, stand strong, and you will be rewarded with heaven's glory, just like Stephen.

NOW WHAT?

Take some time to pray for the safety, encouragement, and faithfulness of persecuted Christians around the world.

DID YOU KNOW?

Stephen's martyrdom kicked off a great persecution of the Jerusalem church, which forced many Christians to flee elsewhere (Acts 8:1). But God used this dispersion to reach even more areas with the gospel!

SEPTEMBER 5

This is a trustworthy saying, and everyone should accept it: "Christ Jesus came into the world to save sinners"—and I am the worst of them all. 1 TIMOTHY 1:15

History's greatest missionary, theologian, and pastor started out as a murderer. His name was Saul.

One day, Saul was traveling from Jerusalem to the Syrian city of Damascus, a 135-mile journey, to destroy the young Christian church there. As a Pharisee (Philippians 3:5) who rejected Jesus as the Messiah, his goal was to exterminate Christians like unwanted insects.

Saul had gladly assisted with Stephen's death by stoning (Acts 7:58; 8:1) and then became a religious bounty hunter of sorts, trekking great distances to imprison other believers (Acts 26:11) and, if possible, sentence them to death (Acts 26:10).

He was every Christian's worst nightmare.

As Saul was traveling to Damascus that day, a bright light shone down from heaven, knocking Saul to the ground and blinding him with the brilliance of its glory.

"Saul!" Jesus said. "Why are you persecuting me?"

"Who are you, lord?" Saul asked.

"I am Jesus, the one you are persecuting!" he replied. "Now get up and go into the city, and you will be told what you must do" (Acts 9:3-6).

By the time Saul regained his sight three days later, he was a completely new man. Jesus had changed his life.

WHAT'S IT MEAN?

Saul's transformation was radical. After Saul's encounter with the risen Lord, Acts 9:20 says he immediately "began preaching about Jesus in the synagogues, saying, 'He is indeed the Son of God!'" He now loved the Savior and the Christians that he had once hated so badly. As part of his ministry to the Gentiles (non-Jewish people), he eventually chose to go by the Roman version of his name, Paul.

Jesus has the power to radically change lives! He saves those who appear beyond hope. Although Paul was the self-proclaimed "worst" of sinners (see today's verse), he realized that "God had mercy on me so that Christ Jesus could use me as a prime example of his great patience with even the worst sinners. Then others will realize that they, too, can believe in him and receive eternal life" (1 Timothy 1:16).

Paul's conversion to Christianity literally changed history. After God called him out of sin and spiritual blindness, he started churches, wrote almost half of the New Testament books, and spread the gospel all over the ancient world.

The Savior who radically changed Paul's life can do the same for you!

NOW WHAT?

Do you sometimes feel like one of "the worst sinners"? Pray to the God who gives mercy and grace to all who humbly ask.

DID YOU KNOW?

Paul took at least three missionary journeys, according to the book of Acts.

SEPTEMBER 6

He called you to this through our gospel, that you might share in the glory of our Lord Jesus Christ. 2 THESSALONIANS 2:14, NIV

Imagine, for a moment, what it must've been like to be the apostle Paul when God called him.

The Damascus Road was a highway in the arid Middle East, and Paul was traveling around midday (Acts 26:13), so the blazing sun was at its apex. It must have been very bright and very hot.

Yet Acts 9:3 (NIV) says that Paul was knocked down and temporarily blinded when "a light from heaven flashed around him." Paul later described this light as "brighter than the sun" (Acts 26:13).

Interestingly, the ancient Greek word translated as "flashed" in English Bibles is the same word the Greeks used to describe a lightning bolt's brilliance. But there were no thunderclouds overhead that day. This was a special light—it was Jesus Christ appearing in his glory!

God's calling was an incredibly powerful event that changed Paul forever.

WHAT'S IT MEAN?

When God called people to serve him in the Bible, it was often quite a spectacle.

God called Moses to lead Israel by appearing in a burning bush that wasn't destroyed by the flames (Exodus 3:2). He called Gideon to be Israel's judge by sending "the angel of the LORD" to visit him while he was threshing wheat (Judges 6). He called Isaiah to be his prophet by giving him a fantastic vision of heaven's throne room, filled with God's glory and special angels called "seraphim" (Isaiah 6:1-4).

When God calls someone, he means business!

On the dusty road to Damascus, God called Paul out of his sin and spiritual blindness and into a remarkable life of world-changing ministry proclaiming the Savior he had long rejected. Today, even though God's calling isn't usually accompanied by such outwardly dazzling displays, it's no less extraordinary. As today's verse says, God calls us to "share in the glory of our Lord Jesus Christ." It doesn't get any better than that.

God's calling miraculously brings life to sinful, dead souls. It brings people "out of the darkness" (1 Peter 2:9) and "into partnership with his Son, Jesus Christ our Lord" (1 Corinthians 1:9).

God is calling you now, through this devotional, to trust in him and serve him. How will you respond?

NOW WHAT?

When God calls people to salvation, he also gives them spiritual gifts and a new life mission, just like Paul. Pray that God would reveal these to you so that you may effectively serve him.

DID YOU KNOW?

These days, God's main methods of calling people to faith and repentance are the Holy Spirit, his written Word, and faithful believers who proclaim the Good News to others.

Because you are stubborn and refuse to turn from your sin, you are storing up terrible punishment for yourself. For a day of anger is coming, when God's righteous judgment will be revealed.

ROMANS 2:5

The apostle Paul's conversion to Christianity was a memory permanently seared into his brain. When the risen Son of God knocks you over with divine glory so brilliant that it obscures the noonday sun, you tend to remember it!

Even twenty-five years later, Paul could still recall specific details of that moment as if it happened the day before. We see this in Acts 26 when Paul shared his life story with Jewish king Herod Agrippa II while standing trial for false accusations.

But as Paul recounted that amazing day on the Damascus Road, he added an interesting detail that wasn't included in the main account of Paul's conversion in Acts 9. When Jesus appeared to Paul, he didn't just say, "Saul, Saul, why do you persecute me?" (Acts 9:4, NIV). He said, "Saul, Saul, why do you persecute me? It is hard for you to kick against the goads" (Acts 26:14, NIV).

WHAT'S IT MEAN?

A goad is a sharp, pointed pole that farmers in ancient times used to guide oxen or cattle. If an obstinate animal tried to resist the farmer, he got a goad in the backside. *Yowzers!* Kicking against the goads hurts!

By Paul's time, the phrase "kick against the goads" had apparently become an expression meaning to stubbornly resist something or someone. This perfectly describes Paul's early years, when he was persecuting Christians. Before he met Jesus, Paul was acting like a hardheaded mule, foolishly kicking against God's will to his own spiritual harm.

Now ask yourself: Are *you* kicking against the goads at all? Is there any area of your life where you are stubbornly resisting God's will for you? Is there a sin you can't let go of, or something you know God wants you to do that you're avoiding?

Fighting against God is useless. It will only bring pain and sadness. Today's verse contains a strong warning for everyone who makes a habit of stubbornly kicking against God's desires for them.

The Lord has a good plan for your life. Entrust yourself to him through faith and obedience to Christ, just like Paul did. Your life, like Paul's, will be so much better for it.

NOW WHAT?

The first step to stop stubbornly kicking against God is simple obedience (Acts 9:6). Take that step, whatever it might be!

DID YOU KNOW?

Paul's trial before Herod Agrippa II was based on the false charges that Paul was speaking against the Jewish law and Temple (Acts 21:27-29).

He fell to the ground and heard a voice saying to him, "Saul! Saul!
Why are you persecuting me?" ACTS 9:4

The apostle Paul was startled, frightened, curious, and confused. Pick an emotion and Paul (then known as Saul) probably felt it during his transformative experience on the Damascus Road.

Immediately after being knocked down by a flash of brilliant light, Paul heard a mysterious voice. "Saul! Saul! Why are you persecuting me?" the voice thundered from above.

"Who are you, lord?" Paul asked, shielding his eyes and perhaps even fearing for his life (Acts 9:5).

The voice, of course, was Jesus', and that moment changed Paul—and the world—forever. But Jesus' question to Paul was interesting. Jesus didn't say, "Why are you persecuting my followers?" or "Why are you persecuting the church?" Jesus said, "Why are you persecuting *me*?"

Paul was on earth hunting down Christians, while Jesus was in heaven (Acts 7:56). How could Paul be persecuting *Jesus*?

The answer speaks volumes about our Savior and his love for us!

WHAT'S IT MEAN?

Jesus identifies closely with believers. In fact, he is so personally connected with them that he feels what they feel.

That's why he said that Paul's attacks against Christians were actually attacks against him. Whatever you do to Jesus' followers, you do to Jesus (Matthew 25:40).

This is a wonderful truth! Our Savior loves us more than we can imagine. Jesus is our "High Priest"—someone who represents humans before God—who "understands our weaknesses" and "faced all of the same testings we do, yet he did not sin" (Hebrews 4:15).

Because Jesus was fully God *and* fully human, he knows exactly what humans go through every day. He experienced the same joy, sadness, and pain that we feel. He cried when people were hurting (John 11:35), stood up for the persecuted (Mark 14:6), and prayed for us (John 17:20-22). Jesus dearly loves his people.

He dearly loves you, too. Like a shepherd caring for his sheep (Hebrews 13:20), Jesus is always with you (Matthew 28:20). He is your Advocate who speaks to God on your behalf (1 John 2:1). He shares your highs, your lows, and everything in between.

He loves you so much that he humbled himself to die in your place so that you could live with him forever. He is not a distant god; he is a close, personal Savior!

NOW WHAT?

Do you have a friend going through a difficult time? Follow Jesus' example of feeling his or her pain, and reach out to help.

DID YOU KNOW?

In the Old Testament, God also closely identified with Israel. See Isaiah 63:7-9 and Zechariah 2:8.

SEPTEMBER 9

Here on earth you will have many trials and sorrows. But take heart, because I have overcome the world. JOHN 16:33

Ananias swallowed hard.

Ananias, a faithful Christian living in the ancient city of Damascus, had just been told by God to visit a house on Straight Street and help a temporarily blinded man named Saul. But Ananias hesitated. Everybody knew about Saul. Some Christians who met this enemy of the church were never seen again.

"Lord," Ananias replied, "I've heard many people talk about the terrible things this man has done to the believers in Jerusalem! And he is authorized by the leading priests to arrest everyone who calls upon your name" (Acts 9:13-14).

But Ananias didn't know Jesus had completely transformed Saul's life. And he didn't know God's incredible plans for Saul (soon to be known as Paul) as a future apostle and missionary.

So God told Ananias, "Go, for Saul is my chosen instrument to take my message to the Gentiles and to kings, as well as to the people of Israel. And I will show him how much he must suffer for my name's sake" (Acts 9:15-16).

Whoa! It all sounded good until that last part. Why did God's plans for Paul involve suffering?

WHAT'S IT MEAN?

Paul's gospel-spreading zeal literally changed the world. But he also suffered more than most humans could endure, including imprisonments, whippings, beatings, shipwrecks, a stoning, and many other life-threatening dangers (2 Corinthians 11:23-28). That's what you call a rough life.

Why did God allow Paul to suffer this way? Well, for one thing, Paul's pain was our gain—and he knew it! (Colossians 1:24). Two thousand years later, his harships still encourage and strengthen Christians worldwide.

Trials and hardships are part of God's mysterious, sovereign plan. He doesn't always reveal to us why we experience them, but he does promise they will come. The Christian life is filled with countless spiritual blessings, but it isn't always a pleasure cruise. Today's verse promises that all believers "will have many trials and sorrows." Trials are God-ordained tools that sharpen our faith (James 1:3-4) and reveal the Lord's power to us (2 Corinthians 12:9).

And never forget: God will always help you in trials. Deuteronomy 31:6 reminds us, "He will never leave you nor forsake you" (NIV).

Trials will certainly come, but you'll never be alone in them!

NOW WHAT?
Read about Paul's most difficult trials in 2 Corinthians 11:23-28. Then read 2 Corinthians 12:9-10 to see his attitude toward them.

DID YOU KNOW?
The ancient Straight Street from Acts 9:11 still exists in the modern-day Syrian city of Damascus.

You must worship Christ as Lord of your life. And if someone asks about your hope as a believer, always be ready to explain it. But do this in a gentle and respectful way. I PETER 3:15-16

The apostle Paul was not someone who sat around twiddling his thumbs. He was a go-getter.

After God restored his sight following his encounter with Jesus, Paul visited the Christians in Damascus briefly to fellowship with them and, presumably, to learn about his new faith.

But Paul was antsy. He couldn't wait to tell others about the life-changing power of Jesus. So he immediately began preaching the gospel in the Jewish synagogues in Damascus, amazing the people with his knowledge and reasoning. In fact, Acts 9:22 says, "Saul's preaching became more and more powerful, and the Jews in Damascus couldn't refute his proofs that Jesus was indeed the Messiah."

Paul's ability to effectively preach the gospel so soon after his conversion is astounding. It speaks to the powerful revelation he received from Jesus on the Damascus Road (Galatians 1:12). But there were other factors too. As a former Pharisee, Paul was well versed in the Old Testament (Acts 22:3). After encountering Christ and spending time with the Damascus Christians, Paul was able to connect the dots and understand how Scripture proved that Jesus was the long-awaited Messiah.

Armed with his newfound faith and knowledge, Paul was quickly off to spread the gospel message all over the world.

WHAT'S IT MEAN?

Paul was a perfect example of today's verse. He understood the gospel well and was eager to share it with anyone who would listen.

Does this describe you? If you "worship Christ as Lord of your life" (today's verse), you need to know what you believe and be ready to share it with others whenever possible. The gospel is too good to keep to yourself!

But sharing the gospel involves lots of Bible study and prayer. How can you know what to believe about Jesus, sin, salvation, and other biblical topics if you don't read God's Word? And when the time comes to share, you'll need God's help to effectively communicate it.

Don't forget to do it in a "gentle and respectful way" (today's verse). That means not shoving your beliefs down someone else's throat. Share the gospel; don't force-feed it!

As Paul would attest, not everyone will accept the message. But your job isn't to change people's hearts; it's simply to be faithful to share "about your hope" (today's verse) in Jesus!

NOW WHAT?

Ask your parents about getting involved with evangelism opportunities at church.

DID YOU KNOW?

Paul eventually had to flee Damascus when he discovered a plot to kill him (Acts 9:23-25).

SEPTEMBER 11

I urge you to live a life worthy of the calling you have received.
EPHESIANS 4:1, NIV

The story of Pat Tillman is as inspiring as it is tragic.

Tillman, an undersized linebacker from California, defied the odds his entire football career. Despite being a low (seventh round) NFL draft pick in 1998, Tillman soon became a starting safety for the Arizona Cardinals and one of the team's leading tacklers. But after the September 11, 2001, terrorist attacks in New York City and Washington, DC, Tillman walked away from a promising NFL career worth millions to serve in the US Army.

While serving as a member of the 75th Ranger Regiment in Afghanistan in April 2004, Tillman was killed in action. He was only twenty-seven years old.

"Pat knew his purpose in life," said former Arizona Cardinals head coach Dave McGinnis, according to the Pat Tillman Foundation. "He proudly walked away from a career in football to a greater calling."

Did you know the apostle Paul also walked away from a promising career to follow a greater calling? Paul was an up-and-coming Pharisee who was "far ahead of my fellow Jews in my zeal" for law-keeping (Galatians 1:14). But Jesus changed his heart on the Damascus Road, and Paul embarked on a completely different life path. He became an apostle of Christ, spreading Christianity throughout the world by taking several missionary trips, starting many churches, and writing nearly half the New Testament.

WHAT'S IT MEAN?

If you are a Christian, "you do not belong to yourself, for God bought you with a high price" (1 Corinthians 6:19-20). That price is the precious blood of Jesus. You are "called according to his purpose" (Romans 8:28) and "called . . . to live a holy life" (2 Timothy 1:9).

Part of this new lifestyle is being willing to give up your desires and pursue whatever calling God has for you, just like Paul did. Nothing—not friends, popularity, sports, school, money, or anything else—should take priority over God.

Every person's ultimate purpose is to glorify the Creator, but he has given different spiritual gifts to different people to achieve that common goal. God has a specific calling and plan for your life.

When God revealed Paul's calling to him, he dropped everything and pursued it wholeheartedly. When God reveals your calling, will you do the same?

NOW WHAT?

Make a list of things you like to do in life. Then ask God to show you if any of those things is your calling. The answer may come quickly, or it may not. Just keep praying!

DID YOU KNOW?

The first book of the Bible Paul wrote was likely Galatians. The last was 2 Timothy.

Peter replied, "I see very clearly that God shows no favoritism. In every nation he accepts those who fear him and do what is right."
ACTS 10:34-35

Bet you've never had a dream like this one before.

In Acts 10, God gave the apostle Peter a fascinating vision of a massive sheet, filled with all sorts of animals, being lowered from heaven. Many of the animals were "unclean" according to Old Testament food laws. Yet God told him, "Get up, Peter; kill and eat them" (Acts 10:13).

Peter objected at first, mentioning his obedience to Jewish dietary regulations. But God answered, "Do not call something unclean if God has made it clean" (Acts 10:15).

As Peter was trying to figure it all out, three messengers from a Roman centurion named Cornelius arrived where Peter was staying and asked for him. In a separate vision, God had told Cornelius to find Peter, bring him to Cornelius's house, and listen to whatever he had to say.

When Peter heard this, he realized his vision was about much more than ancient food laws. God was telling him to preach the gospel to Gentiles (non-Jews)—people whom the Jews considered "unclean." People like Cornelius.

This required a radical shift in Peter's thinking. He had been raised to believe that God's favor rested exclusively on the Jews. Still, he traveled to Cornelius's house and preached to a large Gentile crowd there about Jesus. Peter marveled as many of them were saved. He realized "that God shows no favoritism" (today's verse).

God's message was clear: salvation is for anyone who believes, not just certain people groups.

WHAT'S IT MEAN?

God is not prejudiced. Since he created all humans in his image (Genesis 1:27), he doesn't judge by skin color, ethnicity, or anything external. He is concerned about human hearts (1 Samuel 16:7).

The salvation God provides through Jesus is offered to all people no matter where they're from or what they look like. Whether you're from the United States, Mexico, Ethiopia, Kuwait, France, Brazil, China, Russia, Australia, or anywhere in between, forgiveness of sins is possible *only* through faith in Jesus.

This is a beautiful truth! God is not the God of one specific people group. He's the God of the nations. One day, people from "every nation and tribe and people and language" (Revelation 7:9) will worship before his throne in heaven. What a glorious day that will be!

NOW WHAT?

Befriend someone from a different country. You'll be surprised at what you can learn from him or her!

DID YOU KNOW?

Long before Jesus' birth, Isaiah prophesied that Jesus would bring salvation "to the ends of the earth" (Isaiah 49:6), not just Israel.

*They shared the word of the Lord with him and with all who lived
in his household.* ACTS 16:32

The apostle Paul experienced some crazy stuff on his missionary journeys.
Acts 16 tells one such story.

On Paul's second missionary journey, he and Silas, his companion, were
ministering in Philippi, a Roman colony in Macedonia. One day, Paul cast a
demon out of a slave girl who had fortune-telling powers. This didn't go over
so well with the girl's owners, who were becoming rich off her special ability.

These wicked men stirred up an angry mob against Paul and Silas, beat
them with rods, and threw them in prison without a trial. The city jailer
locked them in his most secure cell and put their feet into stocks. Talk about
a bad day!

But around midnight, God sent an earthquake to shake the jail so violently that all the cell doors swung open and each prisoner's chains fell off.
Frightened and confused, the jailer drew his sword to end his life.

Considering the circumstances, it would have been perfectly understand-
able for Paul and Silas to shout, "See ya later, suckers!" and scamper off. Who
would actually stick around and use the opportunity to tell the jailer about
Jesus?

Paul would.

Amazingly, Paul and Silas stopped the jailer from harming himself and
led the man and his whole family to Christ (see today's verse)!

WHAT'S IT MEAN?

A day that had started terribly for Paul and Silas ended wonderfully—all
because their hearts were sensitive to gospel-sharing opportunities. Even as
they sat bruised and bloodied in a dark, dingy prison, Paul and Silas were
actively looking for ways to tell others about Jesus. What an example for us
to follow!

In previous devotions, we've discussed Jesus' command to preach the gospel (July 20) and our need to know what to share when the time comes (September 10). But equally important is having a heart that is always willing to witness about Christ, no matter what the circumstances. As Paul and Silas showed, any situation can be a chance to proclaim the life-changing message of Jesus to others.

Wherever you are—with relatives, at school, in the neighborhood, on vacation—look for ways to share the gospel!

NOW WHAT?

Pray that God would open your eyes to gospel opportunities this week—even today!

DID YOU KNOW?

Paul wrote his letter to the church at Philippi about ten years after the incident in Acts 16. Perhaps the Philippian jailer who got saved read it!

SEPTEMBER 14

God overlooked people's ignorance about these things in earlier times, but now he commands everyone everywhere to repent of their sins and turn to him. For he has set a day for judging the world with justice by the man he has appointed, and he proved to everyone who this is by raising him from the dead. ACTS 17:30-31

Idols, idols, idols. Everywhere the apostle Paul looked, he saw images of false gods.

Paul's heart was deeply troubled. He was in the Greek city of Athens during his second missionary journey. Athens was renowned in ancient times as the center of Greek culture. Evidence was everywhere of the Greeks' advances in architecture, mathematics, science, art, and philosophy, among other things.

But Paul couldn't get past the idols. The Greeks worshiped hundreds of pagan deities, and the statues and temples built in their honor dominated the city's landscape. Zeus, Hera, Apollo, Aphrodite, Hermes, Poseidon—Athens featured idols to all of them. The Athenians had even built an altar with the inscription, "To an Unknown God," just in case they forgot anybody.

But the Athenians were badly mistaken. There is only one true God, and he calls all people to trust in his Son for the forgiveness of their sins (1 Corinthians 8:4-6). So Paul began preaching the gospel of Jesus Christ in Athens. He didn't mince words, either. He urged the people to repent of their idolatry and turn to God for forgiveness before the final judgment (see today's verses).

WHAT'S IT MEAN?

God has been very patient with sinful humanity. As Acts 17:30 says, he has "overlooked people's ignorance," meaning he has chosen not to completely destroy humankind for their age-old disobedience.

But a day of final judgment is coming (see today's verse). One day in eternity, God will repay everyone according to what they have done (Romans 2:6).

The righteous (those who have trusted in Jesus as their Lord and Savior) will be welcomed into heaven, while the wicked (those who rejected Jesus) will be sentenced to everlasting punishment in hell (Matthew 13:40-43). At that point, there won't be any do-overs, second chances, or timeouts.

This life is a precious gift. Don't waste it on selfish pursuits, Satan's lies, or worldly idols. As Paul told the Athenians, God desires you to "turn to him" through his resurrected Son and live a life that brings him glory.

Some of the Athenians rejected Paul's message (Acts 17:32). What will you do?

NOW WHAT?

Read about Paul's three missionary journeys in Acts 13–21.

DID YOU KNOW?

The stumbling block for most of Paul's Greek audience that day was Jesus' resurrection (Acts 17:32).

You should remember the words of the Lord Jesus: "It is more blessed to give than to receive." ACTS 20:35

Imagine you're enjoying a fun cross-country vacation with your family, but while you're driving from city to city, you keep noticing highway billboard messages that read: WHEN YOU REACH HOME, YOU WILL BE ARRESTED, IMPRISONED, AND EXPERIENCE GREAT SUFFERING.

Your family might think twice about going home. A detour to Tahiti, perhaps?

That's pretty much what happened to the apostle Paul as he traveled throughout the Roman Empire on his third missionary journey. When he came to the city of Miletus, he called some dear friends from the church in nearby Ephesus to visit him. When they arrived, he said, "The Holy Spirit tells me in city after city that jail and suffering lie ahead" in Jerusalem (Acts 20:23).

Nevertheless, Paul felt God was calling him to Jerusalem, so he continued his journey. Before leaving, he encouraged his friends, and then, in his final words to them, he said, "You should remember the words of the Lord Jesus: 'It is more blessed to give than to receive'" (today's verse).

WHAT'S IT MEAN?

At first glance, those seem like strange last words for people you know you'll never see again. Was Paul preparing to pass around an offering plate and collect money for charity?

Nope. These words weren't about money. They were about a heart attitude—an entire outlook on life.

Kings receive. Servants give. In today's verse, Jesus calls his followers to act like servants who give of themselves to others, rather than like kings who expect to receive service from people. We can display a giving attitude with money, yes, but we can also give our time and talents in ways that glorify Jesus.

This giving mind-set should soak into every part of our lives. We should have a generous, servant-like attitude from sunup to sundown. We should probably even tattoo today's verse on our foreheads.

Okay, that last part was a joke. But you get the point. It is much better to think, *How can I give to others?* rather than *What can others give to me?*

Jesus, of course, is our perfect role model in this. As Mark 10:45 says, he came "not to be served but to serve others and to give his life as a ransom for many." That is true giving.

NOW WHAT?

Find a way to give assistance to a needy, elderly, or sick person in your church or neighborhood.

DID YOU KNOW?

None of the Gospels records Jesus saying the words in today's verse. Perhaps Paul was simply repeating what one of Jesus' disciples had told Paul that Jesus said (John 21:25).

This letter is from Paul, chosen by the will of God to be an apostle of Christ Jesus. I am writing to God's holy people in Ephesus, who are faithful followers of Christ Jesus. EPHESIANS 1:1

After studying the book of Acts and the start of the church, our focus now shifts to the New Testament epistles. These are simply letters that the apostles (Paul, James, Peter, John, and Jude) wrote to first-century churches throughout the Roman Empire.

These letters were written to:

- increase readers' theological understanding of God, Jesus, and the Holy Spirit
- explain salvation and all its related doctrines, such as regeneration (see the March 24 deovtion) and justification (see the May 3 devotion)
- teach believers how to live righteously
- correct false teachings that threatened the church

In other words, the New Testament epistles are all about Christian living.

Paul wrote the majority of them, and it's interesting to note how he started all his letters. He began by identifying and describing himself, then identifying and describing his audience. (Today's verse is a great example of this.) Only after that did he start communicating his main message.

Paul always wanted his audience to be clear about his identity and theirs. So as we spend the next few months learning more about Christian living, there's no better place to start than our identity in Christ.

WHAT'S IT MEAN?

Your identity is who you are. It's the specific qualities that make you *you*!

In his letters, Paul often referred to himself as "an apostle of Christ Jesus." But he was equally interested in helping his readers understand who *they* were. So he identified them as follows:

- "faithful brothers and sisters in Christ" (Colossians 1:2)
- "you who belong to God the Father and the Lord Jesus Christ" (1 Thessalonians 1:1)
- "faithful followers of Christ Jesus" (today's verse)
- "God's holy people . . . who belong to Christ Jesus" (Philippians 1:1)

Notice a theme? More than anything, a Christian's identity is in Christ. You might be great at sports, music, art, science, writing, computers, or whatever. But if you have trusted in Jesus, you belong to him above all else.

It's all about prioritizing Jesus in your life. It's about loving him above all other interests and pursuits. It's about making sure your hopes, dreams, and daily activities please him.

There's nothing greater than to be identified with the Savior who loves you and died for you!

NOW WHAT?

If you're a Christian, identify yourself as such when you meet someone new. It's sure to be a conversation starter!

DID YOU KNOW?

In Romans 1:1, Paul identified himself as "a slave of Christ Jesus" to show his full devotion to serving the Savior.

If anyone is in Christ, the new creation has come: The old has gone, the new is here! 2 CORINTHIANS 5:17, NIV

News traveled slowly in 1844.

Without telephones or an official nationwide postal service, long-distance messages were often handwritten letters delivered by a horse-and-carriage service, which could take days or weeks. So it was a momentous day when, on May 24, 1844, Samuel Morse sat down to a mysterious machine in Washington, DC, and successfully sent an electronic message instantly to a colleague in Baltimore. It was the first telegram in US history.

Morse's telegraph system transmitted a series of dots and dashes (known as "Morse code") across a long electric wire to a receiving machine on the other end that printed out the symbols on a strip of paper. This required someone to decipher the symbols into their corresponding alphabetical letters so the message made sense.

Morse's message that day read, "What hath God wrought!" from the King James Version of Numbers 23:23. A more modern translation might read, "Look what God has done!"

Communication is so much easier these days. Smartphones allow us to talk and text with others in real time, browse the Internet, take photos, play games, and more. Phones are one of many examples where the new is definitely better than the old.

Spiritually speaking, the same is true with us. We are far better off as new creations than as old ones.

WHAT'S IT MEAN?

For Christians, "the old" life that today's verse mentions is our former, sinful way of living before we come to saving faith in Jesus. Elsewhere, the Bible describes this old life as "useless" (Romans 3:12), "dead because of . . . your many sins" (Ephesians 2:1), and "far away from God" (Ephesians 2:13). Not good at all.

But when you ask Jesus in repentance and faith to forgive your sins, you become a "new creation." That means God changes your heart.

He does this by regenerating your heart (that is, being "born again," John 3:3) and reconciling you to himself "through Christ" (2 Corinthians 5:18, NIV). He removes the guilt of sin and makes you a new person on a new spiritual path with new desires. Your sinful heart that once thought only about pleasing yourself becomes more concerned about pleasing God. Instead of spiritual death, this new heart brings eternal life!

The new, spiritually transformed life that Jesus gives us is *so* much better than the old. Look what God has done, indeed!

NOW WHAT?

Memorize today's verse to remember who you are in Christ—a "new creation"!

DID YOU KNOW?

In 1866, the first transatlantic telegraph cable was laid across the Atlantic Ocean for international communication.

Put on the new self, created to be like God in true righteousness and holiness. EPHESIANS 4:24, NIV

When was the last time you did any of the following?

- slept in a crib
- played with a rattle
- cried at nap time
- needed a diaper change
- soothed yourself by sucking on a pacifier
- fell asleep to "Twinkle, Twinkle, Little Star"

Hope it's been a while. That's all baby stuff. You did all those things when you weren't as mature as you are now. They shouldn't be part of your life anymore.

The same principle applies in the Christian life. In Ephesians 4:22-24, the apostle Paul instructs believers to "put off your old self, which is being corrupted by its deceitful desires . . . and to put on the new self, created to be like God in true righteousness and holiness" (NIV).

WHAT'S IT MEAN?

All this talk about "old" and "new" sounds a lot like 2 Corinthians 5:17 and yesterday's devotion. But there's a noticeable difference between the two passages. While 2 Corinthians 5:17 mostly talks about the heart change that God performs in us, Ephesians 4:22-24 talks about *our* responsibility after the transformation.

Notice how Paul uses action verbs—"put off" the old and "put on" the new—in Ephesians 4:22-24. When God changes our sinful hearts to receive salvation, he then calls us to action!

Godly character doesn't just happen by itself. We must prayerfully fight a daily battle to put off our old, sinful behaviors. But just like you would never go back to diapers, rattles, and bottles at your age, you also should never resort to the "deceitful desires" of your sinful nature as a follower of Jesus.

Christians must strive each day to live in "righteousness and holiness." Through the power of God's Spirit inside us, we must . . .

- put off hate and put on love
- put off anger and put on joy
- put off lying and put on honesty
- put off cruelty and put on kindness
- put off rebelliousness and put on obedience

How can you accomplish all this? Only through Jesus! Through his death and resurrection, he broke the power of sin "so that in him we might become the righteousness of God" (2 Corinthians 5:21, NIV)!

NOW WHAT?
Make a two-column chart on a piece of paper, listing the sins you struggle with under "Put Off" and the opposite action you should take under "Put On." Pray through your list for God's help.

DID YOU KNOW?
Putting on the new self is not how we earn God's favor. God accepts us based on our faith in what Jesus has already accomplished on the cross for us.

*Put on the Lord Jesus Christ, and make no provision for the flesh,
to gratify its desires.* ROMANS 13:14, ESV

Barry Sanders was kind of like the Tasmanian Devil of *Looney Tunes* fame:
once he got going, he was awfully hard to stop.

Sanders, the Detroit Lions' Hall of Fame running back in the 1990s, was
a human tornado on the football field, piling up 15,269 rushing yards in his
dazzling ten-year NFL career (1989–1998). If he hadn't unexpectedly retired
at age thirty-one, he probably would've broken the NFL's all-time rushing
record at the time.

Sanders's success came from a unique blend of speed, power, agility, and
field vision. His uncanny ability to start, stop, spin, shimmy, and shake left
defenders comically grasping at air.

When facing Sanders, opposing teams had to "mind the gaps," meaning
that defensive linemen had to work together to minimize any holes that
Sanders could exploit. It rarely worked. Sanders excelled at uncovering even
the tiniest weaknesses in a defense—or creating them himself—and turning
them into huge touchdown runs.

"Minding the gaps" is crucial in the Christian life too. Let's check it out.

WHAT'S IT MEAN?

Like an NFL defense playing against Sanders, we must work hard to avoid
leaving any openings for sin in our lives. Sin looks for holes in every Christian's
defense, seeking to exploit our weaknesses and draw us away from God.

Today's verse puts it this way: "Make no provision for the flesh." The "flesh"
is the Bible's term for the ungodly desires that come from our sinful nature.

To make provision for something is to allow—or even encourage—it to
happen. Defenders leaving wide-open holes at the line of scrimmage against
Sanders would make provision for a touchdown run. Not studying for a test
makes provision for a failing grade. Covering yourself in honey and strolling
into a bear's den makes provision for a really bad day.

You get the idea. Christians must be on guard against sinful desires, which are sure to come, both from the devil (1 Peter 5:8) and our sinful natures (Romans 7:18-23). In order to avoid making provision for sin, don't put yourself in spiritually tempting situations.

There's also a positive action to take. Today's verse says, "Put on the Lord Jesus Christ." Like getting dressed in the morning, we are to cover ourselves in Jesus' righteousness.

Mind your spiritual gaps, avoid temptation, and imitate Christ!

NOW WHAT?

Think about your spiritual weaknesses and ask for Jesus' help to fight those temptations.

DID YOU KNOW?

Emmitt Smith (1990–2004) is currently the NFL's all-time rushing leader with 18,355 yards.

SEPTEMBER 20

Let us run with endurance the race that is set before us,
looking to Jesus, the founder and perfecter of our faith.
HEBREWS 12:1-2, ESV

One by one, the statesmen, young and old, filed into the Pennsylvania State House in Philadelphia and took their seats. The date was July 4, 1776.

Outside the building, Great Britain's thirteen American colonies were struggling in their conflict against the mother country and its brutal ruler, King George III. Inside, the Continental Congress's earlier debates about all-out war with England had given way to a much more unified mind-set: it was time for the colonies to break free and form their own sovereign nation.

So the Founding Fathers approved and signed the Declaration of Independence. It was the birth of the United States of America.

John Adams, Benjamin Franklin, Alexander Hamilton, Thomas Jefferson, James Madison, George Washington, and many others poured most of their lives into founding a new nation. These men were willing to risk everything for freedom. The numerous liberties that Americans still enjoy today are, in large part, thanks to the work and sacrifices of the Founding Fathers more than two hundred years ago.

Throughout history, the success of any movement, organization, or country often has depended on the person, or people, who founded it. The same holds true for religion. And as we're about to see, that's what makes Christianity the only true faith.

WHAT'S IT MEAN?

The founder of the Christian faith is not Abraham, Moses, Peter, Paul, or any other godly human being. As today's verse says, Christianity's founder is none other than the eternal Son of God, Jesus Christ. This separates Christianity from other religions. Any other foundation is an imperfect attempt by fallen humans to please God or find purpose in life.

Jesus, however, is the perfect founder of the only true faith because of who he is and what he has done. He is the sinless Son of God who died and rose again. Christianity is built on the unshakable foundation of the cross and the empty tomb.

Jesus isn't just the founder of our faith; he's also the "perfecter" of it (today's verse). While on earth, he perfectly obeyed God the Father (John 17:4), and now he helps all believers in their own gradual process of perfection, or sanctification, that will culminate with flawless resurrection bodies in eternity (1 Corinthians 15:53).

The Founding Fathers were great, but the Founding Son of God is infinitely greater!

NOW WHAT?

When you pray, ask Jesus often to keep perfecting you in his image.

DID YOU KNOW?

Of the four Founding Fathers who became president—George Washington, John Adams, Thomas Jefferson, and James Madison—only Washington did not attend college.

SEPTEMBER 21

The Lord—who is the Spirit—makes us more and more like him as we are changed into his glorious image. 2 CORINTHIANS 3:18

Life is full of unseen realities. Every day, millions of things happen that you can't see.

Take the earth's rotation, for instance. You can't feel it or see it. But at the equator, the earth is spinning at a rate of more than one thousand miles per hour. (Thank goodness for gravity, or we'd all be thrown into outer space!)

Here's more: as you read this, the earth is revolving around the sun at roughly 67,000 miles per hour. Light is traveling at 186,000 miles per second through the universe. Moisture is accumulating in clouds, preparing to fall as rain. Deep-sea creatures are swimming. Ants are burrowing. Hearts are beating. Lungs are breathing. Unborn babies are maturing. Grass is growing—and so are you!

You can't see these things happening. But they are. Just because your eyes can't see them happening doesn't mean they aren't occurring.

Add sanctification to this list.

WHAT'S IT MEAN?

Sanctification is an amazing part of the Christian life. It's a gradual process where we as Christians become less and less sinful and "more and more like" God (today's verse) over our lifetimes. It starts at the moment of salvation, continues until death, and is possible only by Jesus' work on the cross and the Holy Spirit's ongoing work in our hearts.

You can't see sanctification happening inside a believer, but you can see its effects. A liar who now tells the truth, a disobedient kid who now honors his parents, a bully who now shows kindness—these are all examples of people growing in sanctification. When God's Spirit works in someone's heart, the spiritual fruit is visible.

Even though God begins the process, we have a part to play too. God isn't in the magic wand business. He's not going to magically transform you into a Christlike believer while you loaf on the couch. Check out the action verbs in the following sanctification verses:

- "*Walk* by the Spirit" (Galatians 5:16, NIV).
- "*Give* yourselves completely to God" (Romans 6:13).
- "*Put* to death the deeds of your sinful nature" (Romans 8:13).

So take action. Pray for the Holy Spirit's help, strive to be like Jesus, and praise God as you are "changed into his glorious image" (today's verse).

NOW WHAT?

Pray for more of God's love, kindness, patience, joy, and other "fruit of the Spirit" (Galatians 5:22-23). These are all evidence of sanctification in a believer's life.

DID YOU KNOW?

The sanctification process doesn't earn God's favor for you. That comes only when God changes your heart to trust in Jesus' atoning work (his sacrificial death) on your behalf.

SEPTEMBER 22

Do not let sin reign in your mortal body so that you obey its evil desires. ROMANS 6:12, NIV

In 697 BC, a young boy ascended the royal courtroom steps in Jerusalem and sat on the throne. At age twelve, Manasseh had just become king of Judah.

Great hope surrounded Manasseh's coronation. His father, Hezekiah, had been one of Judah's greatest rulers. Hezekiah had led the people back to God through badly needed religious reforms, and he repelled an attack from the mighty Assyrian king, Sennacherib.

Sadly, Manasseh, whose name means "causing to forget" in Hebrew, did not remember or imitate his father's obedience. He ignored God's laws and committed unspeakable evils, including idolatry, planetary worship, building heathen altars in God's Temple, practicing sorcery, and ordering the deaths of many innocent people. Worst of all, he even sacrificed his own son to a pagan deity.

Manasseh led Judah "to do even more evil than the pagan nations that the LORD had destroyed when the people of Israel entered the land" (2 Kings 21:9). Because of Manasseh's unmatched immorality, God promised to judge Judah and "wipe away the people of Jerusalem as one wipes a dish" (2 Kings 21:13). This was fulfilled approximately fifty years later when the Babylonians conquered Judah, destroyed Jerusalem, and exiled many of the people.

When sin reigns, terrible things happen.

WHAT'S IT MEAN?

The language of today's verse, which was written by the apostle Paul approximately seven hundred years after Manasseh's death, calls to mind the reign of an evil king. Just as Manasseh ruled over Judah, he let sin rule over his heart. He devoted his "mortal body"—his thoughts, actions, deeds, and even his very soul—to wickedness and disobedience.

Really. Bad. Choice.

Letting sin "reign in your mortal body" means consistently choosing to following selfish and ungodly desires rather than living like Jesus. That's not what God intended for his children. It's a path that leads to spiritual death (Romans 6:23).

Every person's heart is like a throne. What will you allow to rule on yours—God's ways or sin? Followers of Jesus should never let sin reign in their lives like a wicked king.

Allow God to rule your heart. Trust in Jesus for the forgiveness of your sins. Choose love over hate, forgiveness over anger, and honesty over deceit.

Jesus broke the power of sin on the cross (Romans 8:2) so that the true King could reign in your heart!

NOW WHAT?

Read Romans 6. It's a power-packed study of transferring the reign of your heart from sin to Christ!

DID YOU KNOW?

The first Manasseh mentioned in Scripture was Joseph's firstborn son (Genesis 41:51).

SEPTEMBER 23

There is no condemnation for those who belong to Christ Jesus.
ROMANS 8:1

Late on the night of April 17, 1865, with the US Civil War having ended only eight days earlier, Union soldiers entered the boarding house at 541 H Street in Washington, DC. Before long, they emerged with their prisoner, Mary Surratt.

Three nights prior, John Wilkes Booth had fatally shot Abraham Lincoln at Ford's Theatre in Washington. Surratt was one of many southern sympathizers who were suspected of conspiracy in the assassination.

After a nearly two-month trial, a military tribunal convicted Surratt, who claimed her innocence all along, and seven others. Surratt and three men were condemned to hang. On July 7, Surratt climbed a twelve-foot gallows and infamously became the first woman ever to be executed by the US government.

Even today, historians are still divided on Surratt's involvement in Lincoln's assassination. Now, of course, it doesn't matter. Her condemnation brought death.

Today's verse talks about condemnation. But the news for Christians in Romans 8:1 is infinitely better than the news Surratt received at the end of her trial.

WHAT'S IT MEAN?

The word *condemn* means to declare something to be wrong, pronounce someone guilty, or sentence someone to an undesirable fate. Condemnation is never good.

In Romans 5:12, the apostle Paul wrote that sin condemns all humans to death. Because he is holy and just, God must punish sin, and death is part of the punishment. But three chapters later, in today's verse, Paul says, "There is no condemnation for those who belong to Christ Jesus." How is this possible?

It's possible through Jesus!

On the cross, Jesus suffered God's full wrath toward sin (Romans 3:25). He paid the entire penalty for our disobedience. All the condemnation your sins deserve was nailed to the cross—every last bit. Now, to be free of condemnation, all you must do is "belong to Christ Jesus" (today's verse) through faith in him as your Lord and Savior.

Christians will occasionally experience God's loving discipline (Hebrews 12:5-11), but no true believer will ever be condemned to suffer God's terrifying wrath against sin. Through Jesus, believers will receive only God's love, grace, mercy, forgiveness . . . all the good stuff!

This news is stunning, true, and 100 percent available to you through Jesus!

NOW WHAT?

Memorize today's verse. It's a great reminder!

DID YOU KNOW?

The three other conspirators on trial with Surratt who were not hanged were sentenced to life in prison.

There is no condemnation for those who belong to Christ Jesus.
ROMANS 8:1

Guilt is a tricky thing.

There is perhaps no other human emotion that can produce both good things and disasters in us. Handled correctly, a feeling of guilt after sin can lead to godly sorrow, repentance, and spiritual growth. Handled incorrectly, though, guilt can become an emotional jail cell, imprisoning our hearts with harmful thoughts that interfere with godliness and lock us up in self-pity.

As we consider the amazing truths found in Romans 8:1 for a second consecutive day, it's important for us to take a deeper look at condemnation and guilt.

WHAT'S IT MEAN?

When you sin, it's appropriate to feel regret and acknowledge your guilt. That's spiritually healthy. But what you do with that guilt afterward makes all the difference.

Take Judas Iscariot, for example. He took guilt to terrible extremes. After betraying Jesus in the garden of Gethsemane, Judas was "filled with remorse" (Matthew 27:3). But rather than repenting and turning to Jesus for forgiveness, Judas rushed off and hanged himself. He let guilt overwhelm him.

Guilt should never overwhelm true followers of Jesus. Yes, we all sin—sometimes a lot—and it seems like we can get stuck in the same bad patterns. What's more, Satan, "the accuser" (Revelation 12:10), will remind you of your mistakes and drag you toward unhealthy levels of guilt and self-pity. But that's when it's time to remember the glorious realities of Romans 8:1!

If you have trusted in the risen Savior, your guilt before God is completely removed. Jesus suffered God's condemnation against your sins on the cross so you wouldn't have to.

This means the unkind word you recently spoke, or the lie that you just told, or the way you defied your parents has been forgiven. If you have trusted in the blood of Jesus, God doesn't condemn you, so don't condemn yourself!

But be careful: a Christian's freedom from condemnation is not permission to sin. You must never think, *It doesn't matter how I act because God will forgive me anyway.* That would be wrongly taking advantage of God's grace. As Galatians 6:7 says, "Do not be deceived: God cannot be mocked. A man reaps what he sows" (NIV).

Trust in Jesus as your Lord and Savior, and when you sin, humbly confess it to God. In doing these things, you can say good-bye to guilt and condemnation!

NOW WHAT?

Read all of Romans 8. It's one of Scripture's greatest chapters.

DID YOU KNOW?

Psalm 103:12 says God "has removed our sins as far from us as the east is from the west." No condemnation there!

No power in the sky above or in the earth below—indeed, nothing in all creation will ever be able to separate us from the love of God that is revealed in Christ Jesus our Lord. ROMANS 8:39

Welcome to "the Rock."

In the mid-1930s, as America was struggling with a significant crime problem during the Great Depression, the US Federal Bureau of Prisons took possession of Alcatraz, a former US Army correctional facility on a small, rocky island in San Francisco Bay. From 1934 to 1963, Alcatraz operated as a maximum-security penitentiary and became home to some of the nation's worst criminals, including Al Capone, Robert "the Birdman" Stroud, and George "Machine Gun" Kelly.

Like all prisons, Alcatraz was designed to isolate criminals from the general public to punish and rehabilitate them. But the Rock took that separation to greater levels than virtually any other prison of that era.

Besides the fact that it was an island, Alcatraz employed many other methods of isolation. Unruly prisoners were often sent to "D Block," a wing of forty-two cells that cut them off from the main prison population. The worst offenders were banished to the "Strip Cell," a single unit where inmates were forced to sit naked in pitch-black darkness for up to two days without a sink or toilet—only a hole in the floor.

Whoa.

Separation from others is painful. God created us as relational beings who work best around others. Worst of all, of course, is separation from God. That's why today's verse is so amazing!

WHAT'S IT MEAN?

Every person is alienated from God because of sin (Isaiah 59:2). Not good. In fact, without reconciliation, each of us is destined for an eternity in hell apart from our Creator (Matthew 25:46). *Really* not good.

But in Romans 8:31-39, the apostle Paul describes one of the most glorious truths in Scripture: Christians cannot be separated from God's love. *It's just not possible.*

Once God has saved you by his grace, he will never stop loving you. *Never.* Even when you struggle to obey him, God still loves you. Nothing in this universe—not even the most powerful forces of evil—can hinder God's love for you.

This incredible reality is possible only through Jesus. The salvation he provides is complete and eternal. His death and resurrection bring together the two parties (God and us) who were once at odds because of sin. All you have to do is repent and believe.

Rock on!

NOW WHAT?
Whenever you're discouraged or spiritually struggling, read Romans 8:31-39. It's an awesome pick-me-up!

DID YOU KNOW?
Alcatraz started as a military fortress in the 1850s.

I urge you, brothers and sisters, in view of God's mercy, to offer your bodies as a living sacrifice, holy and pleasing to God—this is your true and proper worship. ROMANS 12:1, NIV

Certain jobs in life are guaranteed to come with a high risk of injury:

1. Hollywood stuntman
2. NFL running back
3. coal miner
4. mixed martial arts fighter
5. military infantryman
6. sheep in ancient Israel

Okay, so being a sheep in ancient Israel wasn't really a job. But boy, was it dangerous!

It wasn't dangerous for just sheep, though. Throw rams, cattle, goats, and even turtledoves on the list too. In Old Testament times, all of those poor animals were acceptable sacrifices to God.

The Israelites slaughtered millions of animals under the old sacrificial system. The Tabernacle (and later, the Jerusalem Temple) was quite a bloody place.

All that blood had a purpose, though. God wanted to show his people the price of their disobedience. Before Jesus' coming, animal sacrifices were God's merciful way of atoning for Israel's sins. The animals acted as substitutes, dying in place of the people. As Hebrews 9:22 says, "Without the shedding of blood, there is no forgiveness."

Why the Old Testament history lesson? Because it helps provide context for today's verse, where the apostle Paul calls all Christians to "offer your bodies as a living sacrifice."

WHAT'S IT MEAN?

By using symbolic language, Paul was clearly calling our attention to Old Testament sacrifices. But don't worry. You're not going to be thrown onto an altar! The key word in today's verse is "a *living* sacrifice."

The difference between the Old Testament system and now is Jesus! By his death, he fulfilled the entire Old Testament (Matthew 5:17) and ended the need for Temple sacrifices (Hebrews 9:11-12). Now, *we* are God's temple (1 Corinthians 3:16), and we worship him by sacrificing our lives for his glory (see today's verse).

That means everything you do with your body should be "holy and pleasing to God":

- the words you speak (mouth)
- the thoughts you think (mind)
- the things you do (hands)
- the places you go (feet)
- the things you look at (eyes)
- the music you listen to (ears)

Thanks to Jesus, your whole life, expressed through all the parts of your body, can be a sacrifice of worship to your loving Creator! (No sheep required.)

NOW WHAT?

Check out Leviticus 1–7 to learn more about Old Testament sacrifices.

DID YOU KNOW?

Paul's words in 1 Corinthians 6:19-20 are similar to Romans 12:1: "You are not your own; you were bought at a price. Therefore honor God with your bodies" (NIV).

Let love be genuine. ROMANS 12:9, ESV

Let's face it: the book of Romans is not always easy to understand.

The apostle Paul wrote it as a letter to Christians living in Rome, the imperial city of the massive Roman Empire, in AD 57 or so. Of his thirteen New Testament letters, Romans is Paul's *magnum opus*—his masterpiece.

For the first eleven chapters, Paul takes us on a marvelous, theologically deep journey through God's salvation plan. He discusses key Christian doctrines and subjects such as sin, divine judgment, Old Testament law, faith, righteousness, justification, sanctification, and much more. Phew! Romans really makes you think.

Then, halfway through chapter twelve, Paul abruptly switches gears from doctrine to practice. In other words, he moves from *what* we believe about salvation to *how* it should affect our daily living.

And the first thing he mentions—in today's verse—is love.

WHAT'S IT MEAN?

It's appropriate that Paul begins the discussion about living the Christian life with love. After all, "God is love" (1 John 4:8), and the goal of all Christians should be to become more like their Creator. Without love, faith is worthless (1 Corinthians 13:1-3).

Love, by definition, is unselfish concern for another. Genuine, God-pleasing love is considering others more important than yourself (Philippians 2:3) and putting their needs before your own. It's having a heart that says, "Others first, me second." One verse later in Romans 12:10, Paul writes, "Love each other with genuine affection, and take delight in honoring each other." Likewise, 1 Peter 1:22 tells you to "love each other deeply with all your heart."

Love that's not genuine is unkind and dishonest. It's acting friendly toward someone when that person is around but then gossiping behind that person's back. It's befriending someone only to get something out of it for yourself. That's not true love, and it certainly isn't pleasing to God.

Genuine love is always sprinkled with kindness, humility, and honesty. The greatest example of genuine love, of course, is Jesus. He was so others-focused, he took the punishment our sins deserved and died in our place. As John 15:13 says, "There is no greater love than to lay down one's life for one's friends."

Jesus showed amazingly genuine love toward you. Go and do the same to others!

NOW WHAT?

Offer to help a friend or family member in a meaningful way without being asked. That's a great opportunity to show genuine love.

DID YOU KNOW?

Paul wrote extensively about love in 1 Corinthians 13, which is sometimes called "the love chapter." We'll look at that in a few weeks.

SEPTEMBER 28

Abhor what is evil; hold fast to what is good.   ROMANS 12:9, ESV

Hate is a pretty strong word.

If you hate something, you have more than a general distaste for it, such as "I'd prefer not to eat spinach" or "I don't like math homework." Hate is an intense dislike. It's the desire to have nothing to do with the object of your feelings. In a moment of unchecked anger, perhaps you've even shouted, "I hate you!" to someone. Those are hurtful words, to be sure.

But in the English language, there exists an even stronger word than *hate*. That word is *abhor*. To abhor something means to hate it . . . times ten. Dictionary.com defines *abhor* like this: "to regard with extreme repugnance or aversion; detest utterly; loathe; abominate."

So it's interesting that in his letter to Roman Christians, the apostle Paul used the word *apostugeó* to describe how a Christian should feel toward sin. In case you're a little rusty on your ancient languages, that's Greek, the language the New Testament was originally written in. The most literal English translations of the Bible render *apostugeó* in Romans 12:9 as—you guessed it—"abhor."

WHAT'S IT MEAN?

Many people have a careless attitude toward sin. It isn't a big deal to them.

But sin is a big deal to God. Sin is breaking God's laws. It's replacing God's perfect plan with selfish, wicked choices. It's trying to rule our own lives without God's help.

Sin corrupted God's perfect creation (Romans 8:20), separated people from their Creator (Isaiah 59:2), and doomed humanity to experience physical death (Romans 6:23). Sin is so serious that it took the death of God's own Son to solve the problem.

That's why we should abhor sin. The goal for every believer is to become like our sinless Savior through the process of sanctification. Sin gets in the way of this.

Here is the great balancing act for every Christian. Yes, we must take sin seriously and abhor it, but there's no need to feel condemned when we do sin (Romans 8:1). On the cross, Jesus fully paid sin's terrible price (1 John 2:2) and broke sin's power (Romans 8:2). Through Christ, we have victory over it in our daily lives and for eternity.

So abhor sin and "hold fast to what is good" (today's verse). Seek God. Love his Word and obey it. In doing so, you'll fulfill what you were created to do!

NOW WHAT?

Memorize today's verse. It's short, sweet, and to the point!

DID YOU KNOW?

In 1 John 3:8, we read that Jesus "came to destroy the works of the devil"—in other words, sin.

Rejoice in our confident hope. Be patient in trouble, and keep on praying. ROMANS 12:12

Cars have instruction manuals. So do refrigerators, microwaves, dishwashers, vacuums, headphones, video game consoles, bicycles, lawn mowers, power drills, remote control airplanes, hot water heaters, toilets . . .

You get the point.

Virtually any product you buy has some sort of instruction manual or a set of directions on how to properly use it. Don't you wish there was an instruction manual for life? Sometimes life can be really difficult. It sure would be nice to have a handbook to tell you exactly what to do when trials come.

Well, look no further! The Bible is exactly what you need. After all, God created you. He knows you inside and out. Why turn to anything else besides God's Word?

Scripture gives very clear guidelines when it comes to life's hardships. Today's verse is a great example.

WHAT'S IT MEAN?

Romans 12:12 is wonderfully practical. In describing how to handle life's curveballs, the apostle Paul suggests a simple, straightforward three-step process. Here's a quick breakdown of each step:

"Rejoice in our confident hope"—Even in life's darkest moments, Christians can experience joy through something that provides hope beyond temporary suffering. That hope is Jesus. According to 1 Timothy 1:1, Jesus is the one "who gives us hope." Likewise, 1 Thessalonians 1:3 mentions the "enduring hope you have because of our Lord Jesus Christ." Life's trials may be great, but the eternal hope and salvation Jesus provides are so much greater.

"Be patient in trouble"—Trials are no fun. And sometimes, they seem never ending. But Scripture calls us to patiently endure. In fact, James

1:12 promises, "God blesses those who patiently endure testing and temptation." The trial won't last forever. You can trust God to help you through it.

"Keep on praying"—Prayer demonstrates trust. When you pray to God during trials, you show him that you're relying on his power, not your own, to pull you through. So keep praying!

Following the three-step instructions of Romans 12:12 won't guarantee that the trial you're experiencing will magically disappear. But resting in and obeying the truths of God's Word will help get you through whatever difficulty you're facing—guaranteed!

NOW WHAT?

When trials rear their ugly heads, remember the winning formula of Romans 12:12—RPP: Rejoicing, patience, and prayer!

DID YOU KNOW?

Jesus, of course, was the greatest example of all three. To see how he rejoiced in hope and showed patience in trouble, read Hebrews 12:2. To see how he kept praying, check out Luke 5:16.

Live in harmony with one another. Do not be haughty, but associate with the lowly. Never be wise in your own sight.
ROMANS 12:16, ESV

Do you remember the story of Jesus calming the storm on the Sea of Galilee? It's a remarkable account of Jesus' power over nature. Less well known, but no less amazing, is what happened immediately afterward.

When Jesus came ashore, he arrived in a Gentile region that most Jews avoided because of ritual purity laws. Immediately, a dangerous, wild-looking man rushed toward Jesus. The man was suffering from severe demonic oppression.

The evil spirits tormenting him had ruined his life and turned him into a monster. Unfit for normal society, he lived naked among the tombs, often screamed at the top of his lungs, and cut himself with stones. Anytime the local townspeople tried to subdue him with metal chains, he ripped the shackles apart. No one dared approach him anymore.

Except Jesus.

With great power and authority, Jesus cast the demons out of the man and completely healed him. When the villagers came running to see what had happened, they were shocked to see the man dressed and sitting quietly at Jesus' feet, listening to him. (You can read about this incredible miracle in Matthew 8; Mark 5; and Luke 8.)

Jesus had a wonderfully sensitive heart toward the lowly.

WHAT'S IT MEAN?

Healing the demon-possessed man is just one of many examples of how Jesus loved people whom no one else cared about. Even though he is the all-powerful, eternal Son of God, Jesus humbled himself to help the poor, needy, rejected, and forgotten. He befriended hated tax collectors (Luke 19:1-5), gave sight to blind beggars (Mark 10:52), healed paralytics (Matthew 9:6), welcomed children whom others were trying to shoo away (Matthew 19:13-15), and showed kindness to the repentant thief crucified next to him (Luke 23:39-43).

The apostle Paul certainly had Christ in mind when he wrote today's verse. Every Christian should share Jesus' heart for the lowly.

Do you know anyone whom no one else likes? Are there people in your school, church, or neighborhood who are hurting, sick, or forgotten by others? Don't look down on them. Befriend them and love them. Seek their welfare. Look for ways to serve them.

In doing so, you will be showing them the love of the Savior!

NOW WHAT?

Get involved with a local charity where you can help the poor and hungry. Perhaps you can do it through your church.

DID YOU KNOW?

Psalm 138:6 talks about God the Father's heart for those who are low on the social scale: "Though the LORD is high, he regards the lowly, but the haughty he knows from afar" (ESV).

Everyone must submit to governing authorities. For all authority comes from God, and those in positions of authority have been placed there by God. ROMANS 13:1

When the apostle Paul wrote today's verse in about AD 57, Emperor Nero was early into his terrible reign over the Roman Empire.

After several years of relative stability, Nero's rule quickly devolved into chaos. He ordered the deaths of his mother, his first wife, his former mentor, and various political rivals, and he personally killed his second wife.

Some historians believe Nero started the great fire of Rome in AD 64 to clear space for the sprawling royal estate he wanted to build, the *Domus Aurea* ("Golden House"). He falsely accused Christians, sparking a deadly persecution of believers in Rome. Early Christian tradition says that both Paul and Peter were martyred during Nero's reign. This guy wasn't up for any humanitarian awards.

By AD 68, the Roman Senate labeled Nero a public enemy and sentenced him to death. Rather than turn himself in, Nero took his own life with the help of an assistant.

This was the type of authority figure that early Christians had to deal with. Yet in today's verse, Paul called those believers (and us) to "submit to governing authorities."

WHAT'S IT MEAN?

Today's verse clearly states that "all authority comes from God." This doesn't mean God approves of wicked rulers like Nero. Anyone who abuses power will answer to God on Judgment Day.

But God has wisely ordained earthly authorities and governments to help us live orderly lives. Otherwise, sinful humanity would disintegrate into self-destructive chaos.

Plus, obeying human authorities helps us learn to obey God, our ultimate authority. After all, how can you submit to the God you *can't* see if you struggle to submit to the authorities you *can* see?

Humanly speaking, your parents are the most important governing authorities in your life. But there are also schoolteachers, church leaders, coaches, local and national governments, law enforcement officials, and others.

Thanks to their weaknesses and your own sinful nature, it's not always easy to submit to their authority. But this is what God calls you to do.

Obey your parents, teachers, and other leaders. Follow your school rules. And definitely don't break the law. Obeying the authorities in your life honors the Lord!

NOW WHAT?

Have you recently disobeyed your parents or another authority? Ask for their forgiveness.

DID YOU KNOW?

Jesus provided our greatest example of obeying authority. The Son of God perfectly obeyed the Father's will (John 15:10) by submitting himself to earthly authorities (Matthew 17:24-27; 22:15-22), even allowing wicked men to crucify him for our salvation (John 19:9-11).

OCTOBER 2

May God, who gives this patience and encouragement, help you live in complete harmony with each other, as is fitting for followers of Christ Jesus. ROMANS 15:5

In 1961, a group of suntanned teenagers from Southern California decided to form a rock-and-roll band. The members included three brothers, Brian, Carl, and Dennis Wilson; their cousin, Mike Love; and a school buddy, Al Jardine.

They began perfecting their sound in Brian's bedroom and by playing small-time local gigs. Soon enough, those humble beginnings led to worldwide fame. A year later, the Beach Boys released their first album, *Surfin' Safari*. The rest, as they say, is music history.

The Beach Boys' catchy, upbeat songs about surfing, hot rods, and love captured the hearts of a generation and are still popular today. Their 1966 album, *Pet Sounds*, is generally considered one of the most influential records of all time. In 1988, the band was inducted into the Rock and Roll Hall of Fame.

What really set the Beach Boys apart were their harmonies—when multiple vocalists sing different musical notes simultaneously to produce beautiful, melodic sounds. Even today, more than half a century after the band's inception, the Beach Boys remain perhaps the greatest harmonic group in rock history.

Harmony, though, doesn't just produce great results in the music world. Harmony is also something that God calls all Christians to share.

WHAT'S IT MEAN?

Perhaps you shatter glass and make dogs howl when you sing. No worries—the harmony God desires between Christians has nothing to do with music.

In nonmusical terms, the word *harmony* means calm, peace, or agreement. This perfectly describes how relationships between Christians should look.

Your interactions with other believers (and everyone else, for that matter) should be marked by love, kindness, and a lack of conflict. As today's verse says, harmony "is fitting for followers of Christ Jesus." If you bicker and fight with other believers, it stains Jesus' name. People will notice and wonder what makes Christians different from anyone else.

Followers of Jesus, after all, are on the same team. We're all working toward the same goal: to glorify God and become more like his Son. This should harmonize you with other believers in love and purpose. (Even if your singing voice makes small children weep.)

NOW WHAT?

For more on Christian harmony, read Psalm 133; 1 Corinthians 1:10; 2 Corinthians 13:11; and Colossians 3:14.

DID YOU KNOW?

The Beach Boys originally called themselves the Pendletones, a reference to the Pendleton plaid flannel shirts popular among surfers back then. (Good switch, fellas.)

OCTOBER 3

Let us go on instead and become mature in our understanding.
HEBREWS 6:1

Babies are cute and cuddly. They make funny faces and adorable cooing noises, and they look like little angels when they sleep.

But babies are also completely helpless. They can't walk, talk, or care for themselves in any way. They need constant supervision. And of course, they still need diapers. (Boy, do they need diapers!)

Babies are one of God's most precious gifts in life. But calling someone a baby isn't a compliment. It implies that the person is acting immaturely.

That's exactly what the apostle Paul called Christians in ancient Corinth, a large, pagan city in southern Greece where Paul had preached the gospel and planted a church during his second missionary journey. After initially believing Paul's message and turning to Jesus, the Corinthian Christians stopped growing spiritually. They were worldly, self-centered, and immature. So here's what Paul wrote them 1 Corinthians 3:1-3:

> When I was with you I couldn't talk to you as I would to spiritual
> people. I had to talk as though you belonged to this world or as
> though you were infants in Christ. I had to feed you with milk,
> not with solid food, because you weren't ready for anything stronger.
> And you still aren't ready, for you are still controlled by your
> sinful nature.

WHAT'S IT MEAN?

By calling the Corinthians "infants," Paul wasn't being nasty. He was simply using figurative language to spur his friends toward Christian growth. What he was really saying was: "Just like a baby has a long way to go in the physical maturing department, you have a long way to go spiritually."

Every Christian starts as an "infant in Christ" after first coming to faith in Jesus. But through sanctification (see the September 21 devotion), believers should become more and more like Jesus. The Corinthians slowed down this process by giving in to their sinful natures.

Choosing sin over godliness stunts spiritual growth. Just like babies outgrow pacifiers, bottles, high chairs—and yes, diapers, too, thankfully—you need to give up old sinful patterns to grow in Christ.

Leave spiritual infancy behind. Say no to sin and yes to God!

NOW WHAT?

Reading the Bible is a must for Christian maturity. You can't grow in godliness if you don't know what God says! Praying and attending a Bible-believing church will help greatly too. So will obeying your parents and picking the right friends.

DID YOU KNOW?

Like Paul, the author of Hebrews used a baby analogy to encourage his readers to grow in godliness (see today's verse and Hebrews 5:11–6:3).

OCTOBER 4

This is how one should regard us, as servants of Christ and stewards of the mysteries of God. 1 CORINTHIANS 4:1, ESV

Time for a pop quiz! Do you know what the terms *steward* and *stewardess* mean?

If you guessed "someone who enjoys eating piping-hot bowls of stew" . . . sorry, good try.

Steward and *stewardess* aren't used much anymore. Not long ago, they were job titles used to describe airline employees who took care of passengers on flights. Now airlines call them "flight attendants." (Hey, we'll call them "Your Royal Majesty" or whatever they want, as long as they keep the complimentary cranberry juice flowing!)

But in the apostle Paul's day, *steward* meant something completely different. It's interesting that in today's verse, Paul describes Christians as both "servants" and "stewards." If they sound similar, they're really not.

WHAT'S IT MEAN?

In the Roman Empire, a servant (or "bondservant") had more rights than, say, the slaves in early America. Servants were often given significant responsibilities by their master, worked for pay, and could eventually buy their freedom. After they were free, some servants continued to work for their former master and even officially took his name as their own to honor him.

Stewards, on the other hand, enjoyed even more responsibility. They were responsible for managing a wealthy landowner's estate, which often included money, property, servants, and more.

Do you see the comparisons Paul was making? Just like servants in first-century Rome, Christians have a job to do for their Master, Jesus Christ. The difference, though, is that we can't purchase our freedom from sin, no matter how hard we work at it (in other words, doing good deeds). Jesus already purchased our freedom on the cross. All we have to do is repent and believe. Once we do, like freed slaves, we should be honored to bear the name of Jesus (1 Peter 4:14), considering how he sacrificed himself for us.

Similarly, just like stewards in first-century Rome, Christians have been given a great responsibility to manage our Master's business on his behalf. Today's verse tells us we are to steward, or take care of, "the mysteries of God." That's the gospel—the good news of long-awaited salvation through Jesus and all the blessings that follow.

The job of a Christian is to faithfully serve Jesus and tell others about him. It's not burdensome servant's work to serve this Master. It's a great privilege!

NOW WHAT?

Check out Jesus' parable of the talents in Matthew 25:14-30. It's all about faithful servanthood and stewardship.

DID YOU KNOW?

The apostle Paul also referred to himself as a servant of Christ in Romans 1:1; Philippians 1:1; and Titus 1:1 (all ESV).

OCTOBER 5

Decide instead to live in such a way that you will not cause another believer to stumble and fall. ROMANS 14:13

When was the last time you thought: *Gee, I wonder if I should eat this juicy, delicious pork tenderloin. The rest of the pig was sacrificed to Zeus in his temple last Tuesday night. Hmmm, decisions, decisions . . .*

Sounds silly, right? But this was a major issue for the first-century Christians in the city of Corinth.

In the apostle Paul's day, Corinth was a bustling hub of idolatry. Pagan temples, altars, and monuments to Greek gods and Roman emperors were everywhere. Oftentimes, the parts of animals that were not used in religious sacrifices were sold in the city's marketplace as food. (Kind of makes you thankful for your local grocery store, doesn't it?)

This presented a moral dilemma for the Christian church in Corinth. Apparently, some Christians with sensitive consciences refused to eat meat from a pagan animal sacrifice. It reminded them too much of when they used to be idol worshipers, before they had turned to Jesus during Paul's first missionary visit to Corinth several years earlier. Meanwhile, more mature Christians were saying, "Who cares if this meat was offered to an idol? The idol isn't a real god anyway!"

News of this problem reached Paul. So he addressed it in his letter to the Corinthian believers, which we now call 1 Corinthians. Speaking to the more mature Christians, Paul wrote, "You must be careful so that your freedom does not cause others with a weaker conscience to stumble" (1 Corinthians 8:9).

WHAT'S IT MEAN?

Even if the question of whether to eat food sacrificed to idols isn't relevant today, Paul's point in 1 Corinthians 8:9 and today's verse *is*! A Christian should never do anything to make other believers stumble in their faith.

Not everyone will share your spiritual convictions on what to eat, wear, watch, and listen to, or who to hang out with. And that's okay. Don't look down on other believers for being more, or less, conservative in their faith than you are. And certainly don't get them to do something they're not comfortable with, even if you are.

Treat these people with kindness and respect. Your job is to love them no matter where they're at spiritually. After all, Jesus died for them just as he died for you.

NOW WHAT?

To learn more about not causing other believers to stumble, read 1 Corinthians 8 and Romans 14.

DID YOU KNOW?

Paul speaks bluntly in 1 Corinthians 8:12: "When you sin against other believers by encouraging them to do something they believe is wrong, you are sinning against Christ."

OCTOBER 6

Don't you realize that in a race everyone runs, but only one person gets the prize? So run to win! I CORINTHIANS 9:24

In 1896, Spyridon Louis was king of the distance-running world.

Louis, a twenty-three-year-old Greek man, won the marathon, an exhaustingly long footrace that at the time was almost twenty-five miles long, during the first modern-day Olympic Games in Athens, Greece. When Louis crossed the finish line in 2 hours, 58 minutes, and 50 seconds, the crowd cheered wildly for their countryman.

Ol' "Spy" was probably feeling pretty good about himself back then. But he was quite slow compared to today's elite marathoners (who now run 26.2 miles). Spy's winning time in 1896 would have placed him dead last in the 2012 London Olympics.

Marathon running has come a long way. In 2014, Kenya's Dennis Kimetto set a new world record of 2:02:57 at the Berlin Marathon in Germany. (Don't worry, Spy, we still love you.)

World-class distance runners aren't made overnight. Marathon running requires a huge amount of time, dedication, and training. This is what the apostle Paul was referring to when he wrote 1 Corinthians 9:24-27:

> *Don't you realize that in a race everyone runs, but only one person gets the prize? So run to win! All athletes are disciplined in their training. They do it to win a prize that will fade away, but we do it for an eternal prize. So I run with purpose in every step. I am not just shadowboxing. I discipline my body like an athlete, training it to do what it should.*

WHAT'S IT MEAN?

The Christian life is like a marathon. It's a long endeavor, not a short sprint. It won't always be easy, but like a tired marathoner at the twenty-first mile, Christians can endure life's difficulties through the strength God provides.

To help with the road ahead, Christians should be "disciplined in their training." This training involves prayer, reading and memorizing Scripture faithfully, and going to a Bible-believing church. These things sharpen us spiritually, just like jogging, stretching, lifting weights, and eating properly help in physical training.

Best of all, the marathon of the Christian life is not all pain and struggle. It's filled with countless joys and blessings from God. And there's a great reward at the finish line: the "eternal prize" (1 Corinthians 9:25) of life in heaven with our Savior!

NOW WHAT?

How are you doing in the spiritual training methods mentioned above? Make any changes needed.

DID YOU KNOW?

Olympic champions in ancient days used to receive laurel wreaths to wear on their heads. Revelation 2:10 says Jesus will give Christians "the crown of life." That's way better!

OCTOBER 7

You should imitate me, just as I imitate Christ.

I CORINTHIANS II:I

Charles Barkley is not a role model. At least that's what he claimed in a controversial TV commercial in 1993.

At the time, Barkley was enjoying the prime of a hall-of-fame NBA career that spanned from 1984 to 2000. During a Nike shoe commercial, Barkley made his now-infamous proclamation: "I am not a role model. I am not paid to be a role model. I am paid to wreak havoc on the basketball court. Parents should be role models. Just because I dunk a basketball doesn't mean I should raise your kids."

Public reaction to Barkley's message was swift and mixed. Some people thought the six-foot-six power forward who made eleven straight All-Star teams was exactly right. Others thought he was avoiding his moral responsibilities as a high-profile superstar.

Either way, professional athletes don't always make the greatest role models. Over the decades, sports stars have been convicted of everything you can think of: murder, assault, domestic violence, burglary, illegal gambling, tax evasion, drug possession, drunk driving, operating illegal dogfighting rings, and more. Barkley himself has been arrested multiple times on various charges.

Even though athletes usually aren't the best option, today's verse makes it clear: it's important to have godly role models in your life.

WHAT'S IT MEAN?

God made humans as relational beings. We were meant to be around others. This was clear during creation when God looked at poor ol' Adam in the Garden of Eden and said, "It is not good for the man to be alone" (Genesis 2:18). So God made Eve.

If you are a Christian, it's important to surround yourself with godly influences. But pick your friends carefully. Hanging out with the wrong people is spiritually dangerous. As 1 Corinthians 15:33 says, "Bad company corrupts good character."

It's also important to have older, Christlike role models in your life, as the apostle Paul pointed out in today's verse. His hope was for the Corinthian Christians to follow his spiritual example. Older, godly Christians can be a huge blessing to you as you navigate life's ups and downs.

Our greatest example, of course, is Jesus. We should strive to be like him more than anyone else. After all, someone who is sinless in every way is a pretty fantastic role model!

NOW WHAT?

Make sure to involve your parents as you choose friends and role models. They have many years of experience in judging people's character and can help you decide wisely.

DID YOU KNOW?

Not only should you have godly role models, you should strive to *be* one (Titus 2:7 and 1 Peter 5:3).

OCTOBER 8

A spiritual gift is given to each of us so we can help each other.
1 CORINTHIANS 12:7

A word of warning: being bitten by a radioactive spider can cause weird stuff to happen to you. Really weird stuff. Just ask Peter Parker.

Peter Parker, of course, is better known as Spider-Man, the web-slinging hero of Marvel Comics fame. Marvel first introduced Spider-Man to the world in a comic series called *Amazing Fantasy* in 1962. Since then, the Spider-Man character has exploded into a gazillion-dollar business, with more comics, animated television series, major motion pictures, toys, costumes, and other Spidey-related merchandise than you can shoot a web at.

Thanks to the spider bite, Peter Parker obtained special powers such as superhuman strength, agility, spider-like climbing ability, and an acute awareness of his surroundings. After that, he had to accept his new alter ego and learn what to do with his unique capabilities. In the 2004 movie *Spider-Man 2*, Uncle Ben, who acts as Peter's father, tells him, "You've been given a gift, Peter. With great power comes great responsibility."

Chances are, you can't scale walls by yourself, shoot webs out of your wrists, or swing between city skyscrapers. But here's good news: if you are a Christian, you have been given special abilities called spiritual gifts that are much better than make-believe comic book stuff!

WHAT'S IT MEAN?

Unlike Peter Parker, you did not get your abilities by accident, and you certainly didn't obtain them from a radioactive spider. You received them—on purpose—from God's Holy Spirit (1 Corinthians 12:11).

There are lots of spiritual gifts: serving, teaching, encouragement, generosity, leadership, acts of mercy, and many more. With Spirit-empowered abilities, you have a responsibility: as today's verse says, God graciously gave gifts to you to build up others.

Think about the abilities you have. Does anything in that list above describe your interests and skills? Are you good at math? Science? Sports? Writing? Art? Music? Something else?

God didn't give you any of those abilities so you'd become famous or make lots of money. He gave them to you to "strengthen the whole church" (1 Corinthians 14:12). You do this by using your God-given talents to serve others and be a blessing to them.

When you use your gifts to do that, you honor the Savior!

NOW WHAT?

Make a plan to use the spiritual gifts you've been given to serve others in your home, church, school, or neighborhood.

DID YOU KNOW?

Romans 12:6-8 and 1 Corinthians 12:4-11 contain lists of spiritual gifts. These weren't meant to be complete. There are many other spiritual talents and abilities that God gives his children.

You are the body of Christ and individually members of it.
1 CORINTHIANS 12:27, ESV

If TV had existed in the first century AD, the church in ancient Corinth could have had their own reality show. The Corinthian Christians were a big, drama-filled mess.

The apostle Paul's letters to this church, called 1 and 2 Corinthians, reveal an unsettling level of conflict and ungodliness among the believers. There were divisions in the church, lawsuits between believers, pride, jealousy, idolatry, disorderly worship, drunkenness during Communion, and confusion about the future resurrection of believers. The Corinthians were drama kings and queens before the terms were even invented!

One of the issues plaguing this church was a misunderstanding of spiritual gifts. It seems many of the Corinthians were clamoring for the most publicly impressive gift—speaking in tongues (1 Corinthians 14). Everyone wanted to mysteriously talk in foreign languages for everybody else to hear.

They seemed to be ranking one another by their spiritual gifts—and that's flat-out wrong. So Paul reminded them about how the church is supposed to function by comparing it to the human body, calling it "the body of Christ" (today's verse).

WHAT'S IT MEAN?

The human body is made of many different parts and abilities. If your body consisted of many eyes but no nose, you wouldn't be able to smell. If your body consisted of many hands but no feet, you wouldn't be able to walk.

Likewise, God has given a variety of spiritual gifts to Christians so the body of Christ can function properly. Whatever your special talents and interests are, they don't make you any better or worse than anyone else. After all, you received these gifts from God (1 Corinthians 12:11), so there's nothing to brag about. God knew exactly what he wanted you to do and made you accordingly (1 Corinthians 12:18). Therefore, rejoice in how God made you, and look for ways to serve others.

Remember, the Christian life isn't a talent show. It's about becoming more like Jesus and serving others. Jesus himself said, "If anyone would be first, he must be last of all and servant of all" (Mark 9:35, ESV).

So don't delay! Put your body to work for the body of Christ!

NOW WHAT?

Pray for a Christlike heart as you seek to use your spiritual gifts to honor God and serve others.

DID YOU KNOW?

The Bible encourages Christians to desire more spiritual gifts. In 1 Corinthians 12:31, Paul tells us to "earnestly desire the higher gifts" (ESV). So pray that God's Spirit would bless you with more abilities to serve him (but not honor yourself).

As for me, may I never boast about anything except the cross of our Lord Jesus Christ. GALATIANS 6:14

If there's anything Muhammad Ali lacked during his legendary boxing career, it certainly wasn't self-confidence.

Ali, who held the world heavyweight title three different times between 1960 and 1981, is considered by many to be the greatest boxer in history. But the Louisville, Kentucky, native's colorful boasts brought him a significant amount of attention too.

Take, for instance, his 1964 championship bout with Sonny Liston. At the time, Liston was the reigning world champion, about ten years older than Ali (who was twenty-two then), and by far the favorite to win the fight. But that didn't stop Ali from confidently proclaiming to reporters, "I am the greatest!" before the fight. He repeated the claim after scoring a shocking seventh-round technical knockout of Liston.

Here are some other memorable boasts from the boxer who earned the nickname "the Louisville Lip":

- "They all fall in the round I call."
- "Float like a butterfly, sting like a bee; his hands can't hit what his eyes can't see."
- "[I've got] muscles so hard it'll break Superman's hands."
- "If you even dream of beating me, you better wake up and apologize."
- "It's hard to be humble when you're as great as I am."

Prideful boasts might make newspaper headlines, but God's Word calls Christians to act differently.

WHAT'S IT MEAN?

Human boasting directs praise the wrong way. It focuses all the attention on us instead of on God.

To understand the error of boasting, we need a proper, biblical perspective on ourselves. We are created beings, helpless apart from our Creator. We rely on God for our very breath (Psalm 104:29). So anything good we do is an achievement that's possible only through him. As the apostle Paul says in 1 Corinthians 4:7, "What do you have that God hasn't given you? And if everything you have is from God, why boast as though it were not a gift?"

Prideful boasting will only bring future humbling (Matthew 23:12) and judgment (Proverbs 16:18). Paul says it best in today's verse: the only one person we should boast about is Jesus Christ. God's Son accomplished true greatness on the cross, far greater than any human deed. His sacrifice purchased salvation for lost sinners.

Give human boasting the knockout punch, and direct all your praise to the Savior!

NOW WHAT?

Since any special gifts or abilities you have are from God (Ephesians 4:7; James 1:17), take some time to praise him for them.

DID YOU KNOW?

Muhammad Ali's real name was Cassius Clay. He changed his name after converting to Islam in 1964.

If I could speak all the languages of earth and of angels, but didn't love others, I would only be a noisy gong or a clanging cymbal.
I CORINTHIANS 13:1

When it comes to musical excellence, few ensembles can match the London Symphony Orchestra.

Started in 1904, the LSO has grown into one of the world's most renowned orchestras by attracting the world's greatest symphonic musicians—those who play instruments such as the violin, the clarinet, the piccolo, and everything in between. In addition to many performances at its home venue, the Barbican Centre in London, the LSO tours worldwide each year to dazzle international audiences. It has also recorded musical scores for hundreds of movies, including the original *Superman*, all the Star Wars films, and five Harry Potter movies.

But imagine if every single member of the hundred-plus-member LSO traded in their tubas, trumpets, and trombones for cymbals. There would be no beautiful music, only a terrible, noisy racket unfit for any audience near or far.

This is the point of today's well-known verse from 1 Corinthians 13.

WHAT'S IT MEAN?

The famous thirteenth chapter of 1 Corinthians is known as "the love chapter." It's often mentioned in weddings, sermons, and Valentine's Day cards.

But the apostle Paul didn't write it for any of those occasions. He penned those Holy Spirit–inspired words in the context of discussing spiritual gifts. Here's Paul's point: when it comes to your God-given talents, even your greatest accomplishments will be as worthless as a cymbals-only orchestra if they aren't done in love.

Among all the important Christian virtues, love is supreme (1 Corinthians 13:13). Love should motivate everything we do in life. If our good deeds are a symphony, the sheet music that guides our performance should be love, informing every note we play. Without love, our righteous acts will sound like an irritating din of clashing cymbals to God, who is concerned with our hearts more than anything else (1 Samuel 16:7).

To be like God, we must show love since "God is love" (1 John 4:8). Love is the foundation of everything God does. Love motivated him to seek a personal relationship with his creation. Love motivated God's Son to endure unspeakable suffering for our salvation. So love—not jealousy, pride, anger, guilt, or anything else—should motivate all our actions and words.

By loving others, your life can produce a beautiful symphony of praise to God!

NOW WHAT?

Read the entire "love chapter" of 1 Corinthians 13, and pray about how you can show more love.

DID YOU KNOW?

The point of love-inspired good deeds is to please and honor God, not earn his favor. We can do that only through faith in Jesus.

Love is patient and kind. Love is not jealous or boastful or proud or rude. It does not demand its own way. It is not irritable, and it keeps no record of being wronged. It does not rejoice about injustice but rejoices whenever the truth wins out. Love never gives up, never loses faith, is always hopeful, and endures through every circumstance. I CORINTHIANS 13:4-7

Today's devotion begins with an easy question:

In which of the following places would you look to find examples of real love?

A. A shopping mall

B. A museum

C. Burger King

D. The local trash dump

E. Church

Most people would guess choice E, right? After all, shouldn't a church be filled with loving people?

Unfortunately, that's not always the case. And it certainly wasn't in ancient Corinth. As discussed in the October 3 and 9 devotions, the Corinthian Christians were a self-centered, worldly bunch who struggled to show true, biblical love.

So the apostle Paul explained love to them in his broader discussion of spiritual gifts. The result was 1 Corinthians 13, Scripture's famous "love chapter" and the leading passage on what Christian love should look like.

WHAT'S IT MEAN?

Biblical love isn't rocket science or molecular biology. It's actually quite simple. In today's Scripture passage, Paul describes God-pleasing love in beautifully straightforward terms.

To show true love, Paul says, Christians must do the following:

- Be patient and kind.
- Avoid jealousy, pride, and rudeness.
- Don't be demanding or irritable.
- Forgive people rather than hold a grudge when they wrong you.
- Don't celebrate when bad things happen to others.

Paul's intent was not to provide a comprehensive list of everything love is and isn't. But can you see the common theme running through his description of love? It's all about treating others with the kindness and respect they deserve as fellow image bearers of God.

It's also about reflecting the love God showed you through Jesus. All those expressions of love listed above were revealed when Jesus sacrificed himself for your sins. As Romans 5:8 says, "God demonstrates his own love for us in this: While we were still sinners, Christ died for us" (NIV).

True, biblical love is sacrificial in nature. When you put others before yourself, you fulfill 1 Corinthians 13!

NOW WHAT?

Show your love for someone today by sacrificing your interests for that person's.

DID YOU KNOW?

While other spiritual gifts will eventually cease one day, love will last into eternity (1 Corinthians 13:8-12).

He comforts us in all our troubles so that we can comfort others. When they are troubled, we will be able to give them the same comfort God has given us. 2 CORINTHIANS 1:4

Sometimes life is like cake and ice cream. Other times, it's like liver and onions. No one knew that fact better than Job.

This Old Testament man was righteous and very wealthy. But God nevertheless allowed terrible disasters to befall Job. He lost all ten of his children and all his property, and he contracted a horrible skin disease.

Most of the book of Job describes Job's interaction with three friends—Eliphaz, Bildad, and Zophar—who came to comfort him. Unfortunately, Job's buddies weren't very comforting. Instead of offering sympathy and a listening ear to their troubled friend, they insensitively (and mistakenly) blamed Job for his own sufferings, insisting his sorrows were divine punishment for some hidden sin in his life.

Eliphaz, Bildad, and Zophar failed "Comforting a Friend 101." Their example is the opposite of what the apostle Paul wrote about in today's verse. At the beginning of 2 Corinthians, Paul discussed the importance of being a friend who comforts those who are hurting.

WHAT'S IT MEAN?

When you experience trials in your life, isn't it nice to have a friend to lean on? Likewise, you should be that type of friend to others in need.

In today's verse, Paul says that one of the reasons God allows Christians to endure trials is to experience his loving comfort so they can eventually share that comfort with others. It's "pay it forward" friendship.

Besides today's verse, God's Word contains many other instructions to love those who are experiencing hardship. Here are some examples:

- "A friend is always loyal, and a brother is born to help in time of need" (Proverbs 17:17).

- "Be happy with those who are happy, and weep with those who weep" (Romans 12:15).
- "Share each other's burdens, and in this way obey the law of Christ" (Galatians 6:2).

No one did this better than Jesus. Isaiah 53:4 says, "He has borne our griefs and carried our sorrows" (ESV). Jesus—God's Son who became flesh—can sympathize with all our weaknesses (Hebrews 4:15) because he, too, experienced the challenges of human life.

To be like Jesus, comfort others in their time of need with the comfort you've received from God!

NOW WHAT?

When someone you know is hurting, be the type of friend who is quick to listen and slow to speak. Sometimes people need a listening ear more than they need advice.

DID YOU KNOW?

In the end, God lovingly restored Job's health, family, and fortune (Job 42:10-17).

OCTOBER 14

We stopped relying on ourselves and learned to rely only on God,
who raises the dead.   2 CORINTHIANS 1:9

The apostle Paul was one tough *hombre.*

During his remarkable life, he suffered more persecution and adversity than perhaps any other Christian in history. He endured multiple imprisonments, beatings, whippings, shipwrecks, and a stoning. He was hated by many, constantly harassed, and often in mortal danger.

But something happened to Paul in the Roman province of Asia that may have been worse than everything else. He described it in 2 Corinthians 1:8-10:

> *We think you ought to know, dear brothers and sisters, about the*
> *trouble we went through in the province of Asia. We were crushed*
> *and overwhelmed beyond our ability to endure, and we thought*
> *we would never live through it. In fact, we expected to die. But as*
> *a result, we stopped relying on ourselves and learned to rely only on*
> *God, who raises the dead. And he did rescue us from mortal danger,*
> *and he will rescue us again. We have placed our confidence in him,*
> *and he will continue to rescue us.*

Paul doesn't give any other specifics about this life-threatening hardship. We only know that he was "crushed and overwhelmed" and "expected to die." But Paul survived. And did you notice whom he relied on for help?

WHAT'S IT MEAN?

Trials are unavoidable in life. At some point, you will face tough times. When you do, the most important question is whom you'll place your trust in.

During a low point in his life, Paul learned to stop relying on his own power and rely instead on the God "who raises the dead" (today's verse). This is an interesting description. Paul could've described God as "the God who can do all things" or "the God who helps those in need." Instead, Paul focused on God's resurrection power.

Here's why: in his darkest hours, Paul took great comfort in remembering that the God who sacrificed his own Son and brought him back to life to save Paul was also watching over Paul during his difficult trial.

This same comfort is also available to you! When hardships strike, remember there's a God in heaven who loves you so much that he willingly sent Jesus to take the punishment that you deserved. If God did that, he is certainly willing and able to carry you through every challenge of life.

NOW WHAT?

Read about some of Paul's most severe trials in Acts 14:19-20; 19:21-41; 21:26-36; 27:13-44; and 2 Corinthians 11:23-12:10.

DID YOU KNOW?

When you're enduring a trial, your prayers and the prayers of others (2 Corinthians 1:11) make a big difference.

OCTOBER 15

We have this treasure in jars of clay, to show that the surpassing power belongs to God and not to us. 2 CORINTHIANS 4:7, ESV

In 1513, Juan Ponce de León landed his ship in what is now St. Augustine, Florida. According to legend, the famous Spanish conquistador was looking for the fabled fountain of youth.

Whether this was the real motivation for Ponce de León's voyage is debatable. Still, the story sounds legit. After all, for thousands of years humans have been (unsuccessfully) seeking to extend life.

One well-known example is baseball Hall of Famer Ted Williams. After he died in 2002, his children paid $136,000 to have his remains cryogenically frozen at a facility in Arizona, hoping he could be brought back to life one day if science advances that far. Creepy!

The apostle Paul, a constant victim of persecution, was well acquainted with how fragile and short human life is. That's why he referred to humans as "jars of clay" (today's verse) and wrote the following in 2 Corinthians 4:16-18:

> *Though our bodies are dying, our spirits are being renewed every day. For our present troubles are small and won't last very long. Yet they produce for us a glory that vastly outweighs them and will last forever! So we don't look at the troubles we can see now; rather, we fix our gaze on things that cannot be seen. For the things we see now will soon be gone, but the things we cannot see will last forever.*

WHAT'S IT MEAN?

Paul's comparison of our bodies to "jars of clay" was a reference to the fragile pottery of his day. Elsewhere, the Bible refers to the human lifespan as being like "a breath" (Job 7:7), "dreams that disappear" (Psalm 90:5), "grass" (Psalm 90:5), "dust" (Psalm 103:14), "wildflowers" (Psalm 103:15), and "the morning fog" (James 4:14).

There's no getting around it: human life is short and weak. But as Paul points out in today's verse, our significant limitations emphasize God's amazing supremacy. That same divine power raised Jesus from the dead (see yesterday's devotion). If we submit ourselves to God's will and power in our lives, we can look forward to "a glory that vastly outweighs" all our troubles "and will last forever"!

Yes, life is brief. But the glorious hope of eternity with the Savior covers all human weakness!

NOW WHAT?

When you're feeling weak or experiencing trials, remember to fix your gaze on Jesus, who promises a new, glorified body and eternal life to all who trust in him!

DID YOU KNOW?

The average American's life expectancy is only about seventy-nine years. That's half the lifespan of some giant tortoises. Talk about humbling!

OCTOBER 16

The love of Christ controls us. 2 CORINTHIANS 5:14, ESV

On November 26, 2011, *Curiosity* launched into outer space.

No, we're not speaking symbolically here. *Curiosity* is the name of one of NASA's latest technological wonders—a two-thousand-pound, six-wheeled robotic rover the size of a car.

Eight months and about 354 million space miles later, *Curiosity* landed on Mars. The rover hasn't found any weird-looking Martians, but it *is* looking for signs of life.

Curiosity's mission is to explore the red planet, extract geological samples from the surface, analyze them, and send the data back to earth, where NASA scientists can determine if Mars has ever supported any life forms, even the most microscopic organisms. *Curiosity*'s ultimate goal is to help us learn if Mars can sustain human life one day.

Most amazingly, *Curiosity*'s every move is controlled from Earth. NASA engineers transmit commands for each action they want *Curiosity* to take, sometimes several days' worth at a time!

What does all this geek-speak mean? It means *Curiosity* is pretty much the coolest remote-controlled vehicle in the universe!

Did you know humans are controlled too? Fortunately, we're not NASA robots. We have a say in who or what controls us. But the choice is of epic importance. It will determine our eternal destiny.

WHAT'S IT MEAN?

Like NASA's creation of *Curiosity*, God designed us for a specific mission: to worship and glorify him. But in Genesis 3, sin got in the way.

Since then, every person who has ever existed—including you—started life under sin's control. Left to itself, sin always leads to spiritual death. But in his great mercy, God offered his Son, Jesus Christ, to suffer the punishment you deserved and provide complete forgiveness. To receive this amazing grace, you have to surrender your life to Jesus and, as today's verse says, be controlled by love for him.

Being controlled by the love of Christ doesn't mean you become a mindless robot like *Curiosity*. God has given us free will to decide between doing what is right and what is wrong. It simply means we choose to follow Jesus rather than selfish pursuits and worldly pleasures.

Are you controlled by sports? Academic success? The love of money? The desire to be popular? If it's anything but Jesus, you're being ruled by something spiritually dangerous.

Allow Christ to guide your life. Let your love of the Savior control you!

NOW WHAT?

Make a list of everything you love to do. Then ask yourself honestly if any of those things controls you more than your love for Christ.

DID YOU KNOW?

The cost of *Curiosity*'s mission to Mars was about $2,600,000,000. That's a lot of zeroes!

We are Christ's ambassadors; God is making his appeal through us.
We speak for Christ when we plead, "Come back to God!"
2 CORINTHIANS 5:20

Being a United States ambassador is a prestigious position and a great privilege. But occasionally, it can be deadly.

In 2012, J. Christopher Stevens was serving as the American ambassador to Libya, an Islamic nation in North Africa, when a group of Muslim protesters attacked and set fire to the US embassy there. Stevens and three other Americans died, marking the sixth time a US ambassador has been killed by foreign militants since World War II.

Fortunately, that tragedy is the exception, not the rule. Being an ambassador is typically a safe job with lots of benefits. An ambassador is a nation's highest-ranking diplomatic official, who acts as a representative to another nation. This person is the main spokesperson for his or her own country in the one he or she has been assigned to. Ambassadors seek to further national interests and encourage greater cooperation between two nations.

In today's verse, the apostle Paul describes all Christians as "Christ's ambassadors." It's the greatest ambassadorship possible!

WHAT'S IT MEAN?

Just like a US ambassador represents American interests to the country he's assigned to, Christians represent Jesus Christ to the world.

For us as Christians, this world is not our true home (John 17:16). We are here only temporarily, awaiting the return of our Savior, who will one day bring us to our eternal dwelling.

Until that blessed day, we are "Christ's ambassadors," placed on earth to represent our heavenly Master and advance his perfect agenda, which is the salvation of humanity. This is a wonderful privilege—and an undeserved one. As sinners, we bring no personal qualifications to the job. But when Jesus saves us, he changes our hearts and graciously appoints us to be his personal representatives to a lost, dying world—the same one he saved us from. Amazing!

Now God appeals to the hearts of unbelievers through us. We have a responsibility to "speak for Christ" and plead to others, "Come back to God!" (today's verse).

We can be successful as Christ's ambassadors, though, only if we live in a way that honors him. A political ambassador who disregards his government's instructions and breaks the law would be a terrible representative. Likewise, a Christian who ignores Scripture and disobeys God can't represent Christ well.

You can be an ambassador for the greatest kingdom ever—the kingdom of heaven! Are you ready?

NOW WHAT?

Pray for God to give you the strength to help you speak for Christ and appeal to others on his behalf.

DID YOU KNOW?

Benjamin Franklin was the United States' first ambassador, to France.

OCTOBER 18

Do not be yoked together with unbelievers.

2 CORINTHIANS 6:14, NIV

When visiting the zoo, have you ever seen a zookeeper put an antelope in the lions' area so they can play together? No, of course not! That would make for a very bad day for Mr. Antelope.

Would a car engineer install a lawnmower engine in a Ferrari? Would a football player take the field wearing scuba-diving gear? Would a concert pianist play Beethoven's Moonlight Sonata wearing mittens? Would you pour tomato juice over your bowl of Froot Loops?

No way! Some things just don't go well together.

This was the apostle Paul's point when he wrote the words of today's verse.

WHAT'S IT MEAN?

The phrase "unequally yoked" is a farming reference. If you recall the March 22 devotion, a yoke is a large, wooden beam attached to the necks of two oxen and tethered to a plow behind the animals. The yoke allows the oxen to do the hard work of churning up the earth by pulling the plow behind them so a farmer can plant crops later.

But if the oxen were unequally yoked—in other words, if a strong ox was hitched to a weaker ox—they wouldn't be able to properly plow the field. The plow would always veer in the direction of the stronger animal, leaving the poor farmer with crooked lines all over his field.

Here's Paul's point: Christians should not "yoke" themselves closely to people who don't know Jesus. Like mismatched oxen, it's a bad pairing.

Christians and non-Christians have different goals and ambitions in life. Christians are Christ's ambassadors (see yesterday's devotion) who want to honor and please their Savior. Non-Christians have other priorities. Being too closely attached to nonbelievers can distract a Christian from his or her true mission.

But we must be careful here in our attitude toward others. Christians should never completely avoid all unbelievers. That's not only impossible but it's also unbiblical.

Scripture tells believers to be "salt" and "light" to the world around us (Matthew 5:13-16). Paul himself spent much of his adult life traveling throughout the world preaching the gospel to the unsaved. When Paul says, "Do not be unequally yoked with unbelievers," he means that you should never be allied with a nonbeliever so closely that the person's sinful behavior negatively affects your life.

Don't yoke yourself to unbelievers. Instead, pray for them, love them, and tell them how Jesus can save them!

NOW WHAT?

For Paul's full thoughts on being unequally yoked, read 2 Corinthians 6:14–7:1.

DID YOU KNOW?

Christians should never think they are better than non-Christians or mistreat them. That would be a poor witness, prideful, and dishonoring to God.

*Each time [the Lord] said, "My grace is all you need. My power
works best in weakness." So now I am glad to boast about my
weaknesses, so that the power of Christ can work through me.*

2 CORINTHIANS 12:9

Paul didn't want to do it.

The great apostle hated boasting about himself. But he had no other
choice. He needed to do something drastic to help the immature Christians
in Corinth, who were in spiritual danger.

By the time Paul wrote 2 Corinthians, the Corinthian believers were following some false teachers who were spreading lies about the gospel. So to
prove his authenticity as a true apostle of Jesus, Paul told the Corinthians
about an astonishing experience that he had never shared with anyone else.

In 2 Corinthians 12:1-4, Paul writes that fourteen years earlier, he was
"caught up to paradise" where he "heard things so astounding . . . no human
is allowed to tell." Many years later, he still wasn't sure if God had simply
given him a vision or actually transported him briefly into heaven.

To keep Paul humble, God gave him a "thorn in [his] flesh" (2 Corinthians
12:7). Paul pleaded with God to remove this painful, mysterious trial, but
God answered with the words of today's verse: "My grace is all you need. My
power works best in weakness."

WHAT'S IT MEAN?

How can power be found in weakness? It's one of Scripture's great paradoxes—
a statement that seems contradictory but is actually true.

God did some amazing things through Paul. But Paul's human limitations and physical weaknesses, including his "thorn," showed that all the
glory belonged to God, not Paul. That's why Paul shared his story with the
Corinthian believers.

If all Christians were superheroes with bionic bodies and otherworldly
powers, we'd probably stop trusting God and keep much of the glory for

whatever we accomplished. But we're clearly not super in any way. We sin often and get hurt easily. And as for superpowers, well, burping the alphabet doesn't count.

God shows his power best through human weakness. Our flaws and frailty highlight God's limitless strength and wisdom. Like Paul's "thorn," God often allows hardships in our lives to remind us where our true power comes from. And the glory for anything good we do should always go to God, who created and sustains us.

When we are weak, God unfailingly proves to be strong!

NOW WHAT?

Read all about Paul's remarkable heavenly encounter in 2 Corinthians 12:1-10.

DID YOU KNOW?

The greatest example of God's power working best in weakness is Jesus, who put aside his heavenly glory to die a humiliating death and offer salvation to all people. Now *that* is power in weakness!

The fruit of the Spirit is love, joy, peace, patience, kindness,
goodness, faithfulness, gentleness, self-control.
GALATIANS 5:22-23, ESV

By the late 40s AD, Christianity was flourishing.

The faith that had started in Jerusalem shortly after Jesus' resurrection and ascension in the early 30s was now rapidly expanding throughout the Roman Empire, thanks to the faithful witness of the apostles, especially Peter and Paul.

During his first missionary journey, Paul traveled throughout the Roman province of Galatia (modern-day Turkey), preaching the gospel and planting churches in cities such as Pisidian Antioch, Iconium, Lystra, and Derbe (Acts 13–14).

But most of the new believers were Gentiles—non-Jews who came from wicked pagan backgrounds, filled with idolatry and immorality. They needed help knowing how to live in a way that was pleasing to God. So in Galatians, his letter to the various churches in Galatia, Paul contrasted "the desires of the flesh" (Galatians 5:16, ESV) with "the fruit of the Spirit" (today's verse).

WHAT'S IT MEAN?

When Paul talks about "the fruit of the Spirit," he's not referring to peaches, pears, pineapples, or pomegranates. He is using a metaphor—a figure of speech to illustrate a point. In this case, he's using agricultural images.

In farming, a tree's health and worth is shown by the fruit it produces. If an apple tree's branches are filled with rotten produce, the farmer will chop down that tree. But he'll keep any tree that bears crisp, juicy apples. A tree's fruit tells you a great deal about the tree itself.

It's the same in the Christian life. If you are a follower of Jesus, people should be able to tell immediately by the "fruit" you display. Are you bearing bad fruit—such as anger, selfishness, pride, and jealousy ("the desires of the flesh")? Or are you bearing "the fruit of the Spirit"—such as love, joy, peace, and patience? These are Holy Spirit–inspired qualities that mark you as a true Christian as the Lord works in your heart to make you more like Christ.

Of course, you won't exhibit the fruit of the Spirit perfectly all the time. No one does. The sinful nature—"the desires of the flesh" that Paul mentions—still wars within us daily (Romans 7:21-23). But Jesus broke the power of sin (Romans 8:2) so that we can choose righteous living over slavery to evil desires.

Don't be a rotten apple! Follow Jesus and produce the fruit of the Spirit.

NOW WHAT?
Spend some time in prayer asking God to give you more of each fruit of the Spirit.

DID YOU KNOW?
Jesus also used the fruit metaphor to encourage godly living in Matthew 3:10 and 7:15-20, and in Luke 6:43-45 and 13:6-9.

Since God chose you to be the holy people he loves, you must clothe yourselves with tenderhearted mercy, kindness, humility, gentleness, and patience. COLOSSIANS 3:12

Patience.

As discussed yesterday, this godly character trait is one of the fruits of the Spirit. But it's also one of the hardest to show!

To better understand this important quality, try to guess which option is the best example of patience in the following situations:

When you're getting tired of being in the car on a long family road trip, you can show patience by:

A. *Telling your dad to speed up*

B. *Asking "Are we there yet?" once every fifteen seconds*

C. *Mentioning how you could've reached the northern tip of Alaska on a pack mule in the time it's taking to reach your destination*

D. *Enjoying time with your family and not complaining*

When that annoying kid who sits behind you at school keeps flicking your ear, you can show patience by:

A. *Turning around and flicking his ear*

B. *Turning around and pouring a bucket of water on his head*

C. *Attempting to turn him into a salamander with a magic wand*

D. *Turning around and politely asking him to stop*

When your older sister has been doing her hair in the bathroom for the last thirty minutes, you can show patience by:

A. *Yelling at her to get out*

B. *Pounding on the door until she opens it*

C. *Threatening to put toads in her bed while she's sleeping if she doesn't come out in five seconds*

D. *Waiting quietly for your turn*

Hopefully, you picked choice D for each question!

WHAT'S IT MEAN?

Patience is the ability to tolerate difficult or frustrating circumstances without showing anger. It's a wonderful, necessary fruit of the Spirit. But it's also easier said than done!

Life is full of challenging situations . . . and challenging people. You will encounter many things in life that will make you want to shake your head, complain, yell, or worse. But a true follower of Jesus shows patience toward others.

After all, hasn't God shown great patience with you? Like everyone else, you have broken God's laws countless times—knowingly and unknowingly. Yet God has offered you forgiveness and salvation through faith in his Son. Now *that's* true patience!

When circumstances, or people, aggravate you, remember the Lord's patience with you, and respond with patience of your own!

NOW WHAT?

Be slow to speak when angry (James 1:19). That's one good way to practice patience.

DID YOU KNOW?

In Romans 2:1-4, the apostle Paul wrote about how God's patience with us should motivate us to show patience to others. Check it out!

OCTOBER 22

We are God's handiwork, created in Christ Jesus to do good works, which God prepared in advance for us to do.

EPHESIANS 2:10, NIV

We live in an age of mass production.

All over the globe, factory assembly lines crank out products at a dizzying pace—cars, toys, kitchen appliances, clothing, and even your favorite sweets. Did you know the Hershey's chocolate company produces about 70 million Hershey's Kisses a day?

Yes, it's a fast-paced, machine-produced world out there. But if you look hard enough—and have enough money—you can purchase handmade brilliance.

Need a new wristwatch? For more than $150,000, you can buy one of the world's finest handmade timepieces from famous watchmaker George Daniels's studio on the Isle of Man in the British Isles.

If your school pen has run out of ink, fear not! You can purchase a handcrafted Italian fountain pen, a limited-edition gold Montegrappa Mayan Calendar model, for only $137,950 (which, coincidentally, can also buy you an extremely nice European sports car).

Speaking of sports cars, why settle for an extremely nice European sports car when, for a mere $1 million, you can buy a handcrafted, 1,200-horsepower Hennessey Venom GT, which set an astonishing world speed record of 270.49 miles per hour in 2014?

Handcrafted items are usually the best. But did you know *you* are handcrafted? It's true! Today's verse says you are "God's handiwork."

WHAT'S IT MEAN?

Psalm 139:13-15, which provides Scripture's most vivid description of how God created humans, says he "formed" your inner parts and "knitted" you together in your mother's womb. You were "intricately woven" together and "fearfully and wonderfully made" (all references ESV).

God showed great care, affection, and intricacy when he made you. He loves you more than you can imagine. Out of everything the Creator made, you are his masterpiece.

Why did God do this? As today's verse says, it was for you to do good works! If you are a Christian, not only did he create you in your mother's womb, he also made you a new creation "in Christ Jesus" to serve and honor him. These good works are things "which God prepared in advance for us to do" (today's verse).

Let this sink in for a moment: well before he lovingly handcrafted you, God already had a plan to save you through Jesus (Ephesians 1:4) and give you meaning and purpose in life. Amazing!

NOW WHAT?

Some of the good works God prepared for you are common to all Christians—such as obeying your parents, serving others, and worshiping God. But some are specific to you, based on your spiritual gifts. Pray that God would reveal these to you.

DID YOU KNOW?

Psalm 139:16 says God knows what will happen every day of our lives before we're even born. Also see Jeremiah 29:11 for more about God's plans for you.

May you experience the love of Christ, though it is too great to understand fully. Then you will be made complete with all the fullness of life and power that comes from God. EPHESIANS 3:19

The universe is a really big place. We're talking huge, gigantic, colossal, enormous . . . no, make that *gi*-normous!

It's super-duper big. But how big? No one knows.

Plenty of theories abound, though. NASA, for one, estimates that it would take one hundred thousand years traveling at the speed of light (186,000 miles per second) to cross the Milky Way Galaxy, where Earth is located. Whoa. But that's just one galaxy. Nobody knows how many others are out there.

What's more, many scientists today believe the universe is expanding, although not everyone agrees. To explain their theories, they talk about quasars, redshifts, dark energy, baryon acoustic oscillations, and lots of other astrophysics mumbo jumbo.

While it's important to learn more about God's amazing universe, we'll never *fully* understand it. It's just too big.

According to today's verse from Ephesians 3, the same is true of Jesus' love for you.

WHAT'S IT MEAN?

We hear about Jesus' love all the time. We sing about it, listen to pastors preach about it, and read about it in books (like this one!). Your family might even have a bumper sticker about it on your car.

But how often do you stop and *really* think about it? When we step back and consider all that Scripture says about God's Son, it becomes quite clear: Jesus' love for you truly is too great to understand (see today's verse).

Let's review: sometime in eternity past, well before creation, the triune God—Father, Son, and Holy Spirit—devised a plan to save humanity from sin. Jesus willingly agreed to become—in the Father's timing—a perfect, atoning sacrifice for a lost, dying world. He suffered a terrible death as our substitute, enduring God's full wrath against our sin. Three days later, he was victoriously resurrected, and now he offers forgiveness and eternal life to everyone who believes in his name.

If that's not "too great to understand fully," nothing is (today's verse)!

Jesus' love for you is boundless. If it were a book, you'd never finish it. If it were a mountain, you'd never reach the top. If it were a jug of water, you'd never taste the last drop.

Forget quasars, redshifts, and baryon acoustic . . . whatever those things are. Keep marveling at the Savior's love for you, and you will be "made complete"!

NOW WHAT?

Read Ephesians 1 and be amazed, along with the writer, the apostle Paul, at Jesus' love for you.

DID YOU KNOW?

The Andromeda Galaxy, the nearest to our own, is estimated to be more than two million light years away.

OCTOBER 24

Do not let any unwholesome talk come out of your mouths, but only what is helpful for building others up according to their needs, that it may benefit those who listen. EPHESIANS 4:29, NIV

Peshtigo, Wisconsin, is a quaint city tucked into the northeastern part of the state, about forty-five minutes north of Green Bay. It's split in half by the Peshtigo River, with a small bridge spanning the water. Outside the city limits, it's known for little else other than the deadly—and still somewhat mysterious—catastrophe that struck on October 8, 1871.

Settled around 1838, Peshtigo started as a logging town. With the river nearby and expansive forests all around, the city's location was a natural place for enterprising loggers to set up operations.

Life continued—and timber fell—in Peshtigo for several more decades. And then it happened. To this day, no one knows how. Perhaps a spark from a logger's fire or a passing steam-engine train hit some grass that had dried out in that year's drought.

Whatever the cause, a fire started—a huge fire. By the time it stopped, it had consumed an estimated 1.5 million acres and killed between one thousand and two thousand people. It remains the deadliest forest fire in US history.

Sadly, a similar destructive power can be found in the human tongue. James 3:5-6 says, "A tiny spark can set a great forest on fire. And among all the parts of the body, the tongue is a flame of fire. It is a whole world of wickedness, corrupting your entire body. It can set your whole life on fire, for it is set on fire by hell itself."

WHAT'S IT MEAN?

Wow, Scripture certainly isn't shy about revealing the dangers of human speech! God wants to make it very clear: our words matter, and if we're not careful, they can cause great harm.

As today's verse says, our words should build others up with encouragement, not tear them down with verbal assaults. So avoid mocking, belittling, and name-calling. The same mouth that praises God should never insult those who are made in his image (James 3:9-10).

In our speech, we must follow Jesus' example. When he was verbally attacked, he never retaliated (1 Peter 2:23). He always lovingly spoke the "words of eternal life" (John 6:68, NIV).

Don't destroy others with a raging inferno of angry words! Build them up with Christlike encouragement.

NOW WHAT?

Have you offended someone with your words recently? If so, ask for that person's forgiveness.

DID YOU KNOW?

The Bible also warns against other improper speech too. Ephesians 5:4 says, "Nor should there be obscenity, foolish talk or coarse joking, which are out of place, but rather thanksgiving" (NIV).

OCTOBER 25

A servant of the Lord must not quarrel but must be kind to everyone, be able to teach, and be patient with difficult people.
2 TIMOTHY 2:24

Alexander Hamilton drew his gun. So did Aaron Burr. To this day, the exact details of what happened next remain a mystery. But the end result was clear: Hamilton had a bullet hole in his stomach.

Hamilton (a Federalist) and Burr (a Democratic-Republican) were bitter American political rivals in the late 1700s and early 1800s. What started out as a quarrel between two men with very different ideas about government had escalated into an all-out personal war.

In 1804, Burr expressed interest in becoming New York's next governor after his vice presidential term under President Thomas Jefferson ended. Hamilton heavily campaigned against Burr, who lost the election and vowed to settle his differences with Hamilton through an "affair of honor"—in other words, a duel. Pistols at dawn. Ten paces, turn, and fire.

Historical accounts differ on what exactly happened when both men met on July 11, 1804, at 7 a.m. near Weehawken, New Jersey. Some say Hamilton shot first at Burr and missed. Others say he fired into the sky, a sign that he wanted a peaceful resolution.

Either way, Burr's shot found its target. The bullet lodged into Hamilton's spine, and he died the next day.

All because of a quarrel.

WHAT'S IT MEAN?

Have you ever had a quarrel with someone? Of course you have. Everybody has.

A quarrel is a disagreement or dispute between two people that leads to a verbal conflict—or worse, in the Hamilton-Burr case. You've probably quarreled with your parents, your siblings, your friends, your neighbors, your neighbor's friends, and your neighbor's friend's third cousin twice removed.

Okay, maybe not those last few, but you get the point. As sinners, quarreling comes naturally to us.

It's no fun to be around a quarrelsome person. This is someone who loves to argue but doesn't like to let others be right. A quarrelsome "I'm right and you're not" attitude is prideful and ungodly.

Does that describe you? If so, ask for Jesus' help. Today's verse commands believers to avoid quarreling, even with difficult people. The Savior can change our quarrelsome hearts into kind ones and our argumentative words into gentle ones.

Patience, love, and kind speech are much better than quarreling. There's no arguing that.

NOW WHAT?

Read James 4:1-3 to find out the root cause of quarrels. It's a great passage that perfectly diagnoses this common human struggle.

DID YOU KNOW?

Aaron Burr avoided a murder trial after the Alexander Hamilton incident and later beat a treason charge too. He died in 1836.

OCTOBER 26

We are not fighting against flesh-and-blood enemies, but against evil
rulers and authorities of the unseen world, against mighty powers in
this dark world, and against evil spirits in the heavenly places.
EPHESIANS 6:12

When the apostle Paul wrote the book of Ephesians, it was about AD 62. The Roman Empire was enjoying an era known as *Pax Romana,* or "Roman Peace," an unprecedented two-hundred-year period of tranquility and prosperity. The mighty Roman legions had fought countless battles to secure the empire's vast borders.

Peace wouldn't last forever, though. After Emperor Marcus Aurelius's death in AD 180, Rome once again found itself on the battlefield, trying to resist barbarian invaders on its frontiers.

Warfare is nothing new. Ever since Cain killed his brother Abel, humans have been fighting against one another.

But as Paul concluded the book of Ephesians, he mentioned a completely different type of warfare—one that doesn't involve generals, infantry, chariots, swords, or spears. He wanted his readers to understand the reality of spiritual warfare.

WHAT'S IT MEAN?

As humans, we often live by what our eyes tell us. We believe something when we see it. But the Bible calls us to have faith in things unseen (Hebrews 11:1), and Paul specifically mentions in today's verse the reality of an ongoing spiritual battle we can't see.

Christians are at war. But our enemy is not human. There's an invisible spiritual war raging on all around us between the heavenly forces of light and the satanic powers of darkness.

The "evil rulers," "authorities of the unseen world," "mighty powers," and "evil spirits" that Paul talks about all describe the demonic realm, which is ruled by Satan (Luke 11:15). These evil spirits are in constant battle against

God's holy angels. Their mission is to fight against God's purposes and destroy his creation. (For more on Satan and demons, see the January 31 and April 16 devotions.)

It's important to be aware of this. God's creation is a marvelous—but sometimes mysterious—place. There's more to it than meets the eye. As soldiers of Christ, Christians must be aware of the great struggle going on all around them.

But remember this: you don't have to fear any satanic power, thanks to Jesus. He triumphed over all evil by his death and resurrection (Colossians 2:15)!

Yes, we are in spiritual warfare, but the outcome has already been decided. Jesus has given us the victory!

NOW WHAT?

Make sure to read tomorrow's devotion on how Christians should prepare for spiritual warfare.

DID YOU KNOW?

The Bible provides some brief but fascinating glimpses into unseen spiritual warfare in 2 Kings 6:8-23; Daniel 10; Jude 9; and Revelation 12:7-9. Check them out!

OCTOBER 27

Put on all of God's armor so that you will be able to stand firm against all strategies of the devil. EPHESIANS 6:11

When the apostle Paul wrote Ephesians, the Roman Empire extended from the Atlantic Ocean to modern-day Iraq, including parts of North Africa, too.

The Romans conquered this immense territory on the strength of their famous legionnaires. These infantrymen were a highly trained, disciplined fighting force that benefited from the latest technology in weaponry and armor.

Every soldier needs proper training and equipment to win in battle. Christians do too.

As discussed in yesterday's devotion, Christians are locked in lifelong spiritual warfare. Jesus has already won the ultimate victory through his death and resurrection, but until he returns to earth for his final triumph, believers must know how to successfully fight evil.

Using a military illustration in Ephesians 6:13-18 (NIV), Paul reveals how we can wage war against our enemy, the devil, in his famous "armor of God" passage:

> Put on the full armor of God, so that when the day of evil comes, you
> may be able to stand your ground, and after you have done everything,
> to stand. Stand firm then, with the belt of truth buckled around your
> waist, with the breastplate of righteousness in place, and with your
> feet fitted with the readiness that comes from the gospel of peace. In
> addition to all this, take up the shield of faith, with which you can
> extinguish all the flaming arrows of the evil one. Take the helmet of
> salvation and the sword of the Spirit, which is the word of God.

WHAT'S IT MEAN?

Let's review our spiritual armor and equipment:

> *"Belt of truth"*—Just as a belt holds an outfit in place, the truth of the
> gospel binds our entire faith together.

"Breastplate of righteousness"—Godly living protects us from Satan's assaults.

"Feet fitted with the readiness [of] . . . the gospel of peace"—The gospel's eternal, unchanging truths empower us to run into life's spiritual battles without fear.

"Shield of faith"—Trusting in God repels the enemy's most wicked attacks.

"Helmet of salvation"—Just as a helmet protects the body's most critical part, salvation in Jesus protects our entire spiritual well-being.

"Sword of the Spirit"—God's perfect, powerful Word is the only offensive weapon we need to achieve spiritual victory.

God has equipped us with everything we need in Christ to fight the good fight of the faith!

NOW WHAT?
Prayerfully ask God to give you more of his mighty spiritual armor, piece by piece.

DID YOU KNOW?
In 2 Corinthians 10:3-6, Paul talks more about using godly spiritual weapons to combat false teaching.

To me, living means living for Christ, and dying is even better.

PHILIPPIANS 1:21

Paul dipped his pen into the inkwell. His ankles were in shackles, and a soldier guarded the door. But the great apostle and pastor still had certain freedoms. So he put pen to parchment and began to write to some dear friends, the Christians in the city of Philippi.

At the time, Paul was under house arrest in Rome. Several years earlier, he had been wrongfully accused of various religious crimes in Jerusalem and put on trial. When Paul realized he wasn't going to receive a fair hearing in Israel, he appealed to Caesar himself, which was the right of every Roman citizen.

When Paul reached Rome, he lived in a rented home under a guard's watchful eye. For two years, Paul waited . . . and waited . . . and waited for his trial to begin. All the while, he had no idea if he would survive the whole ordeal.

But Paul used the time wisely, writing four letters that are now New Testament books, including the one to the Philippians. In this letter, he displayed remarkable courage and faith while facing an unknown future. But Paul knew this much: "To me, living means living for Christ, and dying is even better" (today's verse).

WHAT'S IT MEAN?

Paul wasn't cuckoo. He didn't *want* to be condemned to death, especially since he was completely innocent. Paul just had a proper perspective on life and death. He knew that indescribable blessings with his Savior awaited him in eternity.

All Christians should have a similar mind-set. Today's verse should be your motto. Your life should be completely wrapped up in Christ. Your words, actions, dreams, and goals should all be devoted to honoring Jesus. As Paul wrote immediately after today's verse, "If I live, I can do more fruitful work for Christ."

Even better, Christians don't need to fear death. That's because the end of this life is simply the gateway into a far greater one: enjoying the presence of our Savior forever.

Our current purpose ("living for Christ") and future hope ("dying is better") are beautiful blessings that non-Christians don't have. Without Christ, life turns into a selfish pursuit and death becomes a frightening mystery.

Praise God for purpose and hope! Live for Christ and look forward to eternity with him!

NOW WHAT?

Paul's whole arrest/imprisonment ordeal is a fascinating story. Read about it in Acts 21–28.

DID YOU KNOW?

The book of Acts, which provides the account of Paul's two-year house arrest in Rome, doesn't say what happened next to Paul. Later, nonbiblical Christian writings claim that he was released without a trial.

*Above all, you must live as citizens of heaven, conducting yourselves
in a manner worthy of the Good News about Christ.*
PHILIPPIANS 1:27

In the apostle Paul's day, Roman citizenship was a highly valued commodity. Being considered a citizen of the world's dominant power was a great honor that came with special privileges not available to everyone in the sprawling empire.

The residents of Philippi knew this well. During the Battle of Philippi in 42 BC, Roman generals Mark Antony and Octavian defeated the forces of Brutus and Cassius, two of the conspirators who had infamously murdered Julius Caesar two years earlier. Shortly afterward, the Macedonian city of Philippi officially became a Roman colony, and its residents received the privileges of citizenship, such as land ownership and exemption from certain taxes. Overall, Philippi was a great place to live.

So when Paul wrote the Greek word *politeuesthe* in his letter to the Philippian Christians, it had a special meaning. The term, found in today's verse, can be translated, "live as citizens" or "behave as worthy citizens."

But Paul wasn't telling the Philippian believers to live as citizens worthy of Philippi, or even Rome. Paul was reminding them that they had a far higher calling as citizens of the kingdom of God. And that meant they needed to live their lives in a certain way.

WHAT'S IT MEAN?

If you are a Christian, you are a citizen of the greatest kingdom in history—the kingdom of God. It's not a kingdom that can be found on a map. It's a kingdom of people with hearts changed by the gospel, the good news of salvation through Jesus.

As a citizen of this kingdom, you are expected to live in a way that honors your King, the Lord Jesus Christ, who sacrificed his life for yours. So take a few moments to consider the following: Are you conducting yourself in a manner worthy of Jesus in these areas of your life?

- your speech
- your thoughts
- the way you honor your parents
- the way you treat others
- what you do when no one is looking
- the things you look at (TV, movies, Internet, books, magazines)
- the music you listen to

This isn't a complete list. But it should help as you seek to live a life worthy of the gospel!

NOW WHAT?
Cut out any media or entertainment (music, TV, movies) from your life that might not honor Christ.

DID YOU KNOW?
Remember, living honorably in the areas listed above doesn't save you. Only God's grace, through faith in Jesus, can do that (Ephesians 2:8-9).

OCTOBER 30

Whatever gain I had, I counted as loss for the sake of Christ.
PHILIPPIANS 3:7, ESV

One day, you'll need to find a job. But first, you'll need to create a résumé. A résumé is a document that lists your work history, skills, and achievements so that employers can determine if you're a good candidate to hire.

Résumés didn't exist in the apostle Paul's day, but he had something similar in mind when he wrote Philippians 3. Paul warned the Christians in Philippi to avoid a popular false teaching that said Gentiles such as the Philippians had to follow certain Old Testament Jewish laws before they could be saved.

This was completely unbiblical. To prove the point, Paul described his own past—how he was a "pure-blooded" Jew and a fanatical, law-abiding Pharisee (Philippians 3:5). Then, in Philippians 3:7-8 (ESV), he wrote something shocking:

> *Whatever gain I had, I counted as loss for the sake of Christ. Indeed, I count everything as loss because of the surpassing worth of knowing Christ Jesus my Lord. For his sake I have suffered the loss of all things and count them as rubbish, in order that I may gain Christ.*

WHAT'S IT MEAN?

From a human perspective, Paul's spiritual résumé looked flawless. He boasted the ethnic and moral qualifications that most ancient Jews thought were necessary to please God.

But Paul called these credentials "rubbish." The Greek term Paul used for "rubbish" was *skybalon*, which can literally translate to "dung." In other words, all human attempts to earn salvation are nothing more than a big pile of donkey droppings!

When it comes to gaining salvation, what do you think should be on your spiritual résumé? Christian parents? Frequent church attendance? Generally good behavior? A short-term missions trip you've taken or community service you've performed? If it's anything other than faith in Jesus' atoning work on the cross, God's Word says it's a heap of *skybalon*.

As Paul wrote in today's verse, anything we might list under the "gains" column (things we put our hope in for salvation) other than Christ actually fall under the "loss" column. Jesus is our only hope of salvation because he is the only God-approved sacrifice for sins.

Don't trust in the donkey droppings of human achievement. Trust in the Savior who can make your spiritual résumé sparkle with his righteousness!

NOW WHAT?

List all your recent good works on a sheet of paper and don't read any further until you're finished. . . . Done? Good. Now throw the sheet in the garbage to illustrate today's biblical truth.

DID YOU KNOW?

Isaiah 64:6 says even "our righteous deeds . . . are nothing but filthy rags" to God.

OCTOBER 31

Forgetting what is behind and straining toward what is ahead,
I press on toward the goal to win the prize.

PHILIPPIANS 3:13-14, NIV

Usain Bolt was one fast dude.

At the 2008 Summer Olympics in Beijing, China, the twenty-one-year-old Jamaican sprinter put on a performance for the ages, winning and setting world records in the 100- and 200-meter dashes and the 4x100 relay. But Bolt will be best remembered for the dominance—and flamboyance—of his 100-meter victory.

Bolt surged to such a commanding lead, he actually slowed down a bit with about 20 meters left, twisted his body sideways, and showboated for the cameras. Despite all this, he finished in a blistering 9.69 seconds and decisively beat the runner-up.

In Philippians 3:12-14 (NIV), the apostle Paul used a footrace illustration to describe the Christian life. Only, he described it a little differently than Bolt's historic run:

> *Not that I have already obtained all this, or have already arrived at my goal, but I press on to take hold of that for which Christ Jesus took hold of me. Brothers and sisters, I do not consider myself yet to have taken hold of it. But one thing I do: Forgetting what is behind and straining toward what is ahead, I press on toward the goal to win the prize for which God has called me heavenward in Christ Jesus.*

WHAT'S IT MEAN?

The finish line for sprinters is a horizontal stripe across a track surface. The finish line for Christians—the "prize" Paul wrote about in Philippians 3:14—is eternity with our Savior in heaven.

The race to reach this indescribable reward, which is possible only through Jesus, lasts a lifetime. That's why even the great apostle Paul said he had not yet "arrived at my goal." But how we run each step of our lifelong race of faith is important.

Paul says we must do it by "forgetting what is behind and straining toward what is ahead" (today's verse). In his epic Olympic victory, Bolt did half of that. He blew past the competitors behind him, but he didn't exactly strain forward at the end.

How do you forget what is behind? Don't live in the past. That means you shouldn't dwell on former sins; slip back into old, disobedient patterns of life; or bask in your achievements. Rather, "press on toward the goal" of heaven, always straining forward in your efforts to be like Jesus and honor God.

Don't ease up before life's finish line. Strain forward toward Jesus!

NOW WHAT?

To keep pressing on in your faith, find a new Christian ministry to serve in.

DID YOU KNOW?

Remarkably, Usain Bolt defended all three titles at the 2012 London Olympics.

Always be full of joy in the Lord. I say it again—rejoice!
PHILIPPIANS 4:4

If the ancient Israelites were good at anything, it was complaining.

It all started on the Red Sea's shoreline. No sooner had God powerfully delivered his people from Egyptian slavery than they started complaining. Trapped between the sea and Pharaoh's rapidly approaching army, the Israelites cried out against Moses, "Why did you bring us out here to die in the wilderness?" (Exodus 14:11).

God, of course, miraculously saved Israel by parting the Red Sea. That astounding display of God's power and protection didn't stop the Israelites from complaining, though. In the following months, they moaned about a lack of water (Exodus 15:24) and food (Exodus 16:2-3), the overall hardships of their journey (Numbers 11:1), Moses' authority (Numbers 12:1-2), and his leadership (Numbers 14:1-4). The Israelites had a PhD in the subject of complaining.

They could've used a little help from today's verse.

WHAT'S IT MEAN?

Complaining reveals a heart that is bitter, ungrateful, and distrustful toward God. That's why Paul wrote, "Do everything without complaining and arguing" in Philippians 2:14. Rather, Christians are to "rejoice" and "always be full of joy in the Lord," even in great trials, as today's verse says.

Let's be clear: this does not mean you must be happy all the time. Happiness and joy are not the same thing. Happiness depends on circumstances. It comes and goes. True joy never disappears.

At some point, you will experience great trials in life: a friend may betray you, or a loved one will die. When life stinks, it's okay to be sad. But the Bible tells us to remain joyful in all circumstances. In 1 Thessalonians 5:16, Paul said, "Always be joyful," and in 2 Corinthians 6:10, he put it this way: "Our hearts ache, but we always have joy."

How is this possible? Because joy comes from a proper eternal perspective. Christians can display ever-present joy, even during life's darkest moments, thanks to their righteous standing before God. Through Jesus, believers are forgiven, justified, and loved by the Lord God Almighty, the Maker of heaven and earth. We are his children, adopted into his heavenly family, and heirs of eternal life. This provides great peace, hope . . . and, yes, joy.

Life's difficulties won't last forever. But the joy Jesus provides to his followers will! Rejoice in your Savior!

NOW WHAT?

To develop a joyful heart, make a daily habit of prayerfully rejoicing in God's goodness to you.

DID YOU KNOW?

First Peter 1:8-9 says you can "rejoice with a glorious, inexpressible joy" because your faith will result in "the salvation of your souls."

NOVEMBER 2

I have learned how to be content with whatever I have.
PHILIPPIANS 4:11

When your nickname is "Money," it's pretty obvious what you love most in life.

In 2014, boxing superstar Floyd "Money" Mayweather Jr. became the world's highest-paid athlete after banking $105 million for two fights that year, according to *Forbes*. At the time, Mayweather's total career earnings were estimated at nearly $400 million. That's a lot of coinage.

While Mayweather's personal fortune is staggering, he doesn't keep it, well, very personal. He loves to flaunt his wealth on various social media sites, such as publicizing videos of himself depositing $1.2 million in the bank and counting $1 million in cash on his private jet. He has also posted photos of a $1.1 million bet he made on a college football game, a $500,000 stack of cash he won at a casino, and his Bugatti Veyron, an exotic car with a price tag north of $1 million.

Yes, "Money" Mayweather loves money. But it seems he's not content with his overwhelming riches. You get the sense that he's always itching for more.

The apostle Paul wrote about a much different mind-set in Philippians 4:11-13:

> *I have learned how to be content with whatever I have. I know how to live on almost nothing or with everything. I have learned the secret of living in every situation, whether it is with a full stomach or empty, with plenty or little. For I can do everything through Christ, who gives me strength.*

WHAT'S IT MEAN?

Contentment is feeling happy and satisfied. When you are content, you're fulfilled with what you have, not concerned about what you don't have. Content Christians realize that God's blessings are far greater than temporary earthly treasure (1 Timothy 6:7).

Paul was a great example of true, godly contentment. Despite severe hardships that often left him cold, hungry, sleepless, homeless, naked, or even near death (2 Corinthians 11:23-27), Paul felt satisfied with God's plan for him because of his eternal perspective. He knew Jesus had died for his sins, providing peace and purpose for this life and eternal hope for the next. That's how Paul could be content amidst very difficult circumstances.

How about you? Do you find your heart craving worldly treasure or feeling dissatisfied with your situation in life? That's not what God desires for you. Rest in his provision and in the Savior's love, and you will experience life-changing contentment!

NOW WHAT?

Read 1 Timothy 6:6-10, another great passage from Paul on contentment.

DID YOU KNOW?

Before Floyd Mayweather Jr. became the world's highest-paid athlete for the first time in 2012, golfer Tiger Woods had held that distinction since 2001.

NOVEMBER 3

My God will meet all your needs according to the riches of his glory in Christ Jesus. PHILIPPIANS 4:19, NIV

Elijah was in danger.

The Old Testament prophet had boldly spoken the word of the Lord against Israel's King Ahab, and now he had to run for his life. Ahab didn't take too kindly to prophets who condemned him.

Ahab was a terribly wicked king who plunged Israel into new depths of idolatry. As punishment, God sent Elijah to prophesy a three-year drought in Israel, a crippling blow to an agricultural nation. Ahab was not a happy tyrant.

So God told Elijah to flee to Kerith Brook, a place east of the Jordan River. This was a bare, arid land beyond Israel's borders. Many Israelites would have considered it an unclean, forsaken realm, outside of the extent of God's blessings.

Nevertheless, Elijah obeyed. Hiding all alone in the wilderness, he marveled at God's provision. Ravens brought him food every day, and he drank water from the brook. When the brook dried up, God sent Elijah to a Canaanite town where he met a widow who fed him for many days.

This story, from 1 Kings 17, is one of countless examples in Scripture of God's provision. If you pick any godly person in the Bible at random and read about that person's life, you'll see how the Lord cared for him or her in every situation.

God always provides for the needs of his people.

WHAT'S IT MEAN?

First, let's make something clear: there's a big difference between our needs and our wants.

Our wants greatly outweigh our actual needs. You might think life would be much better if you had the latest phone, received a check for one thousand dollars, won the championship game, became more popular, or got a puppy.

But God knows what's best for us, even more than we know ourselves. He doesn't exist to fulfill our every request, like some sort of divine butler. But he does promise to always give us what we need. He says so in today's verse.

Our biggest needs aren't material; they are spiritual. God met our greatest need in Christ. He looked at our helpless state, mercifully chose to extend grace, and sacrificed his own Son to remove the guilt of our sins.

If God did that, he will certainly meet every other need you'll ever have according to his glorious riches in Christ Jesus!

NOW WHAT?

Psalm 34:9-10; Matthew 6:33; and 2 Corinthians 9:8 also discuss God meeting all our needs. Check them out!

DID YOU KNOW?

Ahab once ordered a man named Naboth to be killed just so he could take his vineyard (1 Kings 21).

NOVEMBER 4

Don't let anyone capture you with empty philosophies and high-sounding nonsense that come from human thinking and from the spiritual powers of this world, rather than from Christ.
COLOSSIANS 2:8

How exciting it must have been to be a Christian in the first century AD!

By the time the apostle Paul wrote his letter to the Colossians around AD 62, Christianity was only about thirty years old, having started after Jesus' resurrection. But the young faith was growing. All over the Roman Empire, Jews and Gentiles alike were leaving sinful lives behind and turning to Christ. It was a thrilling time!

But it was also a period of dangerous spiritual pitfalls. The collection of New Testament books that we enjoy today—with all of its teachings on Jesus, salvation, and godly living—didn't exist yet. Heresy (false teaching) was a common threat. Like wolves in sheep's clothing, false teachers infiltrated many churches and spread bad teaching. Early Christians were left to choose between truth and falsehood.

That's exactly why Paul wrote today's verse.

WHAT'S IT MEAN?

Two thousand years later, false teachings still abound within the church. We're not talking about easy-to-spot false religions such as Islam, Buddhism, or Hinduism. We're talking about so-called "Christian" beliefs that appear legitimate on the surface but are actually destructive lies.

How can you distinguish between spiritual truth and falsehood? This takes much prayerful discernment. It also takes biblical knowledge. To identify false teachings, you need to know God's Word. You can't recognize heresy if you don't know what scriptural truth is.

Test all ideas, teachings, and beliefs with these questions: What do they say about Jesus (1 John 4:2-3)? Do they exalt him as the eternal Son of God, fully God and fully man? Do they uphold him as the sinless Savior, crucified and risen again? Do they proclaim him to be the only sacrifice for our sins? If the answer to any of these questions is no, it's a false teaching.

As today's verse says, Jesus is the measuring stick to determine spiritual truth from errors. Likewise, Ephesians 4:13-14 says "knowledge of God's Son" will help us avoid being "immature like children . . . blown about by every wind of new teaching" or "influenced when people try to trick us with lies so clever they sound like the truth."

Be on your guard against anything that sets itself up against the true knowledge of Christ!

NOW WHAT?

Almost every New Testament book warns Christians about false teaching. Check out these helpful passages: Galatians 1:8-9; Ephesians 4:11-16; 1 Timothy 6:3-5; 2 John 7-10; and Jude 1:4.

DID YOU KNOW?

The New Testament's twenty-seven books were written between AD 40 and 95 or so.

Set your minds on things above, not on earthly things.
COLOSSIANS 3:2, NIV

The human brain kind of resembles a dried prune, only much bigger and with more wrinkles. It's actually pretty freaky looking. But it's one of God's most remarkable creations.

The brain is a three-pound organ that serves as your body's command center. It interprets the five senses, makes decisions, dictates behavior and emotions, controls body functions, allows for imagination, stores memory, solves problems, and much more. It's the most powerful and wonderfully complex part of the human body.

You can live without your fingers, toes, arms, legs, eyes, ears, tongue, teeth, hair, appendix, tonsils, thyroid, portions of your stomach, and even a lung. But you can't live without your brain. No wrinkly blob of tissue inside your skull? No life. *Adios.*

God wants us to put our brains to good use. In today's verse, the apostle Paul says Christians should set their minds on "things above, not on earthly things."

WHAT'S IT MEAN?

Another way to say today's verse is this: Christians should focus their brain-power on the eternal, not the temporary.

It's easy to get caught up in earthly things. This world is filled with distractions such as money, fame, pleasure, and other self-centered pursuits that divert our thoughts from what really matters. But one day, God will destroy all earthly things—even the earth itself (2 Peter 3:10-11). Not much point in thinking about things that will be annihilated with fire!

It's far better to "set your mind on things above." These are thoughts of heavenly, eternal truths. They are thoughts of Christ, who reigns above all else in the universe (Philippians 2:9).

When we avoid worldly thoughts and pursue a deeper knowledge of Jesus, we are using our brains for their true purpose. God wants us to better understand his Son and the amazing realities of salvation.

Immediately after today's verse, Paul details why we should set our minds on such things: "For you died to this life, and your real life is hidden with Christ in God. And when Christ, who is your life, is revealed to the whole world, you will share in all his glory" (Colossians 3:3-4).

Wow! Try to wrap your three-pound, wrinkly blob of tissue around *that*!

NOW WHAT?

When "rebellious," worldly thoughts enter your brain, "capture" them and "teach them to obey Christ" (2 Corinthians 10:5). In other words, train your brain to think godly thoughts!

DID YOU KNOW?

Paul wrote about similar things in Philippians 4:8: "Fix your thoughts on what is true, and honorable, and right, and pure, and lovely, and admirable. Think about things that are excellent and worthy of praise."

NOVEMBER 6

Let the message about Christ, in all its richness, fill your lives.
COLOSSIANS 3:16

Honestly, it's amazing that Christianity not only survived, but thrived in the first century AD.

Think about it: for centuries, the ancient world's religions were fairly stable. The Greeks worshiped their gods. The Romans worshiped their gods. So did the Babylonians, Egyptians, Persians, and many others. In Israel, the Jews followed Judaism. They believed in the one true God and followed Old Testament laws.

Suddenly in the 30s AD, a small group of men and women began boldly proclaiming an entirely unique message that forgiveness of sins and eternal life is possible only through one man, Jesus Christ, the sinless Son of God who was crucified and resurrected. Talk about a radical, new message! But through the faithful witness of the apostles and others, the gospel message spread rapidly across the entire Roman Empire.

This was nothing short of miraculous. In those early years of Christianity, the New Testament didn't exist yet. Young believers had to trust solely in the verbal and written "message about Christ" (today's verse) from eyewitnesses of Jesus' life and other godly men. We see this in 2 Thessalonians 2:15 when the apostle Paul wrote, "Stand firm and keep a strong grip on the teaching we passed on to you both in person and by letter."

Christianity's growth was completely an act of God, who was fulfilling Old Testament promises such as Jeremiah 31:31-34 by spreading the gospel worldwide and transforming thousands of hearts through his Spirit.

The best part is, he's still doing that today.

WHAT'S IT MEAN?

These days, the message about Christ hasn't changed at all. Jesus is still—and will always be—the only way to be reconciled with God. The gospel is still saving lives.

Are you letting this eternal message fill your life? Are you drinking in its richness? Whether it's stories in the four Gospels, spiritual truths in the New Testament letters, or prophecies in the Old Testament, accept Scripture's words about Christ with faith. Soak them up like a dry sponge. Devour them with a hearty appetite. Receive them with joy and excitement like you're opening gifts on Christmas morning.

The message about Christ is rich, glorious, and eternal. It saves souls, matures faith, and glorifies God. That's as true today as it was two thousand years ago!

NOW WHAT?

Reading the Gospel of John is a great way to fill yourself with the "message about Christ." If you read one chapter a day, you'll be done in three weeks.

DID YOU KNOW?

The message about Christ succeeded because God's Word "always produces fruit" and will always "accomplish all I want it to" (Isaiah 55:11).

NOVEMBER 7

Whatever you do, whether in word or deed, do it all in the name of the Lord Jesus, giving thanks to God the Father through him.
COLOSSIANS 3:17, NIV

It was a bad day to be one of the seven sons of Sceva. Out the door they ran—scared, bleeding, naked, and humiliated.

We'd better explain. . . .

Acts 19 tells a brief but fascinating story about the apostle Paul's third missionary journey. While Paul was in Ephesus, God granted him the ability to perform extraordinary miracles. Handkerchiefs that touched Paul's skin became filled with supernatural power and were taken to heal the sick and demon possessed.

One day, seven sons of a Jewish priest named Sceva noticed how Paul was miraculously healing in Jesus' name. These men were traveling exorcists, going from town to town trying to heal people for money. They figured they could get rich off Jesus' name.

But when these con artists tried to mystically chant Jesus' name to heal a demon-possessed man, the evil spirit mocked them and empowered the man to give them a serious whipping. These ungodly fakes thought Jesus' name was nothing more than a magical charm. They had no idea what it means, as today's verse says, to do everything "in the name of the Lord Jesus."

WHAT'S IT MEAN?

Jesus' name brings eternal life (1 John 5:13). There is no greater name in the universe. One day, every knee will bow before the Savior's mighty name and acknowledge his supreme lordship over all creation (Philippians 2:10).

But how do Christians do everything in his name? Does that mean, for instance, that you're supposed to loudly proclaim during Saturday morning chores, "And now, dear parents, I shall go upstairs to clean bathrooms in Jesus' name"?

Uhhh, no.

To do everything in the name of Jesus means to represent the Lord well in all you do. It means living righteously and glorifying Jesus in all your words and actions. Christians are Christ's ambassadors (see the October 17 devotion). When others look at you, they should see Jesus.

When you do things in Jesus' name, you honor him. When you don't, you stain his name. You can't lose your temper or act selfishly in Jesus' name. You can't disobey your parents, steal, lie, or cheat in his name either.

Get the point? Everything you do in life should honor the Savior's name!

NOW WHAT?

Take inventory of your habits and daily activities. Are they things done in Jesus' name?

DID YOU KNOW?

The incident with the seven sons of Sceva prompted Christians in Ephesus to hold a huge bonfire, burning all their pagan magic books (Acts 19:19).

Don't let anyone think less of you because you are young. Be an example to all believers in what you say, in the way you live, in your love, your faith, and your purity. I TIMOTHY 4:12

Young King Josiah started out life with a raw deal.

Josiah, who ruled Judah during the seventh century BC, lived during a terribly rocky period. Josiah's grandfather, Manasseh, was possibly the worst king in Judah's nearly 350-year history. Because of Manasseh's wickedness and idolatry, God promised to bring horrible judgment on Judah, which was ultimately fulfilled after Josiah's lifetime in 586 BC when the Babylonians destroyed Jerusalem.

To make matters worse, Josiah's father, King Amon, followed in Manasseh's evil footsteps. King Amon was assassinated two years into his reign, thrusting little Josiah onto Judah's throne at age eight. Imagine being in Josiah's shoes—a third-grader forced to rule a wicked, doomed nation because of your family's heinous sins.

Thanks a lot, Grandpa. Thanks a lot, Dad.

Remarkably, Josiah blossomed into one of Judah's greatest kings. He cleansed the land of idolatry, repaired God's Temple, reinstituted the Passover celebration, and called the nation to repent. For thirty-one years, "he did what was pleasing in the LORD's sight" (2 Kings 22:2).

Young Josiah, the eight-year-old king, did great things for God. He's a perfect example of today's verse!

WHAT'S IT MEAN?

The apostle Paul wrote the letter we now call 1 Timothy to a young believer named—you guessed it—Timothy, whom Paul had led to the Lord years earlier. In today's verse, Paul encouraged Timothy to lead by example in the Christian church at Ephesus despite his age. Perhaps Timothy was scared that people would ignore him because of his youth. Paul dismissed any such thoughts and told Timothy to model godly character for the Ephesian believers, regardless of his age.

Paul's message to Timothy is for you, too! God doesn't care about your age. It's your heart that matters. If your sinful heart has been forgiven by Jesus, transformed by the Holy Spirit, and is willing to serve God, he can do great things through you.

Forget your age! Follow the Lord and set a Christlike example for others.

NOW WHAT?

Ask your parents to help you find a ministry at church where you can start serving now, no matter how old you are.

DID YOU KNOW?

The Bible is filled with stories of young people who did amazing things for God: Samuel (1 Samuel 3:1); David (1 Samuel 17:42); Joash (2 Kings 11:21); Jeremiah (Jeremiah 1:6); the Jewish slave girl who helped Naaman (2 Kings 5:2); and the little boy whose fish-and-bread lunch helped Jesus feed thousands (John 6:9).

NOVEMBER 9

Be strong in the grace that is in Christ Jesus.
2 TIMOTHY 2:1, NIV

Humans have always been fascinated with physical strength. The ancient Greeks told myths about a legendary warrior named Hercules, who performed mighty deeds. Fast-forward a few thousand years to 1896: the first modern-era Olympics in Athens, Greece, featured weightlifting as one of its main competitions.

Today, we are still awed by strength. Each year, various extreme strength competitions are held, such as the "World's Strongest Man" event. To win the title, these massively beefed-up athletes have to do crazy stuff, such as lugging two refrigerators on their shoulders, towing a tractor-trailer behind them, and carrying six-hundred-pound weights up stairs.

Flex for us, fellas!

Physical strength is cool, but God's Word speaks of a far greater strength. This power doesn't come from weightlifting, protein shakes, good genetics, steroids, or any other human source. As today's verse says, Christians draw true strength from "the grace that is in Christ Jesus."

WHAT'S IT MEAN?

Where do you need strength these days? To obey your parents? To do daily devotions? To show kindness to that certain classmate at school? To get through a family crisis? To make godly choices when all your friends don't?

Whatever you're facing, you can draw strength from the grace Jesus provides. Does that sound like a strange power source? Then perhaps you need a grace refresher.

Grace is God's unmerited favor toward sinners and is available to all true Christians. Here's just a small sampling of the grace every believer experiences:

- Jesus justifies you before God (Romans 3:24).
- God adopts you as his child (Galatians 4:5).

- Jesus saves you from God's eternal wrath (Romans 5:9).
- Jesus breaks the power of sin in your life (1 Corinthians 15:56-57).
- The Holy Spirit dwells inside you (Ezekiel 36:27).
- Jesus becomes your Advocate before the Father (1 John 2:1).
- God promises to work out everything in your life for your good (Romans 8:28).
- You will spend eternity in heaven with your Savior (1 Thessalonians 4:17).

Pretty awesome list, huh? All of it is grace—undeserved and life changing. When you consider all the grace available to you in Christ, it helps you stay strong through all life's challenges. No matter what you're facing, be strong in the grace that is yours in Jesus! (No refrigerators or tractor-trailers required.)

NOW WHAT?
Look up all the Bible references in the list above and on the previous page, and be strengthened in your heart by God's grace!

DID YOU KNOW?
Denmark's Viggo Jensen won the 1896 Olympic men's heavyweight two-handed lift competition at 111.5 kilograms (about 245 pounds). Today's Olympic weightlifters can do twice as much.

If we are unfaithful, he remains faithful, for he cannot deny who he is. 2 TIMOTHY 2:13

Two disciples, two terrible mistakes, and two completely different destinies—that's the tale of Judas Iscariot and Peter on the night of Jesus' arrest.

To study today's verse from the apostle Paul's final letter, let's travel back in time to that sinister night in the garden of Gethsemane.

Judas betrayed Jesus with a wicked kiss. Later that night, Peter uttered bald-faced lies as he repeatedly denied any association with Jesus.

Both were awful sins. But the similarities end there. The reactions of both men show the difference. Filled with remorse but lacking any true repentance, Judas ran off and hanged himself. Peter, too, ran off after his denials, but the tears he wept were filled with godly sorrow.

Judas died, but Peter lived. Jesus forgave Peter, restored him, and empowered him to a life of powerful, effective Christian ministry.

Peter is a prime example of today's verse. In a moment of severe weakness, he was unfaithful to his Lord. But Jesus remained faithful to him.

WHAT'S IT MEAN?

At some point in life, you will fail Jesus. It's inevitable. Because of indwelling sin, all Christians will be unfaithful to the Savior eventually. Your words or actions won't align with his perfect purposes. You might even deny him in a moment of spiritual cowardice.

That's why the truth of today's verse is so uplifting. If you're a true believer, even in moments when you are not faithful to Jesus, he remains faithful to you.

Jesus will never leave you or forsake you. He'll never say, "Forget it, pal, that's one sin too many. I'm outta here." He'll never give up on you. You will always be secure in his love and grace. As he said in John 6:37, "Those the Father has given me will come to me, and I will never reject them."

This is so encouraging! But how is it true? Because true Christians are "in

Christ" (Galatians 3:26, NIV). They are part of Christ's body (1 Corinthians 12:27). God's Spirit dwells in them (1 Corinthians 3:16). If Jesus were unfaithful to a believer, he'd be unfaithful to himself. And that's impossible.

If you acknowledge Jesus as your Lord and Savior, as Peter did, he will always be faithful to you. There's no denying it!

NOW WHAT?

Check out the amazing promise of 1 Corinthians 1:8-9.

DID YOU KNOW?

Jesus' faithfulness toward you should not be treated as permission to sin. That would be wrongfully taking advantage of his grace (Romans 6:1-2).

All Scripture is God-breathed and is useful for teaching, rebuking, correcting and training in righteousness, so that the servant of God may be thoroughly equipped for every good work.

2 TIMOTHY 3:16-17, NIV

Time for a pop quiz!

Today's subject is famous literary quotations. Let's see if you can guess what books they come from.

1. "It was the best of times, it was the worst of times."
2. "All we have to decide is what to do with the time that is given us."
3. "Second star to the right and straight on 'til morning."
4. "Always winter and never Christmas; think of that!"
5. "The sun did not shine. It was too wet to play. So we sat in the house all that cold, cold, wet day."

(The answers are on the next page.)

There's lots of fantastic literature in the world. But there is only one book in human history that is "God-breathed." That book is the Bible.

WHAT'S IT MEAN?

Today's Scripture passage represents some of the last words written by the apostle Paul before he died. In his final letter, Paul wanted to impress on his dear friend Timothy how important it was to understand the truth about Scripture.

The phrase "All Scripture is breathed out by God" is quite interesting. Does that mean God exhaled one day and—*poof!*—a Bible magically appeared? Not exactly.

God used certain holy men—about forty of them—to write all sixty-six books over a span of 1,300 to 1,500 years. But God inspired, or "breathed out," all the words they wrote through the Holy Spirit (2 Peter 1:20-21).

When we read the Bible, we're seeing every single word God wants us to know!

The words of the Bible are:

- completely truthful (Proverbs 30:5)
- pure (Psalm 12:6)
- powerful (Hebrews 4:12)
- wise and righteous (Psalm 19:7-11, ESV)
- eternal (Matthew 24:35)
- able to provide us with eternal life (John 6:68)
- helpful as we seek to obey God daily (Matthew 4:4)

Most importantly, the Bible shows us our need for a Savior and reveals him to us in the Lord Jesus Christ. Through holy Scripture, we can come to saving faith in Jesus and be "equipped for every good work" as we serve him!

NOW WHAT?

Since the Bible is the only God-breathed book in history, we need to know what it says. Read it daily!

DID YOU KNOW?

Here are today's quiz answers:

1. A Tale of Two Cities *(Charles Dickens)*
2. The Lord of the Rings *(J. R. R. Tolkien)*
3. Peter Pan *(J. M. Barrie)*
4. The Lion, the Witch and the Wardrobe *(C. S. Lewis)*
5. The Cat in the Hat *(Dr. Seuss)*

I have fought the good fight, I have finished the race, and I have remained faithful. 2 TIMOTHY 4:7

So what happened to the apostle Paul? It's one of the biggest mysteries in the Bible.

The book of Acts, Scripture's partial biography of the great missionary/ theologian/pastor, ends abruptly with Paul under house arrest in Rome on false charges of stirring up trouble in Jerusalem. No one knows exactly what happened to Paul after that. But we can make a pretty good guess.

Based on 2 Timothy and other ancient historical sources, many Bible scholars believe Paul was released from his house arrest after two years and took a final missionary trip to Spain before being imprisoned in Rome again.

According to early Christian tradition, Paul's second imprisonment was in Rome's infamous Mamertine Prison. Mamertine was an approximately six-hundred-year-old cistern—an underground well carved out of solid rock— that had been converted into a jail cell. The ancient historian Sallust said the prison was twelve feet below ground and "neglect, darkness, and stench make it hideous and fearsome to behold."

Paul was cold (2 Timothy 4:13) and lonely. Most of his acquaintances had deserted him (2 Timothy 1:15). When Onesiphorus, one of Paul's friends, arrived in Rome, he had to search hard to locate Paul (2 Timothy 1:17).

As the elderly apostle wrote his last letter, he knew his life was nearly over. Here are some of his final words to Timothy (2 Timothy 4:6-8):

> *As for me, my life has already been poured out as an offering to God. The time of my death is near. I have fought the good fight, I have finished the race, and I have remained faithful. And now the prize awaits me—the crown of righteousness, which the Lord, the righteous Judge, will give me on the day of his return. And the prize is not just for me but for all who eagerly look forward to his appearing.*

WHAT'S IT MEAN?

To his last breath, Paul remained a faithful follower of Jesus. You are called to be faithful too. Does that mean you'll be imprisoned or executed for your faith? Doubtful. But no matter what your future holds, Christ calls you to stay obedient to him your whole life as you excitedly wait for his return.

For a lifetime of faithfulness, you will receive "the crown of righteousness"—indescribable heavenly rewards. Stay faithful and enjoy eternal blessings with the Savior!

NOW WHAT?

Boldly share your faith with others. It's one way to be faithful to Jesus.

DID YOU KNOW?

According to tradition, the Romans beheaded Paul outside the city on the Ostian Road in the late 60s AD.

NOVEMBER 13

The Son is far greater than the angels, just as the name God gave him is greater than their names. HEBREWS 1:4

One day in the sixth century BC, Daniel, the great hero of the Jewish exile, was walking with some friends along the Tigris River in Persia.

Suddenly, according to Daniel 10, a glorious angel appeared to him with a vision of the future. The angel's appearance nearly gave the poor man a heart attack. As his friends scattered in fear, Daniel's face turned deathly pale, his knees gave out, and he fainted face-first onto the ground.

Don't feel bad, Danny Boy. You're not alone. Scripture is filled with examples of angels scaring people senseless.

Zechariah, John the Baptist's father, "was shaken and overwhelmed with fear" when Gabriel visited him (Luke 1:12). The Roman guards at Jesus' tomb "fell into a dead faint" when an angel appeared to roll the stone away (Matthew 28:4). Isaiah (Isaiah 6:5), Mary (Luke 1:29), the women at Jesus' tomb (Luke 24:5), Cornelius (Acts 10:4), and others all had similar experiences.

You get the point: Don't mess with angels.

Angels are wonderful, highly intelligent "ministering spirits" (Hebrews 1:14, NIV) from God, who serve Christians. They stand in God's presence (Luke 1:19) and carry out his will (Psalm 104:4). But they are also fearsome to behold and wield extraordinary power. They can destroy enormous human armies (2 Kings 19:35) and repel satanic attacks (Revelation 12:7-9). One day, they will accompany Jesus during his second coming (2 Thessalonians 1:7) and commence God's final judgment on evil (Revelation 8, 9 and 16).

Yet despite their power, glory, and privileges, all angels fall on their knees to worship Jesus.

WHAT'S IT MEAN?

Angels are created beings. Jesus is not. Angels are not all-powerful or all-knowing. Jesus is. As today's verse says, Jesus is "far greater" than angels.

And 1 Peter 3:22 says "all the angels and authorities and powers accept his authority." Jesus proved he deserves his exalted position through his death and resurrection (Philippians 2:8-11).

The Son of God's supremacy over these mighty spiritual beings is just another proof of his unequaled majesty and power. The best part is, Jesus' endless power is available to you! The Savior of the world, who rules over all spiritual realms, loves you and wants to empower you to accomplish his purposes.

Rejoice in the unending power and authority of the risen Savior!

NOW WHAT?

Read Hebrews 1 and Revelation 5 to better understand Jesus' superiority over angels.

DID YOU KNOW?

Worshiping anything created, such as angels, is a direct violation of Exodus 20:3 (see also Romans 1:25 and Colossians 2:18). We should worship only the one true God.

NOVEMBER 14

Jesus Christ is the same yesterday, today, and forever. So do not be attracted by strange, new ideas.   HEBREWS 13:8-9

The world is constantly changing. Consider these facts:

- Dinosaurs once roamed the earth.
- In a six-hundred-year span, Assyria, Babylon, Medo-Persia, Greece, and Rome all laid claim to being the world's dominant empire.
- America was once considered wild, unexplored territory.
- For the first 144 years of US history, women didn't have the right to vote.
- Gas-powered "horseless carriages" used to be all the rage on American roadways.
- Video games have been in the mainstream only since the 1970s.
- Prior to the 1990s, cell phones were rare, hardly anyone used the Internet, and smartphones were nonexistent.

Here are a few other things that constantly change:

- weather
- the earth's orbital position in relation to the sun
- gas prices
- fashion trends
- popular music
- teenagers' hairdos (sorry, just sayin' . . .)

Yes, there are very few constants in this world. Things change all the time. But Jesus doesn't. Today's verse speaks a marvelous truth: "Jesus Christ is the same yesterday, today, and forever."

WHAT'S IT MEAN?

Change is often good. Technology and social advancements help improve the world in many cases. But Jesus' immutability—that is, his unchanging nature—is a very good thing. The Bible's words about Jesus were true when they were written thousands of years ago, they're true now, and they'll always be true. As the Second Person of the Holy Trinity, Jesus is no different today than he was in eternity past, or will be in eternity future.

Why is this important? Because if Jesus changed in his nature at all, that would mean either (1) he improved in some area (showing that he wasn't perfect to begin with), or (2) he worsened in some area (showing that he is no longer perfect).

But Jesus hasn't changed. As Hebrews 1:12 says, "You are always the same; you will live forever." Likewise, Revelation 1:4 describes him as "the one who is, who always was, and who is still to come."

The Savior that Christians have put their faith in for two thousand years still loves us, still has the power to forgive sins, and still presents us blameless before God the Father. Jesus is perfect exactly the way he is!

NOW WHAT?

Identify one area you need to change in your life to become more like Jesus. Pray and work hard at making that change.

DID YOU KNOW?

Air conditioning, airplane flight, plastic, electric refrigerators, talking movies, radar, televisions, space travel, lasers, and atomic warfare are all twentieth-century inventions.

Consider it pure joy, my brothers and sisters, whenever you face trials of many kinds, because you know that the testing of your faith produces perseverance. Let perseverance finish its work so that you may be mature and complete, not lacking anything.

JAMES 1:2-4, NIV

The Bible is filled with paradoxes. A paradox is a statement that sounds illogical or self-contradictory but is actually true. Here are some examples:

- "Give freely and become more wealthy; be stingy and lose everything" (Proverbs 11:24).
- "Those who are last now will be first then, and those who are first will be last" (Matthew 20:16).
- "If you think you are wise by this world's standards, you need to become a fool to be truly wise" (1 Corinthians 3:18).

These are all true statements, but at first glance, they look like head-scratchers. Add James 1:2-4 to the list. Today's passage is a humdinger of a paradox!

WHAT'S IT MEAN?

Okay, let's get this straight: We're actually supposed to *rejoice* when life's hardships smack us in the face?

Yep.

It might sound crazy at first (hence, the paradox), but it's not. It's all about perspective.

To understand—and even appreciate—trials, you must overcome your natural sinful tendencies. As weak human beings, we usually try to avoid pain and suffering at all costs. It's easy to wish that life were one big Disney cruise, filled with nothing but whimsy, laughter, and sunshine.

But that's not how life works. Trials are inevitable. When they come, though, we aren't supposed to moan and complain our way through them. God has something better for us!

Life's challenges are not bad luck, random acts of fate, or punishment. Instead, they are God's kindness toward you (paradox alert!). As James 1:3 says, trials are God-ordained tests to increase your faith, mature you spiritually, and bring him more glory. Viewing trials like this will enable you to consider them "pure joy."

This is not meant to minimize pain. It's perfectly fine to feel sorrow when difficulties or tragedies strike. But as you press on, always remember there's a loving God who is conforming you more to his perfect image.

Jesus is our greatest example of rejoicing in trials. He endured the greatest trial of all—the cross—"because of the joy awaiting him" (Hebrews 12:2). He looked past his immeasurable sufferings and took joy in knowing that they would result in our salvation!

NOW WHAT?

When trials hit, get on your knees in prayer. Ask God to help you trust him and persevere. He always proves faithful!

DID YOU KNOW?

Romans 5:3-5; 1 Peter 1:6-7; and 1 Peter 4:12-19 are all great passages on trials too. Check them out!

NOVEMBER 16

My brothers and sisters, believers in our glorious Lord Jesus Christ must not show favoritism. JAMES 2:1, NIV

What do you get when you combine a spoiled seventeen-year-old, ten jealous older brothers, a doting father, and the coolest coat in ancient Canaan?

You get a recipe for disaster!

In Genesis 37, we read about Joseph, the second youngest of Jacob's twelve sons. Jacob loved Joseph more than all his other children (Big Jake's first mistake). So one day, he made a multicolored coat for his favorite son (mistake number two).

Now, a bright, flashy jacket might not sound very interesting to you, but such an ornate garment would have been a pretty big deal to a shepherd used to wearing goatskins and other drab clothing. Joseph became like a Gap model of his day!

Anyway, you know what happened next, right? Seething with jealousy, Joseph's brothers sold him into slavery. Yet through God's sovereignty, Joseph rose to Pharaoh's second-in-command and saved his own family and all of Egypt from a terrible famine.

The Bible's most famous story of favoritism had a happy ending. But Scripture is very clear: Christians should avoid showing favoritism at all costs.

WHAT'S IT MEAN?

Favoritism is unfairly considering one person better than another. In doing this, you're basically saying one person is more valuable than another. And that's just not true.

Every human is made in God's image. Treating someone differently than others is to sinfully judge between people, which is not your place to do. God alone is the judge, and he does not show favoritism (Romans 2:11). He judges all humans fairly and equally, and he calls us to do the same.

In your life, you'll come across all sorts of people: rich, poor, smart, not-so-smart, athletic, clumsy, nice, funny, difficult, and downright nasty. You don't have to be best friends with everybody. But don't limit your kindness to a select few. Show the love of Christ to everyone.

Jesus never showed favoritism. He opened loving arms to everyone, even those who were considered unimportant or outcasts in his day: lepers, the crippled, tax collectors, Gentiles, women, and children. He offers salvation to all people.

Follow our Savior's example and avoid favoritism. (And while you're at it, don't give out any multicolored coats.)

NOW WHAT?

Befriend someone at school or church whom others don't pay attention to.

DID YOU KNOW?

The story of Joseph is also a wonderful reminder of God's sovereignty—how he works good for his people even in bad situations. As Joseph told his brothers in Genesis 50:20, "You intended to harm me, but God intended it all for good."

Faith by itself, if it does not have works, is dead.   JAMES 2:17, ESV

The Bible is God's holy Word. All sixty-six books of Scripture are without error (Psalm 12:6), eternally true (Psalm 119:89), and inspired by God himself (2 Timothy 3:16). Those are facts.

Yet portions of the Bible have often faced criticism, sometimes even from famous Christians! One example is the New Testament book of James, which Martin Luther strongly criticized.

Luther, the well-known sixteenth-century Protestant Reformation leader, hated the book of James. He infamously called it "a right strawy epistle"—in other words, a letter as worthless as straw.

Luther's major beef was with James 2:14-26. This is James's famous "faith and works" passage. In it, James discusses the relationship of faith and good works in the Christian life.

Today's verse really angered Luther. In his mind, it completely contradicted Scripture's clear teaching that sinners are saved by God's grace alone, through faith, and not by any human effort (Ephesians 2:8-9).

Was Luther right in dismissing the book of James? And how should we understand the relationship between faith and works in our lives?

WHAT'S IT MEAN?

First, know this: good works *do not* save us. Neither does faith plus works. Luther was correct in that regard. Sinners are saved by God's grace through faith alone (Ephesians 2:8). No amount of good deeds can produce the spiritual rebirth (John 3:3) that every human heart needs.

However, Luther should not have dismissed James's Spirit-inspired words. James's message was this: while good works don't *produce* salvation, they do *reveal* genuine faith.

Good works are kind of like putting on your favorite team's gear. Wearing an NFL jersey doesn't make you an NFL player. But it does show your allegiance—which team you follow.

It's the same with Christianity. Good works don't save you. But they show where your allegiance is—that you follow Christ. Good works naturally flow out of genuine faith and salvation as proof of the transformation Jesus has done in your heart. If you proclaim faith in Christ yet don't live in a God-honoring way, your faith is "dead," as today's verse says.

The apostle John supported James's message in 1 John 2:3-6. Jesus himself did too. In John 14:15, the Savior said, "If you love me, obey my commandments."

Do you profess to be a Christian? Then show it by your obedience to Jesus and your good works toward others.

NOW WHAT?

Read the whole "faith and works" passage in James 2:14-26.

DID YOU KNOW?

The author of the book of James was—drum roll, please!—James, the earthly brother of Jesus (Matthew 13:55) and the leader of the early Jerusalem church (Acts 15:13).

What is causing the quarrels and fights among you? Don't they come from the evil desires at war within you?   JAMES 4:1

Time to fess up: When was the last time you fought with someone, whether it was a sibling, friend, classmate, relative, or one of your parents?

Was it last week? A few days ago? Yesterday? Earlier today? Five minutes ago? If you're honest, it was probably pretty recently.

We humans are really good at quarreling and fighting. Some of us, in fact, seem to have a college degree in the subject.

Have you ever wondered why it's so tough to get along with people sometimes? Fighting often seems so easy, while harmony seems so difficult. Why is that?

James 4:1-3 has the answer. There's a battle raging inside of you. (And it has nothing to do with indigestion from last night's sausage-and-anchovies pizza.) As today's verse says, there is a conflict of desires "at war within you" for control of your heart.

WHAT'S IT MEAN?

The reason we fight, argue, bicker, and struggle to obey God is because sinful, selfish desires are battling within us. It's that simple. All the conflicts and quarrels you get into ultimately stem from a heart that is evil, prideful, and self-centered.

Think about it:

- When you fight with others, it's because they're not doing what you want.
- When you argue with others, it's because they don't agree with you.
- When you disobey, it's because you don't like what you've been asked to do.

No one put these sinful desires in your heart. They've always been there. Every human was born a sinner (Psalm 51:5).

What we need is a clean heart—one that's free from sinful, combative desires. James 4:8 tells us to "purify [our] hearts."

You can't do this on your own, though. That would be like a heart transplant patient telling the surgeon, "Don't worry. I got this. Can you hand me your scalpel, please?" Bad idea.

You need Jesus' help to overcome the "evil desires at war within you" (today's verse). God's sinless Son died to forgive your sins and break sin's power in your life. When you trust in Jesus, your evil desires won't instantly vanish, but the Lord will sanctify you and give you the power of the Holy Spirit to make the right choices.

For that sausage-and-anchovies pizza still raging inside you, turn to antacid relief. For the evil desires raging in your heart, turn to Jesus!

NOW WHAT?

If you've recently fought with someone and haven't made up yet, seek out that person and ask for forgiveness.

DID YOU KNOW?

Humble prayer can help fight sinful desires of the heart (James 4:2-3, 7-10).

If we confess our sins, he is faithful and just and will forgive us our sins and purify us from all unrighteousness. 1 JOHN 1:9, NIV

King David was quite a guy.

The former shepherd from Bethlehem was the greatest ruler in Israel's long history. He enlarged Israel's kingdom, wrote at least half the book of Psalms, and was "a man after [God's] own heart" (1 Samuel 13:14).

But David was a big sinner, too. At one particular moment in his life, he suffered an epic meltdown of morals, honesty, and justice.

One day, as his army was off fighting battles, David stayed in Jerusalem and fell in love with another man's wife, Bathsheba. Then he arranged for Bathsheba's husband, Uriah, who was one of David's most trusted soldiers, to be killed in battle. After Uriah died, David married Bathsheba.

When the prophet Nathan confronted David for his wickedness, the king repented and admitted, "I have sinned against the LORD" (2 Samuel 12:13). Then David composed Psalm 51, one of the greatest confession songs in the Bible. In it, he admitted his guilt and cried out for God's mercy. "I know my transgressions," he wrote in verse 3 (NIV), "and my sin is always before me."

Despite David's heinous sins, God forgave him and continued to bless him because of his humble confession.

WHAT'S IT MEAN?

This serious episode in David's life is a great example of today's verse. We have a beautifully simple, reassuring promise straight from the Lord in 1 John 1:9: true confession always brings the forgiveness and cleansing that every Christian desperately needs. We need this forgiveness and cleansing because our sin hinders fellowship with God.

Confession is not quickly saying, "I'm sorry" and moving on with life. To "confess your sins" means acknowledging your wrongdoing specifically, by name, to God and repenting. It's a heartfelt admission to God that you have disobeyed his laws and want to be reconciled to him.

If we approach God in humble confession and repentance, we will *always* receive forgiveness and spiritual cleansing—guaranteed—because of God's perfect character. He is faithful and trustworthy and never turns away anyone who comes to him truly seeking forgiveness.

Of course, all this is possible only through Jesus. Faith in his sacrificial, atoning death allows sinners to approach a holy God. So whenever you fall into disobedience, confess your sins to God and experience his wonderful, purifying forgiveness!

NOW WHAT?

Read Psalm 51, and use it to pray through any sin you need to confess to God.

DID YOU KNOW?

Even though Christians are completely forgiven by Jesus at the moment of their salvation, continued confession of sin is necessary so daily fellowship with God isn't obstructed.

Those who have been born into God's family do not make a practice of sinning, because God's life is in them. So they can't keep on sinning, because they are children of God. 1 JOHN 3:9

Sopping wet with bricks in his pockets, Stephen Curry reaches two hundred pounds on the scales.

Maybe.

But despite his slender 6-foot-3, 190-pound frame, the Golden State Warriors' baby-faced guard is one of the best pure shooters in the NBA. As a second-year pro in 2010–2011, Curry set a franchise record by making 93.4 percent of his free throws. Two years later, he set an NBA single-season record with 272 three-pointers.

How does he do it? Practice, practice, and more practice.

During the off-season, Curry shoots baskets daily until he makes 500. During the season, he stays on the practice court until he makes 200 to 350, depending on the team's schedule.

If you compete in sports, play a musical instrument, or enjoy a hobby, you also know the value of practice. Typically, the more you practice something, the better you become at it.

That's why, as today's verse says, you should never "make a practice of sinning."

WHAT'S IT MEAN?

You will sin. That's an unfortunate but undeniable fact of being human. If we claim otherwise, "we are calling God a liar" (1 John 1:10).

But the Bible makes a distinction between falling prey to sin occasionally and making a practice of sinning. To practice sin is to break God's laws in the same way repeatedly, like a basketball player launching bad shots over and over from a difficult angle on the court, despite the coach's instructions to stop. Willfully and consistently disobeying Scripture's commands reveals a heart that is dangerously hardened toward God.

True Christians practice godliness more and more, and sin less and less. This is all part of a believer's lifelong sanctification process (1 Thessalonians 5:23).

Yes, you will have sin struggles. Certain things will tempt you to disobey God more than others. But "when you are tempted, [God] will show you a way out so that you can endure" (1 Corinthians 10:13).

Genuine followers of Jesus confess and repent of their sins, asking for God's Spirit to help them "put off" their old, rebellious ways and "put on" their new, obedient identities in Christ (Ephesians 4:22-24, NIV).

So practice righteousness—in addition to basketball, soccer, ice-skating, piano, painting, writing, yodeling, or whatever you're good at. But don't practice sin!

NOW WHAT?

The next time you practice your favorite sport or hobby, remember today's devotion about practicing righteousness, not sin.

DID YOU KNOW?

Practicing righteousness instead of sinfulness shows others that you are God's child (3 John 1:11).

NOVEMBER 21

Be thankful in all circumstances, for this is God's will for you who belong to Christ Jesus.   1 THESSALONIANS 5:18

With Thanksgiving nearly here, it's a good time for you to meet Bob.

Well, this might be a little tricky. You can't actually *meet* Bob, because he's dead. But it's still a good idea for you to get to know Bob a little better, even after his recent passing. Bob's death was unfortunate for him, but truthfully, more people like him better dead than alive.

Wow, this is getting awkward. An explanation is definitely needed here.

For a while, good ol' Bob had a great life. Every day, Farmer Joe served Bob hand and foot. He fed Bob all he could eat (sometimes too much!), provided him a nice, fenced-in home, and surrounded him with relatives and friends. Farmer Joe was so kind!

Then, one morning last week, the good times ended. Farmer Joe grabbed Bob, dragged him to a nearby tree stump, and stretched his neck over it. Bob, being a bit naive, couldn't help thinking, *Hmm, I wonder why my good friend, Farmer Joe, would—*

Before Bob could finish his thought, Farmer Joe's axe had come down and . . . well, we'll spare you the details.

Poor Bob. You see, dear Bob was a turkey. At this time of year, he and his feathered friends have very little to be thankful for.

Christians, on the other hand, can rejoice in countless blessings!

WHAT'S IT MEAN?

For believers, thanksgiving shouldn't be limited to an annual holiday. As today's verse says, you should give thanks to God in all circumstances. No matter what you're doing, where you're at, or what time it is, you should always be quick to thank God for all his grace.

Giving thanks helps position your heart correctly. It keeps your focus on God, not yourself. By thanking God for the good things he gives you, you're acknowledging his kindness and your total dependence on him. The Lord loves grateful hearts that look to him to provide.

Most of all, thank God for Jesus. Without the Savior, you'd be lost in your sins, condemned to a terrible destiny, kind of like poor Bob. Without any intervention, turkeys are headed for a very unpleasant death. The same is true for sinful humanity! But Jesus intervened by dying on the cross in our place.

Before you gobble up turkey this year, thank the perfect Lamb of God for his great sacrifice!

NOW WHAT?

Start (or continue) a tradition this year by having each person at your Thanksgiving dinner table express gratefulness to God for at least one specific blessing before the meal.

DID YOU KNOW?

President Abraham Lincoln declared Thanksgiving an official US holiday in 1863.

This is his commandment: We must believe in the name of his Son, Jesus Christ, and love one another, just as he commanded us.
1 JOHN 3:23

Life is full of simple pleasures. In the midst of a busy, confusing world, it's nice when you can enjoy the following:

- chocolate chip cookies with milk
- birds singing at daybreak
- a birthday card in the mail
- puppies
- a good book
- popcorn and a movie
- walks on the beach at sunset
- roaring fires on cold winter nights

For Christians, 1 John 3:23 is one of those simple pleasures. The apostle John, who wrote today's verse, had a knack for keeping things straightforward and uncomplicated in his letters.

When he wrote this verse, it's almost as if John wanted to say, "Dear friends, I know things can get crazy and seem so complex at times. But just remember how simple the Christian life can be."

For all the laws, prophecies, heroic tales, jaw-dropping miracles, difficult teachings, and deep theological truths, God's Word is often beautiful in its simplicity. At the end of the day, Christianity is all about believing in Jesus and loving others.

WHAT'S IT MEAN?

Life can be complicated. Living in a sinful world often brings problems, pain, suffering, uncertainties, and hard choices. So it's good to remember how simple our faith really is. If we trust in Jesus and show his love to others, we are fulfilling God's main desire for our lives. It's as simple as that.

Today's verse calls to mind Matthew 22:34-40, when an Old Testament law expert tested Jesus by asking, "Teacher, which is the most important commandment in the law of Moses?" (verse 36). Referring to Deuteronomy 6:5 and Leviticus 19:18, Jesus replied: "'You must love the LORD your God with all your heart, all your soul, and all your mind.' This is the first and greatest commandment. A second is equally important: 'Love your neighbor as yourself'" (verses 37-39). In other words, faith and love sum up what God expects from his children.

Have you put your faith in Jesus for salvation? Are you trusting him daily for the grace and strength you need to live a godly life? Do you show the love of Christ to others? Do you put their needs before your own?

Do these and you'll be fulfilling God's requirements. It's that simple!

NOW WHAT?

Show love today by sacrificing your needs or desires for the good of someone else.

DID YOU KNOW?

The apostle John is believed to have outlived the rest of Jesus' original twelve disciples.

NOVEMBER 23

*Since we have a great High Priest who rules over God's house,
let us go right into the presence of God with sincere hearts fully
trusting him.* HEBREWS 10:21-22

Want an autograph from your favorite pop star or rock band? Have fun trying! Gaining access to famous musicians is not easy.

Most famous singers and musicians keep their addresses or phone numbers confidential, and the biggest superstars sometimes travel with personal bodyguards.

When they arrive at the arena for concerts, rock stars typically park in a special lot that's off limits to the general public, walk through a restricted doorway, and head to a special dressing room, which is restricted to the band, their entourage, and a select few concert officials. Lots of restrictions!

Once the concert starts, don't try approaching anyone in the band. If you jump onto the stage, you'll immediately be greeted by a bunch of extremely unhappy security officials who are much bigger than you and love to tackle people.

After the concert, it's no easier. Occasionally, a few fans can win backstage passes to meet the band. But usually, music stars head back to the dressing room, change clothes, and zip away into the night.

Aren't you glad God is not like that? As today's verse says, Christians can "go right into the presence of God" himself! How do believers gain this incredible, privileged access into the throne room of the Lord God Almighty?

It's only through the name of Jesus!

WHAT'S IT MEAN?

Several times in John chapters 14–16, Jesus told his disciples (and us) to approach God "in my name." To do something in someone else's name means to do it with their authority. Someone who receives special credentials can enter a concert's backstage area by the band's authority. Likewise, Christians can "boldly" (Hebrews 4:16) approach God in prayer by the authority of Christ.

We've done nothing to earn access to God. It's all thanks to Jesus. His sacrificial death satisfied God's wrath toward our sins. Now Jesus is our "High Priest" (Hebrews 4:14) and "Advocate" (1 John 2:1) before the Father. He gives us credentials, so to speak, to enter God's special presence by giving us his righteousness (2 Corinthians 5:21).

As you pray, remember that you can approach the eternal Creator anytime in Jesus' name.

Access granted!

NOW WHAT?

When you pray, you should "never give up" (Luke 18:1), but come to God "on all occasions with all kinds of prayers and requests" (Ephesians 6:18, NIV).

DID YOU KNOW?

Praying "in Jesus' name" isn't a magic formula to get what we want. It's simply a reminder that our prayers are possible only on Jesus' authority. It also reminds us to pray for Jesus' will in our lives, and not for selfish gain.

The grace of God has been revealed, bringing salvation to all people.
TITUS 2:11

The Bible is a big book . . . a *really* big book.

From Genesis to Revelation, God's Word contains sixty-six books written by about forty authors over a span of 1,300 to 1,500 years. The Bible contains about 800,000 words. It also includes 1,189 chapters, meaning that if you read one chapter a day, it will take you three-plus years to finish it.

The Bible features a variety of writing styles: historical narratives, laws, proverbs, poems, prophecies, prayers, and songs. What's more, much of the Bible is arranged categorically, not chronologically. For instance, Ezra is the fifteenth book, but the historical events it describes happened well after those of many books that follow it in Scripture's table of contents, such as Ecclesiastes (twenty-first book), Isaiah (twenty-third), and Jonah (thirty-second).

Are you confused by how the Bible all fits together and what its main message is? Perhaps you need a summary of the whole thing. Look no further than Titus 2:11-14:

> *The grace of God has been revealed, bringing salvation to all people. And we are instructed to turn from godless living and sinful pleasures. We should live in this evil world with wisdom, righteousness, and devotion to God, while we look forward with hope to that wonderful day when the glory of our great God and Savior, Jesus Christ, will be revealed. He gave his life to free us from every kind of sin, to cleanse us, and to make us his very own people, totally committed to doing good deeds.*

WHAT'S IT MEAN?

Here, in four verses, the apostle Paul provides a wonderful summary of the entire Bible and the Christian life! Let's look at the key points of this great passage:

- Born into an "evil world," all humans are guilty of "godless living and sinful pleasures."

- But God revealed his grace, "bringing salvation" through Jesus, who "gave his life to free us" from sin.
- Now, through repentance and faith in Jesus, we can become God's "very own people."
- As Christians, "we should live . . . with wisdom, righteousness and devotion to God" as we "look forward" to when Jesus "will be revealed."

That's it! That's the entire message of Scripture, boiled down to its essence. Let the truth of Titus 2:11-14 sink into your soul, encouraging you and challenging you to live for God.

What a message! What a Savior!

NOW WHAT?

Make it a priority to read the entire Bible. There are many online plans that can help.

DID YOU KNOW?

The longest book of the Bible is Psalms. The shortest is 3 John.

You must remain faithful to what you have been taught from the
beginning. If you do, you will remain in fellowship with the Son
and with the Father. I JOHN 2:24

If you started this devotional book on January 1, you've already read a lot about Jesus Christ.

You've learned about his pre-incarnate state and his fulfillment of many Old Testament prophecies. You've discovered truths about his nature, birth, teachings, miracles, death, resurrection, ascension, and current activities in heaven. You've learned about how salvation is possible through him and how we are to live in Christ-honoring ways.

And now there is only one more book of the Bible left to explore—Scripture's grand finale, the book of Revelation, which we'll begin to discuss in tomorrow's devotion.

But first, the apostle John has an important reminder for you from the first of his three epistles, 1 John 2:22-25:

Who is a liar? Anyone who says that Jesus is not the Christ. Anyone
who denies the Father and the Son is an antichrist. Anyone who
denies the Son doesn't have the Father, either. But anyone who
acknowledges the Son has the Father also. So you must remain
faithful to what you have been taught from the beginning. If you
do, you will remain in fellowship with the Son and with the Father.
And in this fellowship we enjoy the eternal life he promised us.

WHAT'S IT MEAN?

The world is a big place. As you get older, you'll meet lots of people and come across many different ideas. There is seemingly no end to the beliefs and philosophies about life out there. False religions and deceptions about Jesus abound.

How do you tell the difference between spiritual truths and lies? Today's verse has the answer: "Remain faithful to what you have been taught" about Jesus.

This devotional was written to point you to the truth of Jesus. But God's Word is your ultimate source of knowledge about the Savior. Scripture doesn't need to be updated or modernized. As Hebrews 13:8-9 says, "Jesus Christ is the same yesterday, today, and forever. So do not be attracted by strange, new ideas." In life, test everything you hear about Jesus and salvation against God's timeless, inerrant Word.

If you believe the true gospel message, God's Word promises that you will "remain in fellowship with the Son and with the Father" and "enjoy the eternal life he promised us."

NOW WHAT?

Read the book of 1 John.

DID YOU KNOW?

Unlike a computer program that needs constant improvements, there is no Jesus 2.0. That's because he is God—perfect and unchanging.

This is a revelation from Jesus Christ, which God gave him to show his servants the events that must soon take place.

REVELATION 1:1

Dragons, demons, angels, strange creatures, false prophets, and the devil!

Visions, prophecies, famine, disease, thunder, lightning, mountains burning with fire, worldwide war, epic bloodshed, and destructive events!

A rider on a white horse, a lake of fire, a celestial city . . . oh yeah, and some supernatural locusts with really bad tempers!

Is a new Lord of the Rings movie coming out? No, it's the last book of the Bible! As we near the end of this devotional, we fittingly conclude by studying the end times and the fascinating, shocking, troubling—and yes, somewhat confusing—book of Revelation. Task number one: to learn how to understand Scripture's remarkable, perplexing climax.

Buckle up. It's going to be a wild, wonderful ride!

WHAT'S IT MEAN?

The apostle John wrote Revelation around AD 95 after the Romans exiled him to the island of Patmos for his faith. One Sunday as John was worshiping, he received an astonishing vision of the risen Lord Jesus Christ.

First, Jesus gave John various messages for seven different churches in the Roman province of Asia (chapters 2–3). The rest of Revelation is a combination of prophetic and apocalyptic visions that John received. Prophecy, of course, is a prediction of the future. The Greek word we get *apocalyptic* from means "revelation" or "unveiling." In other words, Revelation, uh, *reveals* future events that will take place as God ends this world and begins his eternal heavenly kingdom. Revelation also unveils the unseen spiritual forces at work as God's plan of salvation comes to a dramatic finale.

John's visions are both amazing and puzzling. Many of them include astounding descriptions of events and creatures that are hard to understand. What's literal and what's symbolic in Revelation? Which of Revelation's prophecies have already happened, and which are yet to come? Bible scholars have been debating these questions for thousands of years. God intended there to be some mystery here.

Despite all the question marks, it's important to remember that Revelation is part of God's holy, inspired Word. All of it is true. While many things about the future remain foggy, this much is clear: in the cosmic battle between light and darkness, Jesus wins! One day, God's Son will return to destroy all evil and bring his true followers into his perfect dwelling place to live with him forever.

Christians are victorious through Christ!

NOW WHAT?

Make a plan to read the entire book of Revelation by the end of the year.

DID YOU KNOW?

God promises to bless those who read the Bible's final book (Revelation 1:3)!

NOVEMBER 27

The world has now become the Kingdom of our Lord and of his
Christ, and he will reign forever and ever. REVELATION 11:15

Spoiler alert!

Reading any further will give away important details about the end of the world!

Still reading, huh? Well, we can't blame you for being curious. After all, we're talking about the conclusion of life on earth!

God's Word, especially the book of Revelation, is filled with spoilers about the future. Like a movie trailer, Scripture gives us glimpses—but not the whole picture—of what will happen at the end of time. Here are some amazing facts the Bible reveals to us:

- One day—and no one knows when except God the Father (Mark 13:32)—Jesus will return to earth a final time to condemn the wicked to eternal punishment (2 Thessalonians 1:7-10) and reward the righteous with eternal life (1 Thessalonians 4:16-17).
- Jesus will defeat the devil and all evil (Revelation 19:19-21; 20:7-10).
- God will destroy the current universe—earth, planets, sun, moon, and stars—and replace them with a new heaven and earth (Revelation 21:1–22:5).
- Jesus will set up his eternal kingdom and reign forever (see today's verse).

WHAT'S IT MEAN?

Unlike with movies, it's good to know the ending God has planned. Understanding the future helps us know what to believe and how to live right now.

The Bible clearly says that Jesus will be victorious in the end and will rule over everything forever. Knowing this should change our lives! If you've never trusted in Jesus, it should urge you to submit your life to him. And if you *have* put your faith in Jesus, it should encourage you and strengthen your faith. You're on the winning team!

NOW WHAT?

Knowing that Jesus will reign supreme for all eternity should inspire you to live for him now. As Jesus says in Revelation 22:11-12, "Let the one who is righteous continue to live righteously; let the one who is holy continue to be holy. Look, I am coming soon, bringing my reward with me to repay all people according to their deeds." One day, we will be judged for whether or not we lived for Jesus. What are you waiting for? Start living for Jesus today!

DID YOU KNOW?

Many books of the Bible include passages about the future, but Revelation is Scripture's only book that is devoted entirely to prophecies about the end times.

"I am the Alpha and the Omega—the beginning and the end," says the Lord God. "I am the one who is, who always was, and who is still to come—the Almighty One." REVELATION 1:8

By now, you know your ABCs. But do you know your alphas, betas, and gammas?

Check out the alphabet below. Can you guess what language it represents?

Α Β Γ Δ Ε Ζ Η Θ Ι Κ Λ Μ Ν Ξ Ο Π Ρ Σ Τ Υ Φ Χ Ψ Ω

It's a twenty-four-letter alphabet that shares fourteen common letter symbols with the English alphabet. But even the related symbols have different names. In the alphabet above, *E* is called epsilon, *Z* is zeta, *H* is eta, *I* is iota, and so forth.

Have you guessed the language yet? It's Greek! Understanding more about this ancient alphabet will help you comprehend the powerful truths of today's verse.

WHAT'S IT MEAN?

The New Testament's original manuscripts, including the book of Revelation, were written mostly in Greek. After Alexander the Great conquered much of the ancient world in the mid-fourth century BC, Greek became a common language throughout his empire and stayed that way for centuries. So when Jesus told the apostle John, "I am the Alpha and the Omega—the beginning and the end," the original readers of Revelation would have quickly understood the meaning of this unique figure of speech.

Now look at the Greek alphabet again. Alpha is the first letter, represented by the symbol "A." Omega is the last, represented by the symbol "Ω." Alpha is the beginning of the Greek alphabet, and omega is the end.

At the start of John's magnificent futuristic vision, the eternal Son of God wanted to make it very clear: he is the beginning and the end of all things.

As "the Almighty One," he rules supreme over the present ("the one who is"), the past ("who always was"), and the future ("who is still to come"). Without beginning or end, Christ is the origin and the ultimate fulfillment of all creation. Everything was created by him and for him.

The Savior's perfect, timeless, and exalted character is what assured John—and now us—that every word in Revelation will be fulfilled. Praise Jesus that he is the first and the last, the beginning and the end, the Alpha and the Omega!

(Now, time to polish up on your deltas, sigmas, and upsilons.)

NOW WHAT?

Read the Bible's beginning (Genesis 1–3) and end (Revelation 19–22) to see the starting and finishing points of human history.

DID YOU KNOW?

All modern European alphabets, including English, derive in some way from the Greek alphabet.

His head and his hair were white like wool, as white as snow. And his eyes were like flames of fire. REVELATION 1:14

The apostle John knew Jesus as well as anyone on earth.

As one of Jesus' twelve disciples, John spent several years of his life with the Savior. John was part of Jesus' inner circle, along with James and Peter. Also, John often described himself as "the disciple Jesus loved."

But no amount of previous familiarity could have prepared John for his awesome, frightening encounter with the risen Lord Jesus Christ on the island of Patmos, as John detailed in Revelation 1:13-16:

> *Standing in the middle of the lampstands was someone like the Son of Man. He was wearing a long robe with a gold sash across his chest. His head and his hair were white like wool, as white as snow. And his eyes were like flames of fire. His feet were like polished bronze refined in a furnace, and his voice thundered like mighty ocean waves. He held seven stars in his right hand, and a sharp two-edged sword came from his mouth. And his face was like the sun in all its brilliance.*

WHAT'S IT MEAN?

Have you ever tried staring directly into the sun? (If you haven't, then don't try it!) The sheer intensity of its radiance makes it almost impossible. This is how John described the resurrected Savior.

Jesus' unrestrained glory was too much to behold. "When I saw him," John wrote in Revelation 1:17, "I fell at his feet as if I were dead."

Jesus' overwhelming majesty left John groping for adequate descriptions. So he did the best he could, referencing common items of his day such as wool, snow, fire, bronze, and the sun. But even John's vivid analogies can't fully do justice to Jesus' current appearance.

On earth, Jesus temporarily concealed his pre-incarnate glory with human flesh (Philippians 2:6-7). Now, though, he is no longer a little baby in Bethlehem, a "man of sorrows" (Isaiah 53:3), or a bloodied crucifixion victim. Having conquered death and sin, Jesus sits at God's right hand in heaven, possessing all glory and power.

So ditch any stereotypical images of Jesus as a meek, soft-skinned man with a neatly trimmed beard and long, well-groomed hair. He is the almighty resurrected Savior, exalted and reigning over the universe in complete authority. Worship him in awe and wonder!

NOW WHAT?

Now that you know more about Jesus' true glory, reread the story of his transfiguration (Matthew 17:1-13) with fresh eyes.

DID YOU KNOW?

John's description of Jesus' hair ("white like wool") recalls Daniel's description of God the Father in Daniel 7:9. Check it out!

*I know all the things you do, that you are neither hot nor cold.
I wish that you were one or the other! But since you are like
lukewarm water, neither hot nor cold, I will spit you out of
my mouth!* REVELATION 3:15-16

Lukewarm milk is nasty.

So are lukewarm soda, orange juice, and coffee. Nobody wants lukewarm soup, and lukewarm ice cream is, well, pretty much like milky, lukewarm soup. Gross! Everybody loves a good burger and fries. But if they're lukewarm? No thanks. Room-temperature meatloaf, mashed potatoes, and gravy? Gross, gross, and more gross. And does anyone want a lukewarm helping of steamed spinach?

Gag.

You get the point. Most food is best either hot or cold. But when it turns lukewarm, it quickly loses its appeal and can even upset your digestive system.

In a shockingly blunt rebuke, this is how Jesus described the ancient church of Laodicea in the book of Revelation.

WHAT'S IT MEAN?

In Revelation chapters 2 and 3, Jesus gave spiritual evaluations of seven Christian churches located in the ancient Roman province of Asia (modern-day Turkey). Many churches received both praise and corrections. But for Laodicea, Jesus offered only a severe scolding and an ominous warning. As today's Scripture passage says, Jesus called them "lukewarm" and threatened to literally vomit them up like a distasteful meal that didn't agree with his stomach. Yikes.

The Laodiceans were materially rich (Revelation 3:17) but spiritually bankrupt. They were lazy and indifferent in their faith, becoming bland and unpleasant like food accidentally left on the kitchen counter overnight. Jesus won't tolerate that kind of attitude.

It's one thing to go through a brief period of spiritual struggle and weariness. Jesus, after all, promises to care for needy souls (Matthew 11:28). But living in a state of constant spiritual lifelessness is something else entirely. That's not what Scripture calls us to.

Philippians 3:14 encourages us to "press on" in our spiritual lives, and 2 Timothy 4:8 tells us to "eagerly look forward" to Jesus' return through godly living. No lukewarm attitude there—only purposeful action.

What's the status of your faith? Have you completely given your allegiance to Jesus, or are you halfheartedly straddling Christianity and worldliness like the Laodiceans?

Don't be a lukewarm Christian. Press on in your faith and live for Christ!

NOW WHAT?

Are you stuck in a spiritual rut? Serving others is a great way to get back on track.

DID YOU KNOW?

Despite the Laodiceans' spiritual idleness, Jesus still loved them and gave them a chance to repent. In Revelation 3:19, he said, "I correct and discipline everyone I love. So be diligent and turn from your indifference."

DECEMBER 1

Worthy is the Lamb, who was slain, to receive power and wealth and wisdom and strength and honor and glory and praise!
REVELATION 5:12, NIV

John was heartbroken.

Starting in Revelation 4, the apostle received a once-in-a-lifetime peek into heaven's inner chambers. In this vision, John witnessed God's secret throne room, which was filled with twenty-four heavenly "elders," four supernatural creatures, and millions of angels—all gathered to worship the Lord God Almighty.

In his right hand, God held a tightly sealed scroll, symbolizing his final plan for humanity. But none of heaven's inhabitants could open it. So John began weeping. Why?

Remember: at the time, John was exiled on Patmos for his faith. All over the Roman Empire, other Christians were also suffering persecution under cruel Emperor Domitian. John was probably thinking, "Lord, staying faithful to you is difficult in all these hardships. I want to know that everything will turn out fine and that my faith is worth it."

Then, in his vision, one of heaven's elders told John, "Do not weep! See, the Lion of the tribe of Judah, the Root of David, has triumphed. He is able to open the scroll." But when John turned around, he didn't see a lion. Instead, he saw "a Lamb, looking as if it had been slain" (Revelation 5:5-6, NIV).

Huh? What gives?

WHAT'S IT MEAN?

The Lion and the Lamb in John's vision were the same person: Jesus!

Calling Jesus "the Lion of the tribe of Judah" is a reference to a prophecy about the Messiah in Genesis 49:9 and Jesus' earthly ancestry through Israel's tribe of Judah. Calling Jesus a lamb is a reference to Isaiah 53:7 and John 1:29, where Jesus is described as a "lamb" or "the Lamb of God." As the eternal Son of God, Jesus possesses all power and authority (symbolized by a lion's strength), but he humbly offered himself for our sins (like a lamb of the Old Testament sacrificial system).

In John's vision, as soon as Jesus took the scroll from God's hand, a huge party erupted in heaven. Millions and millions of angels began shouting and worshiping Jesus, saying, "Worthy is the Lamb, who was slain!" (today's verse).

John's fears were relieved! Through Jesus, God's great plan for humanity and future events will be fully accomplished. Jesus' sinless life, sacrificial death, and glorious resurrection have made our salvation possible.

Great is the Lion of Judah! Worthy is the Lamb, who was slain!

NOW WHAT?

Read Revelation 4–5 for a full picture of John's "scroll" vision and Jesus' worthiness to break its seal.

DID YOU KNOW?

The "four living beings" in Revelation 4:6-8 resemble the angelic creatures described in Isaiah 6 and Ezekiel 1 and 10.

Jesus has been taken from you into heaven, but someday he will return from heaven in the same way you saw him go! ACTS 1:11

People in the apostle Peter's day were getting antsy.

When Peter wrote the epistle known as 2 Peter, it was probably the AD mid-60s. Jesus had ascended into heaven only about thirty years earlier. And yet people were starting to lose faith that he would ever return. Check out what Peter wrote in 2 Peter 3:3-4:

> *I want to remind you that in the last days scoffers will come, mocking the truth and following their own desires. They will say, 'What happened to the promise that Jesus is coming again? From before the times of our ancestors, everything has remained the same since the world was first created.'*

Thirty years? That's nothing! It's now been about two thousand years and counting, and Jesus still hasn't returned.

Think about everything that's happened since then. The Roman Empire rose and fell. The Magna Carta was signed. The Middle Ages came and went. So did the Crusades, the Ottoman Empire, the discovery of the New World, the American Revolution, the discovery of electricity, and Europe's unforgivable fashion faux pas of men wearing wigs and tights. (Seriously, guys?)

A lot has changed in the last two thousand years. Nowadays, we have computers, smartphones, fast-food restaurants on every street corner, and microwavable gluten-free corn dogs. Yet Jesus still hasn't returned. Will he ever?

The answer is a resounding *yes!*

WHAT'S IT MEAN?

The New Testament clearly states many times, especially in Revelation, that Jesus will return. Today's verse is another great example. It's the angels' promise to Jesus' disciples after he ascended into heaven. Jesus himself promised to return in passages such as Matthew 24:30; Mark 13:34; Luke 9:26; and Revelation 22:7.

It's a done deal.

This guarantee provides great hope for all Christians. Jesus is coming back to destroy evil, judge all humanity, and welcome true believers into his eternal heavenly kingdom. As he said in John 14:3, "When everything is ready, I will come and get you, so that you will always be with me where I am."

No one knows when, and it might not be according to our timetable, but Jesus is most certainly returning to earth a final time. Is your heart ready? Repent of your sins and believe in the Savior!

NOW WHAT?

Until he returns, Jesus calls his followers to live righteously (Matthew 5:16), love others (John 15:12), and share the gospel with unbelievers (Matthew 28:19-20).

DID YOU KNOW?

Jesus' second coming will not be secretive. It will be loud and impossible to miss (1 Thessalonians 4:16)!

No one knows the day or hour when these things will happen, not even the angels in heaven or the Son himself. Only the Father knows. MATTHEW 24:36

"BEWARE! THE END OF THE WORLD IS HERE!"

Well, not really. But that's what plenty of people thought in 2011.

Early that year, a man named Harold Camping, the president of the Family Radio network, was spreading this message across the United States. Camping predicted that Jesus would return on May 21, 2011, and initiate Judgment Day. Unfortunately, many of his followers sold all their possessions in anticipation of this event.

Of course, May 21 came and went that year, Jesus didn't come, and the world kept spinning. Camping quickly changed his prediction to October 21, 2011. That turned out to be false too, just like a similar prediction he made in 1994. Camping died in December 2013. Today, we are still waiting for Jesus' return.

WHAT'S IT MEAN?

Like Camping, many people throughout history have tried—and failed—to predict Jesus' second coming. But Scripture is clear: no one knows when that day will come except God the Father (see today's verse; Acts 1:7; and 1 Thessalonians 5:1-2).

Waiting is difficult. And if you're a Christian, you naturally long for Christ's return because of the indescribably wonderful heavenly blessings to come. But God calls for us to patiently endure until the end (Matthew 24:13).

Scripture, though, does provide clues leading up to Jesus' return. Wars will increase worldwide, cataclysmic events such as earthquakes and famines will multiply, persecution of Christians will intensify, and godlessness will rise. Also, a satanic figure known as the antichrist will emerge to deceive many people (Matthew 24; 2 Thessalonians 2:1-12; 1 John 2:18; and many references in the book of Revelation, especially chapter 13.) The Bible doesn't give many more details than that.

But don't be discouraged. God's plan is perfect. Because he is eternal and we are not, his timing is different from ours. As 2 Peter 3:8 says, "A day is like a thousand years to the Lord, and a thousand years is like a day."

Jesus *will* return one day. God's Word promises it, so it's guaranteed. And when it happens, Jesus will bring about a glorious era of peace and perfect fellowship with him in a wonderful, eternal kingdom.

Now *that's* worth waiting for!

NOW WHAT?

Don't waste time trying to figure out when Jesus will return. Just faithfully trust in him and follow him in the meantime!

DID YOU KNOW?

By AD 50 or so—only about twenty years after Jesus' death and resurrection—some early Christians were worried that Jesus had already returned and they missed it (2 Thessalonians 2:1-4).

DECEMBER 4

You, too, must keep watch! For you don't know what day your Lord is coming. MATTHEW 24:42

The people of Noah's day were having a grand old time.

Life was one big, wicked party back then. People did whatever they wanted and completely disregarded God. "Everything they thought or imagined was consistently and totally evil," according to Genesis 6:5.

Unfortunately, the people never bothered to figure out why their neighbor was building a massive ark. They never noticed the storm clouds gathering overhead. And before they knew it, God's worldwide flood of judgment destroyed them.

Interestingly, Jesus used this tragic example of humanity's spiritual unpreparedness to describe his own second coming. In Matthew 24:37-39, he said:

> *When the Son of Man returns, it will be like it was in Noah's day. In those days before the flood, the people were enjoying banquets and parties and weddings right up to the time Noah entered his boat. People didn't realize what was going to happen until the flood came and swept them all away. That is the way it will be when the Son of Man comes.*

WHAT'S IT MEAN?

Jesus' message is clear: his final return to earth is imminent, and when it happens, there will be no time to quickly repent and trust in him. Humanity's time will be up. Our spiritual states at that moment—saved or unsaved, trusting in Jesus or rejecting him—will seal our eternal destinies.

No final chances. No do-overs. No going back.

Scripture frequently describes Jesus' second coming as being like a "burglar" or a "thief" (Matthew 24:43; 1 Thessalonians 5:2; 2 Peter 3:10; Revelation 16:15). Thieves do not announce their arrival beforehand. They come when least expected.

This analogy does not mean Jesus is trying to be sneaky or deceptive. It's simply a warning for us to be spiritually prepared for the Savior's return. As he said in Matthew 24:43-44, "Understand this: If a homeowner knew exactly when a burglar was coming, he would keep watch and not permit his house to be broken into. You also must be ready all the time, for the Son of Man will come when least expected."

Jesus could return at any time. Have you turned to him in repentance and faith as your Lord and Savior? Don't be caught unprepared!

NOW WHAT?

If you have never put your faith in Christ for the forgiveness of your sins, do it today! As 2 Corinthians 6:2 says, "Today is the day of salvation."

DID YOU KNOW?

The long wait (by human standards) for Jesus' return reveals God's love, because "our Lord's patience gives people time to be saved" (2 Peter 3:15).

DECEMBER 5

He will release the fierce wrath of God, the Almighty, like juice flowing from a winepress. REVELATION 19:15

Among his many names in Scripture, Jesus is called the Lamb, the Prince of Peace, the Good Shepherd, and the Savior. He blessed infants, healed the sick, fed thousands, and comforted the downcast. He is clearly tender, compassionate, and loving.

And then, like a slap in the face, we read the shocking words of Revelation 19:11-16. . . .

> *I saw heaven opened, and a white horse was standing there. Its rider was named Faithful and True, for he judges fairly and wages a righteous war. His eyes were like flames of fire, and on his head were many crowns. A name was written on him that no one understood except himself. He wore a robe dipped in blood, and his title was the Word of God. The armies of heaven, dressed in the finest of pure white linen, followed him on white horses. From his mouth came a sharp sword to strike down the nations. He will rule them with an iron rod. He will release the fierce wrath of God, the Almighty, like juice flowing from a winepress. On his robe at his thigh was written this title: King of all kings and Lord of all lords.*

Hold on. Is this fearsome, heavenly warrior in the apostle John's vision really Jesus?

Yes!

Jesus is both the Good Shepherd and the fearful Judge. He is the Prince of Peace and heaven's conquering King. He is the loving Savior who provides hope and the divine Warrior who destroys the wicked.

But how can he be all these things?

WHAT'S IT MEAN?

Because he is fully God, Jesus is perfectly unchanging. So the drastic differences between his first and second comings to earth are not because his character has changed in any way. Instead, the differences relate to his purposes.

Jesus' first visit, roughly two thousand years ago, was to fulfill God's plan of salvation for lost humanity through the cross. His second visit, which is yet to come, is to release God's wrath on evil (see today's verse) and begin his eternal kingdom.

For Christians, Jesus' second coming is a wonderful event to be greatly anticipated because it starts eternity with him. But for unbelievers, it's a fearful day because it brings the terrible "wrath of the Lamb" (Revelation 6:16).

The Lord Jesus Christ, beautifully and amazingly, is all these things!

NOW WHAT?

Would you rather meet Jesus as your Savior or your Judge? The choice is obvious. Put your faith in Jesus and be saved!

DID YOU KNOW?

In John's vision, Jesus' white horse signified the victory he has already achieved on the cross over sin and evil.

They will see the Son of Man coming on the clouds of heaven with power and great glory. MATTHEW 24:30

In Luke 2, Jesus entered the world tenderly as a helpless human infant crying in a manger—the unlikeliest of royal births for the King of kings and Lord of lords. In Mark 11, Jesus entered Jerusalem riding on a young donkey—the long-awaited Messiah ironically riding a lowly beast of burden, his only army being a crowd of palm branch–waving Passover pilgrims.

No more.

The meekness and humility that marked Jesus' first visit to earth will soon give way to the greatest display of power the world has ever seen!

WHAT'S IT MEAN?

Throughout the years, there has been significant debate over the nature, details, and timing of Jesus' return in relation to all the other events in the book of Revelation. But if we take everything Scripture says about the Second Coming at face value, a fascinating (if still somewhat mysterious) picture emerges that reveals the limitless power of God's Son:

- Astonishing celestial signs and cosmic upheaval will signal Jesus' return (Matthew 24:29).
- With a loud trumpet blast (1 Thessalonians 4:16), Jesus will appear with countless "mighty angels, in flaming fire" (2 Thessalonians 1:7-8).
- When Jesus' enemies see him, there will be "deep mourning" (Matthew 24:30), and even the mightiest warriors will hide in caves (Revelation 6:15).
- A satanically influenced world leader called "the beast" (also known as the antichrist) will gather the world's armies (Revelation 19:19) for one final, epic battle against Christ at a place called Armageddon (Revelation 16:16).
- With the armies of heaven riding behind him (Revelation 19:14), Jesus

will utterly destroy the antichrist and his armies with nothing more than "the breath of his mouth and . . . the splendor of his coming" (2 Thessalonians 2:8).

- After that, Jesus will throw the antichrist, another wicked world leader called "the false prophet" (Revelation 19:20), and eventually Satan into hell (Revelation 19:20 and 20:10).

No force in heaven or on earth can stand against Jesus! Yes, he is a gentle, loving Savior. But he is also the all-powerful Son of God who will terrify his enemies and effortlessly conquer those who do not worship him.

NOW WHAT?
Read 2 Peter 3:8-13 (focusing especially on verse 11) to see how we are to live in light of Jesus' powerful second coming.

DID YOU KNOW?
Some Bible scholars believe Scripture teaches that the appearances of Jesus detailed in 1 Thessalonians 4:13-17 (the Rapture) and Revelation 19:11-21 (the Battle of Armageddon) are two separate events. Other scholars believe that these events will happen at the same time. Either way, Jesus' return(s) will display his righteous, infinite power!

DECEMBER 7

He will come with his mighty angels, in flaming fire, bringing judgment on those who don't know God and on those who refuse to obey the Good News of our Lord Jesus. 2 THESSALONIANS 1:7-8

Death! Carnage! Fire! Destruction! Pandemonium!

Is this the marketing tagline for Hollywood's latest action blockbuster? Or perhaps what you can expect from the hottest new first-person-shooter video game?

Nope, it's just the Bible's description of the end of the world.

In the book of Revelation alone, we read about devastating seal judgments (chapter 6), trumpet judgments (chapters 8–9), and bowl judgments (chapter 16), where famines, plagues, wars, wild beasts, fire, earthquakes, poisoned water, bizarre meteorological phenomena, and supernatural creatures all bring divine judgment on the world. Revelation 19 discusses how Jesus himself will destroy an army of millions and leave their corpses strewn on the ground as food for vultures.

Gulp.

Scripture's teachings on the end times are both shocking and sobering. It's hard to wrap your mind around the utter annihilation that awaits the ungodly.

In reading this, maybe you're thinking, *Wow, that sounds pretty harsh. Is all that death and destruction necessary? How could a loving God and merciful Savior be capable of such things?*

They are legitimate questions. Is your heart ready for the answer?

WHAT'S IT MEAN?

Fully understanding and accepting the reasons—and even the need—for God's final judgment on earth requires an understanding of God himself.

God is holy—completely free of sin. He also created the universe, including humans, free of sin. But we chose to rebel against our Creator. We are all sinful by nature and in our actions.

God has been extraordinarily patient with his creation, waiting for many to repent (2 Peter 3:9). But because of his holy justice, God must punish sin. Sadly, terrible wickedness deserves terrible consequences. The coming judgment is completely justified, based on God's character and our sin.

But remember this: true Christians won't experience a single drop of God's righteous anger. He already poured the wrath that we deserve on his Son. Now, through faith in Jesus' atoning work on the cross, we can be saved from the wrath to come (1 Thessalonians 1:10).

Yes, terrible judgment against sin is coming, but true followers of Jesus have nothing to fear!

NOW WHAT?

Interested in learning more about the coming judgment? Read the chapters of Revelation mentioned earlier, plus the following passages: Isaiah 66:15; Malachi 4:1; Romans 2:8; Hebrews 10:27; 2 Peter 3:7; and Jude 1:14-15.

DID YOU KNOW?

In Luke 17:28-29, Jesus compared his second coming to the fate of Sodom and Gomorrah, the infamously immoral cities of Abraham's day that were consumed by heavenly fire.

God's holy people must endure persecution patiently, obeying his commands and maintaining their faith in Jesus.

REVELATION 14:12

Let's give it up for cars! They're so much more convenient than chariots.

Let's hear it for women voting and for the civil rights movement! They were long overdue.

And let's give a big cheer for modern medicine, because well, we've heard about medieval "leeching" practices, and that's just plain crazy.

Yes, when it comes to technology, social justice, and medical progress, life in the twenty-first century is far better than long ago. But not everything is getting progressively better.

We are in what the Bible calls "the last days." This is the period of history that began after Jesus' resurrection and continues until his return (Acts 2:17; 2 Timothy 3:1; and 1 Peter 1:20). Scripture says the last days will be filled with increasing wickedness and hatred toward Christians:

- "You will be hated all over the world because you are my followers" (Matthew 24:9).
- "Sin will be rampant everywhere, and the love of many will grow cold" (Matthew 24:12).
- "They will betray their friends, be reckless, be puffed up with pride, and love pleasure rather than God" (2 Timothy 3:4).

Even as God judges the earth, Revelation 9:20 says people "still refused to repent of their evil deeds and turn to God." And Revelation 11 tells about God's "two witnesses" who will be killed and left in the streets of Jerusalem while people "gloat over them and give presents to each other to celebrate the death of the two prophets" (verse 10).

WHAT'S IT MEAN?

Spiritually speaking, things are only going to get worse on earth, not better, until Jesus returns. Evil and hardships will increase, while faithfulness to

Christ will decline (Matthew 24:10). Sadly, this is the natural progression of sin and the unsaved human heart.

Christians are called to stand strong against this rebellious tide. As today's verse says, God wants us to endure patiently, obey his commands, and maintain our faith in Christ. God is fully in control, and he will not allow evil to reign forever (Matthew 24:22).

When Jesus returns, he will destroy all evil and usher in a new, eternal era of peace and perfection. Who gets to enjoy this? Jesus answered that in Matthew 24:13: "The one who endures to the end will be saved."

NOW WHAT?

Pray for the persecuted Christian church around the world.

DID YOU KNOW?

In 2013, there were 2,123 documented Christian martyrdoms around the world, according to Open Doors, an organization that supports persecuted Christians worldwide.

DECEMBER 9

All who are victorious will inherit all these blessings, and I will be their God, and they will be my children.

REVELATION 21:7

Knowing that evil and persecution will only worsen with time (see yesterday's devotion) is troubling. It's easy to grow fainthearted while trying to live righteously in an increasingly wicked world.

But Jesus loves us deeply and "understands our weaknesses" (Hebrews 4:15). That's why eight different times in Revelation, including today's verse, he promises wonderful blessings to his "victorious" followers—those who remain faithful to him for life.

Here are Jesus' promises:

1. To give them "fruit from the tree of life in the paradise of God" (Revelation 2:7).
2. That they "will not be harmed by the second death" (Revelation 2:11).
3. To give them "some of the manna that has been hidden away in heaven" and "a white stone . . . engraved [with] a new name that no one understands except the one who receives it" (Revelation 2:17).
4. To give them "authority over all the nations" (Revelation 2:26).
5. That they "will be clothed in white. I will never erase their names from the Book of Life, but I will announce before my Father and his angels that they are mine" (Revelation 3:5).
6. That they "will become pillars in the Temple of my God, and they will never have to leave it. And I will write on them the name of my God, and they will be citizens in the city of my God—the new Jerusalem that comes down from heaven from my God. And I will also write on them my new name" (Revelation 3:12).
7. That they "will sit with me on my throne, just as I was victorious and sat with my Father on his throne" (Revelation 3:21).

WHAT'S IT MEAN?

Some of these blessings are easier to understand than others. Here's a helpful answer key to understand Jesus' promises:

1. Eternal life.
2. Freedom from eternal punishment in hell.
3. Manna signifies God's gracious provision; a white stone in ancient times was often awarded to victorious athletes.
4. Believers will rule with Christ over the new creation.
5. Jesus' purity and eternal life.
6. A promise of eternal, irrevocable citizenship in God's holy dwelling place.
7. Eternal privileges and blessings in Jesus' presence.

Stay faithful to Jesus and receive the eternal rewards of the victorious!

NOW WHAT?

Pray and ask God to help you remain faithful to him until the end.

DID YOU KNOW?

The reference to the "tree of life in the paradise of God" in Revelation 2:7 recalls the same tree in the Garden of Eden (Genesis 3:22). Eventually, God will restore his creation to a perfect, sinless paradise.

*I am convinced that neither death nor life, neither angels nor
demons, neither the present nor the future, nor any powers, neither
height nor depth, nor anything else in all creation, will be able to
separate us from the love of God that is in Christ Jesus our Lord.*
ROMANS 8:38-39, NIV

Death is everywhere.

It sounds grim, but it's true. In 2012, an estimated 56 million people died
worldwide, according to the World Health Organization. That's an average
of 153,425 people per day.

Death isn't a very pleasant subject. Like it or not, though, it's an inevitable part of the human experience. As Hebrews 9:27 says, "Each person is
destined to die once and after that comes judgment." Death is a result of sin's
terrible curse after the Fall in Genesis 3.

The fear of death is as old as the earth itself. Hebrews 2:15 talks about
people "who have lived their lives as slaves to the fear of dying."

Why do people fear death? Because it seems like a great unknown—a mysterious, uncontrollable event that brings finality to this earthly existence.
Miracles aside, no one has ever returned from death to share its secrets with
the living (Luke 16:26).

But in reality, death is *not* a huge mystery. The Bible, especially the book of
Revelation, has much to say about death and the afterlife. Based on Scripture,
Christians don't have to fear death at all!

WHAT'S IT MEAN?

Jesus took the fear out of death with his victory on the cross. When Jesus
died and rose again, he broke death's power and made eternal life possible.
As the apostle Paul says in 1 Corinthians 15:54-57:

> *Death is swallowed up in victory. O death, where is your victory?
> O death, where is your sting? For sin is the sting that results in*

death, and the law gives sin its power. But thank God! He gives us
victory over sin and death through our Lord Jesus Christ.

Perhaps today's verse says it best: not even death can separate us from God's love. For Christians, death is not the end. It's only the beginning of an eternal, heavenly existence in our Savior's presence that is too marvelous for words.

Yes, death is an unfortunate consequence of sin, but it's not something to be feared when you know what happens next!

NOW WHAT?

Make sure to read tomorrow's devotion for more answers on what happens after a Christian dies.

DID YOU KNOW?

Paul looked forward to the day when God would call him to come home. In Philippians 1:23, he wrote, "I long to go and be with Christ, which would be far better for me."

DECEMBER 11

We are fully confident, and we would rather be away from these earthly bodies, for then we will be at home with the Lord.

2 CORINTHIANS 5:8

So what exactly happens when you die?

That's a question that has both fascinated and troubled humans ever since life began. To find the answer, you must go to the only true authority on life, death, and the afterlife: God's Word.

One day, the Bible says, Jesus will return to earth once more to destroy evil and bring all his true followers into eternity. But what happens between now and then during what's called the "intermediate state"? What is the fate of Christians, past and present, who die before Jesus' return?

While there is plenty of mystery surrounding this subject, Scripture does provide some hints. The apostle Paul's teaching in today's verse is a good place to start.

WHAT'S IT MEAN?

When a Christian dies, that person's physical body is buried and decays on earth, but his or her eternal soul immediately goes into the presence of the Lord (see today's verse).

Jesus himself referred to this during his crucifixion in Luke 23:43. As he hung on the cross, God's Son told the repentant thief crucified next to him, "I assure you, *today* you will be with me in paradise" (emphasis added). There was no delay for the thief. When he died later that day, he immediately entered into "paradise" because of his faith. This is wonderful news for all Christians! Death is tragic and sad, but the immediacy of entering into the Lord's presence afterward provides us with great hope and joy.

But what is this "paradise"? Is it heaven? What will we do there? The Bible remains mostly silent on these questions. But it appears to be a place of wonderful enjoyment and comfort (Luke 16:25). A Christian's soul will experience perfect fellowship with God in paradise until Jesus returns to earth a final time.

At that moment, Jesus will bring with him the souls of those already departed and reunite them to their resurrected bodies (1 Corinthians 15:42-44). All living believers will join them "in the clouds," and then Jesus will take all his followers—dead and alive—back to paradise (1 Thessalonians 4:13-17). Then Jesus will miraculously clothe us with new, immortal resurrection bodies "that will never die" (1 Corinthians 15:53) as we prepare for the new heaven and new earth (Revelation 21:1).

For Christians, to be absent from the body is to be immediately present with the Lord!

NOW WHAT?

To gain further clarity on these remarkable future blessings, read Luke 16:19-31; 1 Corinthians 15:35-57; and 1 Thessalonians 4:13-17.

DID YOU KNOW?

The human soul is the immaterial, invisible essence of a person's being.

DECEMBER 12

The sky was rolled up like a scroll, and all of the mountains and islands were moved from their places.   REVELATION 6:14

Hollywood is infatuated with the end of the world.

Ever since the explosion of 1950s sci-fi movies, the American film industry has generated an endless stream of apocalyptic disaster flicks. There are movies about alien apocalypses, zombie apocalypses, viral apocalypses, weather-related apocalypses, asteroid apocalypses, nuclear apocalypses, and hippopotamus apocalypses.

Okay, that last one is a joke. But you get the point. End-of-the-world movies are everywhere!

While Hollywood's apocalyptic tales are all fictional, this much is true: the end of the world *is* coming. Here's how the apostle John described it in his vision in Revelation 6:12-14:

> *I watched as the Lamb broke the sixth seal, and there was a great earthquake. The sun became as dark as black cloth, and the moon became as red as blood. Then the stars of the sky fell to the earth like green figs falling from a tree shaken by a strong wind. The sky was rolled up like a scroll, and all of the mountains and islands were moved from their places.*

Yes, the world will end one day! But don't worry. If you're a true follower of Jesus, you have nothing to fear.

WHAT'S IT MEAN?

God's current universe is incredible, but it's only temporary. Something even better is on the way.

Romans 8:21-22 says creation is "groaning" under the weight of sin's curse and anticipating the day when it will enjoy "freedom from death and decay." One day, God will remove the old, sin-infected creation and make all things new.

Before then, though, the world is in for—you guessed it—an apocalypse. Cosmic cataclysms will shake the entire universe to its core in preparation for "a new heaven and a new earth" (Revelation 21:1).

These radical transformations will pave the way for Jesus' return. As Matthew 24:30 says, the heavens and earth will be shaken and "*then at last, the sign that the Son of Man is coming will appear in the heavens*" (emphasis added).

Still a little unsettled? Rest in the assurance of Romans 8:39: "No power in the sky above or in the earth below—indeed, nothing in all creation will ever be able to separate us from the love of God that is revealed in Christ Jesus our Lord."

NOW WHAT?

Want to know more about God's divinely appointed apocalypse? Read Isaiah 13:9-13 and 34:2-4; Haggai 2:6; Matthew 24:29-30; Hebrews 12:26-27; 2 Peter 3:7-12; and Revelation 20:11.

DID YOU KNOW?

The English word *apocalypse* comes from the ancient Greek term *apokálypsis*, meaning "revelation" or "unveiling." However, people today usually use *apocalypse* to refer to world-ending doom.

DECEMBER 13

*The Son of Man will come with his angels in the glory of his
Father and will judge all people according to their deeds.*

MATTHEW 16:27

Have you ever watched a courtroom trial firsthand? It's a sobering, eye-opening experience.

Whether the case is for a speeding ticket or a charge of first-degree murder, defendants stand before a judge, hear the charge(s) against them, have a chance to plead their cases, and then await the verdict.

You do not want to stand guilty before a judge.

After Jesus returns to earth once more, he will convene the final courtroom trial of human history. It's called the "Great White Throne Judgment." The apostle John described it in Revelation 20:11-15:

> *I saw a great white throne and the one sitting on it. The earth and sky fled from his presence, but they found no place to hide. I saw the dead, both great and small, standing before God's throne. And the books were opened, including the Book of Life. And the dead were judged according to what they had done, as recorded in the books. . . . And all were judged according to their deeds. . . . And anyone whose name was not found recorded in the Book of Life was thrown into the lake of fire.*

WHAT'S IT MEAN?

The "one sitting" on the great white throne is God, the "Ancient of Days" (Daniel 7:9, NIV). But the Father will grant the Son the right to judge all people (see today's verse; John 5:22; and Acts 17:31).

On that day, confronted by the Savior's glorious majesty, all humanity will bow down and "declare that Jesus Christ is Lord" (Philippians 2:11). Whether you kneel before him in worship as your Savior or in fear as your Judge will be based on your acceptance or rejection of Jesus in this life.

Heaven's books will reveal all your earthly deeds (Revelation 20:12), and the "Book of Life" (Revelation 20:15) will show whether you trusted in Christ on earth for the forgiveness of your sins.

Based on this, Jesus "will separate the people as a shepherd separates the sheep from the goats" (Matthew 25:32)—the righteous ("sheep") to eternal life in heaven and the wicked ("goats") to eternal punishment in hell (Matthew 25:46).

Don't stand guilty of sin before heaven's Judge. Trust in Jesus to be pardoned!

NOW WHAT?

Ask your parents to take you to a local courtroom that's open to the public to experience a real-life trial.

DID YOU KNOW?

Christians don't need to fear the Great White Throne Judgment. Having already clothed us in his righteousness (Isaiah 61:10), Jesus will be our Advocate (1 John 2:1), not our Judge.

DECEMBER 14

Our dying bodies must be transformed into bodies that will never die; our mortal bodies must be transformed into immortal bodies.

1 CORINTHIANS 15:53

What do you look like?

Short? Tall? Long hair? Short hair? Brown hair? Black hair? Red hair? Blond hair? Freckles? Dimples? Green eyes? Blue eyes? Brown eyes? (Sounds kind of like a Dr. Seuss book!)

While we are all "fearfully and wonderfully made" (Psalm 139:14, NIV), no human body is perfect. Our bodies don't always look the way we want. They get hurt easily. They don't always perform like we want them to. Sometimes, they do some really weird stuff. Eventually, they grow old, break down, and die. All this is a consequence of Adam and Eve's original sin (Genesis 2:17).

Enough bad body news. Here's something good: one day, when Jesus returns, he will give every Christian a new resurrection body!

What's a resurrection body, you ask? You're going to like the answer.

WHAT'S IT MEAN?

Just like a small seed must be planted in the ground before it eventually blossoms into a much larger, beautiful plant, our mortal bodies must first die (and be planted in the ground, so to speak) before Jesus transforms them into glorious, eternal bodies when he appears (1 Corinthians 15:36-44, 51-53).

These resurrection bodies are going to rock! Newly clothed in immortality, we will be able to reflect God's glory more beautifully as God's image-bearers (Genesis 1:27) than we ever could before.

What will these new bodies look like, exactly? There's some mystery to it. (No, you won't look like a supermodel or a professional bodybuilder.) However, 1 John 3:2 whets our appetite: "He has not yet shown us what we will be like when Christ appears. But we do know that we will be like him, for we will see him as he really is."

This much is clear: our resurrection bodies will be sinless and "immortal" (today's verse). They won't be subject to all the curses of sin—injuries, sickness, aging, and death. They will be beautifully fit to live in "the new heavens and new earth he has promised, a world filled with God's righteousness" (2 Peter 3:13).

So whatever your current body looks like now, remember this: if you're a Christian, an infinitely greater model is on the way!

NOW WHAT?
The Bible's definitive chapter on our resurrection bodies is 1 Corinthians 15. Take a look!

DID YOU KNOW?
If Matthew 13:43 is to be taken literally, our resurrection bodies might even have a cool, supernatural radiance!

DECEMBER 15

Prepare your minds for action and exercise self-control. Put all your hope in the gracious salvation that will come to you when Jesus Christ is revealed to the world. I PETER 1:13

Each year in mid-February, Major League Baseball pitchers and catchers start trickling into various locales in Florida and Arizona. Other players follow shortly afterward. Their arrivals mark the beginning of spring training and a new season.

Professional baseball's schedule is a grueling marathon. To achieve the ultimate prize, a team must play more than two hundred games between spring training, the regular season, and the play-offs—a span of almost nine months. Phew!

The goal, of course, is the World Series trophy. This glistening trophy motivates players to stay focused, work hard, and endure all the challenges of a tiring season.

Similarly, as Christians our final reward should motivate us to live godly lives. This reward is far better than any shiny trophy. It's the return of Jesus Christ and all the blessings he'll bring!

WHAT'S IT MEAN?

Jesus' second coming isn't just wishful thinking. It's reality. It's also not something to tuck away and forget about, like an old family photo stored in the attic.

No, the truth of Jesus' return should actively affect how we live. In today's verse, the apostle Peter said that you should "put all your hope" in it. Your greatest desire in life shouldn't be money, pleasure, popularity, health, or a nice home with a white picket fence and a big yard. It should be the return of God's Son and the eternal life he brings.

Until then, Peter says, you must "prepare your minds for action." We are to eagerly anticipate Jesus' return, but not by just crossing days off the calendar until he appears. No, there's work to be done! Be a light to those around you. Serve others in love. Tell people about Christ!

Peter also says to "exercise self-control." This means living in a way that honors Christ. Avoid worldly pleasures that would lead you away from Jesus. Show godly restraint in how you act, think, and speak.

The Lord will come back one day. When he does, as Jesus himself said in Luke 12:37, "The servants who are ready and waiting for his return will be rewarded."

NOW WHAT?
Create an action plan of things you can do in the coming weeks/months to serve Jesus as you wait for his return.

DID YOU KNOW?
Verses like 1 Corinthians 15:58; 1 Peter 4:7; 2 Peter 3:11-14; and 1 John 2:28 also mention how Jesus' second coming should affect the way you live today. Check them out!

While they were there, the time came for her to give birth. And she gave birth to her firstborn son and wrapped him in swaddling cloths and laid him in a manger, because there was no place for them in the inn. LUKE 2:6-7, ESV

The countdown is speeding along. There aren't many days left to cross off on the calendar. The big day is almost here.

Christmas is coming!

By now, you are probably waist deep in all the festivities and buzz of the holiday season—the carols, parties, decorating, tree trimming, gift wrapping, candy cane licking, and so forth. It's a wild, wacky, and wonderful time of the year!

For the next ten days, we're going to pause our study of the end times and the book of Revelation and dive headfirst into Christmas. It's appropriate to take some time to think about the glories and blessings of Jesus' birth.

You've probably read today's Scripture passage many times before. The Christmas story—the baby in the manger, the swaddling cloths, the angels, the shepherds, the wise men—is probably as familiar to you as the stories of Bilbo Baggins, Pinocchio, and the Wizard of Oz.

But it's no fairy tale.

Jesus' birth shouldn't be celebrated each Christmas merely as a tradition, like making gingerbread houses or watching *A Charlie Brown Christmas* on TV. Jesus' birth is real history that can change your life!

WHAT'S IT MEAN?

The story of Jesus' birth should amaze you whether you're reading it for the first or the five hundredth time. *God actually became a man!* We call this the incarnation. Two thousand years ago in Bethlehem, God's eternal Son—the second person of the Holy Trinity—took on flesh to be born as a baby boy, fully human and fully God.

Despite all his eternal glory, majesty, and power, Jesus humbled himself and came to earth. He willingly endured all the trials and tribulations of life in a sinful, fallen world, although he never sinned. Eventually, he gave himself over to wicked men to be whipped, beaten, spat upon, mocked, and crucified. He did all this because he loves you dearly—because you desperately needed a Savior.

Jesus' birth is one of the greatest miracles the world has known. So don't become bored or too familiar with it! Let its mystery and magnificence take your breath away again and again this Christmas season!

NOW WHAT?

Plan to read the Gospel accounts of Jesus' birth (Matthew 2 and Luke 2) several times before Christmas.

DID YOU KNOW?

Christmas has its origins in ancient pagan winter solstice festivals that predate Jesus' birth. Christians started observing a December holiday celebrating Jesus' advent in the fourth century AD.

DECEMBER 17

The angel went to her and said, "Greetings, you who are highly favored! The Lord is with you." LUKE 1:28, NIV

Mary was speechless. Was she dreaming? Was her imagination running wild? Did she need to find the best neurologist in Nazareth to see if she was having hallucinations?

No, the dazzling angel standing before her was real.

Gabriel, the angelic messenger, sensed Mary's fear. So he reassured her: "Don't be afraid, Mary . . . for you have found favor with God! You will conceive and give birth to a son, and you will name him Jesus" (Luke 1:30-31).

After thousands of years, God's plan of salvation was nearing its climax. The eternal Son of God was about to arrive on earth in human form and die for humanity's sins. And he was going to do it with the help of a young, very ordinary Jewish girl.

WHAT'S IT MEAN?

Mary had found God's favor. But how?

She wasn't rich, famous, or powerful—God isn't impressed with those things anyway. And even though she was a humble, godly young woman (Luke 1:46-48), she was also a sinner. The Bible is clear that everyone sins (Romans 3:23), and that sin separates us from God (Isaiah 59:2). So why did God bless Mary with the incredible honor of giving birth to the Savior of the world?

Ultimately, it was God's grace.

Grace, by definition, is unmerited favor. It's getting something good that you don't deserve. As sinners, we deserve punishment and death (Romans 6:23). Any good gift we receive otherwise is because God delights in showering us with love and grace.

Mary knew this. After Gabriel's departure, she celebrated God's grace with a song (Luke 1:46-55). "For the Mighty One has done great things for me," she sang. "Holy is his name!" (verse 49, NIV). Notice her emphasis on God's grace, not her credentials.

Like Mary, you have received God's amazing grace. It's the reason, in fact, he has led you to read a devotional about his Son. But that's only one example. Do you have a Bible? Do you go to a gospel-centered church? Has anyone shared the Good News of Jesus with you before? Are spiritual questions stirring in your heart? All of this is God's grace to you!

God could have left you to die in your sins. Instead, he is revealing to you his Son, who can give you new life!

NOW WHAT?

Read the Magnificat, Mary's famous song of praise to God, in Luke 1:46-55. May we respond to God's grace in similar ways!

DID YOU KNOW?

The angel Gabriel also spoke to Daniel, the Old Testament hero, more than six hundred years before Gabriel appeared to Mary (Daniel 8–9)!

*All of God's promises have been fulfilled in Christ with a resounding
"Yes!" And through Christ, our "Amen" (which means "Yes") ascends
to God for his glory.* 2 CORINTHIANS 1:20

Zechariah could barely contain his excitement. It had been almost a year
since words had last come out of his mouth. But now his tongue was loos-
ened, and he had plenty to say!

Nearly a year earlier, the angel Gabriel had visited Zechariah to announce
that Zechariah's wife, Elizabeth, would have a child, John (who grew up to
be John the Baptist). But the couple was old and past childbearing years, so
Zechariah doubted God's promise. Because of Zechariah's disbelief, Gabriel
said Zechariah would be mute (unable to speak) until their son was born.

Nine months later, after Elizabeth miraculously gave birth, Zechariah suddenly regained his speech. Filled with the Holy Spirit, he prophesied about
his son and the coming birth of Jesus, who was born about six months later.

Zechariah praised God for sending "a mighty Savior from the royal line of
his servant David, just as he promised through his holy prophets long ago"
and being "merciful to our ancestors by remembering his sacred covenant"
(Luke 1:69-70, 72).

As Zechariah powerfully discovered, God always keeps his promises.

WHAT'S IT MEAN?

The Old Testament is littered with prophecies about Jesus. The first, as mentioned in the January 8 devotion, is found in Genesis 3:15 right after the Fall.
Moses predicted Jesus' coming (Deuteronomy 18:15). So did David, Daniel,
Ezekiel, Isaiah, Jeremiah, Malachi, Micah, and many others. All told, these
prophecies spanned thousands of years. And amazingly, every single one of
them came true.

In fact, as today's verse says, "all of God's promises have been fulfilled in
Christ." Jesus is the culmination of all Scripture. Whatever promises God
made—whether it was to bring his people into the Promised Land of Canaan,

to bless David's kingly line forever, or to return the Jews from Babylonian exile—they all ultimately point to Jesus. That's because if history is the story of humankind, Jesus' saving work on the cross is the climax.

Jesus is the greatest example—among countless others—that God is faithful to his word. He is 100 percent trustworthy. As Titus 1:2 affirms, God "does not lie."

In a world filled with confusion, deceit, and sin, you can always trust God. You can believe in his Word. He created you, he loves you, and he will never fail you. Zechariah learned it, and Jesus proved it!

NOW WHAT?

Ask God to help you tell the truth and keep your promises, just like he does.

DID YOU KNOW?

The name *Zechariah* means "God has remembered." God always remembers and fulfills his promises!

He redeems me from death and crowns me with love and
tender mercies. PSALM 103:4

What comes to mind when you think of God?

Do you think of a grandfatherly figure with a long, white beard, resting on a heavenly throne? Or a mysterious, impersonal power that governs the universe from afar? Or an angry deity perched on high, just waiting to zap us with lightning bolts when we mess up?

God is none of those things. But it's easy to pick up wrong impressions of God if we don't allow Scripture to properly inform us.

When you think of God, do you think of mercy? The story of John the Baptist's father, Zechariah, highlights this fascinating, yet sometimes over-looked, characteristic of God. When John was born, Zechariah spoke a beau-tiful prophecy about Jesus: "Because of God's tender mercy, the morning light from heaven is about to break upon us, to give light to those who sit in darkness and in the shadow of death, and to guide us to the path of peace" (Luke 1:78-79).

We would be wise to understand God's "tender mercy."

WHAT'S IT MEAN?

Mercy is when God withholds the punishment we deserve (his wrath against sin). God's mercy is often misunderstood because people don't realize they need it. They don't understand that their sins separate them from their Creator.

Because of our sinful nature, we deserve eternal separation from God in hell, not salvation through Jesus. God would have been perfectly within his rights to give us what we deserve, yet he chose to extend tender mercy through his Son, "the morning light from heaven."

God is loving, personal, and relational. As Scripture says, "The Lord is near" (Philippians 4:5, NIV) and "he cares about you" (1 Peter 5:7). His mercy flows from a heart that loves us dearly.

Jesus embodies the mercy of God. He is the great mercy provider. Much like a power cord carries electricity and brings appliances to life, Jesus carries God's mercy and brings life to lost sinners. That's why Zechariah spoke his prophecy before Jesus' birth.

Praise God for his "tender mercy" in Christ!

NOW WHAT?

Because God showed tender mercy to us, we should treat others the same way. In fact, Colossians 3:12 says, "Since God chose you to be the holy people he loves, you must clothe yourselves with tenderhearted mercy, kindness, humility, gentleness, and patience."

DID YOU KNOW?

In the Old Testament, the cover of the Ark of the Covenant was called "the mercy seat." It was a visual symbol of God's loving, forgiving presence with his people. See Exodus 25:17-22 (ESV) for more details.

DECEMBER 20

Suddenly, the angel was joined by a vast host of others—the armies of heaven—praising God and saying, "Glory to God in highest heaven, and peace on earth to those with whom God is pleased."

LUKE 2:13-14

So what's the deal with burning sofas?

In recent years, there seems to be a growing trend of sports fans who set sofas ablaze to celebrate their team's big win. University of Maryland basketball fans lit couches in 2005 after the Terps upset rival Duke during the regular season. Kentucky basketball fans did it in both 2012 and 2014 after the Wildcats beat their own hated rival, Louisville, in the NCAA tournament. And Michigan State football supporters joined the fiery festivities after the Spartans beat Ohio State for the Big Ten championship in 2013.

All things considered, it's a pretty odd way to celebrate.

We love commemorating historic moments (but, hopefully, without flaming furniture). But there has never been a bigger moment than that glorious night in Bethlehem about two thousand years ago.

WHAT'S IT MEAN?

When the Son of God was born, heaven itself exploded into a huge party! Today's Scripture passage in Luke 2 describes how the evening sky in Bethlehem lit up with countless angels, all singing God's praises. The shepherds who witnessed this hurried to the manger and then spread the word around town (Luke 2:17).

Eight days later, two devout God-fearers named Simeon and Anna, who had been waiting their whole lives to see the Savior, rejoiced when Joseph and Mary brought baby Jesus to the Jerusalem Temple (Luke 2:25-38). Sometime later, the wise men arrived with kingly gifts to worship young Jesus (Matthew 2:1-12).

Jesus' birth changed history. It was a life preserver thrown to a world drowning in sin. It was a powerful beacon of hope piercing the darkness of Satan's domain. It was cause for great celebration.

Jesus' birth should cause *us* to worship and praise God too! The same joy that the angels, shepherds, and others expressed at the Savior's coming should be ours, as well.

(But please, no sofa burning.)

NOW WHAT?

Celebrating Jesus' birth isn't just for the Christmas season. Make a point in your prayers throughout the year to thank Jesus for coming to earth to save us.

DID YOU KNOW?

The Bible never says there were three wise men, only that three gifts were given to Jesus. And these men probably visited Jesus at his home when he was a toddler, not at the manger at his birth (Matthew 2:16). Don't let man-made Christmas traditions inform you more than Scripture itself!

*The hearts of these people are hardened, and their ears cannot hear,
and they have closed their eyes—so their eyes cannot see, and their
ears cannot hear, and their hearts cannot understand, and they
cannot turn to me and let me heal them.* MATTHEW 13:15

Nobody likes a party pooper.

A party pooper is someone who ruins a good time. He's the guy who sits in a corner mumbling about how sugar rots your teeth while everyone else is eating Christmas cookies. She's the girl who wants to stay home and do homework while everyone else goes caroling. They don't recognize a good thing when it comes along.

The Jewish religious leaders of Jesus' day were big-time party poopers. While plenty of people rejoiced at the Savior's birth, the priests, scribes, and Pharisees did not. In fact, when King Herod, the wicked, Roman-appointed ruler of Judea, heard rumors about a "newborn king of the Jews" (Matthew 2:2) and asked the religious leaders where the child was to be born, they casually quoted the Micah 5:2 prophecy about Bethlehem . . . and that's it. The Bible says nothing about them sending someone to investigate Jesus' birth—or doing *anything* about it, for that matter.

God's people had been waiting thousands of years for the promised Messiah. Why didn't the religious leaders do something about it?

Their hearts were hardened.

WHAT'S IT MEAN?

Having a hard heart means you are unreceptive and defiant toward God. It means you don't want to listen to him or obey him.

Sadly, the next generation of Israel's religious leaders that came to power during Jesus' adulthood was no different than the one during the time of Jesus' birth. They fought and argued with Jesus constantly. They dismissed his miracles and denied his deity. Not even Lazarus's resurrection softened their hearts toward the Messiah.

So in today's verse, Jesus quoted Isaiah 6:9-10—a long-ago condemnation of Old Testament Israel's unbelief—to describe the Jewish leaders of the first century AD. They were no different than the faithless people of Isaiah's era.

May we never be party poopers when it comes to Jesus! May we never have hard hearts that reject God's Son. Instead, let's rejoice like the angels, shepherds, and wise men at our Savior's coming and worship him!

NOW WHAT?
Say a prayer of praise to Jesus for coming to save you from your sins.

DID YOU KNOW?
Although the Romans ruled Israel in Jesus' day, Rome still allowed the Jews to practice Judaism and gave positions of authority to certain individuals. That's why the Jewish religious leaders had enough influence to eventually convince Pilate to crucify Jesus.

The angel said to them, "Do not be afraid. I bring you good news that will cause great joy for all the people."   LUKE 2:10, NIV

"Joy to the World" is one of the most popular and beloved Christmas carols of all time. During the holiday season, you can hear it everywhere—in churches, on the radio, in shopping malls, from carolers, and more. You probably know the lyrics by heart.

But did you know that Isaac Watts, the song's writer, never intended it to be a Christmas carol? It's true! In fact, the lyrics don't mention anything about Bethlehem, the manger, angels, shepherds, wise men, or anything else specifically about Jesus' birth. Watts's inspiration for his classic hymn was Psalm 98, an Old Testament song of praise celebrating the kindness and power God showed to Israel.

But hey, "Joy to the World" still works great as a Christmas carol, because both the song and Christmas are all about—you guessed it—joy! John the Baptist "jumped for joy" in the womb of Elizabeth, Mary's relative, when pregnant Mary came to visit her (Luke 1:44). When the angel announced Jesus' birth to the shepherds in Bethlehem, he said, "I bring you good news that will cause great joy for all the people" (today's verse).

When Joseph and Mary took baby Jesus to Jerusalem shortly after his birth, a prophet named Simeon said, "This child is destined to cause many in Israel to fall, and many others to rise" (Luke 2:34). And when the wise men saw the star over young Jesus' home, "they were filled with joy" (Matthew 2:10).

Jesus' birth is all about joy!

WHAT'S IT MEAN?

Joy is an unwavering state of delight, peace, and satisfaction in a person's heart. It's deep, meaningful happiness that doesn't fade away. Jesus' birth makes never-ending joy possible!

How? Because the little baby in the manger was the fulfillment of heaven's great salvation plan. Mary's infant son was the eternal Son of God made flesh, come to rescue humanity. The child born in Bethlehem that night would grow up to become the Savior of the world.

Jesus' birth and all the blessings he'd bring to the world were enough to make angels sing, shepherds come running, old men prophesy, and wise men travel great distances. Because of Jesus, we can experience freedom from sin, peace with God, a hope-filled existence, and everlasting life.

Jesus most certainly brings joy to the world!

NOW WHAT?

Read Psalm 98, the inspiration for "Joy to the World."

DID YOU KNOW?

Isaac Watts was an eighteenth-century preacher and theologian in England who wrote more than five hundred hymns.

Wise men from the east came to Jerusalem, saying, "Where is he who has been born king of the Jews? For we saw his star when it rose and have come to worship him." MATTHEW 2:1-2, ESV

So what's the deal with the wise men? Who were these mysterious travelers that visited young Jesus?

The Bible doesn't give a lot of specifics. But we can make some educated guesses based on several clues in Scripture.

Today's verse describes them as "wise men from the east," probably Persia (modern-day Iraq and Iran). The English term "wise men" comes from the word *magoi* in the New Testament's original Greek language. *Magoi*, or "Magi," means "magicians," "sorcerers," or "astrologers."

These were religious men who believed in enchantments and magic spells. They probably tried to predict the future by looking at the stars. They were fascinated by the spiritual realm but almost certainly did not worship the one true God of the Bible.

But something about that special star in the sky captured their attention. Perhaps they were familiar with prophecies about the Messiah such as Numbers 24:17 through Old Testament scrolls left behind after the Jewish exile to Babylon nearly six hundred years earlier. However it happened, they quickly connected the star to old prophesies about "the king of the Jews" (today's verse) and set off on their long journey to Israel.

When they finally arrived, Matthew 2:11 says, "They entered the house and saw the child with his mother, Mary, and they bowed down and worshiped him."

WHAT'S IT MEAN?

We'll never know if the wise men fully understood whom they were worshiping. But give these ancient pagan magicians credit: they followed God's calling and went to great lengths to worship Jesus.

They weren't the only ones. Angels, shepherds, and prophets worshiped baby Jesus too. Many years later, so did fishermen, lepers, tax collectors, Samaritans, Roman centurions, convicted criminals, the blind, the sick, the crippled, and even a couple of religious leaders.

Is it your heart's desire to worship Jesus this Christmas? Jesus doesn't care where you come from. He only wants your worship now.

No matter what's in your past or where you're at in life, take a cue from the wise men: seek Jesus and worship him this Christmas. Bend your knee to the Savior of the world, acknowledge him as Lord, and give him gifts of praise. He is worthy of it all!

NOW WHAT?

Read the full story of the wise men in Matthew 2:1-12.

DID YOU KNOW?

The Greek word *magos* (singular form of *magoi*) is found only once more in Scripture—Acts 13, where it describes a wicked "false prophet" and "sorcerer" named Elymas who opposed the apostle Paul's missionary work.

They opened their treasure chests and gave him gifts of gold, frankincense, and myrrh. MATTHEW 2:11

The long wait is almost over. The moment you've anticipated all year comes tomorrow.

Christmas Day!

You've no doubt made your wish list. Maybe you even ranked the gifts you want in order—you know, just to make sure everyone is aware. Your top three gift ideas are certainly gold, frankincense, and myrrh, right?

Probably not.

Two thousand years ago, when the wise men finally reached the young Jesus' home, they "entered the house and saw the child with his mother, Mary, and they bowed down and worshiped him. Then they opened their treasure chests and gave him gifts of gold, frankincense, and myrrh" (today's verse).

Maybe the Magi's gifts to Jesus don't mean much to you. But these costly items speak a great deal about the special child who received them.

WHAT'S IT MEAN?

Whether or not the wise men realized it, their expensive gifts symbolized Jesus' unique roles as King (gold), High Priest (frankincense), and Savior (myrrh).

Let's take a closer look . . .

Gold is the obvious one. In ancient times, gold was often a symbol of royalty and the measure of a kingdom's greatness. King Solomon, for instance, was renowned for his wealth and gold (1 Kings 10:14-23). The Magi's gift of gold symbolized Jesus' kingship, because he is the "King of all kings and Lord of all lords" (Revelation 19:16) who will one day return to earth to destroy all evil and establish his eternal kingdom.

Frankincense was a type of incense made from tree resin that the Israelites used in Tabernacle ceremonies (and later, at the Temple). Priests would burn this sweet-smelling substance on an altar in the Holy Place as an offering to God (Exodus 30:34-35). The gift of frankincense symbolized Jesus' role as our High Priest who became the ultimate sin-sacrifice to God on our behalf. As Hebrews 10:12 says, Christ is "our High Priest [who] offered himself to God as a single sacrifice for sins, good for all time."

Myrrh was used as a fragrant spice to embalm dead bodies before they were entombed. John 19:39-40 describes how Nicodemus and Joseph of Arimathea covered Jesus' body with myrrh-laced ointment after taking it off the cross. The gift of myrrh foreshadowed Jesus' death and resurrection as our loving Savior!

This Christmas, follow the example of the wise men and worship Jesus as your King, High Priest, and Savior!

NOW WHAT?

Worship Jesus today with the sacrifices of prayer and singing.

DID YOU KNOW?

Apparently, myrrh could be used in drinks. During his crucifixion, Jesus was offered wine mixed with myrrh to dull his pain, but he refused to drink it (Mark 15:23).

The wages of sin is death, but the free gift of God is eternal life through Christ Jesus our Lord. ROMANS 6:23

Merry Christmas!

Today is one of the most wonderful days of the year. On Christmas Day, the cares of life seem to get lost in the hustle and bustle of fun family events, annual traditions, good food, and of course, gifts! All over the world, people of different languages, nations, and cultures are exchanging gifts. It's pretty remarkable when you think about it. And let's be honest: it's just really fun to get stuff!

A gift, as defined by the *Merriam-Webster Dictionary*, is "something voluntarily transferred by one person to another without compensation." In other words, it's a blessing someone gives you out of love even though you did nothing to earn it.

Of all the gifts you'll receive this season, the greatest one is from God. It's his Son, Jesus.

WHAT'S IT MEAN?

Jesus is the greatest gift because of what he has done—and will do—for you. The movies and video games you get this Christmas will entertain you. The books you get will enlighten you. The clothes you get will keep you warm. But only Jesus can save you!

Your family gives you Christmas gifts out of love for you, not because you earned them. It's the same with God. He sent Jesus to earth as a gift to us, not a reward. We did nothing to earn Jesus. Zip. Zero. Zilch.

It's incredible that a holy God would provide his only Son to reconcile lost sinners like us to himself. But God doesn't stop there. When we trust in Jesus as our Lord and Savior, God lavishes innumerable blessings on us.

Here is a small sample of all the gifts that God gives us through faith in Christ:

- love (1 John 3:16)
- mercy (Ephesians 2:4-5)

- grace (Romans 5:15)
- peace (Romans 5:1)
- joy (Romans 5:2)
- hope (1 Thessalonians 1:3)
- the Holy Spirit (Luke 24:49)
- adoption as God's children (Galatians 4:4-7)
- access to God (Hebrews 4:16)
- fellowship with God (1 John 5:20)
- freedom from sin's power (Romans 6:6-7)
- victory over Satan (1 John 3:8)
- eternal life (see today's verse)

Jesus is the gift that keeps on giving—all the way into eternity. The gifts under the Christmas tree will eventually fade away. But gifts that come from salvation through Jesus last a lifetime—and beyond!

NOW WHAT?

Take a break from your gifts today and thank Jesus for the gifts he provides through his great sacrifice.

DID YOU KNOW?

Many historians trace the Christmas tradition of gift giving back to the ancient Roman festival of Saturnalia.

DECEMBER 26

I saw a new heaven and a new earth, for the old heaven and the old earth had disappeared. REVELATION 21:1

Now that Christmas is over and we're back to our study of Revelation and the end times, here's a question for you: Have you ever paused to consider the splendor, beauty, and enormity of God's creation?

For starters, no one—not even NASA's smartest scientists—knows how big God's universe is. Modern astronomy's best guess is that our own galaxy, the Milky Way, includes about three hundred billion stars. That's a lot of stars. It's also believed that the observable universe contains more than one hundred billion galaxies. That's a lot of galaxies. To figure out how many stars are in all the observable galaxies, you'd have to multiply three hundred billion by one hundred billion. That's a lot of billions. And that's not even counting the parts of the universe we *can't* see!

Now consider the wonders of earth itself: the towering majesty of Mount Everest . . . the translucent waters of the Caribbean . . . the mysterious jungles of the Amazon . . . the stunning sunsets of Maui . . . the rolling plains of the Serengeti . . . the frozen Arctic tundra.

Yes, God filled his universe with countless wonders and delights for us to marvel at and enjoy. But this universe is nothing compared to what's in store for Christians in eternity.

WHAT'S IT MEAN?

What do you picture when you think of heaven? The apostle Peter manning a check-in desk at the "pearly gates"? Adorable cherubs flittering about? People floating among the clouds as they gently strum harps?

Over the years, our perception of heaven has become a little wacko.

We often say that Christians will "go to heaven" when they die, and that's true . . . to a point. But the eternal dwelling for all believers is far greater than some mystical, ethereal place in outer space. In Revelation 21, the apostle John described it as "a new heaven *and a new earth*" (emphasis added). It's going to be a huge, physical universe for us to enjoy and explore—only without all the death, pain, suffering, and other junk that comes with this current, sin-cursed world.

One day, God will destroy everything we see and give us a new, sinless creation (2 Peter 3:7-13) to delight in. Considering all the spectacular features of this fallen world, just think how much greater the new, sin-free heaven and earth will be!

NOW WHAT?

Read about the new heaven and new earth in Revelation 21:1–22:5.

DID YOU KNOW?

The new heaven and new earth will be "where righteousness dwells" (2 Peter 3:13, NIV)—a place entirely free of sin.

I heard a loud shout from the throne, saying, "Look, God's home is now among his people! He will live with them, and they will be his people." REVELATION 21:3

John must've been giddy with joy!

When the elderly apostle received his divine vision of "a new heaven and a new earth" in Revelation 21, he probably felt like dancing a jig—well, assuming his creaky, eighty- or ninety-year-old legs would've let him. Eternity's blessings were too marvelous for him to sit still.

But the best was yet to come.

Soon, John saw another vision, this one of a dazzling city slowly descending from heaven to the new earth. The city was enormous and sparkled with gold and precious jewels. John called it the "new Jerusalem" (Revelation 21:2).

Then John noticed something peculiar: the new Jerusalem had no temple. For nearly one thousand years in ancient Israel, the Jerusalem Temple had been a grand, physical representation of God's presence among his people. But in John's futuristic vision, it was gone. Then it dawned on John: "I saw no temple in the city, for the Lord God Almighty and the Lamb are its temple" (Revelation 21:22).

In the new heaven and earth, God will actually dwell among his people!

WHAT'S IT MEAN?

Among all the wonders of the new heaven and new earth, the greatest will be our ability to fully bask in the glorious presence of the Lord God Almighty forever. It's what we were created for.

In the beginning, God designed us to experience and enjoy his full presence. Genesis 3:8 says the Lord actually walked in the Garden of Eden with Adam and Eve. Sin, though, separated us from our Creator. When Adam and Eve disobeyed God, he banished them from the Garden of Eden. This is often referred to as "paradise lost."

But the new heaven and new earth is paradise restored! There, God the Father and the Lord Jesus Christ will sit enthroned in the new Jerusalem (Revelation 22:3), and all the nations will walk in the light of their glory (Revelation 21:24). The temple is unnecessary because we will be able to worship God in person!

Jesus himself will wipe every tear from our eyes, "and there will be no more death or sorrow or crying or pain" (Revelation 21:4). Sin and its curse will be completely destroyed.

There is nothing like being in God's perfect presence!

NOW WHAT?

Compare Genesis 2:15–3:24 to Revelation 21:1–22:5 to see the differences between "paradise lost" and "paradise restored"!

DID YOU KNOW?

If the new Jerusalem measurements in Revelation 21:16-17 are literal, eternity's holy city will be gigantic—1,400 miles wide by 1,400 miles long. That's roughly half the square mileage of the United States!

DECEMBER 28

You make known to me the path of life; you will fill me with joy in your presence, with eternal pleasures at your right hand.
PSALM 16:11, NIV

Eternity is a long time . . . a *really* long time.

It's longer than the book report you have to write for English class. It's longer than the combined lifespan of all your grandparents. It's even longer than—*gasp!*—the wait time for *any* ride at Disney World.

Eternity is forever! It just keeps going . . . and going . . . and going, without end.

So if you're a Christian, it's only natural to wonder: *What will we do for all eternity in the new heaven and new earth?*

Will we have hobbies? Will we get to swim, ride bikes, and climb mountains? Will there even be oceans to swim in, roads to ride on, and mountains to climb? Will we be able to play soccer, read books, and go skydiving? Can we order root beer floats every day?

WHAT'S IT MEAN?

The Bible remains mostly silent on the specifics of eternity. Our future activities in the new heaven and new earth are largely a mystery. Today's verse, though, provides a wonderful hint: in whatever we do, we'll experience unending joy and pleasures in God's presence. In other words, we'll never get bored!

Because sin, death, suffering, and sorrow will cease to exist, every single moment of eternity will be perfectly satisfying and enjoyable. None of the bad stuff that happens here on earth will take place.

According to Revelation 7:15, we will continually serve God in the new heaven and new earth. But incredibly, God will also give us some sort of heavenly ruling power. According to 1 Thessalonians 2:12, we will "share in his Kingdom and glory," and Revelation 22:5 says we "will reign forever and ever." (So forget that class president election you recently lost. That's small potatoes. You're going to rule in *heaven* one day!)

Best yet, we will neverendingly worship the Lord God Almighty in his presence. We'll need all of eternity to adequately thank the Father, Son, and Holy Spirit for what they have done for us!

And so, as the days and weeks and months and years and decades and centuries and millennia pass, we will continually join heaven's angelic chorus (Revelation 5:13) in singing, "Blessing and honor and glory and power belong to the one sitting on the throne and to the Lamb forever and ever!"

NOW WHAT?

Get a head start on eternity and sing praises to God right now in your devotional time!

DID YOU KNOW?

If Scripture passages such as Revelation 19:9 and 22:2 are to be taken literally, eternity is going to be delicious!

DECEMBER 29

The throne of God and of the Lamb will be there, and his servants will worship him. And they will see his face.

REVELATION 22:3-4

The new heaven and new earth can't get here soon enough!

No more sin, sadness, pain, or suffering? Sweet! No more wars, famine, poverty, homelessness, or crime? Rock on! No more bullies, broken bones, math tests, bad hair days, or overcooked asparagus? Sign me up!

Yes, heaven sounds blissful. But none of those blessings is the greatest we'll experience.

Eternity's greatest blessing—by far—will be enjoying God's presence and worshiping him in person forever. *We will actually get to see God face-to-face!*

If that doesn't sound out-of-this-world awesome to you, you probably need a better understanding of God!

WHAT'S IT MEAN?

Seeing God face-to-face in his full glory is an incredible privilege that no one has fully experienced since the Garden of Eden, when God enjoyed "walking about" with Adam and Eve (Genesis 3:8).

Not even the great Moses enjoyed this honor. When Moses asked to see God's full glory, God replied, "You cannot see my face, for man shall not see me and live" (Exodus 33:20, ESV).

God created us for close, personal fellowship with him. But sin ruined that intimacy. That's why God banished Adam and Eve from his holy presence after they ate the forbidden fruit.

As sinners who fall woefully short of God's holiness, we are ill prepared to witness his full glory. It's why people in Scripture reacted to God's appearances in great fear. After eating the fruit, Adam and Eve "hid from the LORD God among the trees" (Genesis 3:8). When the prophet Isaiah saw a vision of God, he cried out, "I am doomed, for I am a sinful man." (Isaiah 6:5).

But in the new heaven and new earth, God will once again live "among

725

his people" (Revelation 21:3)! His glory will illuminate our entire heavenly existence (Revelation 22:5).

Clothed with Jesus' righteousness in new resurrection bodies, all believers will be free to approach God. The barrier of sin will be removed, allowing us to gaze upon the Lord God Almighty and worship him without the slightest fear or hesitation. We will be able to fully soak in God's glory and rejoice in his goodness.

This is what we were created for! This is eternity's greatest blessing!

NOW WHAT?

Read Psalm 27:4 to see how much King David longed to worship God face-to-face.

DID YOU KNOW?

According to Exodus 34:29-35, Moses was allowed to see just a part of God's glory, and it caused his face to glow!

*He who is the faithful witness to all these things says, "Yes, I am
coming soon!" Amen! Come, Lord Jesus!* REVELATION 22:20

Finally, John could exhale.

The great apostle's apocalyptic vision was finished. The Lord Jesus Christ
had just given John an astounding glimpse into the future—and heaven
itself—that no other mortal has ever seen. The revelation answered many
questions but raised many more.

Now, it was John's responsibility to put quill on parchment and record
everything he had just seen. Amazingly, Jesus did not want John to hide heav-
en's forthcoming plans. John's job was to share them with the entire world.
The angel who attended John at that moment instructed him, "Do not seal
up the prophetic words in this book, for the time is near" (Revelation 22:10).

John's heart must've been beating wildly and his thoughts swirling with
excitement, joy, confusion, and faith. So much to write, so little time! Where
to begin?

Then, as if to reassure John one final time and summarize all that John
had seen, Jesus declared, "Yes, I am coming soon!" (today's verse).

The Savior's words must have felt like a safe, calming shelter amidst the
storm of John's emotions and the persecution he faced on his island prison.
So the elderly apostle responded joyfully with four simple words: "Amen!
Come, Lord Jesus!"

WHAT'S IT MEAN?

As we come to the end of this devotional book, it's fitting that we consider
these final words of Scripture.

Jesus' second coming is every Christian's greatest expectation. It's "our
blessed hope" (Titus 2:13, ESV). We should anticipate it, desire it, and pray
for it. We should let it shape the way we act, think, and speak. We should
base our lives on Scripture's rock-solid guarantee that it will happen. It should
affect every area of our lives.

When our Savior comes, he will destroy sin, crush death, cleanse the earth of wickedness, and set up his eternal kingdom where we will enjoy his presence forever. This is why he originally came to earth, suffered in our place, and rose from the dead. This is the grand finale that Christians have been waiting thousands of years for!

Jesus' death, resurrection, and future return mean everything to us. They provide salvation, purpose, and hope to those who believe. And so, may you echo John's faith-filled cry and say with all your heart, "Amen! Come, Lord Jesus!"

NOW WHAT?

Live for Jesus and prayerfully long for his return!

DID YOU KNOW?

Revelation 22:21, the Bible's final verse, says, "May the grace of the Lord Jesus be with God's holy people." God's grace—the undeserved favor he provides us through Jesus—will be with you until Christ returns!

*I will remember the deeds of the LORD; yes, I will remember your
miracles of long ago.* PSALM 77:11, NIV

You did it!

You made it to the end of another year. You survived another twelve
months of life's craziness. You also made it to the end of this devotional book.
Well done—and happy New Year's Eve!

This unique intersection of time—the conclusion of one year and the
beginning of another—provides a great opportunity to recall all of God's
blessings to you over the last year.

Since ancient times, God has called on his people to remember his goodness. Abraham, Jacob, and Joshua all built altars or stone memorials to commemorate God's promises and blessings. After God delivered the Israelites
out of Egyptian slavery, Moses commanded them to "remember the miraculous signs and wonders, and the strong hand and powerful arm with which
he brought you out of Egypt" (Deuteronomy 7:19). And in today's verse,
Asaph the psalmist encouraged us with a similar message: "Remember the
deeds of the LORD!"

WHAT'S IT MEAN?

God has been so good to you. He deserves all your praise for his mercy and
grace—seen and unseen. It's so important to remember all his blessings.
Praise him for all his goodness to you!

The alternative is to become like Israel during the time of the book of
Judges when "another generation grew up who did not acknowledge the
LORD or remember the mighty things he had done for Israel" (Judges 2:10).
That generation spiraled into wickedness and judgment. No thanks!

In addition to looking back, it's also a good time to look ahead and make
some spiritual resolutions for the coming year. Do you want to read your
Bible and pray more? What about starting a Scripture memory program?
Do you want to improve in obeying your parents or sharing your faith with

friends? Whatever your resolutions are, write them down and commit them to God in prayer.

Most of all, make it your goal this coming year to grow in your faith and knowledge of the Lord Jesus Christ. May the apostle Paul's words in Philippians 3:10 be your resolution as well: "I want to know Christ and experience the mighty power that raised him from the dead." Jesus died and rose again so that you could experience complete forgiveness of sins and eternal life with him when he returns.

That's worth remembering!

NOW WHAT?

Take some time today to reflect on God's goodness to you, and then make some specific resolutions for how you hope to become more like Jesus this coming year.

DID YOU KNOW?

New Year's resolutions supposedly originated with the ancient Babylonians about four thousand years ago.

About the Author

Joshua Cooley is a longtime children's ministry director and a former full-time journalist whose work has been featured in a variety of publications, including *Sports Illustrated*, *Sports Spectrum*, *FCA Magazine*, Focus on the Family's *Thriving Family* magazine, and *Bethesda Magazine*. He has written for teenagers and children in *Highlights*, *Breakaway*, *Brio*, *Clubhouse*, and *SUSIE* magazines. Joshua has also authored *Heroes of the Bible Devotional*, cowritten *The One Year Sports Devotions for Kids* and *Playing with Purpose: Inside the Lives and Faith of the Major Leagues' Top Players*, and contributed to Tony Evans's *Raising Kingdom Kids Devotional*. He and his wife have four children.

MORE DEVOTIONALS
— BY JOSH COOLEY —

The One Year Sports Devotions for Kids

This devotional is perfect for kids who love sports, sports trivia, and stories about athletes who overcame odds and performed the extraordinary. From the Polar Bear Club's New Year's Day swim to football to yo-yo records, the stories in this book will encourage boys and girls alike to keep reading day after day. Spiritual insight that connects the trivia to Scripture comes in the "What's the Score?" section. "On the Ball" presents a quick question or phrase to remember, and the "Coach's Comment" introduces the daily Bible verse.

Available wherever books are sold.

Heroes of the Bible

From Noah to Ruth to Hezekiah to Paul, the Bible is filled with stories of ordinary people who had heroic faith and who, through God's power, performed some pretty amazing feats! Their stories can inspire all of us to live like true heroes of faith. Get started on your heroic journey today!

Available wherever books are sold.

CP0964